THE FLETCHER JONES FOUNDATION

HUMANITIES IMPRINT

The Fletcher Jones Foundation has endowed this imprint to foster innovative and enduring scholarship in the humanities.

The publisher gratefully acknowledges the generous contribution to this book provided by The Gladys Krieble Delmas Foundation.

Venice Incognito

Venice Incognito

Masks in the Serene Republic

James H. Johnson

UNIVERSITY OF CALIFORNIA PRESS
Berkeley · Los Angeles · London

Portions of this book appeared previously in different form and are printed here by permission of their original publishers: James H. Johnson, "Deceit and Sincerity in Early-Modern Venice," *Eighteenth-Century Studies* 38, no. 3 (2005): 399–415. © 2005 by The American Society for Eighteenth-Century Studies. Reprinted with permission of The Johns Hopkins University Press. James H. Johnson, "Useful Myths in the Nineteenth Century: Venice in Opera," *Journal of Interdisciplinary History* 36, no. 3 (2006): 533–554. It is included herein with the permission of the editors of the *Journal of Interdisciplinary History* and MIT Press, Cambridge, Massachusetts, © 2006 by the Massachusetts Institute of Technology and the *Journal of Interdisciplinary History,* Inc.

University of California Press, one of the most distinguished university presses in the United States, enriches lives around the world by advancing scholarship in the humanities, social sciences, and natural sciences. Its activities are supported by the UC Press Foundation and by philanthropic contributions from individuals and institutions. For more information, visit www.ucpress.edu.

University of California Press
Berkeley and Los Angeles, California

University of California Press, Ltd.
London, England

© 2011 by The Regents of the University of California

Library of Congress Cataloging-in-Publication Data

Johnson, James H., 1960–
    Venice incognito : masks in the serene republic /
James H. Johnson.
        p. cm.
    Includes bibliographical references and index.
    ISBN 978-0-520-26771-8 (cloth : alk. paper)
    1. Venice (Italy)—History—1508–1797.
2. Masks—Italy—Venice—History.   3. Venice
(Italy)—Social life and customs.   I. Title.
    DG678.4.J65   2011
    945'.31107—dc22   2010036097

Manufactured in the United States of America
20   19   18   17   16   15   14   13   12   11
10   9   8   7   6   5   4   3   2   1

The paper used in this publication meets the minimum requirements of ANSI/NISO Z39.48-1992 (R 1997) *(Permanence of Paper).*

For Lydia

Contents

Illustrations

Preface

I came to this book as many others have come to Venice, drawn in by carnival. I wanted to know what masks tell us about the people who wear them, and Venice seemed like the place to start. Masking there dates back to the thirteenth century. At the height of its carnival, five hundred years later, Venice attracted revelers from across the globe who were eager to change their names and trade their titles for the mask's anonymity. The season also drew smugglers, con men, prostitutes, and thieves, who had their own motives for disguise. Carnival's attractions mixed all social ranks in close quarters: in the city's cafés and gambling dens, in its theaters for music and comedy, before the outdoor stalls of hawkers and touts, and along the crowded lanes around Piazza San Marco. What better setting in which to see the mask's transformations?

Venice appealed to me for another reason. Most agree that carnival freed its revelers from inhibitions and caused them to act on impulse. Consensus calls the effect topsy-turvy, a mad jumble that upended hierarchy and defied mores. In such a view, the Venetian Casanova's jubilant hedonism prefigures a later age. For many, the thought of a happy, tolerant population willing to suspend convention shows Venetians to have been ahead of their time. Might we find sources of the modern self in this carnival city? Did their celebrations reveal human nature freed from social constraint?

As I read more, I learned a surprising fact. Starting in the late seventeenth century, Venetians wore masks in public for six months of the year, a practice they continued until the Republic's fall in 1797. Visitors assumed that carnival had begun to spill into other seasons, driven by a population intent on pleasure. Modern scholars echo that conclusion. But the activities of these maskers were not especially festive. Patricians and diplomats wore masks to solemn receptions and state ceremonies, foreign princes came to the meetings of learned societies in masks, spectators watched plays and heard operas wearing masks, masked patrons came to cafés for conversation.

Understanding why Venetians wore masks in public for more than a century affects how we view their experience of carnival. It also opens avenues that bear little ostensible relevance to the season. The practice grew from a culture in which secrecy was prized and self-revelation not always prudent. It carried traces of a political arrangement that combined exclusive patrician rule with an unchanging social hierarchy. Just as courtly settings elsewhere shaped an identifying etiquette to guide relations, Venetian republicanism produced its own patterns of dress and behavior to smooth transactions in the public sphere. For commerce among unequals, the mask became an essential article.

Masks were the public face of Venice in the eighteenth century. They were also present in less visible ways. Intellectuals spoke of "honest dissimulation," which called a partial truth—as opposed to a half-lie—morally justified. Artists depicted allegorical masks both to condemn and to recommend, with connotations that went far beyond the mere deceit or disguise that modern misreadings see. Women masked their faces with veils, which granted liberty under the guise of protecting modesty. Beggars whose identities were known wore masks to hide their shame. When an economic crisis opened gaping disparities among elites, they still clung to a tradition of identical dress to mask the inequality.

In early modern Venice, masks served purposes that did not depend on anonymity. Their use defies modern notions that identify masks with deception or a mocking rejection of hierarchy. Masking in Venice was more often conservative, preserving distance, guarding status, and permitting contact among unequals through fictive concealment. Rather than obscuring identities, masks affirmed their permanence.

Venice Incognito opens with carnival but looks beyond it to reframe some common assumptions. Did carnival truly free revelers from their social roles? Did it grant them license to mock their superiors and shed their inhibitions? Did the mask actually disguise maskers? To ask such questions with the mask's wider associations in mind exposes currents that are not especially forward-looking, including Venetians' self-policing against unruly revelers, the heavy presence of the state in scripting celebrations that foreigners often took as spontaneous, and the considerable violence that accompanied carnival. Carnival's wider context casts serious doubt on judgments that have linked the Republic's supposedly pervasive frivolity to its decline and fall.

The interplay between the mask's two sides—its function in particular settings and its more abstract invocation by writers, moralists, and deceivers—has shaped the structure of Venice Incognito. The book's twenty-one short chapters are by turns historical and thematic, sketching a broad chronology while occasionally skipping forward and back in time. Vignettes display masks in their many settings: in carnival and commedia dell'arte, among foreign sovereigns visiting the city "incognito" and the local nobles who received them, as rhetorical figures to dissemble the beliefs of those threatened or oppressed, as a tool of "sincerity" used by con men and seducers, and as allegorical features of paintings and drawings intended to warn, counsel, or, in the case of the Venetian artist Giandomenico Tiepolo, pay sad tribute to this city of masks after its defeat by Napoleon.

How past generations have viewed the relationship between appearance and essence—whether the mask of manners is a blessing or a bane—says much about changing ideas of the self. The Venetian intellectual Gasparo Gozzi, convinced that humans were neither equal nor naturally sociable, praised conventions of courtesy as so many "masks, veils, fictions, appearances." Jean-Jacques Rousseau, by contrast, lamenting the corruptions of civilized society, used the language of masks to deplore the sway of appearances. "The man of the world is wholly his mask," he wrote. "What he is, is nothing." Just over a century later, Oscar Wilde reversed the formula and quipped that man was least himself when he talked in his own person. "Give him a mask and he will tell you the truth."[1]

Scholars from several disciplines have written about the promise and limits of altering one's identity in attempts to chart the historical development of selfhood. The literary scholar Stephen Greenblatt traces the roots of modern identity as a "manipulable, artful process" to poems, plays, and religious tracts from the Renaissance. The historian Natalie Zemon Davis locates novel efforts in early modern Europe to forge coherent narratives of the self in cases of imposture and the self-defense of accused criminals. The philosopher Charles Taylor recounts the rise of modern varieties of inwardness and individuality through major works of philosophy, which narrate a greater and greater freedom to shape one's own identity.[2]

Venice Incognito aims to ground these large themes in the lived experience of a particular population. It approaches such changes by enlarging the evidence from case histories and classic works of literature and philosophy to shared beliefs and practices. The book ends with the modern imperative of self-creation still out of reach for most Venetians. The chilling fate of a failed impostor named Tomaso Gerachi, who was expert in counterfeiting nobility, reminds us that in eighteenth-century Venice there were strict limits to fashioning the self.

Masks are a continuing presence in the evolution of selfhood. From the early modern period to our own time, they have gone from marking and reinforcing a hierarchy in which alternative identities were scarcely conceivable, to helping wearers see themselves in other social roles, to standing as an unsettling symbol for freely forged but existentially uncertain identities. From where we stand, somewhere near the end of this sequence, it is hard to imagine masks as doing anything other than questioning identity. *Venice Incognito* tells a different story. To have a good view of masks from an earlier age, we need to set aside our own.

PART ONE

The Carnival of Venice

CHAPTER I

Casanova's Carnival

Casanova celebrated carnival year-round. Where there was revelry, there was Casanova. Where there was gambling into the night, there was Casanova. Where there were freethinking women and frothing champagne, there, too, was Casanova. The neglected son of a small-time actress, Giacomo Casanova embraced every form of disguise this city of masks had to offer. What began as bluster and luck—posing as physician to a decrepit senator named Bragadin, whose gondola he was sharing when the old man suffered a stroke—became for Casanova a lifelong masquerade. Bragadin recovered, grew convinced that Casanova had saved his life, and more or less adopted him. A reckless gambler unafraid of the high-stakes lie, Casanova had struck it rich. Before his big break, Casanova had earned his wages as a mediocre fiddler in a pit orchestra. Now he had the means to transform his roots.

"I hate deceit," Casanova confides to readers in his sprawling *History of My Life*.[1] The truth was that his life consisted of little else. He traveled under assumed names—Farusi, Vetturi—before eventually settling on Seingalt and bestowing upon himself the honorific title of *chevalier*. He changed his wardrobe to suit his serial selves, from a priest's cassock, to the fussy ornaments of rings, medals, ribbons, and watch-chains, to a soldier's uniform that matched that of no known army. He duped patrons with sham numerology and black magic, forged currency, and brought scores of women to bed with the claim that each was the greatest love of his life. The same supreme confidence that had convinced Bragadin earned

Casanova private audiences with kings and philosophers: with Frederick the Great, Louis XV, and the Empress Catherine of Russia; with Pope Clement XIII, who granted him membership in the Order of the Holy Spur; and with Rousseau and Voltaire. By the prime of his life, the Chevalier de Seingalt had successfully erased his past.

Tall, dark-skinned, and muscular, highly polite and even a touch pedantic, old-fashioned in his politics, a gifted storyteller, credulous about the incredible but in religious matters a skeptic, Casanova was a force to be reckoned with. Yet by his own telling, his will had little to do with his rise. On the contrary. It was seldom clear to this master of improvisation what the next step would be. Nor should it have been. "We are but thinking atoms, which move where the wind drives them," he wrote. "Hence anything important that happens to us in this world is only what is bound to happen to us."[2] This is a startling sentiment for someone who defied his origins to move in the highest circles. Following the script of eighteenth-century materialism—a philosophy that likened thought to the careening ricochet of billiard balls—Casanova resigned his life's authorship to Fate. He accordingly undertook to maximize pleasure, minimize loss, and draw whatever lessons, moral or otherwise, his senses might teach.

An encounter with the fifteen-year-old Rosalie, a pious chambermaid in an Avignon brothel, gives him occasion to reflect on ultimate truths. "She devoured me with kisses, and, in short, she made me happy; and since in this life nothing is real except the present, I enjoyed it, dismissing the images of the past and loathing the darkness of the always dreadful future, for it offers nothing certain except death, *ultima linea rerum*."[3] If you asked any foreigner in eighteenth century to describe Venetian carnival, you would likely hear words that applied to Giacomo Casanova, too. It was about forgetting the past and suspending the future, escaping behind the blankness of the mask, minding the muse of pleasure. Carnival, the reveler might continue, was about transforming the self.

It is therefore no surprise that on the last day of carnival, 1754, Casanova was behind a mask, having the time of his life. He would later write that this was one of his happiest moments. Not long before, he had begun an affair with the nun M. M. Her convent was on Murano, the small clump of islands in the lagoon known principally for glassmaking. There was to be a dance in the parlor for the entertainment of the ladies, who were now beginning to gather behind the latticed screens. The scene was improbable, as clowns, peasants, Turks, and pirates spilled out of gondolas in a headlong scramble for the holy ground. Some took inspiration from commedia dell'arte. In his Pierrot costume, Casanova was, as usual, going against the grain. The figure was French, not Italian, a docile simpleton who serenades by moonlight. Casanova wore a baggy white tunic, with loose sleeves and trousers that touched his heels. A large hat covered his ears, and a gauze mask hid his eyes and nose. Provided one wasn't a hunchback or lame, Casanova said, there was no costume better suited for disguise. Not even an intimate would recognize him.

With the ball now at full tilt, Casanova watched as M. M. and the other nuns laughed at him. He danced with clumsy abandon, keeping to Pierrot's character as a boob, blundering through the room, suddenly falling asleep and waking with a start, crashing into other maskers and bumped roughly in return. A nimble Harlequin chased him and, from nowhere, a Punch tripped him hard. Casanova grabbed a leg, wrestled Punch to the floor, and knocked his false hump loose. The crowd cheered, and Casanova streaked from the convent and jumped into a waiting gondola, which took him to the churning sea of revelers in Pizza San Marco.

Shrove Tuesday in Venice, *martedì grasso,* marked the end of the popular celebrations with balls, dinners, and spontaneous dancing in the narrow alleys and packed public squares. The city's official celebration was the previous Thursday, *giovedì grasso,* when maskers of every social class assembled near the basilica and a procession of government officials marched onto the balcony of the ducal palace. Together they watched the same scripted events that Venetians standing in that very spot had seen each *giovedì grasso* for nearly half a millennium. Acrobats risked death on ropes overhead, sword dancers leapt and tumbled, wooden castles were destroyed with clubs, and bulls were beheaded.

The final fling came on Tuesday. Maskers poured into the piazza and along the Zattere to dance with strangers. The winding route between San Stefano and St. Mark's was clogged and virtually impassable. Shrove Tuesday was also the last night of the season for the city's theaters, which staged their best works, hoping for a sellout. Gamblers spilled out of their dens and into the streets, settling scores, nursing wounds, trying to get home safely with their gains. Inside the overcrowded cafés, where the roar grew deafening and the heat was stifling, breathing under the mask was a labor.

As Casanova slipped back to Venice in the waning hours of this *martedì grasso,* he had cause to smile about his disguise. Now fully into his affair with M. M., there was still the problem of C. C., another nun at the convent. She, too, had been watching from behind the grate and had laughed at his antics.[4]

Five months earlier, C. C.'s father had sent her to the convent. She was fourteen and, with the help of a mask, had gone on long walks with Casanova throughout the city, to the opera, to the gambling hall, and eventually to a rented room on the narrow strip of land called the Guidecca. Casanova had assured her that they were married "before God." Asking her father for her hand was a mere formality, he had said. Casanova didn't get the chance. Suddenly C. C. found herself behind the convent's walls, and with that Casanova found religion, joining a handful of lay worshipers in the order's small chapel in hopes of glimpsing her.

It was during his pilgrimage that M. M. noticed him. One evening as Casanova boarded his gondola for Venice, a note was dropped at his feet proposing that he come to the parlor in a mask. Two days later, he was on his way back to Murano in a spacious two-oared vessel with a Countess S., named in the note as a confidant of its author. Both were masked; they spoke of the weather. Casanova could scarcely contain himself. What could the note's farewell—it was signed "your loving friend"— possibly signify? Did she know the real reason for his piety?

Casanova remained masked as they sat down before the screen. When the countess asked for the nun by name, he was astounded by its eminence. Casanova studied M. M. as the women talked. She did not once look in his direction. M. M. was a perfect beauty, he would write, noble and shy, with two rows of magnificent teeth, chestnut eyebrows, and moist lips. "Sure that I should possess her in a few days, I enjoyed the pleasure of paying her the tribute of desiring her."

Furtive notes followed, carried by surrogates. The two met, first at the grate and later at a small apartment nearby. Casanova eventually learned that the rooms belonged to the French ambassador, François de Bernis. A favorite at Versailles, the abbé de Bernis was posted to the city in 1752 with instructions to take special note of what lessons the Serenissima's steady decline ("decadence" was the word the ministers had used) held for France. "The Republic has suffered the sad effects of an ambition that may well exhaust its resources and bring about its utter ruin," the brief read.[5] Diplomats were already saying what is now conventional wisdom: that the catastrophic loss of southern Greece to the Ottoman Turks thirty-five years earlier, formalized in the Treaty of Passarowitz, had sealed the fate of this once-great empire. Venice would henceforth be an observer, and not a broker, of world events.

De Bernis's work did not prevent him from tasting the city's pleasures. Soon after his arrival, he acquired a mistress of elevated birth and furnished their love nest, the *casino* (little house) on Murano, with the latest styles. This was a luxury cultivated by the wealthiest Venetians. At the time of the Republic's fall in 1797, the authorities counted some 130 *casini*, the largest number of which were situated near Piazza San Marco. A pied-à-terre in one's own city, the *casino* was a quiet retreat from the loud cafés: for private dinners and conversation, for politicking or plotting, and for personal business that required discretion. The government was understandably concerned about them, not only for political reasons. In the eighteenth century, it periodically closed *casini* for offenses against morality.[6]

Casanova came to know the ambassador's *casino* well. It had three rooms, an ample fireplace, and a library stocked with works attacking religion, all of them from France and all forbidden. The ambassador kept a collection of pornographic engravings, which included Gervaise de Latouche's *Portier des Chartreux* and the *Elegantiae latini sermonis* of Johannes Meursius. Only after numerous visits to the apartment, and the bouts of athletic lovemaking they inevitably brought, did Casanova learn of one additional extravagance. Just off the main room was a secret alcove that permitted de Bernis to watch his guests through small holes drilled into the ornate woodwork. The ambassador had been a silent witness to their sessions, M. M. informed Casanova, and he hoped to see more.

The revelation led Casanova to find a *casino* of his own, which he rented through the English ambassador's former cook. It was already furnished "for the sake of love, good food, and every kind of pleasure." It included a bedroom, a dressing room, and an English-style water closet. A revolving dumbwaiter connected the main room to the kitchen so that meals could be enjoyed without seeing one's servants. There was a grand marble fireplace, a large chandelier, and mirrors set at propitious angles. Coupling nudes were painted on Chinese tiles, which hung on the walls. The arrangements were worthy of a patrician, Casanova remarked. Here, as elsewhere, he was playing the part to perfection.

As a Venetian, and one whose tastes ran to the forbidden in ideas as well as actions, Casanova knew that his habits strayed toward the far edge of the law. One evening as he left the Murano chapel, he saw another masker dressed in a *tabàro* and *baùta* following him. He got into a gondola bound for Venice. The masker did likewise, disembarking just behind Casanova near the Church of the Apostoli. Casanova ran him down, pressed a knife to his throat, and demanded to know what he wanted. Others approached, and the masker fled.

The man was probably working for the State Inquisition, a secretive council whose army of informants brought back daily reports about who was doing what with whom. One such report, now housed in the archives of the State Inquisitors, named the patrician Marco Donà, a contemporary of Casanova's, as a libertine, atheist, and sodomite.[7] In fact, it was not long after Casanova's affair with M. M. ended that an agent named Manuzzi feigned an interest in purchasing his books and, on the pretext of taking them to an expert for appraisal, presented the Inquisitors with the collection. Along with Ariosto, Horace, and Petrarch, there were works on magic and the Kabbalah, formulas for conjuring the devil, and a fair sampling of pornography. Casanova was imprisoned in a scorching cell beneath the roof of the ducal palace on charges of blasphemy, sorcery, and atheism. His dramatic escape fifteen months later secured his status as an international celebrity. For the rest of his days he charmed polite society all over Europe with its retelling, a performance that took approximately two hours.

The tabàro and baùta, the dress of the likely agent trailing Casanova, was standard attire for eighteenth-century maskers. It consisted of an encompassing black cloak that men wore over their coats and breeches and a close-fitting hood that encircled the face and hid the neck. A white half-mask of waxed carton that extended to just below the nose was normally worn with it. The mask, or *larva,* was wedged against the forehead by a three-cornered hat (figure 1). Women wore the tabàro and baùta over flowing skirts. When they went hatless, they wore an oval *morèta,* a black mask made of velvet or lace. This they held in place by clenching a small button between their teeth, which made speaking impossible. A jewel sometimes adorned the women's morèta, "glittering on the outside," a traveler noted, "to accompany the Sparkling of their Eyes" (figure 2).[8]

The mask gave M. M. the freedom to visit Casanova outside her convent. One evening, he waited for her near the equestrian statue before the church of Santi Giovanni e Paolo. A masker approached, slowed, and began circling him. Expecting to be robbed, Casanova tensed. A hand advanced—open, empty, a gesture of peace—and Casanova suddenly saw that it was M. M. in the clothes of a man, complete with breeches, tabàro and baùta, the white half-mask, and a tricorn. Her gift for disguise extended to other details. Casanova later emptied her pockets, which contained a snuffbox, a case of toothpicks, a scented handkerchief, two fine watches, and a pair of English flintlock pistols. The cook had prepared game, sturgeon, truffles, oysters, boiled eggs, and anchovies, all served on Saxon porcelain. They drank burgundy, champagne, and rum-laced punch. Volcanic lovemaking followed.

On another visit, M. M. came dressed in a full skirt instead of breeches and wearing an oval morèta instead of the *larva.* The couple went to the

FIGURE 1. Couple in the Venetian tabàro and baùta

FIGURE 2. Woman wearing a morèta

Ridotto, Venice's famed gambling hall near Piazza San Marco. M. M. played recklessly, unlucky at first but then winning big. Her luck drew the attention of onlookers. Nobles approached to congratulate her. Gamblers of every social class came to the Ridotto, and, apart from the barefaced patricians who held the bank at each table, most others were masked. This did not necessarily mean that identities were unknown, either to gamblers or to the Inquisitors' agents who were fixtures in the candlelit chambers. Given M. M.'s holy vows and Casanova's low birth, it would be unfortunate for either to be seen here in the company of the other. Casanova began to feel that they were being watched and grew increasingly uneasy. In an instant, they were out the door and moving across the dark waters in a gondola. "This is the way to escape from busybodies in Venice," Casanova wrote.

M. M. receives more attention than any of the roughly 120 other lovers Casanova describes in his memoirs, in large part because she was a kindred spirit. She at once embraced and rejected the reigning order, sincere in devotion but renegade in her vows. "I did not begin to love God until I had rid myself of the idea of him which religion had given me," she says. Casanova writes that he was never sure whether she was a libertine posing as a believer or a believer posing as a libertine. He therefore calls her both. When she comes to him in her nun's habit, she is "disguised as a saint." When she leaves the convent surreptitiously in street clothes, she is "very well masked, as a woman." Casanova gave the same gloss on a scene of passion with M. M. when they were still meeting in the ambassador's *casino* on Murano. They tumble onto a small couch, still mostly clothed. M. M. is wearing the habit, and Casanova is in the masker's tabàro and baùta. Such was the picture of their love, Casanova writes, "sketched out, executed in flesh and blood, and finished off by the great painter, all-wise Nature, who, inspired by love, could never paint another either truer or more interesting."[9] Such was his animating creed: the truth of the mask.

Casanova's carnival—his headlong affair with M. M. wearing masks both physical and figurative—was a telescoped version of the script he replayed in and out of season for the length of his life: embrace a role and call it the truth. Beneath all the masks was a vision of the self as tabula rasa, whose content Casanova spent his days writing, wiping clean, and rewriting. His multiple identities were true, he said, because they were his own creation.

Like the pornographic literature he relished, Casanova's memoirs exist in the perpetual present as if time never passes—a singular feat, given the more than three thousand pages they comprise. It comes as a mild shock to hear mention of lovers Casanova has had fifteen years earlier, or to meet the various adolescent children he has fathered across Europe (at least one of whom he beds, to his professed ignorance). His is an autobiography told from the outside—less a bildungsroman describing growth than a picaresque tale told in ignorance of the hero's thoughts. When Casanova describes his inner life, the effort seems contrived. "On waking in the morning I cast a summary glance at my physical and moral state, and find that I am happy; I examine my feelings, and I perceive them to be so well-justified that I do not complain of not being in control of them."[10]

I do not complain of not being in control. This is not the story of a romantic hero forging his destiny in accordance with the inner self. Casanova may have been a master of self-fashioning, but his selves were successive and serial, made true despite the inconsistencies by his professed sincerity of intentions. An Epicurean who ordered his life to serve his senses, Casanova believed that humans were powerless to direct their larger course. Near the end of his memoirs he strikes a valedictory tone. "My will, far from declaring me free, was only an instrument which Fortune used to make what she would of me" (figure 3).[11]

Altera nunc rerum facies, me quero, nec adsum:
Non sum qui fueram non putor esse: fui.

FIGURE 3. "Now comes another face of things. I seek myself, but I am not here.
I am neither that which once was, nor what men judged me to be: I existed."
Giacomo Casanova in his sixty-third year.

Casanova's unbroken present-mindedness made easier his avowals of undying love, which he voiced to virtually everyone he seduced. This was more than the justification of a cad. It was tied to a self-conception unbound by fixed points of reference, status, or profession. It was intoxicating, free, and liberating, and it contributes in no small way to the tone he maintains throughout his twelve-volume life story: heedless, confident, buoyant no matter how desperate the circumstances.

This was probably why he remembered the Venetian carnival of 1754, when he stepped into the baggy Pierrot costume and launched his crazy dance, as his happiest moment. On some level, he surely knew that his audacious double-dealing would have to stop. Despite his avowed "freedom from prejudice," it was his own discomfort with developments soon after this *martedì grasso* that caused him to end both affairs. These included M. M.'s eventual corruption of C. C., the predictable trios that followed, awkward dinners with the French ambassador, and Casanova's late-dawning realization that he was an unwitting pawn in the grooming of C. C. for de Bernis. Besides, Casanova would soon meet a servant girl and suddenly find himself in love "as I had never been in love with any girl."[12]

But all of this—the two "little houses," the masked encounters, the gambling and fine dinners, the unease and eventual separation—was still in the future when Casanova's gondola plowed through the waters as music and laughter receded behind him. Once in Venice, he waded through the thick crowds of revelers to come at last to the Ridotto.

> I spent two hours playing at all the small banks, going from one to another, winning, losing, indulging in all sorts of antics in complete freedom of body and soul, sure that no one recognized me, enjoying the present and snapping my fingers at the future and at all those who were pleased to exercise their reason in the dreary task of foreseeing it.[13]

CHAPTER 2

New World

Giandomenico Tiepolo's painting *The Minuet* (figure 4) captures carnival in a moment of sheer joy. There is a riot of costumes. Giant white hats tower above a pair of Pulcinella noses. A Turk's striped turban rises nearby. A black-masked Arlecchino holds a baton over his shoulder, and women appear in full and half-masks. At the center a dancer in a gorgeous dress curtsies, lost in her own world and oblivious to her surroundings. She is either an actress in costume—as the lover Isabella from commedia dell'arte, for instance—or a simple girl done up for the occasion. Or maybe Tiepolo is toying with us and she really is Isabella, a make-believe character who has stepped out of the drama and into the city's crush. That would explain the otherworldly blankness in her eyes as she looks out at us and not at her partner, whose chunky calves and courtier's costume make him solidly earthbound. Some in the crowd are fixed on the scene. Others are indifferent. Musicians bunched near the rear are occupied with something out of view.

A girl leans in next to the legs of a massive statue. Three old men stand just behind the dancer. A coachman watches from the back of the crowd with palpable longing. Is he in costume or a hired hand working for one of the revelers? A gentlewoman watches at a slight remove from her window. In the opposite corner, a patrician with his back turned talks to a lady who might well be the dancer's twin. She, too, gazes out frankly. Whatever fantasy world Tiepolo meant to conjure, the human sentiment he captures is real, in the excluded coachman's gaze, in the noble-

FIGURE 4. Giandomenico Tiepolo, *The Minuet*

woman's hauteur, in the bashful interest on the face of the teenager who watches from a wall in the back.

Carnival in Venice began unofficially on December 26, when the theaters reopened after a ten-day break for Christmas. This day, St. Stephen's, signaled the start of a steady flow of tourists, whose numbers grew over the following two months. The government decreed the official beginning of each carnival season, which varied from year to year and was relevant chiefly for knowing which hours of the day masks were permitted. The crowds were largest the week before Lent, when this inveterately private city threw open its doors and became "the hostel of graces and pleasures."[1] Carnival turned Venice into a stage and made everyone a performer. "The entire town is disguised," a French tourist declared upon arriving.[2] The performance is evident in Tiepolo's painting, too, but the disguise is less sure: despite the masks, not all dispositions are hidden.

Revelers of all ranks mingled in cafés and gambling halls, along promenades and before makeshift stages, among the freak shows, fortunetellers, soothsayers, and acrobats, all under cover of the mask. The events of the season were partly scripted and partly spontaneous, blending the ritual of centuries with improvisation. With its overlapping traditions, carnival in Venice played on several registers at once, blending violence, high hilarity, and solemn ceremony. Travelers described a topsy-turvy world, where the plebs and patricians exchanged roles, men dressed as women and women as men, and the powers that be were mocked. Behind the mask commoners were said to mix freely with nobles, women with men, and foreigners with the locals.

Maskers made nocturnal visits to convents to talk to the nuns behind screens. They flooded into cafés to talk to strangers or to gawk at the ostentatious transvestites known as *gnaghe*. They clogged the Ridotto, the dark, vast gambling hall near San Moisè, and mingled in the city's renowned theaters to see plays and hear operas. At mealtime they flocked to the city's inns and *osterie* for duck ragout, a carnival delicacy made from a small black fowl known locally as *diavolo di mare,* "devil of the sea."[3] For visitors especially, carnival was a season outside of time, when roles were suspended, taboos relaxed, and life's practical concerns set aside.

The cacophony of a hundred different sideshows reigned. There were acrobats and rope dancers, exotic animals and human monstrosities, charlatans hawking elixirs, mountebanks with their herbs and ointments, and impromptu performers of all kinds. Maskers moved from one attraction to the next. Con men thrived with their petty scams, and professional card sharks fleeced the innocent. Prostitutes knew what some sought and were eager to serve. Pickpockets worked every corner of the city. Beggars asked alms " in full maske," an English traveler noted.[4] Fortunetellers whispered their news into long pipes to emphasize its intimacy. "When they see a listener smiling," a visitor wrote of them, "or witness some other gesture of approbation, they stop speaking for a moment and ring a small bell with marvelous gravity to show that they have just penetrated a well-hidden secret."[5] Another spoke of the terror and surprise the whispered words could bring.[6] The authorities periodically warned the public about the opportunities such crowds gave predators. It was "corrupting," the powerful Council of Ten stated. But carnival and its yearly rituals were too embedded in the city's history for either Venetians or their visitors to be deterred.[7]

During carnival, Piazza San Marco was transformed into a vast cabinet of curiosities. The atmosphere had aspects of an elegant ball and a county fair. Maskers in silks and lace visited the rustic and inspected the grotesque. In 1750, a lady led a lioness through the piazza, caressing it and periodically putting her hand into its mouth. The next year a rhino

FIGURE 5. Pietro Longhi, *The Rhinoceros*

was on display (figure 5). Camels, elephants, and monkeys appeared; a German displayed a miniature horse dressed in children's clothing; heavy weights were hoisted onto the bellies of strong men. Vendors sold sweets, tooth extractors set up booths, and for twenty-five years running one Giuseppe Colombani cured "hydropsy, paralysis, gout, apoplexy, kidney stones, and phthisic."[8]

Some displays were more edifying than others. For a fee, maskers entered an exhibit just off the square publicizing the wonders of science. It included a wax woman with her stomach opened to expose her organs, a human arm preserved in fluid, and the severed leg of a horse. In the middle of the square, a magic lantern called *Mondo nuovo* (New World) drew people who crowded around "as if they were mad," as Goldoni wrote, all of them keen to see wonderful scenes of battles, regattas, ambassadors, queens, and emperors.[9] A painting by Tiepolo titled *Mondo nuovo* casts us as the excluded outsiders as a man on a chair dangles the device before a group. We see the maskers' backs but can't make out what's happening. The image exerts the same hypnotic pull that carnivalgoers must have felt at every step.

Judging by contemporaries' accounts, Tiepolo's array of costumes in *The Minuet* is accurate. This list comes from two eighteenth-century sources:

> Frenchmen, Turks, Indians, a Hunchback, a Highwayman, Astrologers, Necromancers, Chiromancers, Magi, a Lawyer with Cards, Philosophers, Warriors, Physicians, a Clothing-dealer, Doctors, Actors, Poets, Singers, Captains, Cavaliers, a Nun's Servant with a Basket of Sweets, a Fisherman with a Platter of Fish, Charlatans, a Doctor with a Book, a Street-sweeper, Pulcinella with a Plate of Macaroni, Boatmen, Lackeys, a German with Pearls, a Spaniard, Perfumers, a Hebrew lamenting Carnival, the Devil, a Hunter with Birds and a Shotgun, an Old Hermit, a Gardener with a Cap, a Baker, Clowns, Quakers, a King with a Scepter, a Cavalier on a Stick-horse, Lace-sellers, Sellers of Polenta, Amazons, Moors, Soldiers, a Dancing-bear.[10]

Some maskers opted for plainer garb, the *tabàro e baùta,* which was in many ways the opposite of a costume. It was common, not individual, and its wearers were more likely to blend in than stand out. One French visitor called it the city's "uniform," adding that he was surprised to see that so many chose its black sobriety when the season offered them such freedom.[11]

Maskers traveled in packs, sometimes with a common theme (figure 6). The Seven Deadly Sins paraded around the square in 1756 with a robed demon leading the way. Each held a sign identifying his sin. Most were obvious—the thief was Envy, the prostitute Lust, the "eccentric" Gluttony, and the miser Covetousness—but two carried a barb: the lawyer was Pride and the doctor was Sloth.[12] As the Frenchman Maximilien Misson observed, you were free to dress however you wished but you had to live up to the character you chose. "This is when harlequins converge, scuffle, and say a hundred lunacies. Doctors dispute, preeners preen, and

FIGURE 6. Venetian carnival

so forth."[13] In the final days before Lent the tempo quickened. Costumers passed in a rush of color.

> As the *Carnival* advances, the Dress grows more various and whimsical: the Women make themselves Nymphs and Shepherdesses, the men Scaramouches and Punchinellos, with twenty other Fancies, whatever first comes uppermost. For further Variety, they sometimes change Sexes: Women appear in Men's Habits, and Men in Women, and so are now and then pick'd up, to the great disappointment of the Lover. . . . Their general Rendezvous is the *Piazza di San Marco*, which large as it is, is perfectly throng'd with them, from thence they march in Shoals to the *Ridotto* which is not far off.[14]

Some went as their social opposites. In the 1770s, for instance, "false beggars" were a carnival fashion, as men and women of noble birth dressed in rags, rubbed their faces with grime, and went begging from café to café in the piazza.[15] A more profligate version featured the shredding of fine fabrics to make a tattered suit that at once mocked the poor and flaunted one's own wealth. But reversals also worked from the other direction, sometimes with a political charge. An Englishman on the grand tour was especially amused by six men in lawyers' garb "with very scurvy gowns and weather-beaten wigs" who seized strangers in the crowd and told them they faced charges. The joke was apparently popular. Twenty-five years later, in 1759, two commoners dressed as attorneys went through the streets loudly complaining about the judicial system. They also cited shopkeepers for fabricated infractions and demanded they pay fines on the spot.[16]

This was just the sort of cheek that visitors hoped to see when they came to Venice: a great anonymous frolic in which all participated as equals. Perfect the part and you are whoever you wish to be. "The mask rendered every inequality equal," the nineteenth-century *Lexicon of the Veneto* declared, looking over its shoulder to survey the previous five centuries. It was the coin of the realm for "the greatest nobles, the vilest plebeians, and the most eminent informants."[17] Also writing in the nineteenth century, the historian Samuele Romanin drew a connection between the maskers' borrowed equality and their free mingling. The mask was the Venetians' preferred dress, "worn by the most grave magistrates including State Inquisitors, by the doge himself, by foreign princes and ambassadors, so that, freed of all other designation and greeting one another by no other name than *masker*, they could go everywhere, mixing in with the populace and protected from every insult and offense."[18]

Under the mask, conversation flowed freely among people who would not otherwise have spoken. One approving newspaper termed their familiarity "illustrious," but many others, especially within the Church and government, labeled the conversations dangerous.[19] A 1755 book dedicated to Pope Benedict XIV contended that carnival's pleasures were the work of Satan. It carries a blistering attack on what its author, Daniele Concina, called "modern conversation." "Wise men the world over confirm that these modern conversations are . . . the source of all disorder. They are the cause of divorce among married couples, dissension among families, irreparable loss to youth, and the destruction of the patrimony. They promote luxury, softness, sloth, pomp, and vanity."[20]

Agents of the State Inquisitors faced the nearly impossible task of monitoring what was said, and whenever possible who had said it, in the city's cafés during carnival. Coffeehouses with names such as The King of France, Pitt the Hero, Rainbow, and Abundance lined the arcades that ran along the edge of Piazza San Marco. During carnival, revelers spent entire evenings here shouting over the din in stifling heat.[21]

The eighteenth century saw an explosion in the number of cafés in Venice, with more than two hundred in 1750. The authorities tried to stay ahead of the threat they believed cafés posed to decency. When the Englishman Edward Wright came to Venice for the 1720 carnival, he learned that the government had banned seats in the coffeehouses in order to discourage "Meetings or Cabals of any sort." The explanation is questionable. Standing doesn't keep people from talking. To judge from the transcripts of surveillance agents, moreover, there was no shortage of conversation in these dark spaces.[22]

The cafés of Venice, especially during carnival, provided women with a chance to leave the predictable routine of everyday life. This bothered a good many defenders of tradition. For the patrician Giacomo Nani, women's freedom to speak was a symptom of social decline. When women entered cafés, he observed, they put aside their blushing timidity (which was their major ornament, he added) and assumed that they were equal to others there, "putting themselves so to speak in the arms of all who pass by, even those of basest birth, who display the worst morals and the guiltiest conduct."[23] Others responded archly:

New-fangled Machiavels,
Discoursing on politics
In *casini* and cafés,
On beds and bidets,
Concoct novel systems
As legislatresses,
Assess the Republic
And supplant dogaressas.[24]

Convinced of the moral harm incurred when the sexes spoke freely to one another, the government issued an edict in 1743 forbidding women from entering cafés. Agents fanned out to notify proprietors of the new rule. The exercise had its ironies. When they came to Francesco Righetti's café near San Moisè, they encountered his daughter Eugenia, who was working in her sick father's stead. It fell to Eugenia to refuse women entry and disallow all "women's conversations."[25] A small number of cafés received permission to serve women on procession days but only if accompanied by a man. The order was particularly difficult to enforce, given the pervasiveness of the tabàro and baùta among women and men. As was often the case with laws pertaining to dress, state agents reported violators assiduously, but few were punished. One of them wrote that he had seen women of all ranks behaving "in a manner that does not distinguish gentlewomen from maidservants and ladies of the street."[26] Another said that the atmosphere in a café evoked a brothel—"a continuous bacchanal from morning until night"—with men and women, masked and unmasked, mingling unchecked.[27]

Even as traditionalists expressed their outrage over women's conversations, certain establishments drew a clientele that was still more scandalous. In the century's closing decades, carnival crowds assembled in seedy cafés along the quay just beyond the ducal palace to watch Venice's

FIGURE 7. Cross-dressing
in carnival: a Venetian gnaga

gnaghe. These were men who dressed in full skirts, beads, cloth caps, and flesh-colored masks (figure 7). Some came as Friulian peasant girls, others as Neapolitans with lemons and guitars. The name described their voices, which sounded like cats in heat, a whining nasally *GNAAWW—GAAYY!* Others compared them to crows. The obscenities they hurled were by all accounts stupefying, not just for their content but for being uttered so shamelessly in public.

Gnaghe sometimes pulled boys dressed as babies along by the hand. In a letter to his mother, the Englishman Joseph Spence expressed horror at having seen one such couple during carnival. A fleshy man dressed as a nursemaid suckled a youth in swaddling clothes. When Spence and a companion stared in disbelief, the boy spewed a mouthful of milk at them. Spence just managed to prevent his friend from "beat[ing] the baby's teeth down his throat."[28]

Contemporaries describe what they saw and heard in the darkened rooms of these cafés: gnaghe pressed tightly together, snatches of lewd jokes and insults, rumors of sodomy. Gnaghe gave impromptu performances of songs or scenes from the theater. They brawled and danced and taunted onlookers. Revelers purchased tickets and stood in long lines outside the cafés to see them.[29]

There are scattered reports of gnaghe throughout the eighteenth century, but their numbers in public were greatest in the 1780s. The State Inquisitors sent agents to take notes, which they did with evident discomfort. During the 1788 season, gnaghe crowded into the café Steffano on the Riva degli Schiavoni until no one else could enter. They stomped the floor and beat the tables in rhythm, blew whistles and pounded drums. The reporting agent thought he would go deaf.[30] Masks were de rigueur wherever gnaghe appeared. Anonymity among these revelers was carefully maintained. "Despite the greatest diligence," wrote Girolamo Lioni in a report to the Inquisitors, "I was not able to discover the name of a single masker."[31] Another night, a fistfight erupted among ten gnaghe at the Steffano, with one of them shouting, "Son of a whore!" Again Lioni: "I made many attempts to learn the identity of this masker, but it was impossible for anyone to recognize him."[32]

When an unknown foreigner appeared at the Steffano unmasked one carnival night in 1788 and tried out a familiar insult ("Go bugger yourself!"), he was roundly jeered. One gnaga called out that he should mind his language in such respectable establishments. The visitor had clearly stumbled into the wrong bar and was breaking all the rules. His parting shot, duly noted by the surveillance agent on duty, was tart: "Screw you—you and all of your spying scum."[33] Others who wore masks uttered far worse oaths and were lustily applauded. Little was done to prevent gnaghe from gathering. Agents sometimes followed them throughout the city. Angelo Tamiazzo describes gnaghe of a fresh age parading around the piazza, under the Procuratie, and in restaurants. Not even Geneva, the land of Calvin, he comments with either outrage or cutting irony, hosts such shamelessness.[34] Another agent spotted what Tamiazzo hints at, the fifteen-year-old son of the patrician Alvise Corner engaged in sodomy under the arches of the Procuratie Vecchie.[35]

Carnival's promiscuous mingling—women with women, men with women, men with men—struck a chord with travelers. To them, the carnival of Venice meant a holiday from morality, where disguise made all things possible. Cover the face, alter the voice, and anything could happen. Naturally the most thrilling possibilities were sexual. Englishmen on the grand tour never tired of Venice/Venus puns or of the rhymes they inspired. The Venetian Giorgio Baffo, a noble gone to seed who dabbled in politics, spent his free time composing pornographic verses that ratified the tourists' view.

Anyone seeking a noble amusement
Comes to St. Mark's every evening at dusk.
Here you will find high society eager
To show off its riches and wallow in lust.

If you're looking for fun in this beautiful city,
Then come to the square when the ladies walk by.
They loiter and mingle, these legions of women,
Who are willing and able to make your bird fly.

Then it suddenly seems like a public bordello
As a thousand pink twats start to open their lips,
And the pale little fish with his head above water
Bows to each of them nobly before he commits.[36]

Visitors came to carnival expecting this sort of thing. Their giddy accounts in letters and travelogues give an indication of what they heard and saw. "Carnival is a veritable harvest of love!" gushed the Frenchman Limojan de Saint-Didier. During carnival, he said, masked nuns received their brothers' courtesans in their convents, bringing them into their cells, sharing confidences, calling them sisters-in-law, exchanging caresses.[37] On his first day in Venice for the 1730 carnival, the Baron von Pöllnitz donned a scarlet and silver domino for a walk through the city. He had scarcely entered Piazza San Marco when two masked ladies approached. One began "twitching my sleeve," he writes, and addressed him. "We are inclin'd to think that you are no mean Person. We should be glad of your conversation, and you will do us a Pleasure to take a turn with us round the Square." A conversation ensued, introductions were made, and Pöllnitz duly fell in love with the younger of the pair.[38] Masks exist only "to give occasion to abundance of love-adventures," wrote Joseph Addison on his return to England, "for there is something more intriguing in the amours of *Venice*, than in those of other countries."[39]

Francesco Careri, visiting from Naples, accepted a masked stranger's invitation for a glass of muscat, and the two spoke at length in a café. The woman raised her mask and Careri saw that she was a prostitute. He ended up with the bill. "Look how vigilant you must be to avoid falling into such a trap," he warned.[40] Many of course voiced disapproval—Charles Baldwyn, for instance, called Venice the "Brothell house of Europe"— but it didn't always sound convincing.[41] The eighteenth-century Frenchman Ange Goudar, writing in the voice of a "Chinese spy," begins what sounds like a full-bore denunciation. "One cannot speak of such morals without shuddering." He went on to shudder at some length. "One breathes an air of voluptuousness entering this city, an air dangerous for morality. Everything about it is about show, about pleasure, about frivolous entertainment. . . . Everyone is free to follow every kind of debauchery. License is the *lingua franca;* there is such liberty that all are liberated even from remorse." Marriage is mocked, Goudar continues, fidelity nonexistent, and the only known love illicit. In the gambling dens, servants learn to steal and the young discover wantonness. All of this is the fault of the mask, which allows Venetians to "abandon themselves to their vices without the slightest embarrassment."[42]

The view of Venetian carnival as a time outside of time, when common mores were suspended and identities put in flux, was—and is—powerfully attractive. For connoisseurs of pleasure, it announced a moment when society's artificial rules gave way to the truths of Nature by way of the senses. For the disapproving, it furnished a ready narrative for the Republic's decline and fall: moral decay weakened the foundations and the state eventually collapsed. And for those seeking political meaning in acts of transgression, it granted ample evidence for equality in the moment of disguise. The so-called decadence of Venetian carnival had something for everyone. Its ecstatic celebrations were blinding not only to revelers caught up in the moment but also to many subsequent observers who have tried to understand what was happening. In that sense, Venetian carnival is a bit like the proverbial wayside inn that promises all luxuries, as long as you bring them yourself.

CHAPTER 3

Even Odds

After sundown, maskers not in a café or at the theater were likely to be in front of a table throwing dice or playing cards. Nowhere was the social mix greater than in the city's gambling halls. Here agents of the Inquisitors, expert in penetrating the mask, regularly identified a wide assortment of types: patricians and noble ladies, merchants, Jews, foreign diplomats, vagabonds, prostitutes. Nowhere did the mingling carry more immediate consequences. This was a field where how much you won or lost depended on the sharpness of your wit, how well you judged your opponent, and the whim of fortune, who smiled on all indifferently. Rank held no sway.

Although gambling had gone on in Venice for centuries, its glory days were from the mid-seventeenth to the mid-eighteenth century. As with many social vices, the city rulers first tried to destroy it by an outright ban. When that failed, they tried to limit its damage by heavy regulation. Unlicensed gambling dens, typically in the backrooms of barbershops, fueled a black-market industry. Then the rulers decided to embrace it.

In 1638, the Council of Ten granted nobles permission to sponsor games of chance in their homes. Marco Dandolo, following the letter but not the spirit of the law, petitioned the Council to allow "private" gambling in his sprawling palazzo near San Moisè. Soon hundreds of players were assembling there. The quarters were dubbed the Ridotto, from the verb *ridurre,* "to reduce or abridge." An anonymous poem "In Praise of the New Ridotto" captures something of its atmosphere, which combined burnished opulence, the lure of easy money, and an abundance of masks.

> This is where they come to wager
> Ducats, sequins, silver, gold.
> It has no equal; none can match
> Its splendid air or noble mold.
>
> A sculpted goddess in the foyer
> Keeps stately vigil night and day.
> At the threshold stands a gambler,
> With mask in hand and keen to play.[1]

Two large chandeliers flanked a central staircase, which led to the main gallery. Upstairs were smaller rooms intended for conversation, dining, and the sale of liqueurs, meats, and jellies. One room was called the "Chamber of Sighs," where lovers, the weary, and the unlucky went to rest or nurse wounds.[2] Provided one's clothes were decent, one could engage even the most refined ladies in conversation at the Ridotto, though all insults or offenses were forbidden, since, as one gambler remarked, "the mask is sacred."[3]

In the main room, an eerie silence reigned—"a silence greater than in the church"—as masked men and women sat wordlessly around small tables, their anguish or sudden luck conveyed only by a grimace or twitch.[4] The banker, by law a noble and the sole figure obliged to keep his face uncovered, sat at a central table piled high with coins and fresh cards. The games were simple. In *bassetta*, punters staked bets on the likelihood of a given card appearing; in *faraone*, they wagered on a particular sequence. Skill was relevant, but as much or more depended on luck.

Away from the play in other parts of the building, people milled about in couples or small groups, taking advantage of the mask's liberty to circulate. Local celebrities were sometimes recognized and hailed. After the triumphal premiere of Carlo Goldoni's *Ladies' Tales,* the playwright's friends paraded him from room to room. And after the failure of his *Old Codger,* Goldoni returned there in a mask to hear people condemn the play, an experience he found oddly cleansing. He knew it was bad.[5]

More often, a hush bordering on the funereal prevailed. Contemporaries described what it was like to see scores of maskers moving mutely through the dim candlelight. "The Place is dark and silent, a few glimmering Tapers with a half-Light shew a Set of Beings, stalking along with their pale Faces, which look like so many Death's Heads poking out through black Pouches; so that one would almost imagine himself in some

FIGURE 8. Francesco Guardi, *The Ridotto*

enchanted Place, or some Region of the Dead."[6] The Venetian painter Francesco Guardi conveyed an atmosphere of spectral elegance as maskers trace a circuit that resembles a dance (figure 8).

The Ridotto was also a dangerous place, especially for those who won or lost big. Thieves lurked in the dark streets surrounding the Ridotto, and unpaid debts were sometimes settled by violence. Gamblers could count on finding prostitutes among the masked women, and in the rooms upstairs men sold obscene pictures and illicit verse.[7] There was also the threat of addiction. Portraits of the compulsive gambler appear in virtually every Venetian memoir of the time. The prodigal spender, ravaged by his obsession, stakes his savings on a last desperate attempt to win it all back. Mozart's librettist Lorenzo da Ponte, a Venetian by birth, was drawn into the "vicious habit" by a lover who was addicted. They went to the Ridotto almost every night and were soon pawning their clothes and borrowing from gondoliers in the "fallacious hope" of recouping their losses.[8]

The Council of Ten declared that the tables drew a "detestable mix of patricians, foreigners, and plebeians, of honest women and public prostitutes, of cards and weapons by day and by night [that] confound every status, consume every fortune, and corrupt every custom."[9] Their greatest concern was not for the meager income of playwrights like da Ponte. It was for the patrimony of ancient families, whose younger members were by no means the only noble players to burn vast sums in a single stretch.

Venetian magistrates worried most about two things at the Ridotto: uncontrolled mingling and profligate waste. Even without masks, games of chance eroded the social differences among players and increased the danger and excitement, especially in stratified societies such as Venice. As Voltaire said, gambling's rules grant no exceptions, admit no variety, and brook no tyranny. Denis Diderot made the point more directly. "What a wonderful thing gambling is: nothing establishes equality among men more perfectly."[10] Masks encouraged the recklessness. One critic reasoned that if nobles were to appear barefaced in such establishments, as they did in church, they would set an example of moderation for others.[11] The problem was that they preferred to come masked.

There were attempts to reform the Ridotto, often involving masks. In 1703, moved by a mixture of pragmatism and control, the Council of Ten banned masks outright. Any noble in violation would be banished from the Great Council for two years and fined one hundred ducats; commoners in violation would be sentenced to five years in prison. The effect was immediate, although it was not what regulators expected. People stopped coming to the Ridotto. Strong pressure to readmit masks followed, with much of it coming from nobles, and within a year the Council reversed itself. Masks were made mandatory for commoners and optional for nobles, though few nobles came unmasked. The Ridotto sprang back to life.[12]

Gambling destroyed family wealth, eroded self-control, and fueled an unregulated economy in which money passed from hand to hand and class to class. It drew the opprobrium of the Church and the strong censure of civic leaders. It added little to the economy. Some likened it to usury. Others considered it sinful in sanctioning lies. The deceit of card sharks was well known, as was the way the activity insinuated itself into the mind like a narcotic. In short, gambling was neither socially productive nor personally ennobling.[13] Most nobles knew such arguments and probably rehearsed them to one another.

Yet not all of gambling's effects were damaging. It also forged a temporary intimacy that was otherwise inconceivable in this city of strict boundaries. For hours at a time, Jews and Catholics, Venetians and foreigners, men and women of every class and occupation huddled together to play by rules that applied equally to all. For Jonathan Walker, who has written an authoritative account of gambling in Venetian noble culture, games of chance structured an etiquette of self-control much as the court and its rituals shaped *politesse* in France.[14] In both cases, passions were channeled and rough instincts domesticated for the sake of comity. In Venice, it was a glimpse of what relatively free relations not colored by birth might look like.

It is no surprise that the authorities took a dim view of this. By the middle of the eighteenth century, they were convinced that gambling had become a genuine social evil. Agents sent by the Inquisitors furnished a stream of alarming dossiers: about the damage done under the "pretext" of the mask at a regular pool run by Giovanni Canea, where priests, Jews, patricians, Spaniards, and Neapolitans met; about the two nobles, two priests, one Armenian, and five commoners—all named—who met at Dominico Modetto's *casino;* about the "gentlemen, priests, friars, Jews, and the largest part of vagabonds, thieves, and riff-raff from here and abroad" who congregated in rooms near St. Mark's.[15]

The authorities could not hope to eliminate gambling in these smaller halls, much less in residences or hideaways. What they could do was make an example of the most visible such establishment, the Ridotto. So in 1744, by an overwhelming margin of 720 to 21, the Great Council voted to close the illustrious hall. A medal was struck to mark the event. On one side were overturned tables in an empty Ridotto. On the other was a lion attacking a crouching gambler whose mask and scattered cards are on the ground.[16] Gambling of course continued in Venice, with more than the twenty-one nobles who had voted against the ban no doubt participating. But this central symbol of vice and improbable school for concord among unequals, where bankruptcy and windfall were available to the small and great alike, would not reopen under the Republic.

CHAPTER 4

Blood Sport

The most popular daytime amusement during carnival's closing week was a public sport composed of equal parts glee and gore. *Caccie dei tori,* "bull hunts," were a refinement of games that dated back to Roman times. They had existed in one form or another throughout the thousand-year history of Venice. Almost always sponsored affairs, they were usually organized by Venetian patricians. They sometimes coincided with the visits of foreign sovereigns or other dignitaries. Occasionally nobles received permission to host a hunt for occasions outside of carnival. Despite their popularity, only on scattered rare occasions did the Venetians who flocked to them reflect on their meaning—on why they endured through the centuries, why they accompanied carnival in particular, and what their brutality expressed.

A chaotic procession led bulls from the slaughterhouse near the Jewish ghetto at San Giobbe to whichever square played host. Two young men called *tiratori* (handlers) typically led the animals through the narrow streets by ropes tied to their horns. As the entourage picked up followers, the parade grew rowdier and more dangerous. Some punched or kicked the bulls; others hurled stones; the handlers themselves wrenched the cords from side to side to keep the animals off balance, with the whole heaving mass of people "hollowing in such a frantic manner as tho' they were endeavoring to make the Beasts they follow as mad as themselves."[1] Handlers less frequently transported the animals by boat, with the result that bulls sometimes landed in the water. Approaching the square, handlers held their bulls steady as others whipped them into a rage, knocking them down, landing blows on their heads and horns, singeing them with fireworks or torches.

Now began the hunt proper. Dogs specially bred to inflict harm were let loose among the animals in groups of three or four, ripping into their sides or tearing into their ears and testicles. When the dogs bit into a bull and wouldn't let go, trainers called *cavacani* (dog-extractors) wrested them loose by their tails, first using their hands and then, if necessary, their teeth. The handlers worked to channel the bulls' strength as they bucked and bolted to avoid being thrown off balance. The key was to deprive the bull of any opportunity to charge one of the handlers. Cheers rose when the handlers "threw" a bull, that is, jerked the ropes in such a way as to make it fall (figure 9). A successful hunt exhausted the bull. A failed hunt left dogs, and sometimes handlers, trampled or gored. All hunts ended the same way, with the death of the bull by decapitation either on the spot or, more commonly, at the slaughterhouse.

An anonymous witness to one lavish bull hunt in 1688 called it a patch of paradise on earth. In the compact square of Santa Maria Formosa, a favored site for bull hunts, palazzi were decorated from top to bottom. Banners and colored carpets hung from balconies. Spectators filled makeshift stands erected for the event. The crowd was so large that they also lined windows and leaned out from rooftops. Most wore masks. "They enjoyed the liberty of the mask in this place, and were dressed in so many styles and fashions, in clothes both modern and antique, with rich adornment in gold, silver, pearls, gems, and precious stones." The crowd, which included a Tuscan prince as guest of honor, was "so splendid that no monarchy could possibly match it."

When handlers entered the square with the animals, which on this occasion included bulls and bears, the crowd greeted them with "venomous" jeers and mocking laughter. The spectators suddenly went silent when a gutter gave way and two women plunged three stories to the ground, "leaving, along with their lives, some of their brains on the pavement." Later a priest fell when a balcony in the square collapsed, but he held on to a pipe until others could retrieve him, "more dead than alive."

But the hunt went on. Drums and warrior bugles sounded and men in livery led the animals in, group after group. The crowd watched with "a mixture of cruelty and pleasure" as the cries echoed against the buildings. "The wild beasts, suffering the injustice of an enemy freed of all restraint, bellowed for justice." Handlers worked their way through sixty

FIGURE 9. A bull "thrown" by handlers, to the crowd's delight

bulls and more than three hundred dogs, the former "condemned to live the most painful torments."

They next dragged out bears, which turned on the dogs with unexpected fury, sinking their fangs into the dogs' small backs, pulling off hunks of flesh in their claws, and causing them to "sing" with howls of pain, all to the delirious laughter of the crowd. The day ended with the beheading of an immense bull in the center of the square, "which made all who saw it ecstatic."[2]

Bull hunts ran until the last Sunday of carnival, when a culminating bout took place in front of the ducal palace. Smaller hunts were scattered throughout the city's neighborhood squares—in Santa Margherita, San Polo, San Giacomo dell'Orio, San Geremia, San Barnaba, Santo Stefano, San Simeon Grande—and in large courtyards of structures such as Ca' Foscari or the Fondaco dei Turchi. Usually stands were built in the larger squares. Sometimes spectators were mixed; on other occasions nonnobles were excluded. Handlers wore scarlet vests and black stockings. On occasion, participants dressed in commedia dell'arte costumes as Pantalone or Arlecchino.

Once the Council of Ten granted its permission, sponsors were free to plan the spectacle as they saw fit. They had to buy the bulls and arrange for their retrieval at the slaughterhouse, oversee construction of the stands, draw up a guest list, and make sure there were enough dogs and handlers.[3] Men earned reputations as impresarios of the hunt, vying to outdo one another in the manner of killing and the number of victims. Antonio Costa choreographed a hunt in 1739 for the visiting Elector of Saxony that included 130 bulls and two hundred dogs. Giorgio Celini's 1708 hunt in Piazza San Marco destroyed 150 bulls, with armies of dogs taking them on twenty-five at a time.[4] One four-hour production in 1767 fielded two hundred bulls. It employed forty-eight masked and costumed men representing Spanish, English, Hungarian, and Swiss warriors and enough musicians to keep the music playing until the bitter end, when six butchers lopped off the heads of six bulls in a single stroke.[5]

The extremes to which some went in defending the sport crystallized its lunacy for one Venetian. Michele Battaglia, the author of a slender volume titled *Mindless Chatter on Venetian Bull Hunts*, was standing along the perimeter of the smallish square of San Basilio when a wounded bull let out a moan. Battaglia winced, two dogs continued their attack, and a man standing near him announced that this was truly a beautiful event. Battaglia replied that it would be more beautiful if it featured less cruelty. The man exploded with indignation. Battaglia had the heart of a woman, he raged. If Battaglia had his way, the whole town would starve. No one would have the courage to kill a chicken or a turkey. He went on: "The bull hunts—and all things that are dangerous, bloody, and tragic—make us fearless."

As the man spoke, a bull broke loose and knocked him to the ground. Battaglia knelt by his side. "Get away from me!" the man cried. "I won't be helped by a coward like you." Others laid him across their shoulders. He was still cursing Battaglia as they carried him off.[6]

Battaglia was probably the exception. Jubilation over the gruesome ritual is a feature of most accounts. *Allegrezza*—"liveliness," one might say, or, somewhat more loosely, "giddy fun"—was the word used to describe the atmosphere as two hundred bulls were maimed. On this occasion, the writer compared the hunt favorably to gladiatorial bouts. The Caesars pitted humans against one another, which divided the populace. Attacking animals, by contrast, produced solidarity. It was "pleasing to all, from our greatest ones to the vilest plebeians."[7] A visitor in the early 1720s discerned the same: "You see Dogs, Bulls, and Barcaroles, all in a heap together, within his Serenity's Court: but this is to be taken as another Instance of the *Venetian* Liberty, where the meanest of the People may make thus free with their Prince."[8]

Insofar as the participants considered its significance at all, the joy in such slaughter was experienced as a displacement. As the martyr of San Basilio said just before the bull felled him, the ritual gave Venetians the strength and resolve to confront their enemies. *Everything that is dangerous, bloody, and tragic makes us fearless.* It was a controlled public version of what might follow one day on the battlefield in the mayhem and uncertainty of war. Masks and costumes turned the hunt into a theatrical piece. On this level, it operated as a show of strength, cast as entertainment but meant to convey power. The spectacles' faux English or Hungarian soldiers almost always appeared when foreign princes were visiting. Concluding his account of the 1688 hunt in Santa Maria Formosa, a witness wrote: "All enjoyed the noble entertainment this day, which shows that the sons of Mark's lion are not afraid of even the most ferocious and beastly bulls of our Asian enemies."[9]

CHAPTER 5

Fat Thursday

The climax of Venetian carnival came not on Tuesday but on the previous Thursday, *giovedì grasso*, nearly a week before the silence of Lent put an abrupt end to the long season of festivity. At its center was a lavish spectacle that brought all ranks together in common celebration. The staged events, repeated year after year, century after century, affirmed the Republic's image and put the government's own vision for the season front and center. The state-glorying pageant was high spirited, but it also employed pomp to keep hilarity firmly in check. Anything revelers might do after such a display was bound to be anticlimactic. This was exactly what the day's planners intended.

The events staged on *giovedì grasso* evoked an ancient rivalry between the neighboring coastal towns of Aquileia and Grado, both of them northeast of Venice on the Adriatic. Tensions came to a head in the twelfth century over who held the greater ecclesiastical authority. Both boasted of papal preference, both displayed their credentials with the remains of Christian martyrs, and both claimed the title of Metropolitan, a rank just beneath the Holy See of Rome. The status was important, as it conferred regional jurisdiction in sacred and secular matters. Aquileia, a major port in the Roman empire, traced its Christian origins to St. Mark, who according to tradition had preached there on instructions from St. Peter. But as the Gradenese were quick to point out, Aquileia's patriarch fled to Grado for protection from the Huns, bringing with him the relics of two saints baptized by Mark. This, the Gradenese said, was a de facto transfer of all ecclesiastical authority. In the words of the twelfth-century *Chronicon Gradense*, Grado became "civitatem nove Aquilegie metropolim esse perpetuum," "the new Aquileia, Metropolitan in perpetuity."[1] Religious officials in Aquileia differed.

Resentments simmered until 1155, when Pope Adrian IV granted Grado's bishop, an ally of Venice, jurisdiction over parts of the Dalmatian coast. The German-born patriarch of Aquileia responded seven years later by leading a group of fighters from the surrounding Friulian countryside to invade Grado, declaring it to be a precinct of greater Aquileia. Venice rightly saw the invasion as a challenge to its own authority and intervened.

In popular memory, the glory of what followed obscured the larger struggle behind these events. Patriarch Ulrich of Aquileia was a willing pawn in Frederick Barbarossa's grand strategy to incorporate northern Italy into the Holy Roman Empire. Having claimed the title of emperor, Frederick came to Italy with his armies in 1154 intending to be blessed by the pope. Italian emissaries agreed to his call for a diet, and representatives met in the plains of Roncaglia, but as Frederick's designs grew clear and his army advanced, many, including the Venetians, rose in resistance. In 1161, Barbarossa drew a noose around Venice in the form of a land blockade and prepared to attack. His armies struck Venetian garrisons on the mainland and took captives.

Ulrich was in contact with Frederick when his men assaulted Grado in 1162. What looked to many like a small skirmish in a petty rivalry was rightly seen by Doge Vitale Michiel as a threat to Venetian survival. The move was another step in Barbarossa's quest for the crown jewel. The doge therefore sent a fleet of overwhelming force to Grado, surrounded the city, retook the piazza, and brought Ulrich, a dozen of his canons, and some seven hundred captives to Venice. The priest and canons were marched through the streets to taunts and curses. The doge set a ransom with appropriately insulting terms. The patriarch and his twelve priests would be returned to Aquileia in exchange for a bull and twelve pigs. The animals were duly slaughtered, to the delight of the populace. Over the next decade, Venice and other members of the Lombard League repelled all of Frederick's advances on northern Italy. As for Aquileia, Venice demanded that the city send a bull and twelve pigs yearly on the anniversary of Ulrich's defeat. (By the mid-sixteenth century they were slaughtering only bulls, Doge Andrea Gritti having decided that pigs were not appropriately dignified.)[2]

Although remote, the memory Ulrich's humiliation remained fresh in the minds of the populace. Five hundred years after the event, Marino Sanuto called the events of *giovedì grasso* "a symbol of our lordships' war with the patriarch."[3] A century later, Francesco Sansovino recognized in the festival the "perpetual memory of victory."[4] When a traveler to Venice in 1671 asked a native to explain the ceremony, the Venetian patiently recounted the events and their symbols and explained their relevance. "Much in our ancient history is unknown, which amuses me," he said, "for I know how to take stock reflectively, and with that understanding I can grasp the present."[5]

As carnival of 1789 approached—six hundred years after the original victory—the newspaper *Gazzetta Urbana Veneta* reminded its readers of the venerable history of "this most ancient of festivals, *giovedì grasso,*" and dwelt on the "serenity of the day." Those latter words no doubt surprised visitors who had come expecting debauches.[6]

The ceremony adhered to the same basic form for centuries. Venetians crowded into the small square before the ducal palace and usually spilled into the piazza in front of St. Mark's. Guilds processed carrying identifying banners, with the butchers and blacksmiths managing bulls near the front. Workers from the shipyards followed, their faces blackened or masked, carrying blunt swords and wooden sticks. When all were assembled, a palace door opened above. Magistrates, legislators, and other dignitaries filed out to take seats on the colonnaded balcony, a procession that took half an hour. These included the Ducal Council, the judicial Council of Forty, state attorneys, state censors, the Council of Ten, ambassadors from abroad, senators, and at last the doge and his wife. This was the Republic arrayed and on display. It comprised a fair portion of the aristocracy, which in 1750 accounted for about 3 percent of the population and alone ran the government. They wore their full regalia, with each group in the distinctive attire of its position. The sight was splendid, with brilliant splashes of scarlet and crimson against the salmon and gray stone of the palace.

Soon workers from the Arsenale were executing the complex steps of the *moresca,* an ancient sword dance that, despite its art, retained strong intimations of battle. The pulsing rumble of the wood and steel and the barely suppressed violence of the dance prepared the crowd for a brutal climax: the beheading of a bull with a single blow. The executioner stood before his victim, extending his arm, testing his reach, "sizing it up ever so carefully—three times, in fact—with his massive blade," an eyewitness reports, "wishing to avoid the whistles of the crowd, who said that the bull represented the ancient patriarch of Aquileia."[7] The sword flashed, a head dropped, cheers erupted.

> The populace, their eyes keen and glimmering and their hearts filled with their own glory, erupted in a transport of joy that was also a pledge of new victories to come. They awaited this signal with impatience and seemed to relive their day of triumph, applauding the shame and punishment of their enemy with deafening shouts. This grand execution, or we should say rather the symbolic sacrifice made in the presence of the doge and the Signoria, was always accompanied by uninterrupted clapping, whistles, and loud taunts against the vanquished.[8]

All eyes now turned to the bell tower of St. Mark's, where a boy launched himself in a basket attached to a rope that stretched from the campanile to the palace balcony. If the flight was successful, the child crash-landed somewhere near the doge clutching a bundle of flowers and some lines of poetry to be read to the crowd. Alas, not all were, and citizens gathered up the dead or dying where they fell.[9]

After the flight, acrobats stationed near the two great columns next to the water went through a series of maneuvers called the *Forze d'Ercole,* "The Labors of Hercules," climbing to form pyramids or standing on poles laid across shoulders. In some years, they performed on a massive stage in the middle of the *piazzetta.* In others, they performed at the water's edge or in boats. There were daytime fireworks, spirited music, dancing all around, and spontaneous salutes exchanged between the governors and the governed. When they had seen enough, the assembled dignitaries left the populace to their own celebrations and went inside the palace, where they were given iron-tipped batons and led into a spacious room in which wooden models of historic Friulian castles had been erected. Each Venetian noble then took a turn whacking the structures.

At the end of the day, the doge disbursed meat from the slaughtered bull to the city's residents. This particular carnival custom was among the oldest and longest-lived, dating from before 1272, when Martin da Canal observed the doge giving meat to "the nobles and important men of Venice." In later centuries, meat went to prisoners as well. Eventually a system emerged whereby priests received portions for distribution in their own parishes. The practice persisted into the late eighteenth century, when the doge sent a pound of flesh to each of the city's neighborhoods. The internal organs went to the Ospedale della Pietà, an orphanage for girls whose most famous teacher-in-residence was Antonio Vivaldi. Other gifts from the municipality might accompany the meat, including loaves of bread, carafes of wine, and bowls of rice soup.[10]

That Ulrich's defeat in 1162 coincided with the carnival season was a great gift to the city's leaders.[11] Their elevation of its memory into a crowning ceremony in this season of rebirth was a stroke of political genius. The first mention of carnival in Venice dates from 1094, more than two generations before the victory. Masks, which first appeared in Venice in the late thirteenth or early fourteenth century, were not yet part of its festivities.[12] Celebrating Ulrich's defeat defined Venetian carnival, putting the stamp of collective victory on a season not ordinarily linked to the civic good. It is no wonder that doges and senators, from this moment on, preserved every symbolic detail of the ancient feud on *giovedì grasso*. It put a face on a foreign foe at a time when the spirit of mockery might well have targeted the state or religion. It gave the rambunctious energy of spring a constructive and common solidarity.

Most of all, it kept the power of the Republic uppermost in the minds of Venetians—no small feat, since most outsiders viewed the activities as a series of dazzling if unconnected stunts. To the Venetian memoirist Antonio Lamberti, writing just after the Republic's fall, every detail pointed beyond itself to a shared victory. "The edifice and fireworks recalled the castles destroyed and burned; the moresca was the battle; the boy who brought a palm to the doge, the establishment of peace; the Labors of Hercules showed the strength and fortitude of the Venetians in the war; and finally the beheading of the oxen, celebrated in ancient custom by the killing of a dozen pigs and a bull, demonstrated our hatred of the patriarch Ulrich and his twelve canons."[13]

Did organizers intend Thursday's spectacle to steal Tuesday's thunder? If so, they succeeded. The last day of carnival in Venice was not typically the unhinged blowout that visitors might have expected. Consider the mood as midnight approached on Mardi Gras 1788. Horns blared, drums rumbled, there was a roar of people shouting. By one local newspaper's account, the noise was loud enough to awaken the dead. Yet closer to the scene it was clear that some "invisible restraint" kept the maskers peaceful and even proper. There was no obscenity, wrote a correspondent for the local press, and respect guided the maskers, who comprised young and old, noble and commoner. It was "a masked nation" in high spirits, warmed by food and wine and passing the night as "pleasure's prey, though without a single disturbance arising." The paper lauded the "wisdom of the government, which knows how to shape subjects to follow their duties, even when they seem most at risk of neglecting them, without resorting to troops."[14]

The season's finale was under way. Someone had worked up a chain of several hundred revelers, which was now snaking through the city. Led by a tall masker costumed as a Spanish officer, the procession made its way from St. Mark's to the Rialto bridge, over to San Polo, and back across the Grand Canal, ferried a dozen at a time by the San Tomà *traghetto*. People along the route brought out food and drink as the revelers passed. Some latched on to the chain and joined in the dancing. "There was not the slightest disturbance, which is not surprising to those who already know, through infinite other examples, the admirable docility and gentleness of our nation."[15]

Docility and *gentleness* were two terms that visitors did not normally associate with carnival. *Reverence* was a third. But according to the Venetian Giovanni Rossi, when the midnight bells signaling Lent rang out, most locals dropped whatever they were doing and hurried to the nearest church. "After having spent the whole night amidst dissipation and noise, they did not fail to enter the churches to hear the first Mass." It seemed almost comic to those who did not know Venice, this sudden intrusion of piety with its incense and ashes. Alongside families of the parish and honest workers in their street clothes were harlequins, demons, and men dressed as women. Was it penitence that drew them? Or was church merely the last stop on a reveler's itinerary that had begun hours earlier in the gambling hall? The contrast between the costumes and this final destination was great, Rossi admitted, but he claimed that the impulse was sincere. It just showed, he wrote, that in Venice there were two things you couldn't be by half: a gentleman and a Christian.[16]

CHAPTER 6

Anything Goes?

Assessments of carnival varied widely in the eighteenth century. The Frenchman Ange Goudar was unqualified in his judgment: "It isn't only the rabble who give themselves over to debauchery," he wrote. "All the classes are corrupted."[1] But others, like the German Johann Wilhelm von Archenholz, were disappointed to find in its oppressive crowds and dully similar costumes not the slightest hint of scandal: "Let's conclude from this description that carnival here is infinitely below its reputation."[2] Adjust the tone from boredom to quiet reserve (e.g., the *Gazzetta*'s "admirable docility and gentleness"), and the experience of Archenholz comes close to the way Venetians themselves described carnival in the eighteenth century.

Unlike in other cities, one Venetian wrote, carnival here was innocent. There was no grand bacchanalia, no strident celebrations, no profane curses. Taunts and oaths were rare, and few Venetians went to the brothels. A common sentiment—he called it a "civil police," by which he meant mores understood by all—discouraged it. Out-and-out license "very often offends not only Christian modesty but also the ears of the sensitive, and so the pranks and the fights and the sacrifices to Bacchus are all passed over."[3]

Scholars today by and large take the view of those visitors who saw carnival as unbridled and disruptive. Many find in it signs of dissent. A contribution to the multivolume *Storia di Venezia*, a massive state-of-the-art opus containing encyclopedic articles on all aspects of Venetian history and culture, concludes that the mask made the unthinkable possible and turned pleasure into protest. Carnival was "the other side of life," one article asserts, the "counterpart to social segregation and political repression."[4] This interpretation is widespread. The mask's anonymity was a ticket to liberation, its proponents contend. It conferred on its wearers a power to be anyone they wished, a cover to speak the truth, flaunt convention, and throw off hierarchy.

This is the vision that draws visitors to Venice every February. Based on everything we moderns expect of the mask, it makes sense. Political power in eighteenth-century Venice was held by a relative handful. The social structure was immutable, freedoms were limited, and punishment for any who questioned the system was harsh. It seems fitting that the mask should act as a salutary unsettler, equalizing, challenging, permitting the forbidden.

For many scholars, the work of the Russian critic Mikhail Bakhtin has validated this conviction. In an influential book on the Renaissance author François Rabelais, Bakhtin described carnival in early modern Europe as egalitarian in its irreverence. It was a festival where joyous laughter erased differences, exposed ideologies, and cleared the way for human connections stripped of hierarchy. Bakhtin's term for the spirit was *carnivalesque*. The word has since come to signify more than a season of celebration. Today, *carnivalesque* can describe an attitude, a frame of mind, a joyously subversive stance toward authority in general. The art historian James Steward, for instance, invokes Bakhtin to conclude that "the effect of the mask in providing release from dominant moral codes must have been considerable."[5]

Such readings carry assumptions about how eighteenth-century Venetians conceived of identity. By disguising appearances and exposing hierarchies as arbitrary, masks purportedly revealed a universal impulse for equality. Revelers' behavior, the logic goes, expressed a self-conception at odds with their inherited status. The historian Lina Padoan Urban focuses on the language of maskers to make the point. " '*Buon giorno, siora mascara*' was an egalitarian greeting that leveled social barriers," she writes. Bianca Mazzarotto, another historian of Venice, describes eighteenth-century carnival as "indescribable for its orgiastic madness" when "all regarded themselves as equals in their heedless exuberance."[6]

Danilo Reato, who has written extensively on the carnival of Venice, offers this view of its equality in anonymity: "During carnival the poor can feel rich and happy, they can even approach the noble, the powerful, and the feared; they can affect an unaccustomed rashness, a whim granted to them only for a brief period of time, an illusion that triumphs only by virtue of their disguise, for the renewal of clothes is also a renewal of one's own social imagination."[7] The attraction of such a view is strong in our own time, as ideologies remain entrenched within wealth and position despite assurances of equality. With identities disguised and roles suspended, the genuine self will emerge, unintimidated by power and in celebration of our common humanity. So goes the hope.

Some writers, mindful of the catastrophic collapse of the Republic before Napoleon, have sounded an additional, tragic note in assessing carnival. The festivity may have thrown off the straightjacket of conformism, this reading goes, but in the end it was fatal. The endless celebrations were a willed distraction from dire economic and political crises: a collective forgetfulness for which both the leaders and the populace were responsible. The Republic was defunct, or close to it, and Venetians were too deeply consumed by pleasure to notice. In one of his last essays, the late Feliciano Benvenuti, former rector of the University of Venice and benefactor to the city's cultural patrimony, censures the heedlessness of eighteenth-century Venetians. Intoxicated by their own diversions, Benvenuti writes, they were unable to see the precipice. "While they danced, the Titanic was sinking. The Republic had been dead for a long time; they survived only through their pleasures, which were their last panacea, for pleasure had become a mode of existence, indeed the only way to exist and be alive."[8] The preeminent historian of Venice Frederick C. Lane tempers the indictment but retains its charge: "What distinguished the vice of eighteenth-century Venice was not the depths of its iniquity but the pervasiveness of its frivolity."[9]

Making sense of carnival in Venice takes us quickly from heedless fun to a host of serious issues: about social structure and selfhood, about politics and dissent, about destruction and renewal, about hierarchy, democracy, and equality, and finally about the collapse of the thousand-year-old Republic. There is much to sort out in these large issues, including whether the masks truly conferred a liberating anonymity, whether eighteenth-century Venetians harbored a desire to refashion their identities under cover of the mask, and whether Bakhtin's claim of momentary liberation applies. For Casanova, the answer seems clear. But were his singular gifts for self-creation representative? If not, how did more typical Venetians experience the season?

PART TWO

The Culture of Masking

CHAPTER 7

City of Masks

Throughout his affair with M. M., Casanova relied on the simple half-mask common in eighteenth-century Venice. During his trips to Murano, there was plenty to arouse suspicion—his unlikely devotion in the little chapel, his faithful presence in the convent's visiting room, his regular visits to a certain green door at the top of the stairs. But there was one thing that would not have raised an eyebrow: his mask (figure 10).

In Casanova's day, virtually the whole of Venetian society wore masks as daily dress, and not just during carnival. For six months of the year, beginning in early autumn and ending with Lent, masks dominated the city. They reappeared periodically throughout the summer for civic festivals and ceremonies. Nobles greeted foreign emissaries masked. Venetians entered private receptions and public theaters masked. They heard concerts, watched plays, and danced at formal balls masked. Husbands and wives met for meals masked at inns and hostels. Masked patrons sat in cafés sipping chocolate and reading the gazette, or, at lower-class establishments, eyeing other patrons to rob, swindle, or proposition. The abbé Coyer, visiting from France, marveled that men and women came masked to coffeehouses for conversation "and no one thinks twice of it." Masks, he said, "are honest for both sexes."[1]

Maskers lined balconies and clogged the Grand Canal in boats for regattas and processions. They crowded in windows overlooking the bullfights that were a regular bloody feature of the calendar. Thugs on orders to harass or harm went about their dark business masked. Illicit

FIGURE 10. Masked Venetian

booksellers sold their clandestine merchandise masked. Agents named two such peddlers: Santo Pavan, who had obscene engravings of monks, and Domenico Bruni, who was offering copies of *Candido, ossia l'Ottimiso* "by Signor Dottor Ralph." (Bruni had evidently missed Voltaire's joke.)[2] Depending on the style of the day, prostitutes wore either elaborate multitiered masks or a simple *larva* to the theater. A year before the event, noble girls engaged to be married wore masks to walk with their fiancés in public.[3] When the French ambassador Pierre-François de Montaigu needed to send an urgent message to a theater director, he sent his young secretary, Jean-Jacques Rousseau, in a mask.[4] Keeping perpetual watch over this masked population were armies of internal surveillance agents, who patrolled the gambling dens, sat in theaters, and held vigil in the city's numerous cafés. Naturally, they were masked.

In the eighteenth century, masks were the norm in Venice, and they ranged well beyond carnival season for occasions that were far from festive. Visitors wrongly associated the masks with carnival and concluded that Venetians celebrated it six months of the year, a view still common today.[5] Venetian authorities alone decided when carnival began, which they announced each year by decree. The date rarely fell before January 1. In the eighteenth century, carnival typically lasted about a month. If Easter was late—in 1702, for instance, it was on April 16—carnival might not begin until February.[6] In Venice, carnival of course meant masks, but masks did not always mean carnival.

As an accepted article of clothing, the mask was simple, cheap, and easily had. It was not a luxury item or an exotic fashion. Most of the time, it was not worn to be mysterious or provocative. Masks admittedly made the arrangements of lovers like Casanova easier and gave spies and criminals a clear advantage. These were a minority. Many more intended no deceit when they reached for their mask. "They go mask'd at all public Performances, and go where they have a mind to it," a traveler related in 1730. "People go in masks to take the Air, as well as to Plays and Balls, and 'tis the favaurite Pleasure both of the Grandees and the Community."[7] The Englishman John Moore, who visited Venice in 1780 expecting to see a city teeming with jealousy, poison, and the stiletto, wrote with some surprise and a trace of disappointment that he had instead encountered the "innocent mask."[8] The diarist Giovanni Rossi, looking back to the fallen Republic, remembered the mask as *nobilissima*.[9]

From the 1690s until the collapse of the Republic in 1797, the cape-and-mantle combination called the tabàro and baùta, with its characteristic white mask and black hat, was a common feature of the urban landscape. After appearing first among the nobility of both sexes, the fashion quickly spread to all other ranks but the very poorest. Even here there were notable exceptions. Travelers found the city's masked beggars unsettling. A character in Voltaire's *Princesse de Babylone* called the Venetians "a nation of specters." The Frenchman Maximilien Misson said that the whole town was in disguise.[10]

By custom, the period of masking corresponded with the theater season, which began in October, when the wealthy returned from their summer estates on the mainland. Performances were suspended ten days before Christmas and resumed on the twenty-sixth. The winter season ended with Lent. Theaters reopened for seventeen days during the festival of Ascension, which usually fell in May. Venetians wore masks during this short summer theater season, although wearing the tabàro and baùta during these months was infernally hot. Maskers sometimes stripped off the heavy black mantle and let the hood dangle around their necks.

There were periods when masks were explicitly forbidden—during Lent, for the ten days preceding Christmas, and on selected feast days of the Christian calendar—although the prohibition was not consistently observed or enforced. The board that oversaw city commerce allowed mask makers to open their shops only on days when masks were allowed, "and only after the morning ecclesiastical services are over." Before the late seventeenth century, when masking moved beyond the carnival season, revelers could wear their carnival masks only after Vespers. During carnival, a curfew forbade masks later than four hours after nightfall. As masks spread to the autumn months, officials initially hoped to limit their use to the nighttime hours, but by 1720 daytime masking was common and officially tolerated.[11]

There were other occasions when Venetians donned masks. Nobles wore masks when they received foreign diplomats, attended the marriage of the doge's children, or witnessed the installation of church and city officials. They wore masks on designated dates in the religious and civic calendar: on December 26, when the doge heard Mass at San Giorgio Maggiore and later received ambassadors and senators; on April 25, feast day of the city's patron, St. Mark, when the doge heard Mass in the Basilica and received ambassadors and senators; on June 15, when the doge visited the Church of San Vio in the company of ambassadors to mark the defeat of a plot against the state in 1310; and on July 17, when the doge hosted nobles and guests at a banquet celebrating the reconquest of Padua in the sixteenth century. Nobles and commoners alike wore masks for the three-day celebrations following the election of a new doge or of the powerful procurators of St. Mark. They wore masks to the lavish open houses hosted by foreign governments when new ambassadors arrived. They also wore masks to greet masked heads of state traveling "incognito" with their immense masked entourages.[12]

Paintings from midcentury depict a city brimming with maskers in the tabàro and baùta. In Canaletto's *The Bucintoro Returning to the Molo on Ascension Day,* maskers appear on balconies and in windows, lounging on the prows of gondolas or nestled inside, and inside the Bucintoro itself. This glorious golden vessel transported senators, the doge, musicians, and foreign representatives from the ducal palace to waters beyond the Lido for the annual marriage of Venice and the sea. Solemn and celebratory, the ceremony featured none of the high jinks or hilarity that visitors associated with masking in Venice. Nor did the many other state visits, luncheons, and receptions where masks appeared.

That said, there was plenty of masked mischief throughout the year. The mask, tabàro, and baùta were a godsend to smugglers, card sharks, and thieves. Early in the eighteenth century, the conservative senator Pietro Garzoni attributed an upsurge in crime to the new fashion for masks. People were more likely to misbehave, he wrote, with their faces hidden. He was undoubtedly right. In early winter 1756, two men and woman in masks entered a goldsmith's shop with weapons to demand money and jewels. The same week, a cook who worked for the patrician Angelo Contarini was wounded in the arm by a masker on a bridge near the ducal palace.[13]

The mask brought confusion even when motives were innocent. Lorenzo da Ponte recalls sitting in a café wearing a mask when a gondolier entered and wordlessly summoned him to follow. The boatman led da Ponte to a waiting gondola, where, in darkness, soft hands and a gentle voice greeted him. Da Ponte gamely offered a kiss. The woman, a young aristocrat from Naples, pulled back in horror. Her boatman had made a mistake. "It seeming to me, however, that she was looking upon me with sentiments not unlike those with which I was gazing at her, I took courage and told her all those things which on like occasions one says to a beautiful woman."[14]

A fight erupted between two ladies in a café after a similar misunderstanding. A married couple had entered, the wife masked and the husband not. An acquaintance of theirs arrived, and they spoke; he, too, had planned to meet his wife there. The first husband said he needed to step out—to buy a mask, no less—when, moments later, the second wife arrived, saw her husband with a woman in a mask, and flew into a rage. First came insults, then shoves and slaps. The man returned with his new mask to find his friend trying to separate the women. The scene ended with laughter and apologies.[15] Sometimes the stakes were higher. At an open house, a new emissary from Rome advised guards to bar entrance to anyone masked. As a consequence, some nobles were turned away rudely. It was an embarrassing introduction to local customs.

In general, maskers did not address one another by name. Any indignity or offense was considered more serious when committed against a masker. Piero Tagio, the doorman at one of the city's theaters, was briefly jailed for insulting a masker. With a mask stuck in the hat and a black cape tossed over the shoulders, an Englishman remarked, one could attend any public assembly. "The reverence accorded to masks in general," another observed, "prevented infinite disturbances."[16]

To strip someone of his mask was a supreme insult. When that occurred, people responded with stunned horror, as if they had seen an article of clothing torn away. At a high-spirited party with both patricians and commoners present, one masker, a nobleman, recognized another as the innkeeper at the Queen of England. They apparently had some unfinished business. The patrician confronted the man, launched a few choice words, and pulled off his mask and hood. The music suddenly stopped, silence fell, and the host announced that he alone had the authority to unmask a guest. Similar street scenes brought comparable responses. Signora Santa Conti, a commoner, described her humiliation when a neighbor accosted her, tore off her mask, and spewed insults to the effect that she was becoming too friendly with the lady's lover. "The mask should compel respect in itself," an indignant Santa Conti later testified. "Just because it coincides with carnival does not make it a plaything for everyone." The Frenchman Jérôme Richard had evidently seen a similar confrontation. He wrote that the slightest offense to a masker was not tolerated.[17]

The mask's dual association of formality and concealment kept surveillance agents busy. Unsure of intentions and mindful of the threat of espionage, agents of the State Inquisitors spent much of their time watching maskers for secret signals. Whether they were treasonous or innocent wasn't always clear. During his rounds near St. Mark's one night in early spring, Francesco Faletti spotted maskers lingering near a *casino* that belonged to the patrician Sebastiano Venier. Around midnight, the door opened and a boatman came out, followed by two masked women and a servant, who extinguished his lantern and shut the door. A male masker joined the women and called out, "Polpetta!"—"Meatball!"— in a loud voice to his boatman, who responded, "At your service!" All maskers stepped into the gondola and departed. Agent Faletti took no further action.

G. B. Manuzzi, who also worked for the State Inquisitors, described a suspicious exchange in his report of February 24, 1765. He had been trailing the Austrian ambassador's wife. On Sunday evening, he observed a masker enter the Teatro San Cassiano just before the end of the opera, look directly at the ambassadress in her box, and touch his hand to his mask. "I was unable to understand the significance of this signal," Manuzzi reported.[18]

Masks were so common that a masked agent of the State Inquisitors eavesdropped at length on a conversation between the Spanish ambassador's son and another masker. The masked Spaniard asked about the Inquisitors and the Council of Ten and was told about Venice's network of informants. Neither interlocutor stopped to wonder about the masked man standing nearby.[19] This strange scene, which was duly reported to the Inquisitors, is an indication of just how ordinary masks were. So long as you were masked, you didn't stand out.

CHAPTER 8

Infernal Associations

The earliest reference to masking in Venice dates from 1268, when the Great Council made it a crime to put on a mask and throw perfumed eggs. The absence of earlier references suggests that Venetians did not wear them commonly before the thirteenth century. If they had, surely someone would have been inspired to harass or cause harm, and prohibitions would have followed. What prompted masks now?

There was one event early in the century whose impact on religion, commerce, and public affairs in the daily life of Venetians was immense: the defeat and sack of Constantinople in 1204 by crusaders under Venetian command. The plan for the Fourth Crusade was to liberate the Holy Land, but its crusaders never reached their destination. The Venetians had built and outfitted two hundred ships for the Franks, who arrived in Venice unable to pay for them. With an army at their disposal, Venetian leaders saw an opportunity to recoup their costs and advance their interests. A disputed succession in the Byzantine empire had brought a regime whom the Venetians considered insufficiently friendly at a time when Pisa and Genoa were strong commercial rivals. Control of Constantinople would give Venetian merchant ships unimpeded access to the Middle East and beyond.

Under the dual pretext of restoring the rightful emperor and reuniting a divided Catholic Church, Venetian boats laid siege to the city. Defenses fell, Constantinople was set on fire, and three days of brutal looting followed, with riches, weapons and armor, sacred relics, and antiquities claimed by Venice. The doge declared the Church reunited, and Constantinople was carved into fiefdoms to be governed along Western feudal lines. This arrangement, the crowing achievement of the first successful invasion of the Byzantine capital in nearly a millennium, lasted all of sixty years. The damage was fatal. The devastation and its aftermath sapped the city's morale, crippled its institutions, and hastened its demise in its doomed struggle with the Ottoman Turks.

Venice got the access it wanted—most valuably, to China and southern Asia through the Black Sea—and soon rare commodities were flooding into the city. With Constantinople now a clearinghouse, Venetian merchants acquired goods from Crete, Cyprus, Rhodes, Haifa, Acre, Jiddah, and Cairo. The commercial conquest of the Levant returned precious metals to Venice, along with wood, wheat, exotic spices such as cinnamon and cloves, pepper, cotton, silks, sugar, lemons, oranges, and figs.[1]

And perhaps masks. "According to some," the Venetian historian Pompeo Molmenti wrote in 1880, "the use of masks dates from the conquest of the Levant." Writing in the *Enciclopedia dello spettacolo* nearly a hundred years later, Maria Teresa Muraro likewise cited this moment to explain the appearance of masks in Venice.[2] A reconstruction might go something like this. At the very time sailors were returning with frightful tales of pagans who wore veils and turbans, Venetian youths feeling their oats covered their faces, hollowed out eggs, filled them with rosewater, and looked for the nearest pretty target. The masks were "disguises"—a cover that gave them license to throw—but how much they actually disguised is questionable. How are you supposed to flirt if no one knows who you are?[3]

This is a blind stab—and not especially convincing at that. The fact is, there is precious little evidence regarding motive or use for the earliest masking in Venice. Whatever its origins, the practice persisted. Its contours gradually emerged. Masks became a fixture of carnival, but they were present on other occasions, too. The Renaissance introduced masked plays and mythologically themed masquerades to the city, which were staged in the courtyards and porticoes of palazzi. From the mid-1500s, masked characters of commedia dell'arte appeared regularly in the city's squares with their improvised and often obscene slapstick.[4] Yet even with the spread of masks, the distance separating festive and theatrical masking in the Renaissance and the everyday masking of the Venetian eighteenth century is immense. Masked diplomats, spectators, and gamblers were more typically sober and contained than antic or theatrical.

Everyday masking grew from older Venetian roots, but the practice required overcoming ancient associations of the mask with sacrilege and the underworld—associations that still clung to the mythological and theatrical masks of the Renaissance. Their eventual transformation was the effect of powerful forces in the late Renaissance, when censorship, the demands of secular statecraft, and religious persecution caused many to rethink the essence of masks to find not mischief or deceit but justified self-defense. Some even called the mask honest.

The word *mask* comes from the medieval Latin root *mascus, masca,* as do its cognates in European languages: *maschera* (It.), *masque* (Fr.), *máscara* (Sp.), *Maske* (Ger.), *mask* (Sw.), *maske* (Da.). Linguists trace a still earlier root, *masca,* to pre-Indo-European sources in Italy's Piedmontese and Ligurian dialects. There the word referred most literally to soot or smut, but its more common use designated witches. It appears in a lurid Witches' Sabbath in "The Magdeburg Fantasy," a poem from 1913 by the Italian futurist Paolo Buzzi.

> In the stench of bestial flames
> Shriek *masche,* crones, and witches,
> While friars stretch their bellies out
> On racks, to hump the bitches.[5]

A similar root with the same local use is *masco,* from Provençal dialect, the forerunner of the modern *mascot,* whose sense has shifted from an evil spirit to a lucky charm. *Masca* often appeared with the Latin *striga,* a hag who devoured men, poisoned children, and screeched like a bat (cf. the Greek *strigx,* "screech owl"), as in the opening of this seventh-century edict from the Lombard king Rothari: "Si quis eam strigam, quod est Masca, clamaverit . . .": "If anyone should call her a witch, which is *masca* . . ." *Masca* also appears with *lamia,* from the Greek for voracious. A *lamia* is a monster with the face of a woman and the body of a serpent who, according to ancient and medieval legend, drank the blood of infants. Gervase of Tilbury, writing in the twelfth century, drew the three words together. "Lamias, quas vulgo mascas aut in gallica lingua strias . . . dicunt nocturnas esse imagines, quaegrossitie humorem animas dormientium perturbant, et pondus faciunt." "They say *lamias,* or in common parlance *mascas,* and *stri[g]as* in the Gallic language . . . are burdensome nocturnal apparitions that upset the humors and trouble the souls of those sleeping."[6]

The other principal word Venetians used for mask, *larva,* also has diabolical connotations. Ancient Romans used the term to describe souls of the dead come back to earth to haunt the living. Their torment sent

victims into delirium: hence *larvo, larvare,* "to possess with evil spirits."
In time, *larva* came to mean illusion, fiction, false appearance. Horace
employed the term to describe the masks of actors in the theater.[7] In their
earliest meanings, *larva* and *masca* referred interchangeably to wicked
spirits. Both evolved to denote masks.

The Florentine poet Dante Alighieri points to these infernal associations as the narrator and his guide Virgil emerge from the blackness of
hell.

> Oh, my kind father, if you hear me out,
> I'll tell you what appeared to me,

the pilgrim begins, but Virgil interrupts. He needn't say more, Virgil tells
him. The pilgrim's thoughts are evident to him:

> *Se tu avessi cento larve*
> *sovra la faccia, non mi sarian chiuse*
> *le tue cogitazion, quantunque parve.*

> Although you had a hundred masks
> upon your face, that still would not conceal
> from me the thoughts you thought, however slight.[8]

According to the seventeenth-century French lexicographer Charles
du Fresne, sieur du Cange, a linguistic association links masks with carnival pranks. Citing a fifteenth-century statute, du Cange asserts that
charivari, the mad marriage revels of early modern Europe, was a French
adaptation of *larvaria*. The likely link was the behavior of revelers, who
made noise and shouted insults as if possessed by demons.[9] How have
English-speakers come to associate larvae with wormlike insects? The
route also passes through the underworld. Early definitions for *larva* in
the *Oxford English Dictionary* include both ancient meanings: "a ghost,
spectre, hobgoblin; also, a mask." In 1658, Edward Phillips, in *The Mys-
teries of Love and Eloquence,* combined the connotations to describe a
man as "larvated, masqued or visarded for representing some Gobling or
dreadful Spirit." A larvation, also used in the seventeenth century, is the
"discoloration of the face in a fever-patient, producing a resemblance to
a mask."[10]

The editors of the *Oxford English Dictionary* speculate that Carl Linnaeus used the term *larva* in full knowledge of these associations to describe the wingless grub state of an insect before it undergoes metamor-
phosis. In the larval state, the insect's more perfect form is masked, and
in its mature stage, the larval stage remains only as a ghost. Linnaeus's

use was closer to a crystallization than a coinage; others before him had made similar connections. Writing a generation before Linnaeus's 1735 *Systema Naturae* was published, John Ray described two identical insects at differing stages of development as clothed "under a different *Larva* or Habit."[11]

That both *larva* and *masca* should begin by designating the underworld and evolve to mean mask is a remarkable correspondence, but their common journey is no coincidence. Both etymologies preserve a continuing association that links donning a mask with invoking the spirit world. The connection dates back at least as far as the Greeks. Dionysus is the god most closely identified with masks, and his revelation always summoned unearthly powers. In myth, Dionysus wore many guises, appearing as animals and unrecognizably in human form. The inventor of wine and patron of intoxication, Dionysus also transforms humans, producing madness, laughter, oneness with creation, or murderous rage. The attributes of his mask are qualities of Dionysus himself. Some of these have outlived his cult to survive in the frenzy of carnival.

To his followers, Dionysus's mask was not a mere symbol or likeness. It announced his presence. Images on Greek pots and cups give an idea of how his followers worshiped him. Women ladle wine before a towering column threaded with ivy and topped with an enormous mask of the god. Devotees dance with abandon before the statue as musicians beat drums and play double-flutes. One woman arches her back and looks to the heavens, another bends forward clutching her breast and waving an arm above her head, another's head thrashes as her hand nears the god. Celebrants hoist thyrsi topped with leaves or wave torches, and a satyr, his hair laced with vines, manifests his glory to the god.[12]

Two Athenian festivals celebrated contrasting sides of the god. During the festival of the Anthesteria ("blossoming"), Greeks came to an ancient temple to drink prodigious quantities of new wine in solemn acknowledgment of the dead, whose ghosts were believed to wander among the living for these three days. The atmosphere was akin to an initiation, particularly for children, who were given a small pitcher to consume as well. Worshipers were silent and fearful, although the holy drunkenness also brought singing and dancing. A month later at the City Dionysia, raucous processions paraded through the streets huge phalluses carved from beams and colored with wax. An icon of the god with his mask atop a wooden shaft led the way. Masked Athenians impersonating ithyphallic satyrs (i.e., woodland goat-men with erections) carried the beams, dancing, preening, gesturing obscenely. Some strapped false members to their crotches in the fashion of comic actors. Crowds along the route added their taunts and cheers. The mood was riotous with laughter.[13]

The rites of the Anthesteria and the City Dionysia fell in March, when winter turns to spring, the sap stirs, and the dead earth yields up life. Dionysus's own mythical story retells that annual rebirth. The son of a mortal mother and divine father, killed savagely and ingested by the Titans, then resurrected by Zeus, Dionysus personified the seed that must die in order to live. Some versions of his biography claim that he descended to Hades to retrieve his mother, Semele, before rising to Olympus to live as a god. The philosopher Heraclitus discerned in the narrative elements that linked the two festivals. Had the revelry of the City Dionysia not been dedicated to a god, he wrote, it would have been a disgrace. "But Hades is the same as Dionysus," he explained, "for whom they rave and act like bacchantes."[14]

The rowdy shows of virility, in other words, came from the same source that inspired the dread recognition of specters. To the Greeks, these festivals of drinking and flagrant sexual display were more than a release. They formed a part of the seasonal rebirth that the earth itself was undergoing. "It is from the dead that we receive nourishment, growth, and new buds," runs a saying attributed to Hippocrates.[15] Dionysus was a figure for that otherworldly insemination, uniting the living with the dead and those still to be born. To his initiates, temporary union with the god was possible: in the act of ritual animal sacrifice, in the surge or reverent silence of drunkenness, in the spinning, dizzying dance of forgetfulness. These were instants of Dionysus's own death replayed. Barriers between humans fell; boundaries separating the human from the animal were blurred; a fragmented world was brought to temporary wholeness in a single transforming moment. Members of mystery cults devoted to Dionysus took such moments as glimpses of what the god's resurrection promised believers: eternal life after death.[16]

Why did the Greeks associate the mask with the underworld? Why did they tie it to Dionysus in particular? A mask is pure confrontation. Its features are immobile. Its stare is inescapable. It does not withdraw or avert its gaze. A mask is also incomplete. All surface with nothing inside, an empty facade, the mask announces an absence. As a figure for divinity, its regard is unavoidable, but its incompleteness also signifies the unapproachable. A mask's implacable presence guards a distance.

For the classicist Walter F. Otto these paradoxes contain the essence of Dionysus's epiphany. Otto writes that, unlike the profiles of other Greek gods on ancient pottery, Dionysus looks at the viewer full-face. One encounters him directly or not at all. One cannot see him without coming under his gaze. But that gaze is a mask. "Thus the mask tells us that the theophany of Dionysus, which is different from that of the other gods because of its stunning assault on the senses and its urgency, is linked with the eternal enigmas of duality and paradox," Otto writes. "This theophany thrusts Dionysus violently and unavoidably into the here and now—and sweeps him away at the same time into the inexpressible distance. It excites with a nearness which is at the same time a remoteness."[17]

To the pagan world, the mask of Dionysus—affixed to statues, pictured on pottery, and worn by revelers and believers—embodied something both holy and monstrous. In the simplifying reductions of monotheism, the mask became unequivocally infernal. Among others, Justin Martyr (ca. 100–165 A.D.) was troubled by the resemblance between Dionysus and Jesus. Both were divine though born of mortals. Both died violently and returned to life, a resurrection that promised believers everlasting life. Both descended to the underworld to redeem departed souls. To the followers of both, wine was an initiation and a sacrament. Cannibalism figured in both divine narratives, with the Titans' brutal meal and the words of Jesus at the Last Supper. And every spring brought the celebration of rebirth, in Easter and in the Dionysian festivals. Justin's explanation was that Satan had inspired pagan mythmakers to mislead the weak with false analogies. This had consequences for masking. It confirmed in history what the temptation of Eve had taught by analogy. Satan was the author of masks and a goad to all who wore them. The view was commonplace by the fourth century, when an edict from the Council of the Church of Constantinople prohibited transvestitism and the wearing of masks, which evoked "the detested Dionysus."[18]

Dionysus has of course lost his divine status, and in most quarters today the Dionysian stands only as a synonym for excess. In ancient terms, the carnival passions that modern masks awaken are only incidentally Dionysian. The god is not invoked. Yet carnival can still elicit his attributes: in madness that may be large-hearted or violent, in brazen sexuality, in renewing euphoria and solidarity, and in the frightful or farcical evocation of spirits. This is another way of saying that the mask's power to transform does not depend on a god, or a demon, or an unbroken legacy of associations across time.

Yet if church councils succeeded in killing off Dionysus where the Titans failed, the mask's fundamental kinship with the infernal realm lived on. The connection has been clear to those who believe that spirits from the underworld still visit mortals. Masks found on Egyptian mummies and Mayan kings were meant to escort the dead from the physical to the spiritual realm. Masquerades throughout the world have conjured ancestors, defied death, and cleansed the living.[19] In Christian Europe, the mask's Dionysian trajectory began in the underworld as well, but it ended in hilarity. And unlike in ancient Athens, no latter-day Heraclitus has had cause to observe that reverence for God spares revelers from disgrace.

Arlecchino, the acrobatic jester in black mask and motley costume, first stepped onstage in the late 1500s. Arlequin in French and Harlequin in English, Arlecchino is the most outrageous character of Italian commedia dell'arte. Unafraid to offend and usually driven by the belly (or lower), he can be bumbling or controlled, naive or spry, coarse or witty, depending on what it takes to cadge a meal or get the girl (figure 11). Arlecchino engaged the European imagination long before he joined commedia. Like the mask he wears, he is on a direct line from the underworld. Before he was a scamp, he was a demon.

The earliest versions of Harlequin's story date from the Middle Ages. Walter Map, a twelfth-century archdeacon of Oxford, tells the story of King Herla (Herlaking), an ancient Briton ruler. On the king's wedding-day, an uninvited guest—a red-faced dwarf with hooves instead of feet—brings gifts of gold and jewels. The dwarf asks a simple favor in return. In a year, the king must visit him in his cave. The day comes, and the dwarf hosts the king to a banquet amidst blazing candles. As Herlaking mounts his horse to depart, the dwarf gives him a hound and declares that he cannot dismount until the animal leaves his arms.

Herlaking sees a shepherd outside the cave and asks if the queen is still waiting for him. The man is astonished. "Sir, I can hardly understand your speech, for you are a Briton and I a Saxon; the name of that queen I have never heard, save that they say that long ago there was such a queen of that name over the very ancient Britons, who was the wife of King Herla; and he, the old story says, disappeared in company with a pygmy at this very cliff, and was never seen on earth again, and it is now two hundred years since the Saxons took possession of this kingdom, and drove out the old inhabitants." To this day, Walter Map writes, the hound has not alighted, and Herlaking and his entourage of damned souls still haunt the land without rest or peace.[20]

Versions of Harlequin's story multiplied in the coming centuries. Variations of his name appeared as Hellequin, Helquin, Hoillequin, Hennequin, and Herlequin. The Norman church chronicler Orderic Vitalis examined a scar left by marauders on the forehead of a young priest named Gualchelinus and recounted his experience. Walking along a path on the

FIGURE 11. Arlecchino

night of January 1, 1091, Gualchelinus heard the clatter of hooves. Suddenly a terrible parade was before him. A weary crowd trudged by on foot. Pallbearers carried coffins upon which sat hideous dwarves. A man lashed to a tree trunk was borne aloft as a demon prodded his body with a red-hot poker. Women wailed as they rode on saddles studded with nails. Dark knights on horses carried black flags. "Hæc sine dubio familia Herlechini est," the priest remembered saying to himself. "Surely this is the band of Herlequin." As he watched, a knight paused and urged him to give up his sins. He then touched the priest's brow with his torch.[21]

The dread of Harlequin would recede, but the romantics' recovery of this ancient legend carries something of the young priest's terror into our own age. Goethe's poem *Erlkönig*—a German version of Herlaking—narrates a dying child's delirium as he clings to his father on horseback. Franz Schubert's musical setting captures the onrush of panic. "Do you not see him, Father?—the Erlkönig! . . . My Father, my Father, can you not hear what he is whispering to me?"

The name's infernal associations inspired fresh etymologies among later generations. The fifteenth-century *Chronicles of Normandy* claimed that the spectral *Mesgnie Hennequin*—"the knights of Hennequin"—were the ghosts of the French king Charles Quint and his retinue, who had lived and fought a century earlier. A work from roughly the same period repeats the account. "Regarding the knights of Helquin, these are generally devils who appear on horseback in the guise of men. . . . And whence does this name Helquin originate? . . . From Charlequin, which is to say Charles Quint. Some say Helquin. So that even now when one sees this assembly of men galloping through the night and says, 'These are the knights of Helquin,' others say, 'These are the men of Charle Quint.' "[22]

Other works retained Harlequin's fiendishness but diluted his ferocity. Thirteenth-century stage plays and troubadour songs added quirky, comic features. In the satirical drama *The Play in the Bower,* for instance, Hellequin is a gallant lover who happens to come from the underworld. He participates in a loud charivari staged to mock a character for renouncing marriage. In *The Antichrist's Tournament* and *The New Renard,* Hellequin's gang passes not with shrieks and cries but with the tinkling of bells.[23] It was *The Romance of Fauvel* that secured Hellequin as the buffoon-demon who plays mascot to carnival. On Fauvel's wedding night, a raucous crowd wearing masks and dressed in ridiculous costumes gathers below his window. Some wear their tops and trousers backwards, others come in monks' cassocks or with great humps on their backs. As Fauvel and his bride enter the bedroom, the revelers beat pots and pans, call out obscenities ("Lady, is your oven hot? Your pretty lips will touch my bum!"), and chant lines of nonsense ("Oh Hel-le-quin, Oh Quin-le-hell; Oh Hel-le-quin, Oh Quin-le-hell"). They break windows and pound on doors, dump salt into the wells, and fling excrement at passersby, all the while singing *les lays des hellequins,* "devils' songs."[24]

This is carnival laughter, mocking, derisory, and in gleeful defiance of the established order. Its associations lead less to the Prince of Darkness than to the *diableries* of comedy—to sharp-tailed demons with horns and pitchforks, baiting, poking, squealing with delight. Such are the devilkins of Dante's *malebolge*, the "evil pockets," who tease their prey like malicious cats. These cantos contain the only sustained humor of the *Inferno*, although the pain these clownish tormenters inflict is real. They rip the flesh of their victims and thrust them into boiling pitch. The creatures dart in and out of the sludge as Dante's animal comparisons pile up. They flash above the surface like dolphins or crouch just below like frogs showing their snouts, they are as lithe as otters, as repulsive as wet birds, as vicious as falcons tearing into a duck.[25]

One of these imps is named Alichino, the first appearance of this ancient name in Italian. Harassing the corrupt judges and lawyers condemned to this circle, Alichino trades blows in a sadistic farce with both sinners and other demons. Might Dante have encountered the character and its layered ancestry while studying at the Sorbonne in Paris? The Left Bank was the site of popular fairs that drew minstrels and players in addition to their artisans, merchants, and farmers. Dante's Alichino is a close cousin in temperament and name to the troubadours' Hellequin.[26]

This was the moment when the Harlequin, the fictional character who combined malice with slapstick, stepped off the stage and into the street. A French source from the early 1300s recounts the jarring street celebrations that greeted newlyweds in Paris. "They made a ruckus such as had never been heard; some showed their bums to the wind, others broke awnings, windows, and doors. . . . They carried beer with them, they were drunk. . . . I think that it was Hellequin and his gang."[27] For the German scholar Otto Driesen, who has studied the complex history of the name *Harlequin*, this marked a turning point. Harlequin and his pack are no longer demons of the spirit world. "They are humans who seek to disrupt the nuptial pleasures of their fellow citizens at night with their wild cacophony. And to commit such shameless and serious acts of violence, they act and dress as Harlequin, the comical devil."[28]

Scholars believe that Italian commedia players adopted the name from France. Harlequin continued to appear in French literature as a mostly harmless troublemaker. He retained some diabolical qualities, but they were by and large comical. In the fifteenth century, an anonymous French poem titled "The Virgin's Golden Dream" cautioned against the "false Harlequins" of envy and a wicked tongue, whose dangers were "worse than mere mischief, worse than simple noisemakers." A sixteenth-century collection of French proverbs registers the decline in menace with its entry for a popular expression: "Of Hennequins: said more a fool than a rogue."[29]

It was the 1580s when an Italian actor touring France first called himself Arlequin to create a new persona from the fragments of legend, farce, and street-charivari that clung to the name. One long chapter was ending and another about to begin. The actor, Tristano Martinelli, was such a success that King Henri IV commanded him to participate in ceremonies marking Marie de' Medici's arrival from Italy. Martinelli marked the occasion by publishing a thick volume under the pen name *Don Arlequin*. The book, *Rhetorical Exercises* (1601), bears a mocking dedication to the king. He is liberal in his fusillades, master of half of the Avignon bridge, and "the secret secretary of Madame Marie de' Medici's most secret cupboard." The book's so-called exercises were all deflating. They lampooned learned opinion, the ritual groveling that occurred whenever subjects approached sovereigns, and Martinelli's own access to the king. Its dedication takes up two of the book's seventy pages, illustrations appear on seven additional pages (three of which picture Arlequin on his knees, hat in hand), and chapter headings or obsequious sonnets take up another four pages ("he took Montmélian more easily than eating a macaroon," one line says of the king). The remaining fifty-seven pages are blank.[30]

With *Rhetorical Exercises,* Martinelli affirmed the character of a fledgling brotherhood of stage performers. They were vagabonds and outsiders. Martinelli's hometown was Mantua, but Monsieur Arlechin claimed residence in Novalesca, a postal station in the Alps. The town was not a destination but a way station for mail and travelers. In the coming decades, commedia dell'arte's critics would find plenty to justify the demonic associations that tied it to hell. Martinelli was doing his part, too. On the title page, he listed the place of publication as *Le Bout du Monde,* "The Ends of the Earth." The birth of Arlecchino, as one scholar of commedia writes, came at "the frontier that separated the known from the unknown."[31]

CHAPTER 9

Devil's Dance

In an early commedia dell'arte sketch, Harlequin is visited by his dead mother in a dream. She is a prostitute, unhappily stuck in Hades. She wants her son to retrieve her. Harlequin jumps out of bed, straps on his mask, tucks his wooden sword into his belt, and goes to the underworld. There he soothes the hell-hound Cerberus by scratching his belly and makes Charon laugh with his leaps and contortions. Pluto finds him so funny that he offers Harlequin anything he wants: chief torturer, deputy-god status, privileges in Hades' kitchen. Harlequin sees his chance and names his mother. Pluto flies into a rage—the trollop Cardine is one of his favorites—but Harlequin reminds him that gods never break their word. Pluto submits, and mother and son escape in a boat. Just as they are reaching the shore, Charon brings a flood that sends Cardine tumbling back into hell.[1]

The Pleasant History of Harlequin's Acts and Deeds was a polemic aimed at Tristano Martinelli, whose company of Italian actors, now under royal protection, were drawing enthusiastic crowds in Paris. Its author was a jealous French performer known as Fat William. Madame Cardine was the name of a brothel-keeper, and her recent death had been noted in the wider world. Fat William apparently believed that sending Martinelli to hell was the right humiliation for the Italian interloper. The shot misfired. *The Pleasant History* describes a dazzling, athletic entertainer, and his descent to Hades defined rather than diminished him. Martinelli's response to Fat William took better aim. He composed a prologue and recited it at every subsequent performance. In it, Arlequin returns to Hades and, finding Fat William already there, receives plenary power from Pluto to take his revenge: the slanderer must eat nothing but rice and will earn his keep by emptying chamber pots and dancing naked in winter through the streets of Paris.[2]

When the Church attacked commedia dell'arte as the work of the devil, they probably did not have these sketches in mind, despite their explicit association of Harlequin with his namesakes' storied past. Of the hundreds of surviving commedia plots, *The Pleasant History of Harlequin's Acts and Deeds* and Martinelli's response to it are among the more ephemeral. There were more egregious offenses on the stage: daughters who became pregnant to thwart arranged marriages, for instance, weddings uniting "man" and wife, with the husband a woman in disguise, and any number of crude jokes involving gelding tools, pails of urine, and pigs' blood. To their critics, commedia troupes were sordid and mercenary. They held nothing sacred, made money any way they could, and cheapened everything they touched.

To their followers, they were magical, spinning impossibly convoluted stories with a few simple props and prodigious reserves of inventiveness. The mask was part of the magic, at once freeing actors and fixing their characters. Italian commedia dell'arte characters remained the same— with the same name, clothes, regional dialects, and favorite gags—across scores of plots and despite shifting roles. They were Arlecchino the prankster, who specialized in sexual innuendo; the Dottore, a mincing, officious pedant from Bologna with a mask splayed across his nose like a grape leaf; the Venetian merchant Pantalone, aged, lecherous, and faintly preposterous in a red jumper and long black cape; the Spanish Captain, whose blustering presence nearly always complicates the romance; the hunchbacked Neapolitan Pulcinella in his towering cone hat, white blouse, and loose trousers; and scheming workers and servants with names such as Brighella, Pedrolino, and Burattino, whose swarthy masks betokened manual labor.

The young lovers of commedia—Orazio, Isabella, Fabrizio, Flaminia— were not masked, a feature that drew attention to one of the two sure registers of plots, ardency. The word *zany*, which comes from commedia dell'arte, points to the other. *Zanni*, the Venetian version of *Giovanni*, was a catchall name for the buffoonish lowborn characters who deflated high sentiment with slapstick, sarcasm, and vulgarity.

Beyond their masks, commedia plots were loaded with disguises. Men dressed as women and women as men, Christians posed as Turks and masters as servants, and there was a steady stream of false pilgrims, hunters, beggars, magicians, and slaves. For spectators who witnessed such transformations a question surely arose: is it truly this easy to pass for someone else?

"Improvised Theater," as commedia dell'arte was first known, drew from many sources, including popular farce, Renaissance literary comedy, and court theatricals. Its immediate precedents were the one- and two-man shows by so-called *buffoni*, who flourished in the local squares of Venice in the early 1500s. They were known for their set pieces, like the bravura routine in which Zuan Polo Liampardi stood behind a curtain and imitated the voices of an entire household. A flatulent patriarch tells a spicy tale about Sophie and the Turk, his family follows every twist with laughter or tears, and when the old man drifts off to sleep his servant beds his wife. The playwright Pietro Aretino, who saw the sketch in Venice, said that Polo "made everyone wet their pants with laughter." Zuan Polo and another Venetian performer, Domenigo Taiacalze, entertained with impersonations, songs, magic tricks, and animal stunts. The diarist Marino Sanuto recounts Zuan Polo dressing in the costumes of Moors, Germans, and Hungarians but notes that no masks were worn.[3]

Commedia dell'arte developed alongside such *buffoni*. One distinguishing difference was the use of masks, which its early actors fashioned from the carnival costumes they saw in the towns they visited. By the eighteenth century, its characters and their masks seemed timeless. Luigi Riccoboni, an actor and director, proudly insisted that commedia dell'arte was a direct descendant of Roman theater. The disapproving saw in commedia's excess a darker and still more ancient source. One of them said that in antiquity, clowns, mimes, conjurers, and fools all shared the same bad seed: they were Dionysian.[4]

The first permanent commedia dell'arte troupe got its start a stone's throw from Venice in Padua. In 1545, an enterprising performer named Maphio del Re and two business partners put into writing the governing statutes of what would become the West's first professional acting company. The troupe was made up of a stonemason, two rope-makers, a blacksmith, a soldier, and a harpist. Within a generation, professional commedia companies with names such as "The Zealots," "The United," and "The Confidantes" were common, gaining wide recognition through advertised tours and, in some cases, the patronage of princes.[5] Yet even as their status rose, their common origins still showed. For many, little separated the actor from the charlatan.

Some actors would have agreed. Tradition had it that the inhabitants of Ceretto, a hillside town in Umbria, were expert liars who were particularly skilled in faking amputations or disease to beg for alms. They also imitated traveling monks and priests, earning outrage from those who saw through the hoax and a decent income from those who did not.[6] The term *cerretani* (those from Cerreto) evolved into *ciarlatani*—"charlatans"—and came to refer to itinerant hustlers who jumped up on benches to hawk potions and medicines. These were often the same professional talkers who, having gathered a crowd, pulled on masks and launched into raucous plays. A contemporary describes the transformation.

> They select a place in a public square, where, once the stage is erected, they rise to do first the charlatan and then the actor. A *zanni* or someone like him appears on the stage each day at the appointed hour; and he begins to play or sing to attract the people in a circle to hear him. In a little while another appears, and another, and often a woman, too; and with high jinks and pratfalls they make a concoction of popular seductions. Now the principal comes, the chief seller and arch-charlatan, and with exquisite manners and incomparable eloquence he presents his marvelous medicines. . . . At the end of it they tell the public, *Come to the comedy! The play's beginning!* The boxes are locked, the trunks disappear, the stage changes, and each charlatan becomes an actor. Now they begin their comedy, which holds the audience for the span of about two hours with merriment, laughter, and sport.[7]

Thomas Coryat, traveling through Venice in 1608, reported five or six such stages set up in Piazza San Marco. On one of them, an orator held a crowd of nearly one thousand with patter about tonics and apothecary herbs, mixing his jokes with insult and innuendo. Musicians played and sang; one man held a poisonous snake; another gashed his own arm with a knife and just as quickly healed it with a special salve; and actors came onto the stage wearing "vizards" like "fools in a play." A commedia actor in the eighteenth century who assembled a source book of gags and speeches gave a fitting account of what motivated him. "I work in the manner of physicians who purge the sick," he wrote, "with the evacuation of the body, and that of the purse."[8]

Companies were on the road for months on end, enduring the humiliations of itinerancy. The actor Domenico Bruni complained of "foul inns, shady hosts, wretched horses, broken-down coaches, impertinent boatmen, annoying coachmen, and custom- and tax-snoops."[9] Most performances were outdoors, although from the beginning indoor performances proved important for revenue. An early commedia theater in Florence was Teatro di Baldracca, "Whore's Theater," named for the principal business in the neighborhood.[10] Troupes seldom traveled with more than ten members. Most plots required two old men (Pantalone and the Dottore), three women (the lady, the lover, and the servant girl), two young men (usually suitors), and two or three *zanni* (servants, porters, barbers, butchers). It was the actor, not the plot, that drove the action. Their art was not in conveying emotional depth or development. It was in finding fresh ways to amuse.

Before each performance, the director went over the essential names, places, and events with his players and posted an outline of the action backstage. There were eventually more than three hundred standard commedia stories in circulation. Most featured a confusing sequence of twists and turns involving lost relatives, elixirs of love, pirates, sleeping-potions, kidnapped children, and the like. They were designed to keep the pace at a boil. Details of dialogue and action were left up to the actors, who drew ad libitum from a store of memorized soliloquies, harangues, and laments. Each performer hewed closely to a set of gags and gestures associated with his character. The best played a single role for an entire career, perfecting stunts, polishing speeches, developing new ways to capture the character's essence. Actors kept collections of quips and tags unique to the part that had been assembled and passed down over generations.[11]

Dramatically speaking, commedia characters were scarcely individuals at all. They were comic stick figures, true to type through the pranks that outlived any particular performer. There was one exception. The humpbacked Pulcinella, who joined the band of commedia characters in the early 1600s, did not develop a fixed repertoire of gags and stunts. He was fully mutable, putty for performers. Pulcinella could be noble or servile, a cad or a gentleman, nimble or obtuse, tender or foul (figure 12).[12]

Zanni interrupted the action at will with sallies called *lazzi*. These might be silly (Arlecchino tracks a fly, pulls off its wings, and eats it), acrobatic (sudden handstands or cartwheels), or lewd ("Franceschina comes out again to get a cushion she has left at her kinsman's house, and the Captain begins to fondle her"; "As soon as Franceschina answers the knock, Arlecchino drops the traveling bag and begins to fondle her"; "Flaminia, with much lewd byplay, enters with Franceschina, who also acts lasciviously with Oratio"). Unmasked characters were also capable of shocking audiences. In a climactic scene of *The Madness of Isabella,* Isabella Andreini of "The Zealots" tore her clothes and exposed her breasts.[13]

Priests and theologians condemned commedia performances in the harshest terms, declaring them to be a mortal sin for actors and spectators alike. Many targeted actresses in particular. "What is to come when

FIGURE 12. Pulcinella

one hears women speaking of love with their lovers?" asked the Jesuit Pietro Gambacorta. Another priest furnished a reply: "The blood stirs, youth responds, the flesh comes alive, passions burn. And the devil is waiting."[14] From the 1560s, when women first appeared with commedia troupes, the Church was on the offensive, equating actresses with prostitutes and declaring them to be agents of Satan. Some said that acting was worse than prostitution. Remove prostitutes from society, reasoned the priest G. D. Ottonelli, and there will be a surge of greater evils, including adultery, incest, and "other kinds of the most brutish sins." Remove the theater, he continued, and at worst its denizens will be idle. In other words, prostitution served a purpose, while the theater provides "unending opportunities to commit mortal sins."[15]

If the actions of the character condemned the players, the mere presence of spectators made them guilty. A theologian wrote that poison entered every portal as they watched—through the eyes, the ears, the neck, the tongue ("not to mention other parts")—so that they each became "a furnace of lust." Watch the faces of spectators, a professor of theology in Pavia wrote. See their eyes, listen to their words, interpret their sighs and gestures, "and you, too, will recognize the wickedness of the actions they are committing."[16] The frontispiece to Girolomo Fiorentini's *Comoediocrisis sive theatri contra theatrum censura* (1675) is a summary of the peril to audiences, actors, and the fictional characters alike. Spectators stand in a serried mass before a stage, where a pander recommends a young blade to a visibly reluctant maiden. Winged demons above carry a banner that offers the artist's commentary, drawn from Tertullian's "De Spectaculis." It reads *Negotium Diaboli*: "The Devil's Business."[17]

Credulous audiences, some seeing the marvel of staged fiction for the first time and aware of the Church's view, believed that performers possessed occult powers. They saw servants onstage, an actor reported, and assumed they were servants offstage, too. In the same way, they thought that actors playing sorcerers and magicians were in league with demons. "Hearing the name *istrioni* [histrions], and not knowing the etymology or derivation of the word, they think *istrioni* means *stregoni* [wizards], namely enchanters sent from the devil." Tales circulated of actors who had died during plays but whose bodies were inhabited by demons to finish the performance.[18] Comic descents to the underworld played off such superstitions. The diarist Marino Sanuto recounts a sketch in which the *buffone* Zuan Polo, playing the part of a necromancer, travels to hell to confer with demons. In the commedia dell'arte sketch *Fiammella*, Pantalone is a sorcerer who sends Dottore and his *zanni* Bergamino on a journey to hell, where they drink, sing, and carouse with loose women.[19]

Some claimed to see traces of the devil in the masks and misshapen bodies of commedia characters: the reddened bump on Arlecchino's forehead was a remnant of horns, they said, and Pulcinella, with his humpback, black mask, and priapic nose, was satanic. With such symbols in mind, Carl Jung concluded that, despite its surface hilarity, commedia tapped humans' deepest fears. In the look and conduct of its *zanni*—in their unnerving mix of infantile and obscene, in the insidious way they controlled others' actions, and in their relish in creating chaos—commedia dell'arte evoked an ancient fiend in the collective psyche: the Trickster, the quasi-divine joker who subverts and destroys.[20]

The rhetoric from the Church stoked such fears. To laugh or applaud was to encourage sin in the act of commission. Commedia depicted fornication, adultery, and all things harmful to the Christian spirit; it subverted the customs of city and state; it mocked the aged, taught children to defy their parents, and showed young women how to lose their virtue.

As a summary of plots, the litany was actually fairly accurate. In *The Jealous Old Man,* Pantalone takes his young wife, Isabella, to his country villa to keep a possessive eye on her. She is in love with Oratio, and he with her. Soon Oratio arrives, and Pantalone's servant, with the connivance of the local grocer and his wife, is more than happy to smuggle him inside so that Isabella can make a cuckold of her husband. She does, and then eventually rejoins the garden party in a sweat. When Oratio appears, the grocer whispers to him that they've broken the bedstead. Pantalone gathers what has happened, but Oratio preempts his rage. Isabella, not Pantalone, has been wronged, he announces, for until this very day she was a virgin. The old man is exposed as impotent. In humiliation, he permits his wife to marry Oratio.[21]

The Jealous Old Man is among the more indecent of the forty-odd comedies in Flaminio Scala's 1611 collection of commedia dell'arte plots. Many lack such blatant sexuality, although few are wholly without risqué scenes or suggestions. Their indecency, however, was not all the Church objected to.

The fiery archbishop of Milan Carlo Borromeo voiced a more fundamental criticism. Commedia masks, he said, disfigure God's image and transform humans into beasts. "Abominable mask," Borromeo railed, "behind which it becomes licit for men to utter filthy and dishonest words, to make lewd gestures and commit immodest acts! Wicked mask, impugner of honesty, inimical to gravity, ruin of every charge the Christian soul must keep within and without!" Commedia's countless disguises were similarly destructive, a correspondent with the archbishop observed, transforming women into men and boys into women to arouse "every form of wantonness, every form of lust."[22]

It was certainly true that commedia dell'arte favored disguise, which maximized confusion to draw easy laughs. Disguise also titillated. In *The Faithless One,* Isabella leaves her hometown to escape an arranged marriage with Oratio, who loves her madly. Years pass. She returns home disguised as a young man in order to tell him that his beloved Isabella is dead. Touched by his grief, the "young man" tries to console Oratio by telling him to pretend that "he" is Isabella. "Sir, you see these hands; notice that they are like her very own." Oratio kisses them, and the "young man" caresses him in return. Oratio studies the stranger's face, and praises "his" hair and complexion. And now, staring at the stranger's mouth, he edges closer, sighing at last, "Why can I not thus kiss my dear wife?" A servant enters to find his master and the young stranger in a passionate embrace.[23]

Disguises in commedia plots often put the privileged into subservient positions, usually for the sake of love. Isabella is the daughter of a wealthy Genoese merchant in *The Disguised Servants* and falls in love with a young nobleman on his way to Florence. She disguises herself as a manservant to work in his household. Her brother, also disguised as a servant, travels with her and finds work in another house. In the end, she marries the nobleman and her brother marries the nobleman's sister (whom he has made pregnant). In *The Two Disguised Gypsies,* a wealthy young woman dresses as a gypsy girl to travel the world in search of a lover captured by pirates.[24]

The conventions of commedia emphasized the absurdity of its disguises. Commedia depicted character by well-worn stunts and sallies. It conveyed inner experience chiefly by exaggeration. The laughable fluidity of identity was accepted—if consent without belief is acceptance—for its comic effect. How could lovers who faint at the very sight of their beloved be so easily fooled by a false mustache or a pair of men's breeches? In *As You Like It* and *Così fan tutte,* we look beyond the implausible for what Shakespeare and Mozart reveal about love, faithfulness, and the elements of identity itself. In *The Faithless One* or *The Two Disguised Gypsies,* the transformations are the story. With Shakespeare and Mozart, to suspend disbelief is a sacrifice most spectators are willing to make for the human truths their art probes. In commedia dell'arte, disbelief is no impediment.

Commedia dell'arte's masks create an absurd cartoonish effect that shuns any pretense of holding a mirror to reality. The clergy's howls notwithstanding, this probably helped troupes get away with their signature offenses. A masked clown fondling a servant girl doesn't have the same bite as, say, a barefaced priest doing so. Masks blunted the lowborn's insolence by suffusing it with farce. In *The Jealousy of Isabella,* the masked servant Pedrolino scolds his masked master Pantalone for chronic drunkenness. The result of his delinquency, Pedrolino says, will be a pregnant daughter.[25] A collection of scenes and speeches for use by Pantalones (who were always masked) contains a prologue that delivers gibes equitably across the social spectrum. "Tonight I would give you for dinner a salad of a lawyer's lies, a stew of a merchant's promises, a roast of a gambler's oaths, boiled meat of a woman's cunning, a pie of a lover's advances, a soup of an admirer's compliments, a flavor of whores' wiles, with a pastry of servants' bad judgement and lack of love for their masters."[26]

Defenders of commedia dell'arte maintained that its vices and desires were a version of reality, however distorted. By laughing at commedia's absurdity, they said, audiences laughed at their own flaws. In a sharply worded tract from the 1630s, a writer named Nicolò Barbieri resisted the notion that staging "elderly misers, lawless youths, dishonest women, thieving servants, and ambitious pimps" made commedia itself corrupt. "God in heaven—" he wrote, "as if you could reform an immoral man without naming his vice or depicting his ugliness!" To judge from commedia's popularity, audiences may have grasped Barbieri's point even as the clergy disputed it. Visiting Venice in the eighteenth century, Goethe described spectators who were rapt and delighted. They were seeing "their actual life," Goethe wrote, "presented with greater economy as make-believe and removed from reality by masks."[27]

The masks of commedia dell'arte were not a disguise. On the contrary: they preserved identities. Commedia masks held their characters consistent even as particular plots placed them in different occupations and family configurations. In one play, Isabella was Pantalone's daughter; in another, she was his wife. The unchanging mask maintained the persona across generations.

The mask in commedia dell'arte was not so much a false face, writes Ferdinando Taviani, a leading authority on the genre, as a "lost face": a negation of its features, a denial of interiority, a way of shifting expression to the body. The characters of commedia were superficial, literally. They were all surface. Their behavior came chiefly as a response to events rather than from within. For Arlecchino to change from conniving servant in one play to pimp or porter in the next, "it sufficed merely to change the action, his having no soul, implied or otherwise, to change."

Taviani salutes the early twentieth-century Russian theater director V. E. Meyerhold for having grasped the essence of commedia masks, which fixed identity while freeing character. The expressionless visage of the mask was to Meyerhold "chameleonic." Its lack of expression allowed spectators to see before them all the Arlecchinos they had watched in their lives, and it granted performers greater license to improvise. Taviani comments that the mask "made theatrically credible this absence of character—this absence of psychology, as we would say—that made Arlecchino into a type without making him into a person except through his actions."[28]

This was the very point Nicolò Barbieri had made in his 1634 defense of acting. Clowns, he wrote—*buffoni* like Zuan Polo and Taiacalze—were always clowns. But an actor in the role of a clown only imitates a clown: "by wearing a mask on his face, or a false beard, or makeup, he is able to display the essence of another person." Offstage, an actor has a different identity, is known by another name. "But the *buffone* is always the same in name, look, and approach, not for two hours of the day but for every moment of his life, and not just on the stage but at home and in the public square."[29]

By fixing character, the mask helped to establish what later generations would take for granted, the distance between role and performer. (Barbieri's contemporaries—the ones who believed that servants onstage were servants in real life—didn't always grasp the distinction.) The point may give some insight into an intriguing painting by Domenico Fetti of the actor Francesco Andreini. In its classical pose and sumptuous palette, the portrait plays up the contrast between Andreini's gaunt nobility and the expected silliness of Arlecchino (figure 13).[30]

Barbieri's defense of the craft reminds us how disorienting acting must have been for audiences in the early decades. It also conveys the complexity of the mask. In commedia, it at once protected the position of the actor and preserved the part he played. It kept a distance, in other words, between the person and his persona. It opened a space in the viewer's imagination for fiction, which gave the actor license to offend even as its comical distortions softened the genuinely offensive. That the mask did this with a whiff of sulfur still present helps to explain the mixture of awe and fear that early audiences experienced alongside the merriment.

Tristano Martinelli, the actor who published an empty book of rhetoric from The Ends of the Earth, fully understood the mask's license and power. He occasionally signed the letters he wrote to royal and princely patrons not as Martinelli but as Arlecchino. The forms of address he employed would have been impeachable offenses had they come from any other subject. But the persona of Arlecchino permitted the impermissible, much as the mask did on the stage. He addressed Ferdinando I de' Medici as the "highest master of footgear." Ferdinando Gonzaga was "my fellow rooster of the red crest." Marie de' Medici was "our most Christian, fellow queen hen."

FIGURE 13. Domenico Fetti, *Portrait of an Actor*

Martinelli's mask kept a protective distance, but there are indications that it also granted familiarity. The banter in his letters was usually fond, and on occasion one hears tones of sincerity and reciprocity through the silliness. This is how Martinelli ended a letter in 1614 to Ferdinando Gonzaga, the duke of Mantua. "Meanwhile I pray you to hold us in your grace, because your grace is a grace, that among other graces, one never finds a grace like your grace, and it is not small grace to have as a grace your gentle grace, and with good grace you will have the grace to hold us in your grace, which we receive as a singular grace."[31] Even as it preserved distance, the mask could foster intimacy.

CHAPTER 10

Unmasking the Heart

For critics of commedia dell'arte, carnival masks and their spinoffs in the theater were part of a wider circle of wickedness that stretched from the concrete to the unseen. To them, there was a direct connection between hiding one's face and covering one's heart. Among those to explore this affiliation was Tomaso Garzoni, whose magnum opus *The Universal Assembly of All the Professions of the World, Noble and Ignoble* (1585) claimed to describe every known occupation.[1] For Garzoni, the more obvious link that tied the mask to wrongdoing ran through carnival, when "innocent" pranks sowed seeds of corruption. A more pernicious connection, which put a flimsy piece of cardboard on a continuum with sin, ran through Satan, inventor of the object and purveyor of the deed.

Of all professions, Garzoni writes, mask making alone was founded by Satan. "The inventor of masks, and indeed the first mask ever to be seen on the face of the earth, was without doubt the dark angel, who, in the guise of the malicious serpent, seduced our first mother to horrible excess." For Garzoni, masks are the visible remnant of original sin. They are a sordid inheritance from the first deceiver, who bears "an insatiable lust to mislead at every instant, and who covers his own nature with a mask of seeming beauty."

The excesses of carnival are squarely in Garzoni's sights as he surveys the damage done by masks. His language is scalding. Modern carnival maskers are "bestial"; they dwell in "fetid carnality" and exhibit the "lust of a she-ass." Masks bring out the worst in humans. They inspire impious

words and riotous actions. They debase the good and cause the vulgar to reach beyond their station. "Don't you realize that masks . . . teach artisans to leave their workshops? And doctors to leave their studies? And scholars to pawn their books to visit prostitutes?" Garzoni's horror drew in part from a view of the social order as fixed, which masks grotesquely violated. What does a street-sweeper have to do with Ganymede? he asks, apparently having seen such a costume. What does a filthy peasant have to do with a Doctor of Laws? Masks pervert the common order, which is no surprise given their source. They are "instruments of the devil, offspring of the Adversary, the surest way to Charon's river and the Stygian marsh."

Here Garzoni shifts from carnival masking to hypocrisy, where the deceit is real but the disguise invisible. His examples are from the world around him: an upright merchant who feels a sudden urge to cheat, a steadfast worker who over time grows lazy and dishonest, the religious impostor who affects a gaunt appearance for Lent, women who paint their face with creams and powders. Satan has "granted the mask" to each of these. "Nothing here is true or real but instead false and masked."[2]

Such a connection—tying carnival masks to everyday dishonesty by way of the great Tempter—was characteristic of the age. The anonymous *Discourse against Carnival* (1607), for instance, is vitriolic against the sins of the season. These include theft, fraud, lasciviousness, gluttony, discord, and "other infernal furies that trouble the world." But carnival's real danger goes beyond any momentary mischief. In hiding the face, the sermon declares, masks cover the conscience. To describe both registers, the language shuttles between the physical mask and its more abstract expressions. Terms recur like an idée fixe. An old man convinces himself that he can dance and masks his vanity by saying carnival permits it. A girl goes out alone in public and masks her disgrace by saying carnival permits it. A widow whose tears are still fresh accepts a stranger's arm and masks her betrayal by saying carnival permits it. "Every person with the Devil's mask is disguised." The English doesn't fully capture a redundancy in the Italian that overlays physical and metaphoric masking: *Ogni persona con questa maschera del Diavolo è mascherata.*

In this parade of transgressions the mask is a figure for wickedness. "With a bare face they would not dare to consider such things. Unrecognized, they do them eagerly." Carnival incites corruption that outlives the moment. It fosters "debauchery in the mask of brilliance, dissipation in grandeur's apparel, pride clothed as courtliness, lust covered by facetiousness, and crime pretending to clown." The season elevates "Lucifer himself, in the mask of carnival."[3]

Late in the sixteenth century, artists captured the chain of associations that drew together Satan, the mask, and dishonesty on one side and God, unmasking, and honesty on the other. In the iconography of the time, bestial features and deformed bodies—the clearest expression of original sin—are classic symbols of deceit. Flawless bodies and visible hearts signal immaculate virtue. Masks are prominent in both sets of images.

Consider a triumphal arch erected in 1594 for the entry of Austria's Archduke Ernest into Brussels. One panel bears the allegorical figure of *Sincerity*. A nude man stands on a mound of discarded masks. In one hand he holds a white dove; with the other he points to his heart, visible through a window in his chest. He is stripped to show the naked truth. According to a description prepared for the event, the dove is *sine felle,* "without bile," an expression of purity that is both mental and physical.[4] That double register is in keeping with the force of the allegory, combining symbolic masks with a view inside the body (figure 14).

The same visual language appears in Cesare Ripa's compendium *Iconologia* (1593), which contains images and descriptions for all sorts of things, including states of emotion, illnesses, fields of knowledge, months

FIGURE 14. Triumphal arch, Brussels (detail)

FIGURE 15. *Fraud*

FIGURE 16. *Sincerity*

FIGURE 17. *The Word of an Honest Man*

of the year, the virtues and vices, the seasons, the continents, major rivers, and the planets. *Fraud,* for instance, is pictured as a monstrous two-headed creature dressed in yellow with talons instead of feet and a scorpion's tail. The face of a beautiful maiden is twinned with that of an old hag. One hand holds a blazing, fractured heart. The other carries a mask (figure 15).

Sincerity, by contrast, is a comely young lady in a sheer gown who holds a dove and a heart (figure 16). "Exhibiting the heart denotes integrity," Ripa explains, "for the sincere man, having no base intent, does not hide the heart's interior but places it on display for all to see." This is the sense of a rather ghoulish rendering of *The Word of an Honest Man,* from Pierio Valeriano's 1556 *Hieroglyphica,* which shows the upper torso of a man whose heart hangs on a heavy chain around his neck (figure 17). Ripa offers a similar view in his *Love of God.* Here a man looks upward and opens his robe partway to expose his heart.

Loyalty (Leatà) in Ripa's *Iconologia* appears as a woman holding a flaming torch as she batters a mask against a rocky outcrop. A description explains the image. Her transparent apparel is as the speech of an honest man, which "conveys thoughts to reveal the sincere mind without impediments." The torch stands for the heart and soul; its light, the words and actions that guide others by example. The cracked mask "manifests scorn for falseness and duplicity of mind" (figure 18). Masks appear in *Mendacity (Bugia),* pictured as a youth on shaky ground and holding

FIGURE 18. *Loyalty*

FIGURE 19. *Mendacity*

a bundle of smoking twigs. Adorning his clothes are masks and tongues. Ripa explains that the pattern conveys the liar's inconstancy, which mingles the false with the true and confirms the proverb, *Mendacem oportet esse memorem:* Liars had better have a good memory. The bundle of sticks, a counterpart to *Loyalty*'s shining torch, stands for the brief life of a lie. The allegory extends to the (unneeded) peg leg: "lies have short legs" (figure 19).

In Ripa's *Contrition,* a woman tears her clothes and beats her breast. She has renounced sin and cast off her mask, which lies at her feet. Ripa tells us that the mask stands for things that "flatter, deceive, and impede the honest cognition of ourselves."[5] Note the target of this unmasking. Other images praise truthfulness with others or transparency before God. This image urges honesty with oneself. Its unmasking is for the sake of self-understanding. This gives voice to what has become a modern imperative. Over the next 350 years, the mask would assume different uses, shedding its diabolical overtones to stand instead for evasion, emulation, and at last self-deception: for court etiquette or the falseness of society; for learned professional roles and the play-acting of everyday life; for obstacles the psyche throws up as denials, delusions, and distortions. To Ripa and his contemporaries, it was sin itself.

Ripa's images were in tune with a religious strand of thinking that equated piety with openness. In the wake of the Reformation, both Protestants and Catholics turned the locus of spirituality inward. Desires, thoughts, and motives—and not just actions—were a measure of one's godliness. Writing two generations after Cesare Ripa, the Reverend John Tillotson, the archbishop of Canterbury, linked sanctity with sincerity, which he described as "constant plainness and honest openness of behavior, free from all insidious devices, and little tricks, and fetches of craft and cunning: from all false appearances and deceitful disguises of ourselves in word or action." Sincerity, he went on, was perfect concord between word and thought, a condition in which "our actions exactly agree to our inward purposes and intentions."[6]

How were such exhortations received? Inner states of the long-departed are out of reach, and the responses we do have—in letters, testaments, and confessions—represent a small sliver of humanity. But they are instructive. Judging from the words of many who thought carefully about such things in the sixteenth and seventeenth centuries, and of many more who improvised when forced to justify their beliefs, unmasking the heart was not advisable. As moralists and religious writers urged transparency, powerful pressures of the age were producing its opposite.

In *News from Parnassus,* a satirical author named Traiano Boccalini exposed the delicious double-talk of opening the heart. The book, published in Venice in 1612, is a set of imaginary conversations poking fun at the "passions and habits of private men, no less than the interests and actions of the powerful princes."[7] In the seventy-seventh dispatch from Parnassus, Thales of Miletus proposes the very thing Ripa and others had counseled. Apollo has asked the seven sages of Greece to come up with proposals for general reform of the universe. The privileged follow their own selfish interests, he has said; money is the only authority, nations are at war with one another, and hatred consumes the great and small alike. Thales responds with a rousing speech about the coming age of truthfulness. "When modern men who now proceed with such artifice are compelled to confer and communicate with the window of their hearts open, they will learn the most excellent virtue of being instead of seeming. They will conform their actions to their words and align their tongues—now accustomed to lies—to their hearts, which are incapable of deceit."[8]

The sages cheer and Apollo approves the plan. Surgeons come forth with cleavers to open windows onto all hearts. Suddenly Homer, Virgil, Plato, and Aristotle arrive with misgivings. Since the leaders of the earth rule by example and by reputation, they say, and since their authority would be diminished if they were shamed or embarrassed, wouldn't it make sense for them to purify their hearts before they are opened? Apollo decrees an eight-day postponement. "It was noted by the inquisitive that in the neighborhood of the philosophers—the Platonists, the peripatetics, and moralists—a great stink arose at this time, as if every privy in the quarter had been emptied. And the neighborhoods of the Italian and Latin poets began to reek of overcooked cabbage."⁹

The surgeons reassemble. But now Hippocrates, Galen, and other physicians approach Apollo. Man is a delicately constructed machine with so noble and miraculous a constitution, they caution. The procedure might kill him. The sages are convinced and ask to hear new suggestions for general reform of the universe. At length a proposal is embraced. The Century himself must answer for his misdeeds. He arrives and is decrepit. His voice is weak; his face is flushed. He is a living cadaver, he tells them. Disease overtook him at birth. Look under my clothes, he says and you will see. The sages strip him to find a thick crust of filth covering every inch of his body. After some chipping they come to the bone. The Century has no living flesh. They quickly reclothe him and send him on his way.

Which does not prevent the seven sages from throwing open the palace gates and grandly declaiming their proposal for general reform of the universe. *Limits will hereby be imposed on the price of cabbage, sardines, and squash.* Parnassus erupts in cheers. The dialogue ends with this lesson: the world should be left as it is. The heart will remain covered and the ills of the century disguised.

CHAPTER 11

Age of Dissimulation

Traiano Boccalini's lesson was closer to the experience of his contemporaries than sermons that preached pious transparency. As an anatomist of political power, Boccalini was at once fascinated and repulsed by what he saw. He was equally sensitive to its effects on rulers and the ruled. One of the serious points in *News from Parnassus* is that the ambition of princes is seldom compatible with human freedom. In Boccalini's view, the prerogatives rulers claim—to wage war, destroy internal enemies, and hold the monopoly on force—come at a high cost to their subjects. He remarked sardonically that *ragion di Stato*, the late-Renaissance doctrine that judged the means of amassing power in terms of the state's ends, so pervaded daily life that the term was on the lips of every porter and shopkeeper. Political power traded in appearances, Boccalini believed, not ideals. "The courts of princes are nothing but mask-shops," he wrote, "where all the goods are bogus, made for the sake of deception."[1]

For Boccalini's generation, the noble fabric of civic humanism, according to which the prince was at once a patron of the arts and the protector of his people, was now fraying in a harsh new world. Rule built on brute force replaced an older ideal of clemency and cultivation. In Italy, the Renaissance system of statecraft, which aimed at maintaining a balance among the peninsula's major powers, was in shambles. French and Spanish armies now moved through the land at will. A series of catastrophes came in their train. Florentine stability was shaken and the independence of Milan and Naples lost. Elsewhere in Europe, monarchies with absolutist designs crippled or co-opted noble resistance.

It was also the time of bitter confrontation between militant Protestantism and a Catholic Church fighting to contain the heresy. The violence of the Thirty Years' War (1618–48), a conflict ostensibly between Catholics and Reformers, was a more protracted version of what was played out in book-burnings, imprisonment, torture, and public executions. Authoritarian rule, whether political or religious, brooked little dissent. Secrecy and imposed consent were the order of the day, enforced by sudden arrest, censorship, and the Inquisition. Some faced their accusers defiantly and with principled honesty. Many others devised strategies to withhold, mislead, or falsify. For both the great and the small, on the global stage of statecraft and in the intimate spaces of conviction, the mask was a matter of survival.

Human deceit is, of course, universal. But the cultural contours of seventeenth-century Europe brought fresh preoccupation with its many varieties. Some claimed that its actual practice was on the rise as well. Combine coercive state power with a religiously sanctioned inspection of souls under threat of torture or death, they reasoned, and the result is ever more refined techniques for blurring the truth. "Dissimulation is among the most notable qualities of the century," wrote the essayist Michel de Montaigne. "Innocence itself in these times is unable to negotiate without dissimulation."[2]

Paolo Sarpi, the Servite friar who argued brilliantly for Venice when the city was placed under papal interdict, echoed the view. "In other centuries, hypocrisy was not uncommon, but in this one it pervades everything." Sarpi believed that there was only one recourse. "I am compelled to wear a mask. Perhaps there is no one in Italy who can survive without one." John Milton called Sarpi the Great Unmasker, a sobriquet that, given Sarpi's dogged chronicling of papal self-interest, may well have been accurate. But Sarpi also kept his own mask firmly in place. It is necessary "to remain masked with everyone," he said, "to express conventional opinions while reserving one's convictions." Everything conceals itself "behind the mask of religion."[3] According to his biographers, Sarpi was either an orthodox Catholic, a Catholic reformer, a crypto-Anglican, a Protestant, or an atheist who put on a show of piety—a testimony to his skill in dissembling.[4]

The rhetoric of masking saturates the age. Still more remarkable was the eagerness with which people of various callings and occupations embraced it in defiance of age-old convictions that classed untruthfulness as a moral wrong. Few denied the virtue of honesty or endorsed outright deceit. Rather, they devised ways of parsing words and framing discourse that preserved truth even while concealing it. Again Sarpi: "I never speak falsehoods, but I do not speak the truth to everyone."[5] This impulse to make masking honest was an acknowledgment of two realities. Institutions held extraordinary powers of life and death over individuals, and nonconformists struggled to fashion a defense that was also upright.

Dissimulation equipped such dissenters with the means to protect themselves. "Whether in relation to public or private affairs," writes the historian Perez Zagorin, "the idea that people commonly went masked and habitually dissimulated their true beliefs came readily to contemporary minds."[6] In this age of dissimulation, dissembling was not just about masking the truth. For many, it was about finding a way to do so that was both ethical (or at least not unethical) and protective. Prudence need not come at the expense of rectitude. This was the message of a virtuoso piece of writing by Torquato Accetto, *On Honest Dissimulation.* At first glance, the title seems to yoke incompatibles. But Accetto insisted that dissembling was not deceit and that the mask was sometimes truth's only defense.

Torquato Accetto was born in Naples around 1590, a time of growing tensions between Neapolitans and their rulers, who were regents of the Spanish crown. Accetto was a poet and studied law, but his principal occupation was secretary to the Neapolitan dukes Antonio and Fabrizio Carafa. An early sonnet, "Serving as Secretary," hints at bitterness and buried wrongs. Its narrator longs for sleep as a balm for "grave offenses," finds refuge in "silence, the pen, and wisdom," and faults *la servitù gentil*—the noun is equivocal, meaning domestic service and slavery—for depriving him of the sun's warmth and the solace of nighttime.[7]

A century earlier, Baldassar Castiglione's *Book of the Courier* (1528) had memorialized the princely advisor as a sparkling conversationalist who schooled his master in polish, learning, and virtue. By Accetto's time, the luster was gone. A secretary was now more underling than associate. Expected to maintain accounts, compose letters, and perform unsung duties of administration, his chief task was to answer when addressed but otherwise keep silent. "You must conceal your abilities, feign incompetence, and let yourself be fooled," advised a manual called *The Secre-*

tary. Another said that "it falls to the secretary merely to execute, and to execute only what the master has intended."[8]

On Honest Dissimulation (1641) grew from this twilight world of unacknowledged service, but its reach extends far beyond. Its conclusions set it at a great distance from the trampled masks of fifty years earlier. "My aim is to show that living judiciously is not at odds with purity of soul," Accetto writes near the start of the book. Piety does not demand opening the heart. Dissimulation's masks are akin to the fig leaf, a necessary acknowledgment, he writes, that the Golden Age—when humans lived with the heart "outside the chest, with its imprint felt on every word"—has passed.[9] The lesson of the Fall is clear: self-knowledge awakens the urge to veil our intentions. There can be no return to Eden. The powerful demean the innocent and exert unjust dominion. Falsehood flourishes. Existence overflows with peril. Dissembling is our best defense.

Accetto asserts a clear distinction between simulation and dissimulation. Simulation is the "art of pretending," a show of words and actions. Dissimulation withholds the truth, relying instead on silence and omissions. Simulation cannot be called honest, nor can circumstances make it legitimate. It injures both the deceiver and the deceived. Dissimulation, by contrast, is defensive, a shield and not a sword, a way of avoiding rather than provoking harm. Instead of circulating untruths, it "grants some repose to truth, which can be revealed in its proper time."[10] Dissimulation controls accustomed forms. It interweaves truths with half-truths to create seeming falsehood. It is patient, prepared to endure hardship, reluctant to condemn, and unwilling to meet malice with malice. One simulates what one is not. One dissembles what one is.

Accetto's words go beyond the simple counsel to conceal. Dissimulation is "a veil of honest obscurity and violent propriety."[11] The connection between dissembling and propriety was a familiar theme in the seventeenth century. It was a staple of courtly accounts—and the motor of Molière's comic play *The Misanthrope*—to observe that codes of etiquette employed a healthy dose of dissimulation. The French moralist La Bruyère, a fierce critic of such "propriety," called the courtier who disguised his passions, denied his heart, and spoke against his sentiments a refined hypocrite. Accetto disagreed. Hypocrisy, Accetto observes, feigns virtue to hide vice. Dissimulation preserves virtue by hiding truth.[12]

With the concealment comes a fairly brutal stifling, a point Accetto makes by emphasizing propriety's violence. An undertone of self-mutilation runs through his treatise. The intended book was three times the length of what remains, Accetto writes. Its "wounds" are fresh; the astute will see its "scars"; it is "virtually drained of blood." "Writing about dissimulation has required me to dissemble, and, to this end, I have amputated much of what I wrote at the outset." The admission betrays the dissembler's secret, which is to keep his mask invisible. (Dissimulation, Accetto cautions elsewhere, is a profession of which one cannot make a profession. "Owing to natural curiosity, anyone who wore a mask every day would become better known than all others.") By drawing attention to the unsaid, Accetto puts the dissembler's techniques of self-protection on display.[13] He also hints at hidden meaning within his tightly compacted prose.

The effect is tantalizing. The supposed confession—*writing about dissimulation has required me to dissemble*—admits to concealment but reveals nothing. As a mask that draws attention to itself, *On Honest Dissimulation* highlights the deceptive construction of the verb *to reveal* (L. *re-* + *vēlum*, veil; It. *rivelare*; Fr. *révéler*): to disclose, divulge, make known. The *re-* prefix most commonly means "back" or "again," but in this word and a small handful of others it signifies *un-* (*resign*, to relinquish or surrender; *reclude*, to open; *refix*, to abrogate or annul). The critic Salvatore Silvano Nigro, Accetto's most subtle contemporary interpreter, has written that "the truth of the mask is the mask itself."[14] Another way of putting it is that Accetto's admission of dissembling veils as much as it unveils.

Dissimulation forges a middle course between submission and rebellion. From the outside the strategy may look passive, a sort of extreme modesty that borders on the fearful or insecure. For Accetto this is its moral value. Dissimulation, he writes, is at once a virtue and "the decorum of all other virtues, which are yet more beautiful when in some way dissembled." It is a restraint on pride, cloaking and deflecting qualities that would otherwise "make a vain display of themselves."[15]

As if to underscore the worth of humility, Accetto evokes the powerless in sections on the defense of truth against a greater force. In an extended metaphor on the capacity of the heart to contain all things ("even the world itself"), he sketches the image of a prince in danger who retreats to a secret room inside a palace ringed by guards. "[It is] clear that every man, without expense and exposed to the view of all, may hide his affairs in the vast and secret dwelling that is his heart."[16] Accetto claims that he intends his treatise for "anyone who commands or obeys," but his examples point most often to the latter, for whom dissimulation is not merely a virtue but a defense. And with this, in a book with no ostensible reference to contemporaneous people or events, we sense the threatening presence of overwhelming force.

"Dissimulation in the Face of an Unjust Power" is the title of Accetto's most politically charged chapter. From the first sentence, the rhetoric is pitched in a higher key. "Powers that consume the very substance of those living under their yoke are horrific monsters." The language is as vivid as his similes elsewhere (editing as amputation, the heart as a prince's hidden chambers, etc.), but here it is stripped of all analogy. The head that wears an unmerited crown defies all who possess true wisdom, he writes. Dissembling one's virtue averts the despot's "fear and jealousy." Hiding one's suffering denies him his brutish satisfactions. "When the tyrant forbids breathing, one mustn't sigh; when the sword reddens the earth with innocent blood, one mustn't blanch or shed tears."[17]

Accetto cites the reign of the Roman emperor Domitian as an instance of tyranny, but his readers' thoughts may have run to more immediate atrocities. In Accetto's lifetime, waves of popular protest were met by increasingly vicious repression. When he was in his early thirties, seven residents of Naples were convicted of treason for insulting and throwing stones at the Spanish viceroy Cardinal Zapata. They were stripped naked, bound, loaded into a cart, and paraded through the streets as their captors tore at them with red-hot pincers. They were then stretched across wagon wheels, and their limbs, torsos, and faces were battered with sledgehammers. Once dead, they were decapitated. Their heads were put in iron cages as an example, and their bodies were quartered and dumped outside the city walls for the dogs.[18]

A curiosity in Accetto's text may signal such violence. Roughly half of his twenty-five short chapters end with their closing words fashioned into a calligram resembling a funnel. The device stirs vague unease, as if the very words are being squeezed into silence or perhaps dropping through an hourglass. At the close of chapter 3, "It Is Never Right to Abandon Truth," something more may be happening. The passage itself is inoffensive. Accetto writes that one cannot deceive oneself indefinitely, and that prudent dissimulation, if grounded in truth, is a confirmation of its own value.[19] But phantom words emerge from the line-breaks beginning halfway down on the left: *rogo* (the stake or funeral pyre), *tenendo* (holding, gripping), *temo* (I am afraid), *mostrando* (displaying), *sudo* (I sweat). This is the only calligram where a series of words appears. Their savage kinship is chilling.

Si può nondimeno tralasciar la memoria del proprio male,
per qualche spazio, come dirò;
ma dal centro del petto son tirate le linee
della dissimulazione alla circonferenza
di quelli che ci stanno in-
torno. E qui bisogna il ter-
mine della prudenza che,
tutta appoggiata al ve-
ro, nondimeno a luo-
go e tempo va ri-
tenendo o di-
mostrando il
suo splen-
dore.[20]

The Italian historian Rosario Villari, who learned of the seven protesters' fate in the archives of Naples, argues that dissimulation was deadly
serious. It had affinities with the cunning and intrigue of court society,
but its origins were altogether more menacing. It grew from "a climate
of oppression, conformism, traditionalism, and the spirit of resignation,
which few succeeded in escaping."[21] Accetto's subjects—those who received rather than gave orders, those without riches, those who worried
about moral principles even under the constraint of circumstances—did
not have to read about dissimulation to grasp its necessity.[22]

There were other circles that praised the mask and warned against
putting the heart on view. Arguments advancing Reason of State, the novel
theories of governing that Boccalini had said were on the lips of even ordinary folk, were both symptom and cause of the pervasive distrust of
transparency. In a famous passage in *The Prince* (1513), Machiavelli states
that the ruler should possess the wiles of a fox and the fierceness of a
lion. The prudent ruler, having perfected these qualities, will then know
to hide them. He will be a *gran simulatore e dissimulatore,* a great pre-
tender and dissembler.[23] The view coincides with Accetto's counsel to
gain mastery over one's own affects and passions. In certain respects, this
too was an argument from necessity: the capacity for deceit was needed
to counter the falseness of others. But unlike Accetto, Machiavelli sets
aside questions of right and wrong to discuss how rulers actually rule.
In these terms, hiding the heart was not a necessary evil. It was, however,
necessary. Such advice for gaining and holding power was a revolution
in politics. Its matter-of-fact tone is pitch-perfect for expressing moral
neutrality. This scandalized readers.

In a stroke, Machiavelli shattered the alignment of honesty, virtue, and utility that had been the ideal of effective rule since Aristotle. He dismissed as naive the Christian model of prince as moral exemplar and held that the state's own aims—its demands for the preservation and extension of power as judged by the ruler—transcended moral law. This didn't necessarily urge plunder and illegality or deny categories of good and evil. Rulers ought to be good insofar as they were able, Machiavelli wrote. Nor was "necessity" simply a dodge to excuse dark actions. That said, morality and justice were not in themselves sufficient guides for rulers, who may be called on to act immorally or unjustly to maintain state power. Machiavelli was the first to translate this reality into a systematic view of politics. Such means were not temporary expedients to be abandoned and foresworn once the prince had finished some distasteful business. Machiavellian *virtù*—prudent action chosen of necessity—encompassed deceit, fraud, pretense, and hypocrisy.[24]

A moment from the Thirty Years' War illustrates the novelty and diffusion of such notions. An acquaintance of the Bohemian humanist Wentzel von Meroschwa had written to ask what the cities not yet touched by war should do: side with Emperor Ferdinand, support Elector Frederick, or remain neutral? Meroschwa replied that the threefold choice was "scholastic" in its "ancient candor." Just as modern astronomers have discovered new stars with their telescopes, he wrote, the new politics has its own optics and lenses, "through which it is possible to see other elements and alternatives." Meroschwa enumerated the "new stars": the cities could feign allegiance to Frederick and secretly aid Ferdinand, feign allegiance to Ferdinand and secretly aid Frederick, feign neutrality and aid one or the other, or feign neutrality and aid both. "Regarding such choices, the political man must ask not only what one should or should not do, but also what one should simulate doing." Merchants cheat and lie to sell us their rubbish, Meroschwa added. "Can we not do the same to defend our cities and their regimes?"[25]

It was in this spirit that seventeenth-century political writers defended a version of public deception for the good of the whole. But the influence of the Counter-Reformation is also palpable in tempering what they said and how they said it. Responding to a combination of persuasion and pressure from the Church (Pope Pius V denounced Reason of State as *ragion del diavolo*), some intellectuals after Machiavelli distinguished between good and bad variants of *ragion di Stato*. The former sought the well-being of the whole, for which a state might violate its own statutes but never moral law. The latter was the prince's selfish pursuit of domination, which stopped at nothing.

The post-Machiavellian climate is evident among those who counseled dissimulation in the seventeenth century. Pietro Andrea Canonieri's *Perfect Courtier* (1609) spells out strategies that embrace secrecy and silence, advising princes to frame answers solely in the terms of the question and to fashion their gestures and expressions to conceal the truth. He casts this advice as defensive, which he says makes it unobjectionable. One should not reveal the truth, he writes, but one must not lie. Gabriele Zinano, whose *On the Reason of State* first appeared in Venice in 1626, writes that the statesman is "nothing but artifice" and recommends "all varieties of force and artifice." Yet here, too, artifice could be virtuous or vicious. The latter feigns virtue and religion and is therefore blamable.[26] Ludovico Settala's *On the Reason of State* (1627) urges "concealment of thought, distrust, and dissimulation" and warns the prince against "going about with the breast open," but castigates Machiavelli for recommending deceit, especially in religious matters. Contempt for religion, he writes, has given birth to tyrants by way of temerity, savagery, and finally moral death.[27] With these distinctions, political writers in the century after Machiavelli fashioned a version of honest dissimulation to suit their purposes.[28]

There was a third current that called masking honest. As frontiers hardened between Protestants and Catholics, pressure on nonconformists increasingly set the claims of conscience against the powers of coercion. In contrast to the logic of *ragion di Stato,* morality was paramount at all times in this domain. Believers had to grapple with whether betraying their convictions threatened their souls with damnation. Religious minorities throughout history have, of course, tried to escape persecution by using pretense or concealment. But the pressures of post-Reformation Europe focused these questions with unequaled intensity. Protestantism's elevation of inner conviction and its emphasis on faith rather than works caused believers to live in perpetual examination of their own motives. The terms for understanding appropriate action were new, as well. Rather than resorting to ad hoc evasions and equivocations, theologians now made a case for masking the truth based on Biblical exegesis.[29]

Consider the fate of one of Italy's most discussed religious dissemblers, Francesco Spiera, an attorney who was tried by the Inquisition in Venice for harboring Calvinist beliefs. Under questioning, Spiera confessed to skepticism about the existence of purgatory and admitted to having translated parts of the New Testament into Italian. He also acknowledged having read the *Beneficio di Cristo,* a forbidden book popular among Italian reformers. His interrogations continued, and he finally broke. He renounced his secret Protestantism and promised to reenter the Catholic fold. The punishment was light. He was ordered to recant publicly at the end of a Sunday Mass and to purchase a tabernacle for his parish church.

According to a fellow Protestant who was close to Spiera, the retraction was false. "[Spiera] seemed to want to declare his beliefs openly and hide nothing. Finally, after a long internal battle, he decided on dissimulation. He would keep his opinions firmly but secretly in his heart and with his mouth say something else, namely exactly what the legate wished him to say."[30] After Spiera's public penance, he could not live with himself. Certain that he had damned himself by lying, Spiera fell ill and died in a state of despair six months later. For more than a century, he was familiarly invoked as either reprobate or martyr, and his decision to dissemble was by turns denounced and defended.[31]

The example of Nicodemus, the Pharisee who met with Jesus secretly, was relevant to those like Spiera who faced harsh scrutiny for their beliefs. John Calvin intended scorn in referring to Protestant converts who hid their faith and attended Catholic Mass as Nicodemites. To him, this was idolatry. They should worship in the true faith at home, Calvin urged, and seek to convert as many others as possible, even if it meant death. Those who agreed likened Spiera to Judas.[32]

Others took Nicodemus as inspiration. The view was of a piece with the Lutheran spirit sweeping Europe. Firmly grounded in scripture, it privileged the intimate, open channel that each believer had with God and acknowledged no obligation to earthly institutions. Otto Brunfels was a monk who left his monastic orders in Strasbourg and, in 1527, published a work that was to become the locus classicus for religious dissimulation. *Pandectarum veteris et novi Testamenti,* also called the *Pandectae,* or *Compilations,* strongly countered the view that Christians were obliged to make themselves martyrs for their faith. Brunfels wrote that the tactics of papists justified deception. "Before the ungodly it is legitimate to feign and dissemble in order to both prevent and avoid peril."

Brunfels used Luther's message of Christian freedom to support his argument. The believer was lord of all and subject to none. Jesus himself evaded Pharisees when they pursued him. By resisting the ungodly and their intrusions, "we may temporarily humble ourselves before them for the glory of God."[33] Brunfels likened Protestants to Jesus' early followers, who worked from within the Mosaic law they had renounced to avoid offending those they hoped to convert. He quoted Paul's letter to the Corinthians: "To the Jews I became as a Jew, that I might win Jews. . . . To the weak I became as weak, that I might win the weak. I have become all things to all men, that I might by all means save some" (I Corinthians 9:20, 22). Paul had Timothy circumcised so that Jews would not be scandalized. He gave his flock—"babes in Christ," he called them—only as much truth as they could digest (I Corinthians 3:1–2).

To dissemble belief or feign Catholicism was therefore excusable. Brunfels denied that this justified willful prevarication. God saw into the heart's recesses, and any selfish or groundless deception was sinful. Still, the margin for misleading words and actions was wide, extending to worship within the full Catholic rites if judged necessary.[34]

Brunfels's *Pandectae* was read eagerly by Protestants throughout Europe. Fifteen Latin editions were published between 1528 and 1556, and five German editions appeared between 1528 and 1562. By midcentury, there were three editions in French, four in English, and two in Italian. Its cities of distribution—London, Paris, Wittenberg, Frankfurt, Amsterdam, Venice—map a widening circuit of pious dissembling. "In this sense, the forgeries and disguises demanded by circumstances revealed the deepest characteristic of this book," writes the historian Carlo Ginzburg. "Namely, the expression of a piety indifferent to institutional boundaries and therefore assimilable to all."[35]

There were many cases in Venice and the Veneto that showed the need to dissemble: that of a renegade monk named Giorgio Siculo, who was hanged for preaching Anabaptist tenets and writing in defense of religious simulation; of Giulio di Milano, who received a life sentence from the Inquisition for having read and spoken favorably about the *Pandectae;* and of the dyer Zuanbattista Sambeni, who, after months of unremitting interrogation about his heretical views, was lashed to a large stone, rowed to the Adriatic, and thrown overboard. The number of religious dissemblers is impossible to know. One of the many ordinary Venetians caught in the Inquisition's web spoke of "a world of heretics" who worshiped secretly in the city. Experience, not books, taught them to master their words and actions. By 1600, the Catholic Church had succeeded in ridding northern Italy of the Protestant threat. But ideas of dissimulation—its rationale, techniques, and plausible honesty—remained embedded in the culture.[36]

The conditions that prompted writers to justify dissembling worked on all who had to reconcile prudence with conviction. People hid their reactions and schooled their gestures to remain within communities. These were ways of enduring inequity, of muffling dissent, of protecting rather than transforming one's identity. If the anguished end of Francesco Spiera is any indication, their dissembling was not undertaken lightly. In the constricted intellectual climate of the seventeenth century, when challenging orthodoxy could be fatal, their masks were natural and understandable. Wearing one's heart on a chain was not an option. The dominant image for the age went from window to mask.

Three paintings from the 1640s mark the distance traveled since Cesare Ripa had pictured *Fraud* as a two-headed beast carrying a mask. Lorenzo Lippi's so-called *Allegory of Simulation* is an enigmatic portrait of a young woman with a mask in one hand and a pomegranate in the other (figure 20). She has just pulled off the mask—or is she about to put it on? A finger covers the mask's mouth, and, like the girl's own face, the mask is without expression. Her eyes are alert, her mouth almost pursed, her chin slightly raised in pride or defiance. Perhaps an eyebrow arches. Pierio Valeriano, whose *Hieroglyphica* had depicted *The Word of an Honest Man* one hundred years earlier as a heart dangling from a neck-chain, had also written that pomegranates were a symbol of duplicity. Inside their beautiful exterior corruption may fester, he wrote. Some viewers of Lippi's painting have accordingly grouped the fruit with the mask and called the painting a warning.[37]

But the slice in the rind reveals no corruption. What we see instead are lusciously abundant seeds, some red and others still green. The more common associations of the pomegranate in the late Renaissance ran not to deceit but to regeneration: to plenitude, fertility, and an encompassing oneness-in-variety. In Christian symbolism, its juice signifies blood and its seeds promise rebirth. In Botticelli's *Madonna of the Pomegranate,* for instance, the baby Jesus holds the fruit and offers a blessing. Such connections argue against seeing this painting as a caution. Its title, *Allegory of Simulation,* is modern, appearing only in the twentieth century. Earlier it was known simply as *Lady with Mask and Pomegranate.*[38] Unlike Ripa, Lippi shows no monster in the possession of a mask. The girl's face is unblemished, aloof but not a threat, supremely inscrutable. The pomegranate as plausibly holds secret wealth as any supposed rottenness. This, combined with the girl's own inscrutability, hints at something more complex than simple deceit—something closer to dissembling than to feigning. It is arguably a version of the honest mask that hides all things securely within the heart, "even the world itself."

The painter Salvator Rosa, who knew Lippi when they both lived in Florence in the 1640s, executed two works that touch on similar themes. One shows a man in a frock pointing to a mask he holds. Behind him is a youth whose stare contains both disgust and fascination (figure 21). Many have taken the image to be an admonition against duplicity. Its most frequently used title, *La Menzogna,* or *Falsehood,* presents the image as an

FIGURE 20. Lorenzo Lippi, *Woman Holding a Mask and a Pomegranate*

admonition against duplicity.[39] In a biographical sketch, however, Rosa's contemporary Filippo Baldinucci refers to the canvas as a "philosopher showing a mask to another person." That phrase served as the painting's ungainly title until the mid-nineteenth century, when *Falsehood* replaced it.[40] It is far from clear that the philosopher intends censure. His index finger, more John the Baptist than *Noli mi tangere*, seems to announce or recommend, not to warn off. The mask's features bear a plausible resemblance to those of its possessor. Is this a lesson in masking? In a letter to

FIGURE 21. Salvator Rosa, *Philosopher Showing a Mask to Another Person*

FIGURE 22. Salvator Rosa, *Self-Portrait*

a friend about his service to the Medici family, Rosa wrote: "I go about advising on the best way of wearing a mask, i.e. those acts of abasement and flattery that are so necessary in this court if you want to get ahead."[41] Clearly, he was familiar with the uses of unseen masks.

Rosa's notebooks trumpet honesty in categorical terms. "It is a slavish thing to speak lies and trade in fraud." "Nothing is more damaging to human society than pretense [*simulazione*] and broken promises." "Men win honor with valor, not with fraud." "Liars are traitors to nature."[42] Such statements appear to contradict his advice to wear the mask of flattery to get ahead, unless Rosa followed the practice of his contemporaries and distinguished simulation from dissimulation. If so, the invisible masks he urged were not incompatible with his stubborn refusal to betray principle. There is a space in Rosa's prose for honest dissembling.

A self-portrait done by Rosa underlines the stance (figure 22). Here Rosa rests a tense hand on a tablet inscribed with Latin. A heavy cloak has slipped from one shoulder. The painter's grim face looks small against the sky, and its features, especially the strong nose, chin-strap beard, and creased mouth, resemble the would-be philosopher holding a mask. The tablet's motto reads *Aut tace aut loquere meliora silentio,* "Say nothing unless your words are better than silence."[43] We might imagine the man having just shrugged off his cloak, deciding perhaps to disclose a secret truth that he has been hiding. Now we see it, and it reveals nothing. Rosa has manifestly opted for silence.[44]

The modern renaming of both Lippi's and Rosa's paintings is a sign that our own associations with masks have narrowed since the seventeenth century. Feigning and falsehood conform to a view that instinctively links masking to disguise, guile, and deception. There have always been versions of such views, and in the seventeenth century many were eager to call masks the devil's invention and a symbol of human duplicity. But even as priests and moralists railed against the evils of the mask, others found in it a defensible escape.

The masks of Accetto and Brunfels, of the political minds who split off the bad from the good in *ragion di Stato,* and of the unremembered many who kept silent to conceal a truth were a curious kind of cover, one that obscured and concealed but steadfastly resisted charges of deceit. These invisible masks, evoked figuratively and depicted by artists, were not identified with pranks, mischief, or attempts to undermine the power structure from within. They were by and large defensive, intended less to manipulate than to survive.

The effect was to habituate large parts of the population to viewing the mask not as an accomplice to guile or trickery—and still less as an intimation of the underworld—but as a modus vivendi, intended to preserve rather than disrupt. To call dissimulation honest recast the mask from the devil's tool to an instrument of virtue. That its honesty mattered so much was a sign of its particular value. Given the right circumstances, the mask could be conservative.

PART THREE

The Honest Mask

CHAPTER 12

Legislating Morality

The discourse of honest masking was widespread when Venetians took up the mask as common attire. Its particular terms—what distinguished feigning from dissembling, for instance, or which circumstances might justify employing one or the other—were not likely to have been familiar to the great majority of Venetians, who did not live their lives guarding secrets that could put them at risk. They nevertheless understood and accepted its basic premises: that masks were not always sinful or demonic, that their use extended beyond commedia and carnival, and that they served purposes other than disguise. Honest masking had various sources, which together widened the mask's associations. In Venice, for reasons unique to the setting, it moved from weighing one's words and controlling one's gestures to covering one's face.

Once Venetians began wearing masks in public, the fashion caught on quickly. Their appearance substantially altered the texture of public life, prompting visitors to speak of Venice as a city of libertines and deceivers. The public record attests to this extraordinary shift. Consider two statutes, one from 1608 and the other from 1699. The first forbade Venetians and foreigners from moving through the city by foot or boat in a mask except during carnival. The second, a version of the customary prohibition forbidding masks during Lent, included the observation that many people were now wearing masks "accidentally" during Lent, "to the scandal and complaint of the upright."[1] Accidentally? The word suggests habit. Three decades later, when Monsignor Jacopo Oddi was invested as the new papal nuncio to the city, the formal events fell during Lent. Religious officials, Venetian nobles, and foreign dignitaries took part in the proceedings. "The rejoicing was great," an account reads, "and large numbers of masks were seen throughout the city."[2]

For decades, legislation had prohibited carnival maskers from entering churches, but in the eighteenth century their tone grew more urgent. In 1718, the law warned maskers to stay clear of the vicinity of the church; in 1739, it deplored the impiety of those who entered churches wearing masks; and in 1744, it explicitly forbade anyone from hearing Mass while masked.[3] Judging from a report filed in October 1736 by a surveillance agent assigned to watch a man named Vilio, the vigilance was merited. "About an hour after sunset, just as he had last night, Conte Vilio arrived in a gondola and alighted at the same spot wearing a mask and with a scarlet tabàro, a red velvet suit, golden buttons and button-holes, and sleeves made of sable. The said gentleman went straight into the church, where he noticed me in the sacristy, although I, too, was masked."[4] In 1608, it was still thinkable for the authorities to limit masks to the days before Lent. A century later, they were common in the streets and on the water for half the year. And nearing the mid-eighteenth century, despite the explicit prohibitions, neither spies nor the spied-upon considered it strange to wear them inside a church.

Severe penalties for visiting holy places in masks were in place but imposed unevenly in the eighteenth century. Any noble who appeared masked in the visiting area of a convent risked a two-year banishment from the Great Council; commoners were liable to four years in prison or eighteen months chained to the bench of a galley. The penalties were similarly harsh for entering churches masked. But when the nobleman Francesco Battagia was arrested in November 1770 for stepping into St. Mark's Basilica wearing a mask, he was "corrected" with house detention.[5] Francesco Guardi's 1746 painting *Il parlatorio delle monache di San Zaccaria* shows a great gathering of maskers in one Venetian convent during the carnival season. The mood is graceful, refined, and notably lacking in anything clandestine or corrupt.

Venetians of course wore masks before the tabàro and bàuta made them common attire. In addition to theatrical and carnival references, statutes and surveillance records cite their use for crime and concealment. This explains the draconian penalties threatened against maskers who entered convents and churches, as well as their later neglect in practice: the original decree came from 1603, three-quarters of a century before the Venetian mask assumed connotations of modesty and reserve. An eighteenth-century manuscript in Venice's Correr Museum details crimes committed in masks stretching back two hundred years: in 1556, V. Molin is killed by a masked assailant; in 1615, F. Loredan dies of wounds inflicted by a man in a mask; and in 1616, G. Rasaro is killed leaving a wedding by an attacker wearing a mask. In 1628, the Great Council, expressing its outrage over those who "take the occasion to mask themselves in order to pursue detestable designs, including homicide and other grave offenses, without being known," conferred sole authority on the Council of Ten to regulate masks. Edicts followed forbidding maskers from carrying weapons of any sort, including canes, steel-tipped batons, and knives.[6]

Laws strictly regulated the dress of prostitutes in early modern Venice, and masks were a matter of concern. Regulations swung between requiring them to wear masks and forbidding them outright. How respectable women dressed at any particular moment was relevant, since prostitutes often heightened the scandal and allure of their trade by dressing as patricians. Early in the seventeenth century, for instance, prostitutes imitated respectable women by covering their heads and faces with long veils. The *veléta*, which reached nearly to the ground, was made of semitransparent silk. Virgins wore white; wives and widows wore black. Prostitutes naturally chose white.

There were laws that "absolutely prohibited" the practice, but they had little effect.[7] At midcentury, the Venetian council policing blasphemy reported that prostitutes were "mixing in among honest women, causing uproar, laughter, rumors, and talk." They appeared in public places wearing "the mendacious clothes of married women and other intolerable styles." In 1681, prostitutes were again explicitly forbidden from wearing the *veléta* or any other clothing normally associated with noblewomen. (Appearing respectable wasn't the only trick in the Venetian prostitute's playbook. Another law, repeated with the same weary regularity, condemned those who "dressed in lewd clothes and made a great din with their scandalous speech.")[8]

The intent of such laws was to maintain ways of distinguishing "honest" from "dishonest" women at a glance. Noblewomen appeared infrequently in public, and when they did they often covered their faces with a veil or mask in modesty. Forbidding prostitutes from wearing the veil was one important way of matching appearances with identities. Masked prostitutes risked humiliating penalties. A 1608 edict specified that any "woman of ill-repute or public prostitute" found wearing a mask would be chained for two hours between the two columns of the Piazzetta or forced by the lash through a gauntlet of jeers from St. Mark's to the Rialto. In addition, they received four years' banishment from the city and a fine of five hundred lire.[9]

One hundred years later, with the fashion for masking firmly established, the goal of distinguishing prostitutes from respectable women was dropped. Now prostitutes were required to wear masks in public. A 1709 decree from the government council responsible for regulating dress observed that barefaced prostitutes in patricians' clothes were seating themselves in the first rank of theater-boxes. Calling this an example of "audacious impudence and fearful gall," the law expressly forbade prostitutes from appearing in theaters or the Ridotto without a mask. It was reissued numerous times throughout the century.[10] In 1732, the decree introduced a refinement: prostitutes were to appear masked only if seated on ground level or the first or second boxes. Elsewhere—which is to say in the less visible upper boxes—they could go unmasked but were to conduct themselves with "the greatest reserve and dignity."[11]

What accounts for this about-face? One essential difference, the presence of theaters in Venice, made the context for the eighteenth-century laws requiring masks for prostitutes considerably different from the 1608 decree forbidding them. The first public performance of opera came in the late 1630s, with performers appearing before paying audiences that comprised a broad social range. Prostitutes grasped that a prominent box in these enclosed spaces gave them a stage, too. With respectable women attending the theater masked or in veils, prostitutes' naked faces seemed obscene. The 1732 decree identifies masks with modesty, not extravagance or wantonness. Those required of prostitutes were the same white *larva* or oval black morèta seen throughout the orders. In the presence of so many masks, the thinking must have gone, it was better to have anonymous indistinguishability than hold to a distinction that showed off the prostitutes.

The notion that masks could promote modesty appears in a surprising initiative undertaken by conservatives within the government in the late eighteenth century. On instructions from the State Inquisitors and promulgated a month later by the Council of Ten, what had been a choice now became mandatory. *All* women, foreigners excepted, had to wear masks in the theater. In the Council's decree, issued in late 1776, prostitutes were not the primary concern. It was the dangerous immodesty of the supposedly decent classes. As the Council warned, the "excessive liberty and license of females" were a primary cause of moral decadence. In a Republic, morals and customs were "the most essential thing." By dressing as they pleased, women placed "pristine civic discipline" at risk. The solution was to make them cover their faces. "Be it proclaimed," the decree announced, "that henceforth it shall not be permitted to our noble women, nor to any other woman of civic and honest condition, to enter a theater unless masked, with the usual accompanying dress."[12]

Enforcement fell to the doorkeepers, who turned away all unmasked women attempting to enter. Certain ladies were clearly unaccustomed to receiving orders from such people. Masking by choice was entirely different from masking under orders, particularly when told that the fate of the Republic was at stake. Tense encounters persisted through the late 1770s and 1780s, as adamant doormen, insisting on masks, recorded the names of violators and in some cases chided them in their boxes.

A doorman at the Teatro San Luca informed two noblewomen without masks what the law required. One them shot back, "Siete pazzi!"— "You're crazy!"—as they breezed by. Other spectators followed the letter but not the spirit. When another doorman asked a lady to don her mask, she sent her boatman to fetch it, put it on as she walked through the door, and then returned it to the boatman. Domestic agents from the State Inquisitors were assigned mask duty at the theaters, with instructions to report on any offenders. They responded with lists bearing names of the city's most powerful families: Grimani, Tron, Bembo, Contarini, Dandalo, Gradenigo. Agents expressed frustration when they couldn't identify the offenders. "I did not know her name," one of them wrote of an unmasked woman at the Teatro San Moisè, "but she was surely noble, because others addressed her as 'Your Excellence.'"[13]

Reports convey spotty and reluctant compliance, citing women whose masks rested atop their tricorns, whose baùtas drooped about their shoulders, or who had managed to slip by doormen without masks. Some came all'Inglese, that is, with the baùta encircling the face but without a mask. One agent counted twenty women who were stopped by the doorman at the Teatro San Benedetto on a single evening in May. Five months after the decree, audiences were still greeting orders to mask with bewilderment. "In general, the unmasked women who are informed by the porter that they must mask themselves are surprised, as if this were some sudden novelty; and many cover their faces with their baùtas in a ridiculous manner." But there were also scenes of cooperation. When the doorman reminded a lady that she needed to pull her baùta up, she responded with an apology (though not without condescension): "Sorry lad, I wasn't thinking." At the San Moisè, a noblewoman who appeared at the door with her baùta down let the doorman assist her in pulling it over her head.[14]

The order requiring women to mask was one small sign of the unprecedented demographic and social strains Venice faced in the late eighteenth century. A fragmented ruling class, economic stagnation, and increasingly blurred boundaries between patricians and commoners had prompted officials and intellectuals to look for culprits. In the decree, the Council of Ten had called the bare face immodest, a sign of the "indecent licentious liberty" that was wrecking age-old custom.[15] In women especially, individual freedom was considered a threat to the civic order. The playwright and poet Carlo Gozzi, a self-described moralist with a gift for scalding prose, made the point in his memoirs with characteristic venom. Modern women, emboldened by French *philosophes,* have filled their heads with "fashions, frivolous inventions, rivalries in games, amusements, loves, coquetries, and all sorts of nonsense." They have bolted from their houses, he continued, "storming like Bacchantes, screaming out 'Liberty! Liberty!' " while neglecting their children, servants, and household duties.[16]

But the effort to contain women is not the full story of masks in the theater. It may have even been the lesser part. An earlier directive from the State Inquisitors requiring masks differed from the final version in two key respects. Men were included in the initial order to mask, and it applied only to patricians. There is evidence that the Inquisitors' first intention made its way to some theaters. An undated, unsigned document in the files of the State Inquisitors and among handwritten reports from theater doormen on their efforts to enforce masking reads: "No patrician gentlemen may enter the theater or the orchestra seats unless masked." While women constituted the preponderance of violators in reports of doormen and government agents, they also named noblemen who came to the theater without masks. One man wearing a mask who approached the Teatro San Moisè in 1781 with his baùta around his shoulders was told that he must pull it up before entering.[17]

In first proposing that all nobles wear masks, the State Inquisitors implied that the risk to public mores was in the blurring of social difference rather than female immodesty. The view was widespread. In a 1780 report expressing unease over public mores, Pietro Franceschi voiced support for the original initiative requiring patricians of both sexes to wear masks in the theater. He offered a portrait of pervasive social sickness: vice and luxury had sapped the military spirit, the young wrongly believed that they could discuss public affairs freely and publicly, and social distinctions were disappearing. He quoted a speech, delivered in the Great Council, in which the patrician Carlo Contarini had deplored the "confusion of classes." With each person now dressing as he pleased, Contarini had said, the "patrician character" was at risk of vanishing.

Franceschi extended the point. Although the four-year-old decree requiring women to mask was respected by many, he observed, it was openly mocked by the young. For Franceschi, the crumbling of the social order was attributable to the abandonment of traditional Venetian values. These were discretion, obedience, and submission to hierarchy. His description of the original proposal is telling. "It obliged honorable persons to recover the use of the mask."[18] The verb "to recover" is key. *Ripigliar* might also be rendered "to take up again." Social disorder stemmed in part from the decline in public masking. Its use, especially among patricians, had to be recovered.

It was no accident that these officials singled out the theater, the heart of Venice's public sphere, as the focus of their concern. This was where locals and foreigners of all classes mixed in close proximity. What these officials remembered as an ordered commingling earlier in the century had become a dangerous, promiscuous, undifferentiated mass. In ordering the return to masks for patricians, they hoped to recover its earlier function among spectators, which, they suggested, preserved noble distinction. Perhaps masks could once again act as guardians of modesty.

CHAPTER 13

Saving Face

To think of the mask of Venice as a defender of rank rather than a tool for disguise runs counter to a powerful line of interpretation stretching from the eighteenth century to our own time. The French traveler Ange Goudar, writing more than two hundred years ago, summed up the judgment. "For six months of the year, Venetians give themselves over to madness and extravagance, and so that they can do so more freely, the Republic allows them to disguise themselves." One of today's leading historians of dress in Venice, Doretta Davanzo Poli, describes eighteenth-century Venetians as having had a "craving for disguise," which she compares to an addiction.[1]

To disguise literally means to alter the customary dress, manner, or mode in order to conceal or mislead. Masks in eighteenth-century Venice could, and did, conceal identities. It was their role in crime that prompted the powerful Council of Ten to regulate them. But the principal purpose of masks for most Venetians was not disguise. Their motives lay more often in ritualized reserve than in concealment, and the collective effect was on balance conservative, not deceptive, disruptive, or lewd. The everyday use of the mask was a response to changes in how and when diverse members of this stratified society came together in public. The history of dress in the sixteenth and seventeenth centuries shows ample precedent for covering the face in similar situations and for comparable purposes. The mask was less a departure from customary dress than

FIGURE 23. Beggar in a mask

the general diffusion of practices employed earlier among small segments of the population.

Travelers to early modern Venice were puzzled to see beggars asking for alms while wearing masks. An artist named Giovanni Grevembroch, who filled hundreds of pages with drawings and descriptions of every rank and occupation in Venice, conveyed the strangeness of the scene. A man on his knees extends a palm before a sheet of paper that tells his story. His mask, mantle, and hat are identical to the combination worn by the city's privileged residents (figure 23). Grevembroch names the beggar. He is the "Very Revered" Bernardo Marconi, a member of the middling class of *cittadini*—"citizens"—who staffed the Venetian bureaucracy. His mask, Grevembroch writes, is "compassionate." Its use reflects "our own goodwill." Marconi was once an honorable man but has lost his wealth, Grevembroch explains. He is now among the many who "blush in asking for alms to feed their poor families."[2]

More than a century earlier, the engraver Cesare Vecellio also had pictured a beggar wearing a mask. These are the "disgraced poor," Vecellio writes. Once rich, they have fallen into ruin through misfortune or adversity. Most are cittadini, he continues, and would rather hold a note asking for alms than beg with words or gestures.[3] He could have been describing Marconi.

Grevembroch and Vecellio relate the shame felt by those born to status but living on handouts. Masks covered their pride and hid their humiliation, and they may well have obscured their identity. But Grevembroch and Vecellio also show that Venetians sometimes knew the rank and even the names of those behind the mask. In such cases, donors' compassion caused them to pretend otherwise. The fictive anonymity the mask granted preserved the dignity of their neighbors.

The veils and masks Venetian women wore worked in similar ways. Although they typically weren't used to cover shame or spare humiliation, they were viewed as a kind of protection. Vecellio called the veil the "highest mark of honesty in the rearing of patrician girls in Venice." He went on: "This keeps them well protected and properly cared for." When girls left adolescence or became engaged, they exchanged the white silk veil for black, which they wore when they paid visits to other homes in the city, received their husbands-to-be, attended church, or took chaperoned strolls in the evening (figure 24). The Frenchman Maximilien Misson observed with some disappointment that women of quality were so cloistered that one rarely saw their faces, "even at church, which is the one place where they appear in public."[4]

The practice of women veiling themselves in public was not unique to Venice, but it was so closely identified with that city that three different styles of Venetian veils appear in Jean-Jacques Boissard's catalogue of international costume, *Habitus variarum Orbis Gentium* (1581). Veils also appear in women's dress from Padua, Ferrara, and Naples. Boissard includes no veils in dress characteristic of Rome, Florence, Siena, Bologna, Ancona, Mantua, or Pisa.[5] There was historical precedent for the use of women's veils to segregate and distinguish. In ancient Athens, courtesans, slaves, and tradeswomen moved freely through the city barefaced, while respectable women appeared in public only if veiled. Tertullian reports veils among Jewish women in the third century B.C., and noblewomen of the Middle East wore veils to separate themselves from commoners in pre-Islamic societies.[6]

As with most Venetian dress before the eighteenth century, differences in the style and fabric of veils segregated women by social rank. The silk *veléta* that the upper ranks wore was only one of the ways women covered their faces in the name of public decency. The *zendà* (sometimes called *zendado*), originally worn only by nobles and cittadine, was an encom-

FIGURE 24. Venetian engaged to be married

passing sheer bonnet that covered the face and fell to just below the shoulders. Women could raise or lower it as they liked. Some called the zendà the national dress for refined ladies of the eighteenth century.[7] The *faziòl* (also called *ninzioléto*) was the commoners' version of the zendà. It was worn by the wives and daughters of merchants, tradesmen, and artisans. A thin muslin veil of white cotton or linen, the faziòl formed the upper part of a flowing mantle that covered the head and most or all of the body. Over the course of the eighteenth century, these sharp distinctions were lost. By 1750, noblewomen were wearing the faziòl and nonnobles the zendà.[8]

The morèta, the black fabric mask women held in place with their teeth, served similar purposes. Grevembroch relates that husbands escorted wives and daughters in morètas to Piazza San Marco, to homes of relatives, and to see friends or family in convents. By the simple means of a mask, he wrote, families could avoid "dissipating the dowry" with costly makeup and extravagant hairstyles. The black mask, he went on, "set off the skin's whiteness to make a young person even more noticeable."[9] Given the description, which combines miserliness with delectation, it is hard to tell whether Grevembroch was writing as a father or an aficionado.

In Venice, women's masks and veils were evidence of a condition that most contemporaries considered part of the natural order: the subservient role of females in society and the family. Masks and veils kept their supposedly vulnerable virtues at a protective distance wherever they appeared. Women who abandoned their families to become prostitutes, writes the Venetian historian Gaetano Cozzi, cast in high relief the qualities of the "honorable young woman," who was "restrained, silent, modest, and God-fearing, with every thought fixed upon her family." Cozzi goes on: "Enclosed within her *zendado,* her eyes lowered, jealous of her honor, and obedient to her parents, her very innocence made her prey to others' unscrupulousness."[10] Covering the face was the visible mark of a society defined by hierarchy, which extended to the family.

From within this context of hierarchy, however, Venetians did not view women's masks or veils as a mere sign of servility. Adolescents and brides-to-be, accompanied by guardians for the rare venture outside the home, were deemed to be in need of the veil's protection. Married women who covered their face as they slipped out of doors were more autonomous. The psychological distance masks and veils guarded may well have protected modesty. But it also protected against charges of immodesty, which is not the same thing. That difference gave Venetian women a freedom in public that they could not have had otherwise.[11]

A character from one of Goldoni's comedies gushes about the freedom covering the face brought to women. "What a great convenience masks are in Venice! Here a decent woman, once she is married, can go by herself to visit friends and do as she wishes without the slightest remark." A character in another play says that in Venice "masks permit women to go everywhere honestly."[12] In the context of veiling, that last word inverts common assumptions about the mask. Here putting on a mask conveyed decency. To be alone in mixed company outside the home with a bare face would be brazen. The veil's liberty was not the license of disguise for a more immediate reason. The sheer silk or cotton made genuine concealment difficult.

In this sense, women's masks and veils shared a feature with beggars' masks. They were a token of reserve and guardian of distance whether or not they hid identity. In both cases, they served important purposes not tied to disguise. By holding their wearers at a distance they preserved a space for self-respect and granted a circumscribed liberty. This is the context for understanding the spread of masks to others in the population.

Venice is famous for having the first public opera house in Europe, the Teatro San Cassiano, which opened with *Andromeda* in 1637. Its stunning success brought new productions and transformed the city into the continent's operatic capital. This particular revolution grew in the fertile soil of a city already known for its theatrical life. But before *Andromeda,* performances had been largely private affairs, often mounted on provisional stages. Sponsored by great families or elite fraternities called *Compagnie della Calza,* they drew audiences from a narrow slice of the population.[13] In the first enclosed theaters—at the first theater at SS. Giovanni e Paolo (1579), for instance, or the Teatro Michiel (1581) near the church of San Cassiano—spectators were still by and large elites. A document from the time describes theaters as "gathering-places for the whole of the nobility," who rented "virtually all of the boxes."[14]

As more theaters were built, impresarios seeking profit hoped to widen the pool for audiences. The expulsion of the Jesuits in 1606, who for nearly two decades had convinced the Council of Ten to suspend dramatic performances, was a boon to entrepreneurs and wealthy patrons. Opera and drama returned to the darkened halls. Other theaters opened their doors for the first time: the San Moisè in 1613, the Vendramin in 1622, the first of three Grimani theaters in 1639, the Novissimo in 1641, and the Sant'Aponal in 1651. When the Teatro Grimani opened near San Giovanni Crisostomo in 1678, audiences were sizable enough to support seven active theaters for music and drama.

By the middle of the seventeenth century, and in contrast to the semi-private gatherings of a century earlier, Venice offered truly public performances at an array of locations. Relatively modest prices permitted a broad social spectrum to attend. The papal nuncio, Monsignor Francesco de' Pannocchieschi, reported that virtually anyone who wished could purchase a ticket without great inconvenience. In another hundred years, when Goldoni dominated the stage, popular classes filled the cheaper seats, prostitutes sat intermingled with wealthier spectators along the balconies, and gondoliers kept abreast of reputations.[15]

It was during the theatrical boom of the mid-seventeenth century that spectators took to wearing masks in public. The practice was spontaneous and was soon considered natural by the population. The English traveler Philip Skippon, who visited Venice in 1663, described seeing noblewomen approach and enter the theater masked. They kept their masks on until they reached the relative seclusion of their boxes, "where they pull'd off their vizards." Limojan de Saint-Didier, who published *La Ville et la république de Venise* in 1680, detailed the attire he saw among men and women in the theaters. It consisted of a cape, a black hood encircling the face, and a shimmering white half-mask. "Most everyone goes to the theater and the opera in masks," he commented, "to enjoy greater liberty." Both accounts describe masking as a practice of patricians, but it soon spread to nonnobles. A newspaper from the late 1680s reported the delight evident among commoners who came to the San Cassiano and San Samuele theaters wearing masks.[16]

Over the next one hundred years, masking grew common enough among all classes of spectators to become a distinguishing feature, astonishing visitors and confirming them in their belief that this was a city devoted to intrigue or celebration. The Teatro San Luca was the scene of a near-catastrophe involving masks when the Frenchman Casimir Freschot was visiting the city. Freschot's noble host was known for his temper. As the performance began, he amused his guest by pointing out clergymen in the audience who were wearing masks. Presently there came a ferocious pounding at the door. A masked figure thrust his way in. The noble leapt up and drew a stiletto from his cape, whereupon the masker exploded in laughter. It was the groundskeeper of a convent near the man's estate on the mainland. Their familiarity had given the commoner "the liberty to come find the patrician in his box and listen to the opera, which is exactly what he did, taking a seat next to us in his mask and staying until the end."[17]

In Carlo Goldoni's *The Respectable Girl,* the title character, Bettina, wears a mask to the theater to watch a respectable play and, she says, learn something useful. An illustration from an eighteenth-century edition of the play shows masked spectators converging at a booth outside a theater to buy tickets (figure 25). Goldoni must have relished the effect: masked audiences applauding a masked "spectator" on the stage.[18] A 1749 novel narrating the fantastical journey of one Enrico Wanton through a landscape of apes takes its hero to an operatic performance. The spectators and performers are all monkeys, but the setting is recognizably Venetian. Wanton is told that he cannot enter the theater without a mask, and, after finding one suitable for humans, he takes his place

FIGURE 25. Spectators buying tickets outside the theater

on the right side of the pit. "From the start, this habit of masking seemed to me a strange and incongruous thing," Wanton comments. "But then I became tolerant of using it, and finally enjoyed it."[19]

Cristoforo Ivanovich, a librettist, critic, and historian of the city's theaters, witnessed the coming of masks in the middle years of the seventeenth century. He attributed them to the presence of diverse social ranks in so close a space. Venetian theaters differed from the vast open amphitheaters of ancient Rome in three ways, Ivanovich wrote. Venetian theaters were enclosed, they were much smaller than their Roman predecessors, and their walls were lined with private boxes. The boxes Ivanovich mentions were a Venetian innovation in theater design and a sign of social segregation. Boxes were the precinct of patricians, who rented them to showcase their own eminence and keep a distance from the lowborn in attendance. Nonnobles rarely appeared in the first- or second-tier boxes, which were occupied largely by members of prominent families, government officials, and foreign dignitaries.[20]

Ivanovich explains that noble women remained unmasked in their boxes, where they enjoyed perfect freedom. But it was another matter for those nobles who sat in the parterre. "Each night, seats are also sold on ground level without distinctions among spectators, where the use of masks removes the necessity for respect. Roman senators and patrician women, who always appeared with majesty, were accustomed to such respect. Venice, born free, wishes to preserve the freedom of all."[21]

As long as nobles stayed in their boxes and did not mingle with commoners, they went without masks. But when they sat shoulder to shoulder with other spectators on ground-level benches, the mask preserved the liberty of all. How? By eliminating the need for public displays of hierarchy and status—"the necessity for respect"—that greeted Roman patricians whenever they appeared in the theater. (An example of the kind of public respect Ivanovich might have had in mind is in the background of figure 26, an early eighteenth-century engraving depicting typical noble attire. To the right, a commoner bows deeply before a patrician [detail, figure 27].) The effect was twofold. Masks excused nonnobles from acknowledging their superiors as such, and they freed nobles from expecting this ritual. As a consequence, the mask preserved privacy in the theater's close quarters. Where the physical distance was lacking, wearing a mask, like wearing sunglasses on the bus, preserved a mental distance.

The actor-director Luigi Riccoboni commented on the effects of masking among audiences. Masks were "a great conveniency" to patrician men and women, senators, and those in high office, he wrote. "While they are masked, they have no occasion to distinguish themselves by the habit that is peculiar to their quality or employment." If they were so inclined, they could go with their faces uncovered, "which gives an opportunity for the women of quality and distinction to be seen."[22]

Masking did not necessarily mean that nobles went unrecognized, although undoubtedly many did. Disguise was not its main purpose. It was, rather, to preserve a measure of liberty by dispensing with ceremony. As with beggars and veiled women, this liberty was not license to act out of station. On the contrary, it was an assurance of rank even as others enjoyed the freedom to act as if in ignorance of it. Masks were apparel in the subjunctive mode, upholding the hierarchy by temporarily effacing it. In this way, they were conservative.

Ivanovich offers a similar account of why masks appeared in other public places where nobles mixed with commoners. One of these was the learned academy, a quasi-public assembly of like-minded individuals that flourished throughout Europe in the 1600s. Independent of the universities, separate from governments, and often formed in the proud absence of organizing statutes or rules, academies cut across class and

FIGURE 26. Venetian noble in winter dress

FIGURE 27. Venetian noble in winter dress (detail)

gender lines. Loosely understood, their raison d'être was to bring truth to light by promoting the arts, sciences, and letters, in printed works, lectures, and unhindered conversation. The names of Italian academies announced a dismal state of letters and drew attention to the task ahead: The Deaf, The Dull, The Sluggish, The Drowsy, The Moody, The Obtuse. When the nobleman Giovanni Loredan was working to launch what would become Venice's most distinguished academy, he voiced misgivings about one name under consideration, Gli Incogniti. He worried that the name would wrongly suggest that its members were unknown or disguised rather than conveying their ignorance before all that awaited discovery. His associates convinced him otherwise, supported by the 1612 dictionary of the Florentine Accademia della Crusca, which includes among its definitions for the word: "Not known, not noted, not understood; that about which one has no cognition or information."[23] In the end, Loredon embraced the name.

Ivanovich probably had the Accademia degli'Incogniti in mind. Whenever nobles alone met, he wrote, masks were not worn. When "other private persons" were present, however, members wore masks.[24] A 1663 biography of Giovanni Loredan confirms this, with the additional detail that it was typically women and distinguished attendees who wore masks on such occasions. "To exempt others from exercising due regard, to permit greater liberty, and to feel themselves truly free, ladies and princes came masked or incognito."[25] The phrase nearly repeats Ivanovich's claim that masks in the theater removed the necessity for respect.

The Accademia degli'Incogniti met on Mondays during the winter months in a palazzo near Santa Maria Formosa. An undated roster of roughly half of its 250 members names 57 nobles and 49 nonnobles from Venice and other Italian cities and includes 3 mathematicians, 7 attorneys, 7 physicians, and 15 clerics. "Our academy, being itself a republic, can similarly exist without a head, preserving its own vital substance within the bosom of its subjects," one of its members wrote of its rough equality. As if to hold themselves to it, members sat side by side on benches without distinction during lectures and for conversation that followed.[26] At the Incogniti and in other academies, masks played a role in the republican ideal. Without denying members' status they eliminated the need to acknowledge it.

According to Ivanovich, another prime venue for masks was the Ridotto, which opened one year after the Teatro San Cassiano inaugurated public performances with the opera *Andromeda*. In his discussion of masks at the gambling hall, Ivanovich does not describe license or disguise. Masks are instead "noteworthy for their modesty." As the maskers gamble, Ivanovich continues, "one never hears clamor or complaint, even when the losses are huge; and each is permitted the liberty to leave the game at any time without offense to the company."[27] This description is consistent with accounts throughout the eighteenth century. Self-control was expected from all players.

Despite a 1704 law making masks at the Ridotto mandatory for commoners but optional for nobles, the reigning preference among nobles was to mask themselves, too.[28] A surveillance agent was stunned to see a respected judge gambling without a mask, which he said was not the practice. The judge was met with derision from other gamblers. Edward Wright, who traveled from London to Venice in the 1720s when the requirement for masks was still fresh, tied the easy commerce among gamblers of all ranks to their seeming equality. "What is a Privilege only in other Places, is here turn'd to an Obligation; perhaps for the better maintaining that Appearance of *Equality* which is requisite to the profess'd Liberty of the Place; that is a Reason I have heard given for it." He elaborated. "A Tinker, by Virtue of his Masque, may come to a Basset-Table, and set a Ducat with one of the Princes of the People."[29]

Note Wright's wording. Masks maintained the appearance of equality. The social cleavages that masks covered were known to all; anecdotal evidence suggests that they were often obvious. Maskers judged the status and sometimes guessed the identities of one another by the quality of their clothes, the sound of their voices, and the nature of their gaits. They studied small things—gloves, buckles, stockings, shoes—for telling details. They knew that reading one's opponent was part of winning. Although the tabàro and baùta dominated at the Ridotto, gamblers shed these heavy mantles when it got too hot, revealing a motley collection of tattered clothes next to elegant silks.[30]

Surveillance records contain long lists identifying gamblers at the Ridotto and smaller halls where masks were also worn. These logs characterizing clientele are from the files of the State Inquisitors:

Ponte dei Fuseri: every station of person excepting none (1713).

Rio Marin: courtesans and clergy (1732).

Ruga di S. Giovanni Elemosinario: gentlemen and wearers-of-tabàros, priests, artists, and those of every other condition except, however, certain dregs of society (1737).

Calle dei Bambaseri: foreigners, priests, shopkeepers, cutpurses, commoners and nobles, soldiers, women, Jews (1753).[31]

Agents also named names. The Spanish ambassador to Venice came masked to the Ridotto three nights running in 1743 with his masked attendants, whom a surveillance report identified by name. It also named every Venetian to whom the ambassador spoke. Another report gives the name, status, and occupation of thirteen talkative gamblers there, including two nobles, a solicitor, an officer, a lawyer, a visiting Armenian, two priests, and five commoners. One amused agent described a masker on all fours rummaging under the tables for money someone might have dropped. Play slowed and people whispered. Wasn't that the patrician Alvise Corner? they asked, shocked "that a Venetian noble would so degrade himself." (It wasn't only masked gamblers whom agents identified. An agent in 1743 named two maskers who were spreading counterfeit coins throughout the city. Another named a noble recently back from Udine who "goes about everywhere in a mask without a care or notice.")[32] Much of the time, maskers probably had a good idea of who was winning and losing.

What was the point of wearing masks if others could figure out who you were? The answer is that the mask did not have to conceal identity to save face. It allowed nobles to play "anonymously" and off the record—

to avoid the censure gambling drew, and often deserved; to share the room with society's outcasts; to lose large sums to commoners. The benefits went beyond protecting noble pride. Masks also worked to preserve the hierarchy. A critic of gambling in Venice had worried about the effects of commoners gambling alongside patricians. "Someone born poor or perhaps still young but favored by fortune soon imagines himself great and, mindful of his status and place, will raise the stakes carelessly, heedlessly, scorning all sense. Ultimately he will not tolerate his superiors."[33] The mask was a fig leaf that provided an assurance to those superiors, however weak or unjustified, that this would not happen. How can your authority be defied if it isn't publicly acknowledged? The commoner on a roll who kept raising the stakes was a brutal confirmation of Ivanovich's observation that masks dispensed with the need for respect. The appearance of equality at least took away the sting.

At the Ridotto, the mask was a symbol of formality, a purveyor of intimacy, and a token of anonymity. It permitted a wide social and economic range to interact freely and spontaneously and was a mercy to those whom fortune did not favor. Masks placed in abeyance a hierarchy that was never in doubt and served a purpose that did not depend on disguise.

In these ways, masks perfected the self-control that public gambling encouraged. This was the Ridotto's rougher version of the modesty veils were said to protect among women. Under the pressure of the game's bluffs and wagers, players learned a discipline that mastered sudden anger or swift delight and policed even the smallest gestures. Masks made this easier. "The tranquillity and calm with which players lose very great sums is an extraordinary thing," a French visitor observed. "One might say that gambling is a school established to learn moderation in good and bad fortune rather than an entertainment." Another made the point more vividly in fewer words: here huge sums change hands without gamblers unclenching their teeth.[34] Insofar as the habits of equanimity and self-mastery learned at the Ridotto were applied in other times and places, masked gambling played its part in maintaining social cohesion in this stratified society.

The fluid interaction of maskers was also seen in the city's cafés, which first appeared in Piazza San Marco in the early 1680s. Maskers of course went to cafés during carnival, but they also met there at other times of the year. The privileged gathered at upscale establishments like the Golden Mast or the Great Cross of Malta in the square. On Sundays during Lent and again in early summer, the latter offered instrumental concerts that drew masked nobles, cittadini, ambassadors, and wealthy nonnobles. Maskers visited the grittier cafés along the narrow commercial strip just beyond the piazza called the Frezzeria, where the Inquisitors' professional eavesdroppers heard masked nobles and merchants speaking freely.[35] During the theater season, maskers met after performances in the cafés along the Riva degli Schiavoni and in private *casini* near San Moisè.

State agents recorded the turns conversations took, and the officials who read them responded with concern, convinced that they put the secrets of the Republic at risk. At a café in the piazza, patrons talked freely about things "that ought to have been respected." At another near the steps of the Rialto bridge, a handful of older men "spoke publicly about the most secret business of the Senate." At the Hungarian Queen café, a certain abbot Palermo "advanced expressions that were disrespectful toward the patrician class," while a foreign sea-captain named Cima spoke loudly against the Republic's military policy. The journalist Gasparo Gozzi, writing in the *Osservatore Veneto,* commented tartly that the newest schools needed no masters of rhetoric but only a café and conversation.[36]

Historians of Europe have pointed to the café as a seedbed of public opinion, a concept new to the time and of political significance before the rise of participatory politics. It was in the cafés of eighteenth-century Europe—and most especially those of London, Paris, and Vienna—that ideas of the high Enlightenment were refined and disseminated. Here the literate read about reform in pamphlets, books, and newspapers and exchanged their views. Conversation in cafés cut across classes. Its codes of reciprocity ran counter to the etiquette of deference that social hierarchy demanded elsewhere. Cafés provided the setting for the population to recognize itself as a public—critical, unfettered, and independent of the official line.[37]

In Venice, the mask promoted exchange among clients that cafés naturally fostered. As elsewhere, its presence in cafés testified to social differences separating those who gathered. As one masked patrician was overheard saying to two others in a café, the mask gave nobles the same freedom in the city that they enjoyed unmasked in the country.[38] Yet if masks manufactured distance for elites in certain venues—when crowded cheek by jowl on theater benches, for instance, or bunched in among the riffraff at the *faraone* table—they could also work in the opposite direction, drawing together instead of repelling. In cafés, the accent fell on closeness. They were places of willing sociability where gathering was an end in itself. An article in the *Pallada Veneta* observed that conversations among maskers were remarkable for their "illustrious familiarity."[39]

What gave such conversations their thrill was not that masks disguised their wearers, though they often did that. It was that they lent plausible deniability to direct contact. From this, temporary intimacy could develop. Masks encouraged conversation among those unaccustomed to speaking by providing an emotional defense the bare face lacked. Their anonymity, whether genuine or fictive, granted permission to disregard the chasm of rank and prestige. Masks in Venice operated much as elaborate codes of etiquette did among courtiers at Versailles, or as common protocols of politeness would do in the nineteenth century. They eased the awkwardness of communication among unequals.

Masks began to appear in other public places around the same time they were first seen in the theaters, academies, cafés, and gambling halls. There was something grand and superb, the Frenchman Limojan de Saint-Didier commented in 1680, in the masked noble procession to install the new procurator of St. Mark. The news sheet *Pallada Veneta* wrote in 1687 that the exuberance of maskers pouring into the streets to mark Vicenzo Fini's installation as procurator would have cheered even the gloomiest soul. The summary of an ambassador's public reception in 1682 suggests that masking had taken hold but was not yet universal: "The crush of nobles and of gentlemen, some masked and others uncovered, was truly great, this being the sole occasion on which entering the house of an ambassador is not a capital crime for nobles."[40]

When Maximilien Misson described Venetian culture in 1688, masks were more numerous. "You must realize that it is not just during carnival when one takes up the mask in Venice. It appears in all public celebrations. One rushes to meet ambassadors wearing masks. On Ascension Day, they are not confined to the Bucintoro, on which nobles are masked. In the city, the entire population is masked."[41] A handful of maskers are among the noble fashions in Luca Carlevarijs's *Entry of the British Ambassador the Count of Manchester into the Ducal Palace,* painted in 1707.

Records of the Commissioners of Display, the council established to regulate and monitor dress, confirm what this scattered anecdotal evidence suggests. Over the 1680s and '90s, masks were covering the faces of more and more Venetians, noble and nonnoble, on a widening circle of occasions. The council was in charge of the city's famed sumptuary laws, which limited how much citizens could spend on clothes and restricted public display of jewels and precious metals. Reading between the lines of its decrees from the early years of masking, one can sense officials quietly acknowledging the shift. For most of the seventeenth century, the boilerplate prose concluding each of the council's sumptuary decrees was the same. Its provisions applied to all Venetians, both male and female, whether noble or plebeian. In September 1677, an additional clause appeared. These terms apply to all, a decree concludes, "whether masked or not."[42]

The moment marks official recognition of what Ivanovich and others had already noted. Over the next several decades, masks would become the public face of this famously inscrutable city. The origins of masking outside the carnival season point to an emerging public culture within a rigidly stratified society. Compared to Paris or London, the public sphere in Venice was not especially robust. In the middle of the eighteenth century in Paris, there were 600 coffeehouses; in Venice, there were 206.[43] Newspapers were few, censorship was effective, and surveillance created the uneasy sense that someone was always watching.

Nevertheless, the Ridotto and the city's cafés and theaters were without precedent in providing common spaces for relatively free mingling. Here Venetians came together freely for occasions neither sponsored by nor in explicit praise of the state, to match wits, tempt fate, share news, cheer or mock performers, complain, silence rumors, or spread falsehoods. For the merchant or artisan who until now had dealt with the ruling elite only as a subordinate, these places offered interactions on the mask's unique terms, the fiction of similitude. A French traveler grasped this when he observed in 1709 that in Venice "the mask, which most everyone wears to the opera by custom, assists in all manner of exchange, which would be terribly difficult without it."[44]

A remarkable essay narrating the progress of humanity by means of the mask gives an insight into these uses. Its author was Gasparo Gozzi, editor of the *Osservatore Veneto* and brother of the playwright Carlo Gozzi. Humans are not equal, Gozzi writes. We possess no natural sympathy, and, given our true nature, there are good reasons to keep our urges and impulses veiled from view. "Led to live in the company of others, the heart has found exterior signs to convey its goodness." Shaking hands, kissing cheeks, small signs of friendship, sitting here rather than there, extending the right as opposed to the left hand: these and a hundred other conventions are for Gozzi so many "masks, veils, fictions, appearances."[45]

This vision set Rousseau's famous broadside against society on its head. For Gozzi, there was nothing noble about man's savage state. In it, humans knew only conflict—the language of fists, scratches, and bites, as he put it. Modern displays of politeness are an advance over that natural condition. Those who claim otherwise are "enemies of humanity." Gozzi writes that acts of courtesy—his masks, veils, and fictions—are "the effects of good cultivation and of the best qualities of the human heart." The position was a defense of convention phrased in the Venetian dialect of masks.[46]

The mask spared ceremony while preserving respect. It furnished a common footing without denying status and saved face when one's dignity was at stake. It was a token of privacy instead of the real thing, a manufactured buffer that licensed genuine aloofness and unaccustomed closeness. Its ritualized "anonymity" could be acted on or ignored at will. The mask honored liberty in the Venetian sense, which meant a measure of autonomy within jealously guarded limits.

CHAPTER 14

Venetian Incognito

In mid-January 1782, a season when cold rains pelt the lagoon and the days alternate between brilliant sun and dark gloom, the Serenissima staged one of the century's grandest parties for foreign guests. Officially, the visitors were known as Counts of the North. For a full week, from Friday morning until late Thursday night, the city was host to events that clogged the waterways, filled theaters for command performances, and drew thousands of Venetians to Piazza San Marco for a last bloody bull hunt. At their own request, the visitors arrived and toured in the "strictest incognito." Participants in the weeklong extravaganza, following the prescribed protocol, wore masks of their own. The guests' official anonymity was respected, even as they rubbed shoulders with nobles and basked in the attention of wave upon wave of commoners struggling to get a glimpse. The ritual of false names and covered faces was thought necessary, although from the moment of the guests' arrival everyone knew their identity. They were the future czar and son of Catherine the Great, Paul Petrovich, and his wife, Maria Feodorovna.[1]

In the eighteenth century, Venice was a prime destination for sovereigns on holiday. Drawn by its famous festivity and the lure of the mask, they invented fanciful names, outfitted themselves in tabàros and baùtas, and headed for the balls, boat races, and theaters. King Frederick IV of Denmark came early in the century as the Count of Oldenbourg. Sweden's Gustavus III visited as Count Haga. Prince William Henry, the Duke of Gloucester, fashioned himself as a Frenchman and took the title Comte de

Gaveau. Joseph II of Austria came twice incognito, first in 1769 as the Count of Falchenstein and again in 1775 with his three brothers.

Writers and artists savored the idea of unrecognized potentates on the loose in Venice. In Voltaire's *Candide,* six deposed kings and four former princes who have come for carnival find themselves in the same little inn. Giovanni Paisiello's opera *Il Re Teodoro in Venezia* treats the city as a holiday resort where foreign princes mix freely with the natives, disguise abets seduction, and rulers and the ruled alike taste the "happy liberty" of sensual delights. The plot pokes fun at human vanity. A penniless king in exile devises a scheme to get rich by marrying a wealthy innkeeper's daughter. In the end, his identity is revealed and he winds up in debtors' prison.[2]

In reality, not much was left to chance when foreign rulers came to town. Preparations began months in advance, and an approved agenda governed each day. This allowed maximum extravagance. On Joseph II's first visit, the government proposed a series of floating gardens on barges between the Giudecca and San Giorgio Maggiore. They were to have flowers, trees, and lakes stocked with fish for Joseph to see as he walked to a feast in his honor. When he learned of the plans he balked, and the idea was scrapped. Other arrangements were only slightly less extravagant. A "royal hunt" in Piazza San Marco celebrated the presence of the "Count of Oldenbourg" (Denmark's King Frederick IV). Fences were erected, stands were set up, and 150 bulls were brought into the square to be attacked by dogs.[3]

No welcome was more lavish than the one staged for the Counts of the North. Their visit was part of a European tour orchestrated by Catherine the Great to reorient Russian policy away from Prussia and toward Austria. The itinerary included Vienna, Poland, Paris, the papal states, principalities along the Rhine, and the Netherlands. From the Venetians' perspective, the visit had three important diplomatic aims, which internal government correspondence spelled out. It was to strengthen economic relations with personal ties, to introduce the grand duke to Venetian products available for export, most especially ships and luxury glass, and to convince him of the strong health and standing of the Republic.[4]

With regard to the third, Venetians themselves had cause for doubt. Internally, the ruling class was divided and weak; externally, the Republic was virtually powerless. This was a sad fate for an empire that had once stretched to the Black Sea. Over the previous three centuries, the Republic's possessions had steadily shrunk, from "a quarter and a half of the Roman Empire," as the doge's sovereignty had once claimed, to a meager strip of northern Italy and a few scattered islands and fortresses. Its ships had once held mastery over the Adriatic and much of the Mediterranean. Its strongholds had stood along the Dalmatian coast and in Cyprus, Crete, and the Peloponnesus. With the New World's riches flowing into Spain, the shift from Italian mercantilism toward capitalism, and an unending war with the Ottoman Turks, Venetian power dwindled. One by one, its colonies were lost: Negropont in 1470, Cyprus in 1573, most of Crete in 1669, and southern Greece in 1715. When the Treaty of Passarowitz was signed in 1718, bringing an end to the long struggle with the Turks, the frontiers of the Venetian Empire were again reduced, this time for good. Venice would retain isolated outposts in the Mediterranean and along the Adriatic coast and land holdings in Bergamo, Brescia, Cremona, Verona, and Vicenza, with territory as well in Polesine, Rovigo, Treviso, and areas of Friuli.

Many in the eighteenth century feared that Venice had reached the tipping point. Some searched for causes. The French ambassador to Venice in 1786 said the government had neither the force nor the resolve to influence events. It exhibited "a sort of terror before the future," he wrote. It was true that Venice had watched from the sidelines during the War of the Spanish Succession and the Seven Years' War, a notable departure from its close involvement in continental politics before the eighteenth century. From the nineteenth century until our own time, many have sided with the French ambassador, arguing that the last hundred years of the Republic's millennial existence was witness to a sad, slow decline, from austere civic virtue to aimlessness and distraction.

For this one week in 1782 there was no sign of weakness or irrelevance. During the days, the imperial couple toured Venice as other tourists might. They saw the glassworks on Murano, paintings and churches, the Great Council in session, Sansovino's National Library, and the Arsenale. Unlike other tourists, they were surrounded by secretaries, diplomats, royal relatives, and guides. Crowds of onlookers trailed after them everywhere they went. The state procurator Francesco Pesaro, one of the most politically astute of the governing class, was their perpetual escort. A small band of dignitaries made up the inner circle. These included the grand duchess Maria's brother, Frédéric-Eugène of Würtemberg, three Russian princes, two ladies-in-waiting, the Viennese ambassador to Venice, and members of the Austrian diplomatic corps. A division of Russian knights constituted the traveling court. Venetian hoteliers recruited two hundred servants to staff the daily receptions, balls, and dinners. Venetian nobles, summoned by the government's official invitations, exhausted themselves dancing, dining, and proposing eternal friendship in the salons, theaters, and reviewing stands that served as gathering points throughout the city.

Whenever they appeared in public, Paul wore a scarlet tabàro with a baùta and mask, which delighted the locals. Maria wore a Venetian zendà, the black chiffon veil that covered the head and face. Venetians were free to approach the pair, which they did in large numbers. A witness saw commoners approach the grand duke and heard one of them say, "There he is! There he is! He's just like a Venetian, he's wearing the tabàro—he's got to be good, he's human, sure enough, he's wearing the tabàro!"[5]

Others were less adoring. In a gossipy letter to the Venetian ambassador in France, Luigi Ballarini wrote that Maria Feodorovna had "a most Germanic physique, very fleshy, with a colossal chest, spoiled teeth, and bad sight that obliged her to use an eyeglass continuously." But she did show great feeling and talent, Ballarini went on, "in contrast to the grand duke, who is offensively unattractive, childish, and without experience of the world."[6]

The guests watched opera seria at one theater, opera buffa at another, and commedia dell'arte at a third. Audiences at each performance were "packed with maskers," all of them noble, who visited the grand duke and duchess in the box for conversation.[7] On Sunday, they listened, masked, to sacred music performed by girls from the city's orphanages. On Tuesday, they attended a masked ball that ended with a feast for eighty-five noble women on the stage of the theater. (Paul and Maria dined later on ostrich and truffles at the Leon Bianco on the Grand Canal, the government having explicitly forbidden any meals with Venetians during their stay.) On Wednesday, the couple presided over a regatta, having arrived at the event in two eight-oared vessels with crystal window-panes. They watched, masked, from the water's edge.

On the final day of the Russians' visit, Venetians gathered in a vast oval amphitheater built for the occasion in Piazza San Marco. The stands, decorated to recall the hanging gardens of Babylon, were filled with nobles and cittadini wearing "masks of every sort." Eight orchestras played. Spectators, also masked, leaned from windows above the square. The uninvited had arrived early in the morning and pressed in around the perimeter. Five chariots, each drawn by eight white bulls, entered the arena through a triumphal arch decorated to hail Agriculture, Abundance, Commerce, the Arts, and Peace.

Paul and Maria appeared on a balcony, and the sport commenced, as some eighty handlers dressed in the national costumes of various countries unhitched the bulls from their chariots and dragged all forty of them into the enormous arena. The dogs were then set loose. Maria became ill. When the wounded bulls were led away, four wide gates opened to let spectators rush onto the field, where they crowded at the far end near the royal balcony. "Viva San Marco!" they chanted. Some threw wigs into the air. Grand Duke Paul remarked that their discipline was surely a sign of good government and that the people resembled a single family.[8] As darkness fell, Grand Duchess Maria lit the fuse of a mechanical dove on a wire that went screaming through the square, lighting torches and setting off a chain reaction that illuminated a triumphal arch and the portals of St. Mark's. As the Russians and invited guests withdrew to a glittering ballroom, the populace danced where the bulls had bled.

The exclusive reception that followed was one of the week's three invitation-only gatherings in the Procuratie Nuove overlooking the piazza. Typically used as a concert hall, the space served as the principal rendezvous for the Russians and their hosts. As one of the guests put it, this was where the "incognito Republic" received its "august incognito guests." Invitations to Venetian nobles specified dress for each event. This evening, they were to come "masked, with the baùta down"—that is, with masks in place but with the close-fitting hoods left free around the shoulders. Notes from the State Inquisitors who planned the reception make clear that the masks were intended for what they called "private noble conversations." Any foreigner who attended would have to wear a mask as well.[9]

Giustiana Wynne, whose mixed English and Venetian parentage gave her unequaled access to foreign and local elites, was present that night. She credited the mask with helping to allay the awkwardness of approaching royalty. "The ease of the mask and the open invitation to all the nobility brought a prodigious crowd to the building. The desire to approach the Counts of the North—to see them face to face, and perhaps be remarked by them, too—encouraged even the most timid." Accounts of this and other encounters describe frank and open conversation between masked Venetians and their "incognito" guests. The grand duke flattered the men by asking them specific and probing questions. The grand duchess spoke to the ladies in "honest" and "personal" terms. "Everyone was in a mask," Wynne wrote to her brother. "You know the Venetian mask: it is more a convention than an embellishment."[10]

The image Wynne conveys is arresting: elites speaking face-to-face with their faces covered, masked Venetians desiring to be remarked by their incognito guests. As odd as the etiquette was, planners within the government insisted on the masks. Their logic went something like this. When diplomacy requires, Venice must lavish all appropriate honor on foreign princes, sovereigns, and ambassadors. All appropriate honor requires the presence of Venetian nobles. But given the Republic's vulnerability to treason or corruption, Venetian nobles must never mix with foreign princes, sovereigns, or ambassadors. Such discrepant aims were destined to produce the kinds of contradictions Wynne expressed. Guidelines prepared for the visit by the State Inquisitors contained a similar paradox. Nobles would be permitted to "approach" their guests but not "mingle with" them, their ministers, or any other foreign officials.[11]

Masks helped Venetians meet these aims. They gave access but preserved distance. In this case, the distance they preserved was at once deferential (acknowledging royalty among mere nobles) and defensive (inserting a screen between patricians with state secrets and powerful foreigners eager to probe or lobby). From the Inquisitors' perspective, incognito, like the "honor" of the ever-present escorts, showed all due respect while containing the risk. In a phrase that echoed Ivanovich's account of masks in the theater a century earlier, the Inquisitors observed that incognito "dispenses with all ceremony, etiquette, and compliments."[12]

This is the first definition of *incognito* in the *Oxford English Dictionary:* "*adj.* Unknown; whose identity is concealed or unavowed, and therefore not taken as known." Venetian incognito did not signify an identity concealed. It signified an identity unavowed and therefore not taken as known.

When Jean-Jacques Rousseau went to Venice as secretary to the French ambassador, he was no candidate for incognito. In due time, he collected a handful of acquaintances: the wretched Vitali, who as a servant in the ambassador's household did all he could to undermine Rousseau; the Spanish consul's secretary Carrio, who went with Rousseau to concerts and the theater; the merchant captain Olivet, whose ship Rousseau helped to save from seizure by the Venetians; and Olivet's mistress Zulietta, offered by the captain to him in return, whose malformed nipple caused Jean-Jacques to recoil in horror. Rousseau picked up local customs. "I have slightly disturbed my philosophy to dress like other people," he wrote to a friend. "I am wearing the mask and baùta in the theaters and public squares as proudly as if I had spent my entire life in such clothes."[13] This wasn't incognito. Masked or not, the young Rousseau was assured of going unrecognized by the general public as he wandered through the labyrinth of alleys and canals.

To go unavowed or unacknowledged, you first have to be known. A prince in a mask (or a celebrity in a ballcap and sunglasses) is a public face hidden, which, if recognized, brings the voyeur's thrill of having glimpsed the private person. The public person, seen in a royal carriage, or on the red carpet, or in a televised address, brings another set of responses: reverence, scorn, evaluation, outrage. Strangers, unmasked, are unremarked. They may disguise themselves, but they are incognito only to those who would otherwise recognize them. The known, unmasked, are recognized. In the eighteenth century, Venetians used the term *incognito* to designate notables who had temporarily changed their names or altered their appearance. They were not necessarily disguised. Venetian incognito countenanced the fiction of anonymity.

Rousseau's superior, the Comte de Montaigu, understood the complications and indirections of Venetian incognito. As a foreign ambassador, he was closely monitored and well known to the city's rulers. Over the previous one hundred years, surveillance of all foreign diplomats had increased dramatically. In 1618, a plot to invade Venice by sea, lay siege to the ducal palace, and burn the Arsenale was uncovered, and the Spanish ambassador was thought to have been an organizer. The ensuing panic was the culmination of a series of disasters that had terrified the Republic. Calamitous fires ravaged the Arsenale and the ducal palace, and two waves of bubonic plague each killed more than a quarter of the population. Plots to murder the doge were discovered in 1606 and 1607, and a series of high-profile cases revealed that Venetian nobles were willing to sell state secrets. Other crises followed. Venetian agents assassinated the patrician Angelo Badoer in 1630 for having passed sensitive information to the papal nuncio and the Spanish ambassador; Girolamo Grimani, who shared state secrets with Spain, met a similar end after seeking refuge in Rome and Naples.[14] The government responded to these cases of treason with fresh regulations. No patrician was to mix with foreign ambassadors, ministers, or representative without the explicit permission of two-thirds of the Great Council. The penalty for violators was ten years' banishment from the city.

Nobles took the prohibition seriously. An ambassador whose page had just died reported that "not a single noble or cittadino" had attended the funeral, "since they avoid ambassadors' staffs like the plague."[15] Yet there were numerous state occasions that both patricians and foreign ministers attended. These included official receptions, civic celebrations, weddings, and banquets. At such events, those present wore masks. The practice began in the second half of the seventeenth century, when masks also started appearing in cafés and among theater audiences. By 1710, when the French foreign ministry assembled a memoir laying out Venetian protocol, masks were a fixture.[16]

Masks did not hide the fact that nobles spoke with ambassadors. Rather, they functioned at diplomatic events as they did elsewhere in their seeming equality and formal distance. Most such occasions were so tightly scripted that there was little chance to pass secrets. The benefits of the mask outstripped its risks. A Frenchman visiting Venice near the end of the century wrote that in receptions following the installation of a new doge, masked nobles of both sexes sought out ambassadors for conversation. "In such ceremonies, the constraints that ordinarily obtain between nobles and foreign ministers are suspended."[17]

The doge hosted four large receptions each year—on Ascension and on the feast days of Saints Mark, Vitus, and Stephen—to which ambassadors and nobles wore masks. A more exclusive banquet followed. For a time, the French diplomatic memoire notes, masked "women of quality" were also permitted to enter the dining hall, "where they remain up to half an hour, satisfying their curiosity and standing alongside the doge and ambassadors."[18] An engraving by Giovanni Battista Brustolon depicts one such feast. Nobles dine along the perimeter of the room while masked men and women mill about the interior (figure 28).

Masked ambassadors and their staff attended three days of celebrations in the ducal palace after the election of a new doge. Ambassadors also wore masks when they attended the weddings of prominent families. Diplomats wore masks to convey their congratulations to Giovanni Badoer upon his elevation as cardinal in May 1706. They did the same a month later to congratulate Badoer's successor as patriarch of Venice, Pietro Barbarigo. On both occasions the crowds of Venetians in masks were immense.[19]

Commoners and elites wore masks to events marking the installation of new ambassadors. By tradition, diplomats visited a monastery on the island of Santo Spirito to hear Mass the night before presenting their credentials. When the Marquis de Durfort made the voyage "incognito" in 1759, a "prodigious concourse of maskers" lined the four-mile route between his embassy and the island, in boats, on bridges, in windows, and along the quays. Members of the high judicial councils—the state attorneys, heads of the Forty, and ducal councillors—witnessed his installation in the ducal palace wearing masks.

That evening and the next, Ambassador Durfort hosted two open houses in the French embassy that lasted until sunup. His residence, in

FIGURE 28. Masked ambassadors at a banquet in the ducal palace

the same spacious palazzo where generations of French ambassadors had lived and worked, was near the Church of Madonna dell'Orto, not far from the Jewish quarter. Its land bordered the Fondamenta Nuove, the long quay facing Murano. Torches lit the garden, where coffee, chocolate, wine, lemonade, relishes, and confections were served. Inside, eighty servants in wigs and black robes served refreshments from silver basins.

"Virtually the whole town came," Ambassador Durfort wrote with evident pride. All were in masks, from the "baseborn"—who crowded around tables in the garden—to Venetian nobles and "foreigners of distinction," who greeted the ambassador one by one in an upstairs salon. Despite the presence of armed soldiers, pieces of crystal and porcelain went missing. "A considerable crowd of Jews and other persons of base extraction, who entered thanks to their disguise, took everything they could lay their hands on," the ambassador reported. The sentence is curious. Either the masks didn't disguise the thieves very well or Durfort was jumping to conclusions. But the remark does indicate the range of guests who attended wearing masks.[20]

Durfort's reception was lavish, but it paled in comparison to the welcome given to Louis XIV's ambassador Charles-Arnaud de Pomponne a half-century earlier. On his arrival, the Republic presented him with great wheels of cheese, smoked tongue, assorted meats, sixteen basins of sauces and jellies, and a cooked sturgeon. In return, the ambassador showered opulence upon his guests at his open house. Thirty life-sized statues outside plus four living Moors provided light with blazing torches. A thirty-two-piece orchestra and two smaller ensembles played inside the palace. Potted orange and lemon trees stood in the garden. Food was dispensed in such profusion that one guest ate himself sick ("petrified and unresponsive, he was taken home as though dead"), and armchairs upholstered in silver and scarlet were available "as a service to distinguished persons of quality who wish[ed] to repose."

Guests made their way through the mansion by the flickering light of candelabra. The half-mask allowed them to eat flavored ices and to sip tea or heated chocolate. On the second floor, they inspected tapestries of hunting scenes, rivers, forests, and the four seasons in allegory. In an upper room were immense portraits of the Sun King and of French princes and princesses in gilded frames. Along the Fondamenta Nuove, Turkish rugs and velvet cushions covered benches, "which masked women of the highest distinction employed."[21]

The masks' token anonymity suspended differences sufficiently to permit common access to the ices and sweetmeats, even if distinctions were still evident in the details of comportment and appearance. By its very presence, the mask was a barrier, a stubbornly immovable obstruction to the nonverbal cues that feed close conversation. Or so we might think. But from within the world of prohibited interactions, the mask could also give access to surprisingly personal conversation. This was not for the reasons we might suppose—that they disguised their wearers, for instance, or prompted maskers to assume false identities. Rather, the figment of anonymity, mutually accepted and acted on, was freeing in ways that resembled the professed liberty of veils.

What else might explain the "highly private and confidential colloquy" between Doge Alvise Pisani and the future Holy Roman Emperor, Charles Albert of Bavaria, which was approved by the Council of Ten on the condition that both be masked?[22] Or the "liberty" the French ambassador François de Bernis said the mask conferred as he spoke with senators following the installation of a new procurator of St. Mark? The senators expressed their goodwill toward France, de Bernis reported to Versailles, and declared the Republic's intention to remain neutral as the storm clouds gathered before the Seven Years' War. "The assurances of friendship that they conveyed to me over these three days did not seem to be mere politeness," de Bernis wrote to the king.[23]

On another occasion, de Bernis's account of the intimacy of masks was altogether more vivid. "During the festivities, I had occasion to speak with all the nobles and had two conversations with the doge while masked. In these large assemblies, I gave and received the most flattering testimony— the *sincerest* testimony, I would even dare to say—of esteem and mutual friendship. The frank and open manner with which I expressed myself, my civility, and the individual distinctions I professed in these various occasions, produced the intended effect in the minds of the nobility." This was an extraordinary testament to the mask's sanctioned liberty. Not only did it make illicit talk licit, it brought sincerity, openness, and candor.

De Bernis understood the fine line between exploiting a back channel and compromising a good source. In this instance, the mask's advantage— its conspicuous secrecy—was also its danger. De Bernis manipulated its possibilities with consummate skill. The "intended effect" he mentions was to persuade influential nobles to support tariff reductions on French sugar. Fees on Portuguese sugar were substantially lower, and French producers were at a disadvantage. In a coded section of his communiqué, de Bernis told the king that the procurator Zuanne Emo and his son appeared supportive. A month later, the tariffs were lowered.[24] (In another dispatch, de Bernis named a patrician who had refused to hear him, thus demonstrating "the faithfulness with which the Chevalier Morosini has executed the instructions of his superiors."[25] De Bernis did not write this in code, a nice touch.)

De Bernis's correspondence is a glimpse into the workings of Venetian incognito, in which "anonymity" served its purposes without hiding identities. As masks became a familiar presence in formal settings, their full strangeness may have gone unappreciated by the councils who planned incognito visits and masked Venetians who welcomed the visitors: the 150 nobles, for instance, who attended a reception for the Duke Elector of Saxony, who came to the city incognito in 1684; or the three hundred nobles who attended the reception at the Arsenale for a brother of the Duke of Parma in town, incognito, in 1700; or the scores of nobles who greeted Austria's Joseph II in his theater box as the Count of Falchenstein.[26]

The ritual of Venetian incognito was so ingrained that the very face of subterfuge, the mask, came to define encounters between Venetians and foreigners. This was an extraordinary sequel to the Bedmar conspiracy of 1618. Just two months before the fall of the government, with Napoleon's armies already in northern Italy, poor nobles wearing masks approached French diplomats pleading for liberation from an oppressive and high-handed regime.[27]

Foreigners who participated in masked state rituals were often baffled. The Venetian priest Giovanni Cattaneo was a diplomatic liaison for visiting dignitaries who also kept the State Inquisitors abreast of all he saw and heard. His report about an exchange with the new Austrian ambassador captures the ironies of the mask in the last years of the eighteenth century. Members of the Hapsburg family were coming to Venice incognito, and Cattaneo was finalizing plans to have several foreign ambassadors, including the Austrian Baron von Praüner, meet with them publicly. When he mentioned to Praüner that he would need to wear a mask, the ambassador took exception.

The request was "particularly strange," Praüner told him, since that very morning the procurator Francesco Pesaro had assured him he could come however he wished. Cattaneo replied that it was inconceivable that Pesaro had intended him to appear without a mask, "not only because this is unalterable protocol, but also because ministers wishing to attend such gatherings, placed as they are on the same level as heads of government, also wear masks." In this way, Cattaneo added, wearing a mask would bring Praüner public honor.

Praüner took the logic to its absurd conclusion. If the Hapsburg guests truly wanted to escape public notice, he asked, and if the mask identified them as dignitaries, then shouldn't they simply go without masks? Cattaneo's response was as irrefutable as it was bewildering to a newcomer like Praüner: "without a mask they could not expect to receive any more respect than other foreign gentlemen receive ordinarily."[28] Uncovering their faces, in other words, might cause them to go unremarked. By 1791, Venetian incognito, never really intended to hide identities, was publicizing preeminence.

The presence of so many maskers in Venice was, and continues to be, deceiving. For outsiders, masks in Venice could mean only one thing—carnival—and carnival must have meant disguise. Montesquieu was closer to the prosaic truth of the matter when he wrote that in Venice "the mask is not a disguise but an incognito." His *Voyages de Gratz à la Haye,* more reflective than other travelers' accounts, describes a city whose residents recognized each other despite their masks. "One rarely alters one's clothes, and everyone knows everyone." His example was a Venetian who encountered the papal nuncio in the street. The nuncio was wearing a mask. Seeing him, the man fell to his knees to receive a blessing.[29]

CHAPTER 15

Democratizing Dress

For officials who monitored apparel in Venice, the changes in dress that ushered in the mask were part of a movement that constituted the greatest threat to the public identity of nobles in memory. The transformation was driven by nobles themselves, who, over the last third of the seventeenth century, exchanged the venerable toga for the capelike tabàro. This was met with strenuous objections from the Commissioners of Display. Their fears were well founded. The period marks the start of a series of internal political and social crises that would continue for more than a century, from which the patrician class would not recover. The mask is part of this story. Its appeal to patricians—in protecting rank through manufactured distance, in saving face, in producing a common etiquette for necessary transactions—was clear, but it was not without peril, since it entailed the appearance of equality. The effects of relying on clothing that by turns preserved and suspended social distinctions were consequential, especially since nonnobles also wore the mask. In the end, the ways in which masks were useful to nobles were trumped by a simple fact. Masks can also mask.

In 1650, anyone familiar with the dress codes could have sketched a social topography of Venetians based on appearance. All nobles wore the *vesta da zentilomo*. This "gentleman's toga," a heavy robe that reached to the ground, announced majesty. The oldest mosaics in St. Mark's Basilica, depicting local nobles alongside Byzantine officials, was a testament to its antiquity. To some, it conjured Roman senators. Nobles were required by law to wear the robe whenever they appeared in public or in the Great Council. In addition to the toga, nobles often wore a stole across one shoulder. Sumptuary laws prohibited most individual ornaments, although particular details denoted state service. Nobles who had served as foreign ambassadors wore golden buckles on their belts or gold-trimmed stoles. The togas of senators and of the six doge's counselors were scarlet, and those of the procurators, state attorneys, ministers, and chiefs of the criminal court were violet. On feast days, the procurators wore golden stoles. Subtle differences in cut designated more specific functions. Cittadini, the honored second class of the population, dressed as the nobles did but could not wear the noble stole.[1]

Dress for noble women varied significantly over time, though an overall modesty characterized public styles, with the ample zendà often covering the face and shoulders. Nonnobles wore what they could afford that was in keeping with the nature of their work. The Jews of Venice were required to wear a yellow "O" on their clothes. "It is a shameful and ignominious offense to the name of Christ that Jews are not distinguished from Christians," read the statute, with the identifying O drawn from *offesa* (offense). If the yellow letter was not visible, they were to wear a cap or turban of either yellow or red cloth.[2]

Visitors to the city commented on several striking features of these codes. They noted that rich and poor nobles dressed identically, and that individual differences signified not wealth, power, or personal taste—as might be the case in courtly settings—but civic title or position. Many were intrigued by the closeness in patrician and cittadini attire. One popular explanation hinted at conspiracy: perhaps it was intended to make the noble class seem larger than it actually was to discourage rebellion.[3]

Identity among patricians was first and foremost political. Its attributes, though heritable, were cast not in the language of blood or biology but of governmental duty. All noble males older than twenty-five sat in the Great Council, which assembled on Sunday afternoons in a cavernous hall in the ducal palace. Each was eligible, according to certain conditions, for any additional council. In theory, any one of them might become doge, a largely ceremonial position determined by a complex system combining deliberation with selection by lot. Closely watched by councils finely tuned to detect conspiracy or corruption, the doge lived as a magnificent bird in a gilded cage.[4]

Sovereignty was divided among all nobles equally in the interest of preserving the state from faction or clan. The watchword was virtue, the self-described mainspring of the Republic and guardian of liberty. This was substantially different from honor, the self-regarding spirit animating monarchies. Commentators throughout Europe since the Renaissance had been drawn to the Venetian experiment. In particular, they marveled that incentives and constraints might be devised to produce a governing class whose actions were politically virtuous (i.e., in defense of liberty, averse to favoritism) without assuming moral virtue among its members. The city's celebrated rule combining the one, the few, and the many was said to be an essential condition. Administration was a complex mechanism of controls and duties set within a paternal structure that included surveillance and correction. At the center of government were committees of nobles, elected or appointed by their own class, who kept vigilant watch over their peers.[5]

The political virtue of Venice rested on a clear, evident, and fiercely preserved hierarchy. Vettor Sandi, an eighteenth-century historian who chronicled his city's institutions, wrote that proper modesty relied on "maintaining each thing in its place, which, in this context, means not abasing oneself below or elevating oneself above one's proper condition or power." Clothes were the surest indicator of this hierarchy, with each rank distinguished by dress. The Commissioners of Display did everything in its power to prevent deviation. Its descriptions of clothes were often freighted with moral and religious language. By its own description, the council's charge was "the defense of religion, liberty, and country." Its laws held "incomparable wisdom," and its vision was "purgatorial." It was the Commissioners' duty to "correct and form" Venetians by deciding what could be worn by whom.[6] Beyond the moral taint of luxury, the government believed that rivalry and emulation in dress would squander the noble patrimony, transfer domestic wealth to foreign producers, and drive local artisans out of work.

Sumptuary decrees from the council restricting the public display of expensive ornaments and fabrics appeared with regularity. Declaimed in Piazza San Marco and posted on church doors, they carried the full authority of the state. Forbidden items included any fabric with gold or silver stitching, precious furs, and imported cloth. Laws limited the public display of most jewelry to brides married less than a year.[7]

Venetians by and large accepted the principle that republican virtue required the regulation, in Sandi's words, "of ornament and dress according to the condition, state, age, and authority of persons." A small group standing near the Procuratie Vecchie in Piazza San Marco saw a foppish young aristocrat dressed in the latest international fashion, with a long tailored coat, a hat tucked under his arm, and a towering wig. "All he needs is a sword and he'll be a true Englishman," one of the men said. "Bah—true liberty is done with when you can go about however you wish." The Commissioners of Display framed freedom in these very terms. "Alter the dress, and everything is transformed—even liberty itself—into arbitrariness and disorder."[8] Noble dress was therefore "inalterable," as the council declared in a 1676 decree. Venetians understood the deeply conservative nature of the council's codes. They helped to preserve a hierarchy that was virtually unchanged since the Middle Ages.

A newspaper from just before the Republic's fall contrasted the city's policies with the practice of other European countries, where comparative freedom to dress meant that "the character of a man is on many points revealed by the way he dresses himself." Not so in Venice, where the dominant tone was to conceal rather than express character by dress. This was especially important for patricians, whose common togas were a visual embodiment of the Republic's governance by equals. As the Commissioners put it in 1668, the toga "necessitates similitude in the exterior appearance of each." The toga was a kind of uniform. Its role in producing "singleness of purpose and concord" was "not insignificant."[9]

In the late 1600s, the crisp visual map of status began to blur. A note of unease crept into the language of the council as it warned of disorders, alterations, and confusion in accustomed dress. Its members worried that wealthy nobles were starting to distinguish themselves as individuals with expensive personal touches. Many neglected to wear the toga in public, and by midcentury some nobles had begun attending the Great Council without it. In 1668, that body, affirming the toga as an "outward sign and testimony of noble worth," voted to punish any patrician who failed to wear it in the assembly.[10] By then, however, the battle was lost.

In these decades, the noble style among males for indoor dress—for receptions, dinners and banquets, weddings, and the like—moved toward the *velada,* a long tailored coat worn with a vest, breeches, and silk stockings. The fashion came from Paris—its early devotees were singled out for dressing "alla francese"—and spread quickly to become the principal attire for well-to-do Venetians throughout the eighteenth century. It was sleek and elegant and could be loaded with glittering ornaments. The velada's accompanying vest, called a *camisiòla,* earned the particular ire of the Commissioners of Display, who denounced its imported silks and exotic colors. The wig, introduced to Venice in 1668 and promptly prohibited by the authorities as extravagant, was a necessary component. Despite the vow of Antonio Correr and 250 fellow nobles never to wear wigs, their advocates were persistent enough to convince the Senate in 1701 to allow them.[11]

As if to compensate for the luxury, nobles at the same time began wearing the tabàro, the somber black cape that reached to midcalf. Versions of the tabàro went back hundreds of years in Venice and elsewhere in Europe. Most recently, it had been worn locally by the popular classes as a simple all-purpose cloak. In the early seventeenth century, the Commissioners of Display declared it off-limits to nobles and cittadini, but by the century's end it was the preferred public dress of the city's elites.[12] There was a good reason for this. At a moment's notice, you could sweep up your tabàro, fling it across your shoulders, and cover your sparkling French suit before stepping outside.

This was a classically Venetian solution to the dilemma of how to remain "virtuous" in public and stylish in private. In the Republic, you hid your individuality under a mantle. To Giacomo Casanova, the ultimate nonconformist who lived to be noticed, this enforced egalitarianism was depressingly dull.

> The citizen who wants to avoid persecution must, if he is not like everyone else or worse, bend every effort to appearing to be so. If he has much talent, he must hide it; if he is ambitious, he must pretend to scorn honors; if he wants to obtain anything, he must ask for nothing; if his person is handsome, he must neglect it: he must look slovenly and dress badly, his accessories must be of the plainest, he must ridicule everything foreign; he must bow awkwardly, not pride himself on being well-mannered, care little for the fine arts, conceal his good taste if he has it; not have a foreign cook; he must wear an ill-combed wig and be a little dirty.

The tabàro's function as a cover for new French styles helps to explain the timing of its appearance. It allowed nobles to have it both ways, to respect the spirit of the law while dressing as they pleased. Some stretched even the spirit by wearing sky-blue, scarlet, or dove-white tabàros.[13]

The appearance of the baùta, the close-fitting hood made of velvet, lace, or satin, owed to a similar convergence. When worn with a mask, the baùta was a streamlined, masculine version of the noblewomen's zendà. Both fell from the head and covered a portion of the face. An Italian dictionary from 1829 identifies the origin of word in the German verb *behüten,* "to guard or protect."[14] The definition describes the function of women's veils and the baùta-and-mask combination. Its use was akin to wearing the tabàro. Both signal a turn inward, an effort to protect one's privacy in public. What appears in retrospect an odd and sudden departure in dress begins to make sense. With the growing appeal of international styles, a determined ban on their public display, new venues for gathering in public, and a precedent for covering the face in order to mingle "modestly," donning the tabàro, baùta, and mask was logical for both sexes.

Believing that new fashions would impoverish and diminish the ruling class, the Commissioners cast those who wore lavish velade beneath their tabàros as ostentatious self-seekers set apart from their equals and as a featureless mass indistinguishable from the populace. In a sense, both descriptions were correct. The government's first line of attack, which came in 1704, targeted men's dress in general and the tabàro in particular. On the express command of the Council of Ten, a decree was read monthly in the Great Council that deplored the "abuse," "scandal," and "licentious freedom" of nobles who wore the tabàro in place of the noble toga. Appearing publicly in apparel other than the toga would bring a penalty of five years in prison and a fine of one thousand ducats or banishment for twenty years.[15]

The Commissioners' second strike, aimed at reforming women's fashions, was more sweeping. Hoping to reduce the demand for expensive foreign fabrics and as worried as ever about ostentatious display, the council forbade women of the patrician and cittadini classes from wearing any color other than black in public. Black suited their status, as the 1707 edict said.[16] Later decrees completed the policy. To keep the orders distinct, women who were not noble or cittadine were explicitly barred from wearing black in public (although young women of the noble and cittadini class could wear other colors publicly until they married). Noble and cittadini men, constrained to wear the toga in public, were by implication included in the order for black dress. Young men of the same classes, whether married or single, had to wear black in public.[17]

The decrees were a resounding failure. The muscular rhetoric did little to resuscitate the toga. Insofar as elite women complied with the new order, it inspired a new fashion for black among nonnobles. This defeated the larger goal of segregating the orders by dress. With reports of prostitutes now eager to dress in black, one wag quipped that noble ladies would have to go naked to distinguish themselves from the rabble.[18] Still more tabàros, not all of them black, appeared in the streets, theaters, and cafés, with their usual complement of baùtas, tricorns, and masks. Patrician women just as often dressed as they pleased: in black tabàros and baùtas, in colorful silk dresses in the French style, and sometimes with a mask and black baùta pulled over a colorful silk dress.

In response, the council devised elaborate and faintly comic plans to observe who was wearing what. Agents trained to sniff out traitors and unearth spies found themselves taking notes on fabrics, cuts, and colors. These reports are dated August 11, 1747:

> This evening around 5 P.M., the nobleman Marco Antonio Corner was seen under the arcade of the Procuratie Vecchie wearing a silk velada of undulating violet hues and a grey wig.
> Around 7 P.M., the nobleman Agostino Nani of Cannaregio was seen in St. Mark's Square . . . wearing his usual cinnamon-colored velada and wig *à la Mirliton.*
> Around 5:30 P.M., the nobleman Domenico Guerini was seen under the arcade of the Procuratie Vecchie wearing an ash-grey tabàro and blond wig.[19]

Penalties for nobles who violated the new dress code were absurdly draconian, the effect of which was that they were seldom applied. The council responsible for enforcement was the State Inquisitors, whose agents detailed violations but made few arrests. One noble apprehended for not wearing the toga received a strong rebuke from the Inquisitors, declared himself contrite, and was dismissed with these words: "Because we can see that you are ashamed of having committed this detestable and imprudent action, we will at this time send you away with this just reproof."[20]

Such was the context as more and more nobles wore masks in public: a government unable to enforce its will in required dress; a class accustomed to clothes that both leveled and distinguished now tired of the toga; and a populace eager to imitate noble styles. When worn by assembled nobles—as at the invitation-only receptions for dignitaries or alongside ambassadors in the ducal palace—the mask took on qualities akin to the toga, asserting overall uniformity. By the 1730s, when a traveler noted that the doge himself attended state events in a mask, its quasi-official status was confirmed.[21] On such occasions, the mask served as a marker of collective identity. Joseph Jérôme de Lalande, traveling through Italy late in the century, called the patricians he saw at official ceremonies "*masque-emissaires,* who come as it were on behalf of the state and who signal its presence."[22] In one respect, the tabàro, baùta, and mask combination went further than the toga had gone in expressing equality among the ruling class. While the tabàro and baùta, like the toga, rendered bodies largely indistinguishable, the white half-mask obscured the face.

The power of the mask to bridge differences within the patriciate was of additional significance as the class endured severe strain in the seventeenth and eighteenth centuries. The crisis was principally demographic—

the number of nobles was plunging—but its implications reached into governance and finance. In 1664 there were 300 noble families in Venice; by 1715 that number had slipped to 216. In 1761, the noble population had shrunk by one-third from its numbers a century and a half earlier. The decline threatened the operation of a government uniquely dependent on patricians for its administration. In the mid-1600s, Venetian elites began to view the situation with alarm. "Our State cannot stand on few and weak supports," one of them observed. Another warned that the day was not far off when "there may be more offices than subjects."[23] One hundred years later, the situation caused some to wonder about the very survival of the patrician class.

Plans were advanced to address the aristocratic crisis. In 1736, Scipione Maffei proposed expanding the ranks by recognizing local nobles under Venetian jurisdiction on the terra firma whose status could be traced back three hundred years. It was hardly liberal, much less revolutionary, but the government gave it scant notice.[24] In a separate effort to replenish the stock, the Great Council passed legislation permitting wealthy commoners to purchase noble status, but the dwindling numbers of families who joined was a reflection of just how few could afford the privilege. Eighty entered the nobility between 1646 and 1669, forty between 1670 and 1704, and only eight between 1704 and 1718. A similar initiative was passed in the late eighteenth century to keep the wheels of government turning. The assembly voted to accept forty new families. Only ten entered.[25]

At the same time, economic forces were dramatically changing the living standards of Venetian elites. With the loss of overseas colonies, the main source of noble wealth shifted from maritime trade to agriculture. Elites living inland grew wealthier as ancient families in the city fell into need. A substantial decline in marriage rates among nobles, which plunged from 49 percent in the sixteenth century to 34 percent in the eighteenth, was a measurable indication of distress. Limiting marriage to a single son within patrician households concentrated dwindling inheritances in a single heir. By some estimates, only one in three noble girls married in the eighteenth century, leaving large numbers with few choices beyond entering a convent. From just after the fall of the Republic until our own time, observers have attributed this fatal decline to a heedless taste for festivity among Venetians, a myth fueled by the mistaken identification of the mask with endless carnival and a passion for disguise. A more accurate explanation lies in the structural changes of the European economy.

Yet if it is wrong to say that Venetians danced while the *Titanic* sank, it is also wrong to conclude that they did all they could to avert disaster. The sustained demographic crisis of the eighteenth century offered the patriciate an opportunity to transform itself from a rigid caste into a flexible elite able to replenish its ranks. It steadfastly resisted this chance by setting the price of admission too high and maintaining a forbiddingly inhospitable front to potential newcomers. Nor did the strategy of limiting marriage to a single son prevent noble families from falling into poverty. The sobering fact was that de jure equality, the immemorial hallmark of the Venetian patriciate, was now severely undercut by economic inequality. In 1756, a patrician named Giacomo Nani classified noble families by wealth to announce that only 20 percent were either "rather wealthy" or had "more than their needs." Nearly 45 percent possessed "less than their needs" or "nothing at all." Close to one-third of all ancient patrician families, the so-called *Case vecchie,* fell into this latter category. The poorest nobles, numbering about one in four patricians and comprising some 125 families, were no better off than some manual laborers.

With their means depleted, many of the poorest nobles migrated to a forsaken corner of the city in the parish of San Barnaba, where, under the name of *Barnabotti,* they lived as pariahs, uneducated and unemployed, at the state's expense. Nani recommended wholesale redistribution of noble wealth to revitalize the ranks. His proposal got nowhere. Others recommended stripping the poorest members of their noble status. This was not done either, and the *Barnabotti* held on to their right to sit in the Great Council.[26]

It therefore seems fitting that nobles met this crisis of identity by covering their features and enwrapping themselves in the baùta and tabàro. By putting on a brave face of equality, the mask helped to hold a class together that was in serious danger of falling apart. Here is how one historian describes the so-called war of the theater boxes, a competitive scramble among nobles to appear in choice seats at performances: "A box at the opera and a mask on the face: two ways of asserting moral behavior and the norms of civic protocol. The box itself was a mask that covered the truth of social misery, of political weakness, and of an institutional decline that Venice had never known."[27]

In this account, the mask is an analogy for the loge, but one could add that the real thing—the mask on the face—accomplished the same end. It, too, covered the truth of misery, weakness, and decline. The mask asserted a uniformity that was effectively absent among nobles. Some of them, especially those in Nani's lower strata, probably had this in mind when they covered their faces to appear in public. They may also have shuddered at the closeness of their own condition to that of the masked beggars they passed in the streets.

There was a harsh irony in all of this. As the tabàro and baùta spread to other ranks, all hope of distinguishing social position at a glance was gone. From one point of view, this was a gain for common civility. Codes of respect that masks taught in daily life resembled the restraint noted at the Ridotto. But from another, such interactions eroded noble uniqueness. Traditionalists pointed to one activity in particular that rivaled the nobility's impoverishment as a scourge of the Republic: conversation.

The senator Pietro Garzoni had sounded an early warning in the 1720s when he traced a path from masks in the theater to masks in the streets for "calls, visits, conversations." Their liberty, he said, was a grave threat to traditional virtues.[28] The fact is, such critics were probably right about the effects of conversation on the established order. "I have heard some say with a note of pride in their voices that the world today has become sociable," cautioned a priest named Masotti in a published sermon. "Everyone talks about everything." For Father Masotti, this *libertà del parlare,* "the freedom to speak," disrupted the divine order by dismissing innate differences of status.[29]

In his memoir on public mores, Pietro Franceschi castigated those who "reason about the government" in the name of conversation. "Driven by their own passions and desires, and inspired by designs drawn from their own fantasies, they promise themselves a better state." Franceschi evoked an image of dreamers following misguided notions of liberty who met in homes, *casini,* and cafés. "A mask of zeal for the common good covers the motives of these disastrous gatherings. In the meantime, our ancient constitution is destroyed in both form and public tranquillity." Franceschi furnished proof that speaking freely endangered state security. In broad daylight on the morning of March 29, 1777, without provocation and in plain view of passersby on the Fondamenta Nuove, a commoner punched the patrician Pietro Giovanni Semitecolo in the face.[30]

Others found conversation among men and women in cafés, salons, and *casini* equally disturbing. After sixty centuries of embroidery and the spindle, a poet of the time asked, do women suddenly think that they can set aside their work, neglect their own relations, and spend their days in visits? These were liable to stir up dangerous passions and undermine the family. To another author this "deformity of custom" was a "breeding ground" of lust.[31]

For Giacomo Nani, the patrician who documented the impoverishment of his fellow nobles, free conversation denied the principle of hierarchy on which the Republic rested. It was a sign of the times, he wrote in *Principles of a Calm and Ordered Administration* (ca. 1781), that Venetians were mingling without regard to sex, age, or status in the city's cafés. The mask has aggravated the peril, he went on, since it "has the effect of eclipsing every difference of rank and putting all men on the same footing." Nani warned that the outward equality of this "legal eclipse"—by which he meant the official toleration of masks for six months a year—was now taking on all the attributes of "material equality."

Nani spoke ominously of the harm to come. "The thinking of a wise man will show no superiority to that of a woman or an imbecile, nor the words of a man of experience prevail over those of youth."[32] Conversation, and the masks that encouraged it, were symptoms of the Republic's demise. Of course, one man's demise is another man's opportunity. Or woman's.

On a January afternoon in 1793, the widow Laura sat reading the newspaper in a café called the Thistle. She was alone and masked. Her eye fell on a letter by a self-described enemy of deceit. Signor Calofilo ("Sir Lover-of-Beauty") protested that masks denied connoisseurs like himself the pleasure of watching women. "You women—you who are the beautiful half of mankind, who bring delight to all men who see you— why do you renounce this sovereignty? Men vaunt you as the most perfect work of creation. Why do you deform yourselves in this way?"

The widow Laura felt patronized. She took up her pen. "Will you refuse to read further if I tell you I am a masker?"—she begins.

> I do not know if you respect the gentle sex, but you are reading the words of a woman. Without the aid of the mask, do you think I would be able to write? The gentlemen around me all think I'm a man. They leave me in peace to scratch out these lines without annoying me with their elaborate bows and handshakes and the pretty little phrases whispered in my ear and all the other artful things that men do when they talk to members of my sex. The delight of responding to you therefore comes from the very thing you so scorn.[33]

The image is rich: a solitary women in black mantle, hat, and mask bent over her table first reading and then writing feverishly, ordering another cup perhaps, speaking in muffled tones, hoping that no one will disturb her or notice that she was a woman. Her letter mixes exaggerated politeness with an occasional taunt. She urges Signor Calofilo to come out of his attic, saying that she will recognize him by his horror among so many masks. "Then I'll introduce myself."

Is it possible that Laura's mask emboldened her, urged her to think of herself differently, caused her to imagine holding her own, as a woman, in public—to suggest, in a deliberately patronizing tone of her own, that she might introduce herself to a stranger?

Variations of the scene were probably repeated by others who used the mask to purchase an afternoon's independence. It attests to a population not so much lost in pleasure as one ready to use the customs of dress to live and flourish in a society built on an unequal distribution of power. The mask's ability to separate and distinguish was still acknowledged, but its diffusion to the Lauras of the city devalued whatever currency it retained as a carrier of status. In this sense, those who warned that maskers' seeming equality was becoming substantial equality were not far from the truth.

Great differences still separated elites from commoners at the end of the Republic—differences of fortune and heritage, of property and prestige, of possessions, living standards, and access to power. But in the public commerce of daily life, masks had so smoothed relations among unequals that their subjunctive equality was becoming increasingly declarative. First worn to preserve—to preserve modesty, distance, distinction, class identity—they ended up subverting. Carnival was not the occasion for this subversion, which ran deeper and was less visible than a sudden flash of mockery or irreverence.

Laura's pluck at the Thistle sounds a faint echo of those women from an earlier time who claimed that the veil brought them liberty. But unlike women's veils, it wasn't modesty that Laura's mask asserted. It was equality.

CHAPTER 16

Taming the Devil

Venetian audiences must have been stunned when they first encountered Carlo Goldoni's Arlecchino. The character was nothing like the ridiculous figure who belched and groped his way through a century and a half of improvised skits. Instead he was substantial and oddly sober, with depth and personality and the capacity to feel sentiment. In Goldoni's play *Jealous Women*, Arlecchino is a working-class porter, honest with his masters, efficient in his rounds, and proud of his work. He is solicitous, polite, even a touch dull. And now, approaching the end of act II, he's also feeling extremely awkward.

Arlecchino has just entered the Venetian Ridotto with a shapely young woman on his arm.[1] Both are masked, in keeping with the custom of the place. Signora Lucrezia, a happy widow with a sharp tongue, has asked him to come with her to the gambling hall. Her flattering invitation has unnerved him. It doesn't matter that she has warned him to keep quiet so that no one will know he's working-class, or that she'll probably drop him as soon as she sees someone she knows, or even that his friends mock him for presuming to call Signora Lucrezia pretty. He may be near the bottom of the ladder, but he has as much right as anyone to be smitten with a proper lady.

Signora Lucrezia is playing a cruel game in *Jealous Women*, tormenting two ladies she detests by toying with their husbands. She has come to the Ridotto to continue the fun. The husbands arrive wearing masks of their own and approach to pay their doting respects. They are artisans, one a haberdasher and the other a jeweler, and they both owe Lucrezia money. Excited by her attention, the men warble on about how and when they will repay her. Their wives, also in masks, have followed them here. They spot Lucrezia at once. She recognizes them, too, and their growing fury only feeds her pleasure. Others notice and begin to watch: an unattached woman is basking in the attention of two suitors while a pair of unhappy maskers in commoners' clothes eye their every move.

At last the wives explode. Chaos erupts, the husbands flee, and in a rage Lucrezia turns on Arlecchino for letting the women insult her. He has fallen asleep. She slaps him and calls him a swine and a jackass. With all gambling now stopped and other maskers watching merrily, Arlecchino, slow-witted and in love, pleads with her by name again and again— *Siora mascara Lugrezia, Siora mascara Lugrezia*—as laughter fills the hall. Gamblers take up the chant—"My masked Lucrezia, My masked Lucrezia"—and force her from the place in humiliation. Arlecchino leaves the building mortified. His shame is real, and it draws a wince.

In the long history of commedia dell'arte, this moment—and many others like it in Goldoni's oeuvre—was epoch-making. Arlecchino is no longer a devil but an artisan you might recognize from the neighborhood. His emotions aren't superficial or silly but lifelike and complex. And although he is still capable of comedy, he can also elicit sympathy. With Goldoni, commedia figures were being reborn into the daily rhythm of Venice as respectable artisans, shopkeepers, seamstresses, and washerwomen. But what was truly revolutionary, the thing for which audiences were altogether unprepared, was that these figures—Arlecchino, Pantalone, the Dottore from Bologna, other lovers, and *zanni*—were starting to show their faces.

After nearly two centuries on the stage, characters of the commedia dell'arte were now asked to take off their masks. The change was disorienting to both audiences and actors, who thought they knew what to expect from commedia. Taking off the mask meant that characters could emerge as individuals, to grow, to change, to feel love or pain or disgrace. In the process, the commoners they personified were endowed with passions and activities no less worthy of the stage than the affairs of the privileged.

No sooner had Goldoni begun to unmask his characters than the defenders of tradition, led by the poison-penned Carlo Gozzi, launched a vicious campaign that would ultimately drive him from the city. Seeing subversion in the plays, Gozzi attacked the "dogs" and "blustering fanatics" who had opened "a splendidly hideous field" for dangerous ideas. In uncovering the faces of the city's servants and workers, Goldoni had

FIGURE 29. Carlo Goldoni

given them a voice. The unmasking was meant to be empowering. In a city where masks and the social structure were bound so closely together, the idea did not sit well with conservatives. Goldoni had also opened a line of thinking that questioned the very foundations of the city's supposedly immutable hierarchy.

Until his early forties, when he became a full-time playwright, Goldoni divided his adult life between the bar and the stage. His early work, done when he was still an attorney, revealed a prodigious pen, the ability to produce under pressure, and fluency in a range of styles. These talents would stay with him for the rest of his life. Goldoni's comic universe embraces the whole of Venetian life. Its inhabitants include patricians and councillors of state, members of the military, bureaucrats and intellectuals, teachers, poets, professionals, and an immense stock of artisans, merchants, and manual workers (figure 29).

Carlo Gozzi represented another world, that of the culturally dominant aristocracy. Gozzi's mother was the last descendant in her family's branch of the ancient Tiepolo line. That the line was now impoverished

FIGURE 30. Carlo Gozzi

made Gozzi's own reactionary defense of tradition all the more visceral. His writing exudes haughtiness and resentment. In his *Memorie inutili,* Gozzi describes his dispute with Goldoni with the fall of Venice fresh in his memory. He was a neglected Cassandra, he writes in these "useless" memoirs, who warned of disaster while audiences flocked heedlessly to the new comedies. The wounded tone, like his autobiography's mock-modest title, is disingenuous. His polemic against Goldoni carried the day (figure 30).

As a lawyer, Goldoni spent his time in the company of actors, a group almost always on the margins of society in the eighteenth century. Gozzi, by contrast, gathered the most conservative young nobles, collegians, priests, and scholars to join in opposition to all things modern, especially French. They called themselves the Accademia Granelleschi, organized for the defense of tradition in language, taste, and style. Founded in 1747, when Gozzi was twenty-seven, the circle's unwavering defense of letters as an elite enterprise echoed its founders' claims to privilege. Its variety of wit (*granelli* are testicles) aimed to be Rabelaisian, but it usually came off more mean-spirited than merry. "Human existence is a continuous war," an anonymous academician wrote, "and those who love peace realize that there are more pricks in the world than men." The academy's mascot, a dwarf, was by Gozzi's telling too vain to know he was being mocked when members crowned him with a wreath of shriveled plums.[2]

The Testicular Academy met regularly to hear learned lectures, issue prizes, and publish works of their own. When the final reckoning came between Goldoni and Gozzi, it was played out on the boards but hatched in the Academy. On a dare, Gozzi wrote plays that reintroduced masks, traded real life for fable, and hammered home the theme that hierarchy—in the family, in society, in language itself—was the glue of human relations. They were a complete success.

When Carlo Goldoni returned to Venice in 1748 from his most recent legal work in Pisa, he was intent on transforming the genre of comedy. At the time, the Venetian stage offered a miscellany of imports, experiments, translations, and adaptations. Given the flourishing theatrical culture of Venice, some entrepreneurs had tried, and mostly failed, to bring commedia dell'arte indoors. Its gutter talk, somehow less offensive in the market square, was wildly out of place in a proper theater, and its traditions were anathema to the discipline of scripts and schedules.

The San Samuele in previous decades had mounted a steady diet of these plays with titles such as *Pantalone the Medicine-Man, Pantalone the Bankrupt Merchant,* and *Pantalone the Bully.* Critics responded with disgust. They were "unworthy of being heard by civil persons," "entrusted to ignorant men who stop at nothing for a laugh," "stuffed with obscenities."[3] Goldoni himself complained that their jokes could turn the strongest stomach. "The comic theater in Italy had for more than a century been so corrupt that it was an abominable object of scorn for the rest of Europe," Goldoni wrote in the preface to a new edition of his plays in 1750. He continued:

> Nothing appeared on public stages except filthy harlequinades, dirty and scandalous love scenes and jokes, poorly developed plots, with no morals and no order, and which, far from correcting vice—the original and most noble purpose of comedy—fomented it instead. It made the ignorant lower classes, dissolute young men, and mannerless boors laugh, but it bored and angered people of culture and good morals.[4]

When the plays weren't crude, they were inane. Goldoni recalled seeing a Don Juan who excelled in turning somersaults while holding a lighted candle. Connoisseurs who followed theater elsewhere cited Molière as a model for modern comedy, but his brand of refined satire had few followers in Italy. The Milanese critic Gorini Corio surveyed the scene to offer universal condemnation. Serious drama was a mere handmaiden to music, he said, tragedy was derivative, and comedy in its banality attracted only the ignorant.[5]

Goldoni's vision was for theater to be a school for virtue, with commedia its improbable carrier. He came to Venice prepared, with a talented commedia dell'arte troupe in tow whose director, Girolamo Medebac, he had befriended in Tuscany. They arrived in the summer, Medebac picked up the lease on the San Angelo theater, and the acting company began preparations for an October opening. Titles from this first season of reform convey the middle-class virtues Goldoni would accentuate over the next fourteen years: *The Lucky Heiress, The Crafty Widow, The Prudent Man, The Respectable Girl.*[6] By the end of his company's first season, Medebac believed that the project was sufficiently launched to announce a new direction for comedy. In the traditional envoi just before the curtain fell on the last day of carnival, 1749, Medebac proclaimed in local dialect that the comic stage was no longer an embarrassment.

El mondo vederà
Ch'el Teatro no xe più scandoloso.

The Testicular Academy had its cause. Led by Carlo Gozzi, the Granelleschi began leaving snide sonnets in cafés and theaters. Either outraged or energized by Goldoni's gambit, and goaded by the brilliantly scathing pamphlets that materialized daily, spectators took sides. Gozzi recalled seeing quarrels during religious ceremonies, civic festivals, and in the marketplace. "In Venice, hawkers and charlatans, gossips and boatmen, gentlemen and adventurers, ladies and merchants all disputed the rules of comic theater and made loud displays of their preference," writes one of Goldoni's biographers.[7]

Gozzi himself set the tone, calling Goldoni's output "a diarrhea of dramatic works." The shot was well aimed. In the 1750 season alone, Goldoni promised and completed sixteen comedies, a quantity that he later said damaged him physically and mentally. Over his career, Goldoni wrote more than 150 works for the stage. Gozzi claimed that their sheer number dazzled rather than persuaded audiences and likened them to the barbarian invasions. He cast Goldoni's flaws in terms of class. Greedy for applause, he charged, Goldoni flattered the lower ranks (who are "always too disposed to envy and malign the great") and drew promiscuously from all quarters for inspiration, including "the swamps of the lower classes." Goldoni's plays might well contain truths, Gozzi continued, but they were "so low, so vulgar, so common" that they fell far short of theater's dignity. Goldoni had boasted about wanting to clean up commedia dell'arte. In fact, Gozzi said, his plays were a hundred times "more lascivious, more indecent, and more injurious to morals."[8]

Carlo Gozzi and the Testicular Academy targeted Goldoni's language, which was a mixture of Venetian dialect and proper Italian or, in some plays, entirely in Venetian. This was a sharp departure from the ornate diction of everything else on the Venetian stage. For Goldoni, capturing the melody and cadence of everyday speech situated plays "within the grasp of all." One member of the Academy characterized Goldoni's "atrocious Italian" as a mongrel mix of Venetian, Lombard, and Roman dialects. As always, Gozzi was more cutting. Goldoni's plays offered "scraps and tags of erudition, stolen Heaven knows where, and clumsily brought in to impose upon the crowd of ignoramuses."[9] As with his content, Goldoni's use of language allegedly betrayed poor judgment. His critics' objection wasn't that the lower classes never used the crude expressions Goldoni gave them. It was that Goldoni gave their coarse talk a public platform.

On this last point the accusers were correct. The language of Goldoni's plays is startlingly rough. He regularly stages private quarrels that spiral out of the comic and into a realm of genuine unease. In *The Coffeehouse,* Vittoria, the simple wife of a compulsive gambler who has spent two nights hemorrhaging their savings, tracks him down only to be cursed and physically threatened. "Go ahead and kill me, you dog," she shrieks through tears in the middle of a public square. "Murderer, traitor—kill me then, you disgrace, you failure. You have no principles, no heart, no honor." Goldoni freely admitted to transcribing confrontations he had witnessed and said that some might even recognize themselves on the stage, but he was unrepentant. The blame was not his for staging brutality, he said. It was on the brutality and those who committed it.[10]

If traditionalists condemned Goldoni for degrading drama and pandering to the masses, a different sort of complaint came from his actors. Playing ordinary people was frightfully difficult. Doing so while reciting prepared lines was even harder. "This different way of directing has cost me a huge effort," Goldoni wrote in the preface to *The English Philosopher.* In another preface, he described two commedia actors who broke character during a performance to vent their anger, "perhaps out of unhappiness with me." Some simply found the transition unmanageable, and, like silent-screen actors whose careers sank with the coming of sound, they suddenly began hearing catcalls after years of acclaim. Francesco Rubini, a veteran Pantalone of the San Luca theater, tarnished his reputation when he first performed without his mask. He was "so ill-at-ease and embarrassed that he lost all grace, all wit, all common sense," Goldoni recalled. The play failed "in the cruelest, most humiliating manner conceivable for him and for me."[11]

Actors called the new plays "premeditated." Goldoni reasoned that the best way to restrain the obscene banter that was commedia's stock-in-trade was with the yoke of memorized lines. There were other benefits. Treating comedy as drama—shifting the play's engine from actors to the author—permitted sustained dramatic development. Now, over the course of a play, an honest café owner might convince a bad husband of his harm; an honest patrician might show a profligate friend the value of thrift.

The stage techniques that unmasking brought served these dramatic ideals. Goldoni believed that performers in masks overacted, exaggerating their gestures and distorting their speech. It wasn't so much that masks were incapable of conveying feeling. It was that they hid the subtler emotions Goldoni wanted to depict. The face, he wrote, was the interpreter of the heart. Today we want our actors to have soul, he explained, and "the soul under a mask is like a fire beneath ashes."[12]

In *The Comic Theater,* Goldoni depicts actors grappling with an unnamed playwright's reforms. They are moving from improvisation to memorized lines, from slapstick to more cerebral comedy, and from masks to faces. It is one of Goldoni's cleverest works. The play's action takes place backstage, but the fictional actors retain their characters' names. Arlecchino's real name is Arlecchino, Pantalone's is Pantalone, and so on. The message was the same as when he named his porters, shopkeepers, and servants Arlecchino, Pantalone, Brighella, and the like. Actors had private lives, too. That said, the effect of naming an actor Arlecchino who plays a character named Arlecchino is bizarre. It's as if after two hundred years of playacting we're finally seeing what he's really like.[13]

What we learn about him is that in private Arlecchino speaks in a polished and elegant Italian. He needs a director to coach him in the vulgar dialect of his character. We hear the prima donna Rosaura praising a certain local playwright for writing sixteen plays in a single season, especially one called *The Comic Theater.* And nervously pacing backstage is Pantalone, who is paralyzed by stage fright because, for the first time in his career, he must memorize his lines. Once again, Goldoni was transforming the everyday life of Venice into material for the stage.

Despite Pantalone's jitters, the actors of *The Comic Theater* stand solidly behind the playwright's reforms. When a self-pitying poet named Lelio shows up to peddle his plays, the performers rib him for being behind the times. His tirades are hollow, they say, his soliloquies are tiresome, and his mindless gags are a relic of the past. Brighella, whose onstage persona is buffoonish, is earnest and wise offstage. He states that comedy should "correct vice and ridicule bad habits." How? By drawing from "the great sea of nature," so that those who watch it will learn from people like themselves. He adds that the popular classes of the city are now talking about the elevating effects of theater.[14]

The actors are, of course, a mouthpiece for Goldoni, and by the time *The Comic Theater* premiered, three and a half years after the reform was launched, everyone knew it. Winking in the direction of his supporters, Goldoni has the sad sack Lelio tell Brighella: "You sound more like a poet than an actor." Brighella responds with pride, "With a mask I am Brighella, but without a mask, though not a poet, I am a man of discernment, which is necessary for my *métier*. An ignorant actor cannot succeed as any character."[15] The comment goes to the core of Goldoni's rationale in unmasking his players. A century earlier, the actor Nicolò Barbieri had defended commedia masks as an aid in distinguishing performers from their characters. Clowns in comedies, Barbieri had argued, were no more clowns in real life than sorcerers or kings onstage cast spells or ruled kingdoms offstage.[16] After more than a century of seeing fictions on the stage, audiences now grasped that the actor was not the role (which gave the joke of calling Arlecchino Arlecchino its relish). Goldoni was pointing to a different distinction. By setting actors backstage and barefaced, Goldoni drew attention to their real-life counterparts as professionals who worked hard at their craft.

When *The Comic Theater* premiered, Goldoni was still moving slowly on his project of unmasking. He omitted masks entirely in *The Respectable Girl,* which had premiered during carnival, 1749, only to use them a year later in *The Antiquarian's Family.* It was therefore appropriate that halfway through *The Comic Theater* the actors, until now unmasked, don their identifying masks to rehearse the next night's performance. When Florindo briefly steps out of character to ask Ottavio if they can try performing without masks, the director defends their use. "It's not yet time to do it," he says, adding that the populace would develop a taste for genuine wit only by the apprenticeship of plays both with and without masks.[17]

Ottavio's reasoning was a fair reflection of Goldoni's thinking in 1751.

Even after he decided to unmask commedia characters, he acted with deliberation, assessing what had worked and what had not, gauging spectators' reactions, making adjustments where needed. "In the first and second years of this experiment, I did not dare to present a comedy without at least some masks, but they slowly became less necessary," he explained in a new preface to *The Gentleman and the Lady.* "I showed the populace—taking it by the hand, as it were—that laughter did not require masks, and that laughter in response to intelligence and wit is only proper to men of judgment."[18] Such spectators of judgment were presumably not limited to elites.

In the 1750s, satisfied that his audience was now sufficiently prepared, he began revising earlier works to show the actors' faces. His *Father of the Family* had masks in its 1750 version but none in its reprise three years later. Commedia masks appeared when *The Lucky Heir* premiered in 1750 but were written out of the play in 1752. In the 1752 revision of *The Gentleman and the Lady* (1749) he also omitted the masks. *The Comic Theater* was at the turning point, and it takes only a slight suspension of disbelief to believe that his own characters in the play convinced him that it was now time to take the masks off for good.

The unmasking gave the lowborn an ethical seriousness otherwise unimaginable. When an arrogant patrician talks down to an honest merchant in *The Gentleman and the Lady,* the merchant replies that the real plebeian is the man who inherits a title, does nothing productive with his estate, and shows his strength by abusing his powers. Ridolfo, a hardworking café owner in *The Coffeehouse,* says he would not exchange his position for any other, even if it meant more money and status. "I'm in an honest line," he says, "a trade of the artisanal class that is dignified, clean, and civil." Unmasking Arlecchino helped tame the demonic energies that had driven the character for centuries. "I am a decent man," he asserts indignantly in *Jealous Women* when asked to do a job he thinks is beneath him.[19] His rise to respectability would continue. In Goldoni's Paris plays, he falls in love, marries, and settles down.

Goldoni's readiness to depict industrious commoners was not naive. He lampoons pettiness, brutality, and corrosive distrust wherever he finds it, which is often among the working class. The human squalor of a play like *The Bickering Chioggians* is harrowing. In it, two families of fishermen erupt in violence over a trifle, and the lovers at its center careen into howling fights.[20] Yet even such ugliness places commoners on comparable moral footing with the nobility, whose idleness and corruption Goldoni also puts on full view. Both groups are capable of tremendous bloody-mindedness. The taint of guile and rancor that clings to so many of his plays also serves to humanize them. Goldoni was careful not to mock those deserving of compassion. His smile is sardonic but seldom sneering. Citing the poor fishermen and modest shopkeepers who sat in Venetian theaters alongside the rich, Goldoni said that he hoped all spectators would see their own "customs, defects, and, if I might permit myself to say so, virtues."[21]

That sentiment was at the heart of Gozzi's objections to Goldoni. It was worse than his pandering, worse than his vulgar parade of working-class speech in the name of truth. To exalt the loyalty or so-called honor of the lowborn was for Gozzi unacceptable. It obscured the fact that values must come to the servile from above. Moreover, Goldoni's plays made patricians into objects of ridicule by imputing to them iniquity and un-earned ease. Goldoni's fault was to suggest that the uneducated might have something to learn from watching their own kind. In Gozzi's view, the populace already despised "the necessary yoke of subordination."[22] Goldoni's plays made them question it altogether.

Whatever the merits of his prescription, Gozzi showed himself an acute reader of Goldoni's message. Scattered throughout his plays runs one consistent theme, which flies in the face of the strict hierarchy on which the Venetian system depended: that on a fundamental level, social rank is artificial. "Nature teaches that we are all made of the same putty" *(Mother Nature's Wondrous Effects);* "We're all formed from the same dough, and it is the merest accident that one is the master and another the servant" *(Torquato Tasso);* "Slip off that glittering coat and you'll see that our natural state is equal" *(Bertoldo, Bertoldino, and Cacasenno).*[23]

Yet it would be wrong to call Goldoni a revolutionary, or to suggest that he advocated the reordering of society. Goldoni punctures aristocratic pretense and champions the virtues of the lowly, but class distinctions remain firmly in place. Pantalone, the lecherous merchant of commedia dell'arte, becomes a model citizen over the course of Goldoni's comedies. He grows generous, honest, and hardworking. He sometimes outshines Goldoni's patricians in dignity and common sense. As a wealthy merchant in *The Antiquarian's Family,* he urges his daughter, who has married a young noble, not to let the title go to her head. "Be modest, be patient, be good, and then you will also be noble, rich, and respected." Yet he always shows deference to his superiors and urges other merchants to do the same.[24]

Goldoni's plays question the terms of social worth, not society's basic arrangement. He shifts public value from birth to deeds. Nobles are judged by their usefulness; political virtues are present in the middle classes; and the lower ranks are praised for honest work. In Goldoni's view, social order relies on mutual respect rather than fear or blind tradition. Conveying this on the stage required eliminating masks.

Goldoni's declared intent in unmasking his actors was artistic. The mask was a physical impediment that limited dramatic expression and the development of character, he claimed. Once freed of the mask, however, his characters developed in ways that conservatives found disturbing. This, too, was probably by design. In commedia dell'arte, keeping the lower orders in masks held them at a distance from their betters. Goldoni's unmasking forced a proximity among all ranks that commedia masks had blocked. Resisting that proximity was a part of what had first prompted masking among theatergoers and at the Ridotto one hundred years earlier. Goldoni's gesture asserted what masks in the audience and on the streets denied: the rough equivalence of character among all classes.

That moral vision, framed in similar terms and motivated by the same general aims, would resurface in Venice in 1797 during the Provisional Municipality, a body inspired by ideals of the French Revolution that governed the city after the fall of the Republic. Scorning the "grotesque scandal of commedia dell'arte," its Committee of Public Instruction called on authors and directors to make the theater a school for virtue with examples drawn from ordinary life. A popular playwright of the period named Simone Sografi followed suit with plays in dialect about civic harmony and the virtues of the common folk.[25]

In Goldoni's day, this was an ideal ahead of its time. The verdict came in late January 1761, announced by a boy from the stage of the San Samuele theater, who proclaimed the return of the *comici vecchi,* "the old comedians." They have been dismissed, the boy says. They have been condemned as old-fashioned and exhausted. This is a fraud, he says, and to prove it, just look who is entering from the wings.

With this, Pantalone the courtier enters in his ancient mask to be told by the King of Hearts that his only son, Prince Tartaglia, will die of a mysterious disease unless he is made to laugh. Pantalone enlists the masked jester Truffaldino, who tries every gag in the old commedia playbook, shrieking, stuttering, and stumbling, examining Tartaglia's eyes, taking his pulse, inspecting his sputum, and declaring in the end that the prince has been poisoned by a steady diet of stinking verse. Nothing works until an elderly woman totters to the public fountain to fill her pail. Truffaldino flies to her side, ridicules her looks, and mocks her age, and in the confusion she falls headfirst into the fountain with her legs sticking straight up. Prince Tartaglia nearly topples from his throne in laughter. He is cured. Commedia dell'arte is back.

Unbeknownst to most of his friends, Carlo Gozzi had been at work on what he hoped would be the final nail in Goldoni's coffin: a set of plays to revive old comedy, restore the hierarchy weakened in the flood of recent comedies, and show the world that Goldoni's fame was a passing fad. His instant success with this first effort, *The Love of Three Oranges*, surprised even him. Enlisting veteran commedia players whose own careers had suffered during Goldoni's reforms—actors like the seasoned Arlecchino Antonio Sacchi and the career Pantalone Cesare D'Arbes—Gozzi followed with more "fables" the following season, including *The Stag King* and *Turandot*.[26] By early 1762, the popular preference was clear, as audiences left the San Luca, Goldoni's theater, to see Gozzi's latest productions at the San Samuele. In April, Carlo Goldoni left Venice for good, beaten down by a decade of attacks. The Venetian public had found a style more attuned to its own taste.[27]

Gozzi's fables were a defiant riposte to Goldoni's reforms on his own turf. He fashioned them to show that the future of comedy need not follow nostrums about utility and moral equality. He took his shots against "enlightened" ideas wherever he found an opening: "Figuring out the world and getting what you want by hook or by crook—*that's* the real modern philosophy," says the clown Truffaldino in *The Green Bird*.[28] He praised himself for returning masks to commedia actors, whose innocent throats, he said, Goldoni had wanted to slit. The restoration of those masks, coupled with the sort of pranks that opened *The Love of Three Oranges*, signaled proper subordination. In his fable *Zeim, King of the Genies*, Gozzi puts his views in the mouth of a slave girl, who recounts what a wise old man once taught her:

> He always told me that sacred, inscrutable Providence had planned everything, and that the position of great men was a wonder of God. He said it was a heavenly sight to see all the people, rank by rank down to the most humble peasants, subordinated to their betters. "Oh," he said, "don't be led astray by those malicious sophists who claim that there is liberty outside this beautiful order which Heaven has given us. They only sow confusion and disturb the peace, and often they are murderers, thieves, and heathens who end up on the gallows. Daughter, respect the great ones, love them, and however heavy your state may be to you, do not be envious of them."[29]

The "beautiful order" of a population aligned in ranks, from kings down to slaves, is immaculately preserved in Gozzi's fables, whose stratification extends to character and speech. Nobles exhibit magnanimous sentiments and speak in polished verse. The professional classes speak in prose. Members of the popular classes—Arlecchino, Brighella, Truffaldino—improvise in dialect, as the former commedia players had also done, from a sketch. There is little mingling among the ranks, and nothing is said about the human struggles or hopes of those in masks.

This was the social vision that conservatives found threatened late in the century. Its preservation would prompt elites to call for honorable persons to "recover" wearing masks when attending the theater. Gozzi's commedia characters who regained their masks and those noble spectators asked to do the same were, of course, social opposites. But the motivation was the same in both cases: to preserve hierarchy and protect distinction. Masks eroded individuality and upheld the status quo. This was a point on which Goldoni and his attackers agreed, although their conclusions were vastly different.

By the end of the dispute, another similarity had emerged. Both Gozzi and Goldoni had corralled the lusty irreverence of Italian comedy. In his one concession to Goldoni's reforms, Gozzi did not reinstate the broad sexual humor of earlier commedia. Whereas Goldoni had replaced it with realism, Gozzi aimed for magic. He achieved this effect by cutting all ties to the everyday world. His plays were designed to seduce and enchant, not to critique or provoke. Audiences were meant to be captivated, swept away, dazzled—and not to think too much. Gozzi followed his fables with a series of Italian adaptations from the Spanish stage of the seventeenth century that continued the formula of imaginary kingdoms, a strongly marked social order, and ample opportunities for improvised slapstick among masked commedia characters.[30] These works drew crowds through the 1770s.

In cleaning up commedia dell'arte, Goldoni and Gozzi did much to bury one of the longest associations of the genre, that linking masks to the underworld. By taming the devil in the theater, the playwrights also had a hand in domesticating the other main stage where boisterous Arlecchinos and Pulcinellas regularly performed, Venetian carnival. That pacification was already under way.

PART FOUR

Carnival and Community

CHAPTER 17

Redeemed by the Blood

In late winter 1679, the Venetian Giovanni Corner staged a spectacle that linked images of renewal to the pressures of an empire beginning to come apart. The event was called an equestrian ballet. It was a masquerade on horseback that combined music, costumes, and symbolic killing in choreographed maneuvers. As an orchestra played, riders systematically pierced, stabbed, and shot their victims. Although it is unlikely that the participants thought of it quite so abstractly, the event was a highly refined version of an immemorial ritual, repeated for centuries each spring: rebirth through blood.

Corner was among the more powerful patricians of Venice. The former rector of Šibenik on the Dalmatian coast, he was the scion of an ancient Venetian line that included three doges. His guest of honor, who played a prominent role in the masquerade, was Ferdinando Gonzaga, the Duke of Mantua. As for the rest of the players, Corner cast the cream of Venetian society—officers, high government officials, even a future doge. Many were battle-seasoned, some against the very antagonists they were called on to impersonate. To a flourish of trumpets, four groups entered the field outfitted for battle: Turks, Moors, Tartars, and Indians. A singer led the procession.[1]

The thirty years on either side of Corner's masquerade saw some of Venice's fiercest sea battles since Lepanto in 1571. The stronghold of Crete had just fallen after four and a half centuries as a Venetian colony; safe harbors all across southern Greece hung in the balance; the Turks were advancing steadily through the Balkans and eastern Europe and would soon be at the gates of Vienna. The Moors continued to launch raids on Venetian convoys loaded with goods from the East. Conflict with the Moors, a loose designation for Muslims of north Africa, southern Spain, and more generally throughout the Mediterranean, had been perpetual for close to seven hundred years and would continue into the eighteenth century. In the minds of Venetians, the Turks and Moors were a barbarian menace: heretics, savage, and without honor in peacetime or in war.

Guests invited to the equestrian ballet took their seats in a large temporary amphitheater. Corner had spared no expense. Each rider had an escort of two heralds, four grooms, and two servants, whose dress matched that of their warrior. The Turks were done up in red silk turbans adorned with flowers, the Moors wore broad sashes with crescent moons and stars, the Tartars had open vests, and the Indians wore rich brown fabrics. The warriors' tunics were weighed down by heavy gold braid. There were strangely delicate touches, too, details that would have been absurd on any soldier's uniform. Plumes of yellow, blue, orange, and green trailed from their turbans and helmets. The Turks had flowers on their shields. Pearls adorned the Moors' turbans. The masquerade's dénouement—the symbolic slaughter of six "monsters"—intensified the oddity of these ethereal touches, as if Botticelli had been called in to add garlands and gauze to a scene from Goya.

Every warrior was a Venetian noble. The Turk Allesandro Molino had served as the commissioner of Venetian ports in the Peloponnesus. The Tartar Francesco Morosini was the once and future captain general of the Venetian fleet in the Aegean; he would eventually become doge. Francesco Loredon, also playing a Tartar, was the ambassador to Vienna and a future procurator of St. Mark. The Indian Giacomo Marcello was a decorated general. His fellow Indian Piero Venier was procurator of St. Mark, a coveted lifetime position of influence in a city where real personal power was rare. The host, Giovanni Corner, was a Turk and his guest Ferdinando Gonzaga a Moor. Such were the heroes of Corner's masquerade, leaders of the Republic who dressed as enemies and infidels.

The singer's name was Cecchi. He walked to the center of the field to open the masquerade. The orchestra played, and Cecchi began:

> I am the Goddess who rules in the Orient.
> Where the day breaks forth and is born
> I am Goddess, I the Ruler,
> Where the sun sends her rays,
> I am Queen supreme.

The lyrics personified Venetian claims in the East, which, given the recent loss of Crete, probably struck spectators as some combination of defiance and reassurance. The text was steadfastly hortatory. In the fifth stanza Cecchi shifted to address spectators directly, urging them to imitate the actions of the Venetians before them.

> As they destroy the monsters with their swords,
> So shall you do the same with your countenance.
> No further delay, my victorious champions!
> The earth is destined to witness war.
> To battle, to battle! To war, to war!

And with that, riders mounted their horses to bear down upon the monsters, a series of carton targets mounted on barrels.[2] They moved with military precision in this vicious ballet. From opposite sides, first one by one, then two by two, and three by three, they attacked their victims:

> Having struck with his lance, the first cavalier performed a caracole and executed a turn as he drew forth his firearm, crossing paths with another cavalier from the other side who had just done the same. The second cavaliers took their turn, and, while the first went on to attack using firearms, they struck with their lances, and so on successively, so that when the first were wounding the beasts with scimitars, the second were striking with their firearms and the third with their lances. Thus were the six beasts each wounded at the same instant. In this manner the cavaliers were always either at full gallop, attacking, or turning to take another weapon.

Cecchi returned to the field:

> Now cease the battle, heroic equestrians,
> The arena is covered in blood,
> And the slaughtered beasts are your trophies of war.
> Leave off fighting, my dread cavaliers.

The riders answered Cecchi's song with a kind of victory dance on horseback as the orchestra and its mounted trumpeters played martial music. The riders came in groups of four that included a member of each "nation." As one group circled the track in close ranks, the others performed dressage in the center. The horses reared up on their hindquarters, executed small hops to bring all four legs off the ground at once, and traced out interlacing patterns at a gallop. As the orchestra played a stately piece, riders performed singly in succession. Then the musicians played a livelier air, and the steps were repeated with the "nations" united. A "beautiful confusion" reigned, marrying pomp with delight. It was a feast thrown by the elite for the elite.[3]

Corner's masquerade was a pantomime of violence with the bloodshed sublimated. But Cecchi's lyrics dispelled any doubt as to what the monsters had suffered. Spectators were well acquainted with blood-covered arenas from the city's bull hunts, and *giovedì grasso* regularly produced trophies of slaughtered beasts for its residents.

In earlier decades, Venetians had watched spring theatricals much like that of Corner's masquerade, but with the bloodshed real. A carnival masquerade in 1529 portrayed civilization's triumph over brute force. It started with the killing of six pigs and twelve bulls. Four young couples then mounted a stage in the center of the piazza and began a series of dances. Savages rushed in to seize the women, setting off a complicated series of steps that fell somewhere between dance and battle. The civilized youths brandished mallets, halberds, and shields. The savages carried rocks and primitive swords. Four savage women appeared, armed with weapons of their own. Eventually the captives were freed and the savages disarmed. The masquerade ended with the original couples and the redeemed barbarians dancing a happy tarantella together.[4]

A masquerade the following year featured Neptune, Mars, Mercury, the Sun, Hercules, Cacus, and Cerberus. Masked horsemen killed bulls and pigs, seven mythological characters danced an elaborate set of steps, and in the end Cacus and Cerberus were slain. The Venetian diarist Marino Sanuto wrote that it was "a beautiful thing to see." "The lengthy and varied dances, the sacrifices, and at last the deaths of Cacus and Cerberus." Sanuto also describes a bull hunt that was followed by a ballet representing Orpheus's return from the underworld.[5]

The animals slaughtered in such masquerades were among the season's many deaths, real and symbolic. In the early modern period, revelers in Venice and throughout northern Italy killed pigs, bulls, turkeys, goats, and bears. They personified carnival in the figure of a straw mannequin and devised ways to brutalize it. In Lombardia on *martedì grasso*, for instance, a dummy was burned in the main squares of towns. In the Marches, villagers hailed the incineration of a giant carnival puppet with wailing lamentations. In Friuli, effigies of carnival were pulled through villages as residents shouted, *To the wall with him!* Pulcinella and Arlecchino figures from the commedia dell'arte were sometimes the victims, with mock trials, charges, confessions, and formal sentencing. In the Italian Alps, Arlecchino's trial was followed by a crashing sword dance. Revelers shot, kicked, drowned, beat, burned, and bayoneted carnival effigies, all to unfailing hilarity.[6]

In Renaissance Rome, bloody bull hunts were a high point of carnival. For two days, processions took animals along the Tiber, through every neighborhood, and across the principal squares in preparation for the massacre, which usually came on Sunday. The site was St. Peter's Square, with the pope himself sometimes in attendance. In 1502, Cesare Borgia drew cheers when he killed a bull with his bare hands. An early description of these festivities gives a Christian gloss on the butchery. According to a canon at St. Peter's, the killings represented the death of the devil, pride, and lust so that participants might lead upright lives during Lent.[7]

The combined farce and bloodshed of carnival made such acts neither wholly tragic nor fully comic. In Monferatto, a town in Italy's Piedmont region, a turkey was borne into the main square in a cart pulled by six oxen. The turkey's head was secured to a post and its body hung free. One by one, youths on horseback galloped past and clubbed the torso, until the head broke loose, showering the victor with blood. The turkey's last testament was then solemnly read, which recounted the year's accumulated gossip detailing the villagers' vices, infidelities, blunders, and embarrassments. In death, the victim thus mocked his tormenters.[8]

Carnival was also the season of "wild man" hunts, which took place in the Pyrenees, German- and French-speaking Switzerland, the Italian Alps, Austria, and the eastern Czech lands. The belief that forests were populated by creatures who were half-man and half-animal fueled a yearly purgation. Although the hunts took various forms, a basic narrative prevailed. Youths chose or were chosen to blacken their faces, dress in leaves and vines or animal hides, and frighten their neighbors by rampaging through the community as if mad. In such disguises, "the performer regarded himself and was regarded as the living recipient of the wild man's power, in deed as the living wild man himself." They willingly endured the taunts and humiliations of their neighbors. Hunts were organized, captured men were put in chains, and public "executions" followed. The condemned ruptured small sacks of pigs' blood they carried as villagers fired blanks or made as if to stab them. Feigning death, the youths lay motionless on a bier and were carried through the streets. Some were thrown into lakes or ponds.[9]

The moresca, the sword dance that workers from the Arsenale staged every *giovedì grasso*, is a part of this history of ritual killing. The first European notice of sword dancing dates from 1350, although versions probably existed earlier. Some believe that the dance was originally part of a fertility ceremony for the land and all living things. As with other rituals of violence, it was staged most often during the carnival season. Its central ritual act, the folklorist Cecil J. Sharp writes, was "the killing and subsequent restoration to life of a man who, from the character of his dress and other considerations, represented, apparently, the animal world."[10] Choreographed fights and individual duels punctuated the dance. Dancers interlaced swords to create stars and other geometric figures, at times encircling a participant's neck in a simulated beheading. The "execution" was followed by a "resurrection," as dancers raised the victim aloft on their linked swords. In some versions, dancers blackened their faces to depict demons and other spirits from the underworld. Dancers sometimes enacted symbolic confrontations or transitions: between summer and winter, life and death, or the old and the new years.[11]

Even as it grew more refined, the dance's associations with battle remained. There was a reason for this. The moresca was by name a reference to the Moors. The dance spread throughout the Mediterranean world, from Spain to Italy and southern France. It appeared in many Italian cities during the Renaissance, often performed by elites: in Sienna during the 1465 visit by the Duchess of Calabria; in Faenza for the 1482 wedding of Galeotto Manfredi; in Ferrara for the 1502 marriage of Lucrezia Borgia and Alfonso d'Este; and on similar occasions in Milan, Rome, Florence, and Sicily.[12] It migrated to England and was danced on May Day by performers with blackened faces and bells on their feet. The English called it the *morisce, morisk,* and *moresco* before eventually settling on Morris dance. The final dance in Monteverdi's 1607 opera *Orfeo* is a moresca. The setting suits the oddly discrepant worlds the dance had come to straddle: high culture, sacrificial death, a return from Hades, resurrection.

When Venetians blackened their faces or wore masks to dance the moresca, it was at once an appropriation and an expulsion. Dancers mastered demons—or Moors—by impersonating them. The move was familiar in Venetian masquerade. Shortly after the 1683 Ottoman siege of Vienna, a battle that cost the lives of some ten thousand men, two rowdy masquerades with Islamic invaders swept through the streets of Venice. In the first, a group of noblemen and noblewomen posing as Moors in shiny fabrics and sparkling jewels wove its way to the courtyard of the San Lorenzo monastery, where there was a great ball with dancing and laughter. Later, twenty-four young patricians in Venice donned vaguely Eastern dress and danced through the streets to the sound of drums and whistles. In 1760, on the terra firma in Treviso, more than one hundred men and women donned the clothes of Turks, Moors, and slaves to stage, as a witness reported, "an agreeable spectacle with marvelous success."[13]

Such masquerades shared the spirit in which Corner and his fellow patricians dressed as heretics to show off their horsemanship. Here the masqueraders were costumed but not disguised. The message turned on knowing the participants' identity. And although the reversals were striking (Venetian-as-Moor, Christian-as-Moslem, master-as-slave, lord-as-subject), they involved no raucous humiliation, no mighty-shall-be-made-low carnival reversal. The costumers defeated their enemies by impersonating them. The displays were exorcisms staged as entertainment.

Venetian carnival, which staged power in a tightly choreographed spectacle, shared a number of these elements. As one observer had said, every detail pointed beyond itself to the larger story—in the battles of its armed dances and fireworks, in the military resolve of Hercules' Labors, in the victory of demolished wooden castles and the punishing justice of the slain oxen and twelve pigs. How such rituals functioned to bind and unify the community was possibly their most important feature, an element that was more potent and lasting in staging power than the words of Corner's singer Cecchi or the evocations of the defeated patriarch Ulrich on Fat Thursday each year.

One of the first scholars to study the communal function of carnival violence was Sir James Frazer, whose *Golden Bough* (1890–1919) brings together religion, myth, and magic under a single unifying vision. Criticized as patronizing and present-minded in his scorn for "primitive superstition," Frazer nonetheless set the terms for an anthropological reading of carnival.[14] According to Frazer, deaths staged in connection with carnival bear the stamp of ancient fertility rites. In "dateless antiquity," such killings did more than mark the turn from winter to spring by a lavish show of power. They were a magical rite to insure the revival of life. "Led astray by his ignorance of the true causes of things, primitive man believed that in order to produce the great phenomena of nature on which his life depended he had only to imitate them."[15] To Frazer, modern carnival was a mostly hollow echo of that primal violence, a last degenerate remnant of the barbarous past.

Frazer's conclusions rest on several interlinked assumptions. First, spring sacrifices were a symbolic murder of the "spirit of vegetation." By uprooting the feeble vines and plants, actions for which the sacrifices were a bloody symbol, primitive humans, ignorant of the seasons and terrified by winter's waning light, thought that they could hasten new growth. (There was a grain of truth in the thinking: pruning regenerates.) Second, confirmation of these rites' supposed success in longer days and new buds brought celebration and the experience of renewal in sacrificial death. Third, carnival was the direct successor of such celebrations in an unbroken legacy that still carried vestiges of ancient sacrifice.

As evidence, Frazer cites the agricultural associations of many myths. He believed that Dionysus was one embodiment of the spirit of vegetation. So were Osiris, Tammuz, Adonis, and Attis, all of whose followers commemorated an annual death and resurrection. "In name and detail the rites varied from place to place: in substance they were the same."[16] The cult of Attis in particular was for Frazer a principal source of carnival.

Born of a virgin, lover to the fertility goddess Cybele, Attis died violently to be reborn as a pine tree. From the third century B.C., Romans paid him homage in raucous celebrations each year on March 25. They went about disguised. Social roles were exchanged. Insolence and insult were common. The climax came as initiates underwent a rite designed to produce union with the god. As they crouched in a pit near the temple of Cybele, a bull wreathed in garlands and gold leaf was led to stand above them on a wooden grating. Priests advanced, prayers were offered, and celebrants slit the throat of the bull. "Its hot reeking blood poured in torrents through the apertures and was received with devout eagerness by the worshiper on every part of his person and garments, till he emerged from the pit, drenched, dripping, and scarlet from head to foot, to receive the homage, nay the adoration, of his fellows as one who had been born again to eternal life and had washed away his sins in the blood of the bull." The Roman poet Prudentius, whose graphic account Frazer has not embellished, also notes its significance to initiates. The worshiper—"dreadful to see"—comes forth convinced that the blood "has purified him while he was hidden in those shameful depths." The ritual took place where the Vatican now stands.[17]

The festival of Attis provides a chilling example of Frazer's view of the scapegoat. Such bloodshed did more than mark the turn from winter's sleep to spring's awakening by a lavish show of power. It was part plea and part prayer, a propitiation to God or the gods for the guilt of the community. It was as well an entreaty for blessings on the land and the expression of a common desire for purity, rebirth, and renewal. Frazer names societies in which the ill or deformed were made a scapegoat. But for Frazer, the more common agent of atonement was a divine victim. Rebirth was conceivable for believers if their god had also been reborn.

According to Frazer, Saturnalia was another source of carnival. Saturn was the god of sowing and husbandry. Romans pictured his mythical rule as a Golden Age, when crops were abundant, property was unknown, and all humans were equal. They celebrated his memory with a riotous seven-day festival. Frazer writes that during this period, slaves were freed, servants insulted their masters, the rich served meals to the lowly, and a mock-king issued absurd and willful orders. The population gave free reign to extravagant celebrations, in which "darker passions" found vent, the "pent-up forces of human nature" burst forth freely, and unbridled joy degenerated into "wild orgies of lust and crime." "The resemblance between the Saturnalia of ancient and the carnival of modern Italy has often been remarked; but in light of the facts that have come before us, we may well ask whether the resemblance does not amount to identity."[18]

There are, of course, similarities between this description of Saturnalia and European carnival. The main question is whether carnival is in essence a vestige of pagan fertility rites or an evolving tradition with different meanings and motivations. The late Spanish anthropologist Julio Caro Baroja believes that it is the latter. In *Carnival: An Historical and Cultural Analysis* (1965), which offers a wholesale critique of *The Golden Bough*, Baroja writes that the Christian calendar was stronger than pagan custom. Carnival's common denominator—a collective release before Lent—is anchored by the religious calendar, Baroja argues, but he goes on to say that any particular tradition is eminently local, varying from region to region and from one age to the next. Given the wealth and variety of carnival, Baroja doubts that any single concept—he had Frazer's spirit of vegetation in mind, but the same might be said of Bakhtin's carnivalesque—can meaningfully describe practices stretching over generations and across continents. And rather than seeing in carnival's violence a heritage of fertility rituals, he proposes a more immediate meaning. It is, he argues, a means of strengthening the social bond, which is expressed in a collective impulse to seek scapegoats. Carnival's particular practices, in other words, serve functions fitted to the community.[19]

To deny an unbroken line tying carnival to antiquity is not to ignore pagan precursors. There are clear correspondences between Roman festivals and later carnival traditions. Both marked the same changes in the season and on the land. Customs were inherited, adapted, and incorporated. As Baroja puts it, people worked, loved, rejoiced, and suffered much as they had before, even as they fashioned new habits. Such echoes and affinities do not depend on a legacy inherited from Saturnalia and other pagan rites. Carnival is self-generating, creative in its own right, and expressive of the needs and customs of particular communities.[20]

And yet the persistent violence of carnival is undeniable. Pigs, turkeys, goats, Corner's monsters, Pulcinellas, and "wild men" were killed symbolically or in actuality throughout Europe. In Venice, the blood of bulls flowed freely in ritual beheadings and hunts, and the charged symbolism of the moresca suggested human victims. The thirst to kill and to revel in cruelty exposes a dark, enduring undercurrent in modern hilarity.[21] Giordano Bruno, the astronomer who believed the earth circled the sun, was burned at the stake for heresy by the Roman Inquisition the day after Ash Wednesday, 1600. The timing was not exceptional. From the mid-1650s, Roman officials reserved public executions for the last days of carnival. In 1654, four criminals were hanged during the week before Lent. Revelers sang, drank, and danced around the scaffold. From the Middle Ages through the seventeenth century, Jews in Rome opened each carnival season to taunts as they were paraded down the Corso in red and yellow clothing. Later in the week, a "Jewish footrace," whose participants were made to run naked, traced the same route. Humiliating mock trials of Jews as Judas figures were staged to great laughter. To their perpetrators such acts were no doubt warranted, for the sake of "fun" or "justice." Combining the two, a unique prerogative of carnival, turned community bonding into bloodlust.[22]

The visceral energies that rose up among a population at such moments gives credence to the claims of some theologians that ritual violence is related to a fundamental human impulse that operates on both the collective and individual levels.[23] From as early as the ancient Israelites, major religions have acknowledged and sought to redeem guilt in ceremonies involving banishment or violence. While some symbolic repetition carries religious meaning within it (the blood and body of Christ in the Eucharist, for instance), scapegoating may persist without explicitly religious connotations. The differing inflections of words associated with it bear this out, turned variously as they are toward the deity, the wrongdoer, the victim, and the community: propitiation (to placate or appease an offended deity), expiation (to acknowledge one's sins and seek to have them cleansed), scapegoating (to load one's guilt onto another), atonement (reconciliation, harmony with others or between God and man, "at onement," as the earliest rendering of the word had it).

The collective and individual regeneration of the latter two terms, marked by the deadly blow and rush of blood, may endow the moment with something akin to religious experience in its terror, bliss, and awe before an irreversible act. Walter Burkert, a classicist who has studied the violent origins of myth and religion, reasons that this may explain how such rituals become "sacred" and self-perpetuating even in the absence of an explicit animating idea. "The fact of understanding is more important than what is understood. Above all, then, ritual creates and affirms social interaction."[24]

There is no evidence that Venetians consciously considered the slaughtered bulls of *giovedì grasso* as anything other than stand-ins for the renegade bishop and his twelve canons. Similarly, the monsters slain at Corner's masquerade affirmed prowess and valor on the battlefield. Nothing suggests that Venetians imagined their acts as a plea to an angry God, or a collective cleansing for the year to come, or the ritual sacrifice of scapegoats. The willful cruelty of the city's bull hunts was an entertainment. It was a show of skill and daring, a spectacle of power to foreign visitors, and an assurance to oneself of salutary hardness. As for the moresca, some Venetians may have mused about the epic struggle with Islam as they watched shipyard workers pound out the dance on *giovedì grasso,* but their thoughts were more likely on the dancers' skill and quickness. Some may have liked the idea of an enemy's head tumbling to the ground when the swords ringed a dancer's neck, but they probably just laughed, or fretted, to see a neighbor menaced so theatrically. Whatever they thought, they probably didn't take the moresca, or the bulls' destruction, or the equestrian ballet as a fertility rite.

But this does not mean that such spectacles could not bring a kind of rebirth. The elation in such moments was real, the participation renewing, and the solidarity it nurtured deeply felt. Revelers did not have to be mindful of the theology of propitiation to feel the shudder and thrill of collective action, repeated over centuries, that resulted in the loss of innocent blood. Nor did they have to know about the mechanism of scapegoating to feel satisfaction in the atonement such bloodshed offered. The deaths strengthened civic unity in a shared act of violence and regeneration. In many rituals, the threat was named and overcome. The priest and his canons were thwarted, the savages were civilized, the Moors and Turks were subdued.

These narratives were simple, but their function was fundamental: to bind together a community. The fierce condemnation of Michele Battaglia as a coward when he winced at the suffering of a bull was framed as a betrayal. He had disturbed the deep chords of community. *Everything that is dangerous, bloody, and tragic makes us fearless.*[25] This same impulse for solidarity in violence may account for the crowd's unsettling eagerness to continue with a bull hunt after the gruesome deaths of two women. The holy awe of such moments may also explain one observer's view that the day was "the very portrait of paradise on earth." The mocking jeers that greeted the animals were "venomous," he wrote. The last bull's beheading rendered all who saw it "ecstatic."[26] In Venetian carnival, the bloodlust and its atonement were channeled and contained, but nonetheless deeply felt.

Might this communal function and its associations both conscious and unknown explain the bizarre scene Denis Diderot described in the early 1760s? He relates that an acquaintance, coming into Piazza San Marco, saw barkers and commedia dell'arte actors on a makeshift stage and, a little further on, a priest standing on a plank holding a crucifix. The priest said: "Turn away from those wretches, gentlemen. The Pulcinella who draws you over there is a fool." Raising the crucifix and its dead Christ high above his head, he said, "This is the true Pulcinella. This is the great Pulcinella!"[27] Venetians probably sensed on some level that spring sacrifices—the bulls, pigs, turkeys, cardboard monsters, and puppets— were a ransom.

CHAPTER 18

Carnival Tales

Over the past few decades, the term *carnivalesque* has come to be short-hand for a theory of carnival set forth by the Russian critic Mikhail Bakhtin. Bakhtin's book *Rabelais and His World* was completed in 1940, published in the Soviet Union in 1965, and translated into English in 1968. According to Bakhtin, the ribald irreverence of the French Renaissance writer François Rabelais offered glimpses of authentic human freedom, a utopia still recoverable whenever carnival laughter unites the powerless in mockery and defiance. Since its publication, *Rabelais and His World* has become a field guide to the season.

Mikhail Bakhtin stands in an ongoing tradition of interpretation. The liberation he finds in the rites and passions of carnival is a stark contrast to Frazer and his followers, who saw in the season not emancipation but "a monument of fruitless ingenuity, of wasted labor, and of blighted hopes," as Frazer wrote.[1] Yet despite their opposing views, Bakhtin shared Frazer's premise that carnival could be understood under a single rubric. By studying carnival as such, both Bakhtin and Frazer comment on its human import across time, a perspective that has clear attractions. Whether the approach can describe the significance of carnival in particular times and places, however, is less certain.[2]

As a young man, Mikhail Bakhtin earned the distrust of Soviet authorities for his association with dissidents within the Orthodox Church. In 1929, he was arrested for private lectures in and around Leningrad. His sentence was six years' exile in Kazakhstan, where he wrote books on language and literature and, on orders from the state, taught courses in bookkeeping to pig farmers whose lands had been collectivized.

In 1940, Bakhtin submitted his doctoral dissertation, "Rabelais in the History of Realism," to the faculty of the Gorky Institute of World Literature. Seven years passed before the formal defense. In 1946, Stalin's chief party ideologist, A. A. Zhdanov, outlined the orthodoxy of socialist realism for artists and intellectuals, which called for the elevation of the masses through triumphant images that shunned anguish and uncertainty. As Czeslaw Milosz would later write, human suffering was drowned in the trumpet blare.[3] Humor was also suspect. Bakhtin's examiners criticized his emphasis on "the so-called folklore realism of Rabelais" and for dwelling on images "of a crudely physiological character." They deferred judgment on his doctorate. Four years later, a review board denied him the degree. The authorities' doubts were well founded. Although the dissertation described the vision of a writer living four hundred years earlier, its emphasis on the liberating irreverence of laughter spoke to the present.[4]

Rabelais and His World is wide-ranging, learned, and immensely appealing. It describes a turning point in European culture, when the language of the marketplace entered the sanctum of literature. For Bakhtin, the comedy of Rabelais, Boccaccio, Cervantes, and Shakespeare distilled a millennium of jolly oaths and insults. Bakhtin's term *carnivalesque* denotes humor that deflates pretense, embraces community, and celebrates life in its highest—and lowest—impulses. Nowhere is the carnivalesque more concentrated than in *Gargantua* and *Pantagruel,* Rabelais's two novels, in which laughter "asserts and denies, . . . buries and revives." Here the organic cycle of life, death, and rebirth is fed by hilarity. Topsy-turvy treatments of hierarchy, learning, and the sacred signify the destruction of the old and birth of the new. The verbal and physical abuse that appears in *Gargantua* and *Pantagruel* is creative and renewing—"steeped in merry time," as Bakhtin writes. The violence associated with the carnivalesque (Rabelais features bloodshed, dismemberment, burnings, beatings, blows, and curses) is, according to Bakhtin, essentially comic. Insult and injury imply fond praise.[5]

Bakhtin saw laughter in Rabelais's world as wholesome, hearty, and universal. This is a world where gigantic infants emerge from the womb preceded by a parade of sixty-eight mules loaded with salt, seven camels carrying eels, and twenty-five cartloads of leeks, garlic, onions, and chives. It is a world of mock-erudition catalogued in pitch-perfect Renaissance pedantry. Among the 139 titles in the monastic Library of St. Victor are

The Mustard-Pot of Penitence, The Fart-Puller of the Apothecaries, On Peas with Bacon (With Commentary), The Batwing Headgear of the Cardinals, Monkey's Paternoster, and *The Backgammon of the Banging Friars.* It is a riotous world of schoolyard pranks and cruel jokes—where a character plays a trick on professors, for instance, by smearing the streets outside the Sorbonne with a concoction of garlic, warm turds, and ooze from open sores.[6]

For Bakhtin, laughter gave power to the powerless. It challenged impregnable institutions, the "official, ecclesiastical, feudal, and political cult forms," as Bakhtin writes, that perpetuated their influence through ceremonies and spectacles. Laughter flattened hierarchies and allowed people to interact as equals rather than as rulers and ruled. Seen this way, the howls and indecencies, the obscene gestures and crude jokes, were not harmful or demeaning. "People were, so to speak, reborn for new, purely human relations. These truly human relations were not only a fruit of imagination or abstract thought; they were experienced. The utopian ideal and the realistic merged in this carnival experience, unique of its kind."[7]

According to Bakhtin, masks encourage and affirm what the carnivalesque reveals. In place of dogma, certainty, and a fixed order on earth, the carnivalesque offers a universe that is open-ended and forever in flux. In the clarifying light of a world inverted, truth becomes relative. Masks convey to all that rank is arbitrary and status is only skin deep. Masks wean their wearers from conformity to the self and blur the line between reality and make-believe. For Bakhtin, the metamorphoses of the carnivalesque and of masks are interchangeable.[8]

In hiding the face, masks also accentuate what all humans share. To Rabelais, nothing human was foreign, including the body's odors, urges, orifices, fluids, and functions. To put private parts on display—to render bodily life "grandiose, exaggerated, immeasurable," as Bakhtin puts it—is to celebrate the collective identity of creatures who drink, eat, copulate, defecate, die, and give birth.[9] It shifts the center of gravity down, away from "rational" or "economic" man. One chapter in *Pantagruel* offers 166 encomiums to the testicle (Shining ballock, Magisterial ballock, Shrewd ballock, Affable ballock, Thieving ballock, . . .). Another answers it with 171 aspersions (Sunburned ballock, Numbstruck ballock, Beery ballock, Disgusted ballock, Burglarized ballock, . . .). For Bakhtin, even the stuff of Rabelaisian insult is an affirmation of creation. "Excrement was conceived as an essential element in the life of the body and of the earth in the struggle against death. It was part of man's vivid awareness of his materiality, of his bodily nature, closely related to the life of the earth."[10]

Bakhtin's rhetoric in *Rabelais and His World* is immediate and encompassing. The tone is heroic, with descriptions often cast in the present. The effect is to convey a psychological state as much as evoke the distant past. "Everyone participates [in the carnivalesque] because its very idea embraces all people." "The individual feels that he is an indissoluble part of the collectivity, a member of the people's mass body. In this whole the individual body ceases to a certain extent to be itself; it is possible, so to say, to exchange bodies, to be renewed (through change of costume and mask)." "While carnival lasts, there is no other life outside it."[11]

This tone is consistent with Bakhtin's attitude toward historical instances of carnival. While he acknowledges that carnival has appeared in a variety of forms over time, Bakhtin also asserts that any particular carnival can be measured by the standard of the carnivalesque. This certainty grows from the dual conviction that Rabelais's affirming, leveling laughter revealed an ageless human essence and that carnival continues to be the reservoir of that laughter. Throughout the medieval and early modern periods, local feasts and rituals coalesced into what Bakhtin calls "classic carnival forms," a process of unification that "corresponded to the development of life itself." Although medieval charivaris, the Feast of Fools, and the Feast of the Ass disappeared long ago, Bakhtin writes, their identifying humor lives on during carnival.[12]

The effects of assessing historical events by an ideal type are evident in the disappointment Bakhtin voices about Goethe's *Italian Journey*. The poet landed in Rome at the height of carnival in 1788 and, according to Bakhtin, ignored its most important features. The "central philosophy" of carnival flourished during Goethe's lifetime and beyond, Bakhtin asserts. Yet Goethe reported no collective spirit, no affirming rebirth, no revolutionary moment. The fact that Goethe was describing an event two and a half centuries after elements of the carnivalesque appeared in Rabelais is "of no importance." Goethe failed to grasp the true meaning of what he saw.[13]

Bakhtin is not oblivious to history, but its influence recedes before what he takes to be the timelessness of the carnivalesque, where "the utopian truth is enacted in life itself." To consider carnival's essence as unchanging means that the reveler (or the scholar) can find its liberation in a variety of times, places, and manifestations. Its promise is permanent. The carnival spirit "offers the chance to have a new outlook on the world, to realize the relative nature of all that exists, and to enter a completely new order of things."[14]

This rhetoric held special resonance in Bakhtin's circumstances. Two authors of a critical study of his life and work note the irony and danger of writing about egalitarianism under a regime that employed coercion in its name. "In a time of authoritarianism, dogmatism, and official heroes, [Bakhtin] wrote of the masses as ebullient, variegated, and irreverent. At a time when literature was composed of mandated canons, he wrote of smashing all norms and canons and ridiculed the pundits who upheld them."[15] As with other tourists to carnival, actual or of the imagination, Bakhtin tells us as much about his own hopes as he does about the actual event.

Historians have not hesitated to apply Bakhtin's terms to carnival across the globe. Guido Ruggiero's *Binding Passions. Tales of Magic, Marriage, and Power at the End of the Renaissance* (1993) makes a strong case for their continuing relevance to Venice. The book opens with a vivid account of a confrontation during carnival in 1571. In Ruggiero's retelling, two unruly revelers, Zaccharia Lombardini and Giacomo Zorzi, dressed themselves as priests on *giovedì grasso* and went through the streets mocking the Church and taunting other maskers. One of them carried a broom, which he thrust about obscenely while calling out *Asperges me:* "Lord, sprinkle me." They invited a married lady named Letitia Parisola to join. She declined. Later they spotted her and her servant with four other maskers, all men and all in high spirits. They were outraged. They enlisted others to chase the group through St. Mark's as they shouted, "Kill! Kill!" The four men escaped, but Lombardini and Zorzi seized Letitia and her servant, held knives to their throats, and forced them through the crowded streets.

Lombardini and Zorzi were denounced, arrested, and brought before the Holy Office. Witnesses were called, testimony was heard, and the pair's status came out: Zorzi was a patrician and his friend Lombardini was a lawyer in the ducal palace. They were cleared for lack of evidence. Connections, power, and the tacit understanding that this sort of thing happens during carnival apparently were enough to acquit them.[16]

This is the first of five highly engaging tales Ruggiero has retrieved from the archives to illustrate what he believes is a historical turning point in Renaissance Venice. Natural urges that had before been given free reign were now increasingly "bound," that is, corralled, disciplined, and denied. The carnival context of this opening tale gives Ruggiero occasion to generalize, using Bakhtin's terms, about the period as a whole. Late Renaissance culture, Ruggiero argues, was beginning to turn from the carnivalesque toward a perpetual Lent that is modernity. The "late-carnival" scenes he describes—stories of prostitutes, corrupt priests, love potions, and witchcraft—are glimpses of unbound passions, exceptions to the increasing constraints in bodily desires that would take hold in the coming decades.

Ruggiero sees the carnival of 1571 as an affirmation of what Bakhtin called the folk-urge to mock institutions, defy orthodoxies, and construct its own set of shared values. Its significance lay in what it unleashed: unbridled sexuality, masculine assertiveness, the temporary unmasking of social power. It was "the season of festivities, when the passions and the flesh were unbound and ruled for a moment openly and when people came out into the streets to play at turning their world upside down." Zorzi's and Lombardini's threats were signs of freedom. "Rather than destroying all social organization, as the theories of the licit world would have it, [these passions] seemed to become themselves one of the organizing principles of a counter society and order with a history and at times a culture and values of its own."[17]

Yet one must ask just how liberating Zorzi's and Lombardini's carnival frolic really was. Their supposed priests' surplices were their wives' skirts turned backward, a silly costume to be sure but not especially cutting as a lampoon against the Church, if that was their intention. The others' costumes were not especially topsy-turvy. Letitia dressed as a market girl, and her companions, a merchant and three workers from the Arsenale, dressed as two clowns, a Turk, and a Spanish cutpurse. Little turned on the mask's anonymity. Two witnesses recognized the noble Zorzi; another identified Lombardini and knew his profession. Just before they held knives to the women's throats, Zorzi and Lombardini stripped off their costumes.[18] It is hard to see in this an upside-down world where the constraints were dropped by common consent and shared hilarity erased divisions. It was more likely simple jealousy that drove Zorzi and Lombardini. They look less like revelers than bullies avenging a slight.

Another way of putting it is that as soon as Zorzi and Lombardini saw Letitia with other men, the fun was over. They acknowledged as much when they took off their costumes. In an essay sharply critical of Bakhtin, Umberto Eco makes a similar point to question whether the carnivalesque can ever be genuinely liberating. His argument is this. The upside-down world of carnival is fundamentally comic, and by definition comedy is the violation of a recognized rule; without such rules, carnival is impossible; comedy and carnival are therefore authorized (as opposed to genuine) transgressions; and authorized transgression cannot be truly liberating. However much one might feel an indissoluble part of the collectivity in the midst of carnival's intoxication, life with its accustomed inequities and divisions will return to normal.

Eco classes the comedy of carnival as clownishness rather than satire (a point that Bakhtin also makes). If carnival risked real revolution, Eco writes, then "it would be impossible to explain why power (any social and political power) has used *circenses* to keep the crowds quiet; why the most repressive dictatorships have always censured parodies and satires but not clowneries; why humor is suspect but circus is innocent; why today's mass media, undoubtedly instruments of social control (even when not depending upon an explicit plot) are based mainly upon the funny, the ludicrous, that is, upon a continuous carnivalization of life." For Eco, in a genuine (as opposed to authorized) carnivalization of life, the comic evaporates as revolution takes over. Hilarity disappears and revolutionaries grow earnest. Eco's examples of the true carnivalesque are urban riots, violent campus confrontations, and political coups.[19] A historical example is the prohibition of masks during the French Revolution, which occurred by order of the government one year after the fall of the Bastille. Officials who had once skewered the king in high Rabelaisian style now expressed scorn for carnival as unworthy of free peoples. "The fun of carnival this year was all serious," observed the Parisian *Modérateur* in February 1790. In its denunciation of carnival the *Révolutions de Paris* wrote, "We are not buffoons." In a world of revolutionaries, sincerity replaces banter and ardor resists the mask.[20]

This isn't to say that carnival can have no unsettling social effects or that it is incapable of triggering political upheaval. Carnival's brand of comedy can be explosive, socially and politically. On such occasions, the task is to understand how features of its upside-down world lasted beyond carnival. The historian Natalie Zemon Davis looks to gender in addressing the question. According to Davis, sexual inversions in early modern carnival—men in dresses acting coyly, women in trousers acting mannishly—likely emboldened women to act out of station in more serious moments, to chastise husbands, rebuke priests, and stand up to local administrators. Davis does not embrace Bakhtin's sweeping claims of carnivalesque liberation. Role reversals were as likely to strengthen traditional hierarchies as weaken them, she observes. But carnivalesque reversals in early modern carnival may well have schooled women "to rise up and tell the truth."[21]

In cases of upheaval, the answer is not to call carnival in itself revolutionary but to seek the specific conditions that occasioned it. The 1580 carnival in the French town of Romans, expertly analyzed by Emmanuel Le Roy Ladurie, was such an event. The holiday fell at a time when major cleavages among residents in wealth, property, and tax debt threatened open conflict. Class antagonisms between craftsmen and wealthy merchants in the city, and peasants and landed seigneurs in the country, were high. Insurrections had broken out in the countryside, and manifestos proclaimed the people's right to rebel. When carnival protesters in 1580 targeted the moneyed elite, their reversals looked liked sedition. The response was deadly.

In the spirit of the season, local officials had posted a mock price list of foodstuffs, with turkey, pheasant, and partridge set at pennies and straw, oats, and hay priced exorbitantly. Given the tensions, the gesture was seen as a provocation. Craftsmen and peasants danced in their carnival costumes and sang that the rich were fat at the poor's expense. On Monday, rumors circulated that the populace planned to massacre elites. On Mardi Gras, violence exploded as armies wearing masks fought with knives and clubs in the streets. Battles in the days that followed claimed a dozen lives. Fifteen people were hanged as instigators. Six weeks later, violence in Moirans, some thirty miles to the northeast, killed between fifteen hundred and eighteen hundred peasants.[22]

Le Roy Ladurie calls the violence a pure expression of class struggle. He includes the episode in a series of antiseigneurial protests stretching from the Middle Ages to 1789. The will to rebel was already present; the threat of violence preceded carnival. With tensions high and the social order threatened, carnival lost its clownishness. The officials' price lists and the lower classes' mocking songs were standard fare and in most other years would have drawn laughter. But the mood in 1580 stripped the buffer of fun from the mockery. In such an atmosphere, the carnival's authorized transgression became genuine.[23]

Despite the upheavals he chronicles, Le Roy Ladurie views most carnival reversals as conservative, not utopian or revolutionary. The inversions he describes rely on and reinforce the dominant order. The commoners' taunts acknowledged the power structure, for instance, even if the holiday allowed them to pretend otherwise. The price list posted by elites was thought absurd only because all understood why meat was more expensive than hay. "If men exchanged roles during carnival," Le Roy Ladurie comments, "it was only to reaffirm the strength and permanence of the social hierarchy."[24] The assertion seems counterintuitive. Isn't mockery the purest form of defiance? Hadn't Bakhtin seen in it the essence of revolution?

Le Roy Ladurie notes that the only alternative to an upside-down world is one turned right side up. Reversals may shuffle the placeholders, but the structure of the status quo remains. Moreover, in depersonalizing positions, reversals clarify their function and underscore their necessity. As the anthropologist Victor Turner has put it, "Cognitively, nothing underlines regularity so much as absurdity or paradox." He continues:

> Emotionally, nothing satisfies as much as extravagant or temporarily permitted illicit behavior. Rituals of status reversal accommodate both aspects. By making the low high and the high low, they reaffirm the hierarchical principal. By making the low mimic (often to the point of caricature) the behavior of the high, and by restraining the initiatives of the proud, they underline the reasonableness of everyday culturally predictable behavior between the various estates of society.[25]

This describes how carnival can act as a safety valve. Fix the time and place for celebrations, the analogy goes, open the plug, and a year's worth of simmering resentments will spew out without causing major damage. Between the sixteenth and nineteenth centuries, illustrators turned out an unending series of reversals under the rubric of the world turned upside-down that, according to commentators, served this function. They touched virtually every category of experience, from sex roles and family duties to nature and the seasons. Women dress as soldiers and patrol the streets, men tend babies, monstrous rabbits roast hunters, mice chase cats, a chicken mounts a rooster, and cattle guide plows behind yoked men. "Their intention seems clear," write the authors of a survey of such images. It is "to show to all an order in which nature and society are solidly unchangeable." The reversals "dissipate subversion through amusement."[26]

The safety-valve theory helps to explain how carnival celebrations that seem subversive can leave the order undisturbed. The model does not deny genuine grievances. It acknowledges an appetite to challenge the power structure but assumes a willingness to return to it once the thirst for rebellion is slaked. This is what the medieval Feast of Fools and Feast of the Ass accomplished, briefly and at sanctioned moments: the exaltation of the lowly. The festivals, which flourished between the eleventh and sixteenth centuries, were largely a French phenomenon and clustered around the New Year. In late December, choirboys were given permission to chase church canons from their stalls and drape their elders' capes around their shoulders. One of them became bishop for a day, or was named the Pope of Fools, to be paraded through the church wearing the trappings of office. He did everything a priest would do except preside over Mass.

In the Mediterranean town of Antibes, Franciscan monks held their books upside-down, wore orange peels as eyeglasses, and blew ashes from the censers into each other's faces. In Paris, clerics wore masks, dressed as women, and played dice at the altar. In place of incense, the sanctuary filled with the smoke of old shoes set on fire. The feasts culminated on January 1, when an ass was led to the altar and, as congregants brayed, the clergy and choir recited a donkey's antiphon in mock-imitation of the psalms: "The Lord spake: *Hee-haw!*" "The Virgin spake: *Hee-haw!*" "The Holy Word is: *Hee-haw!*"[27]

Officials in Paris deplored the "pernicious and detestable corruption" of such displays, which "profaned the sacraments and ecclesiastical dignity." A church council in Rouen condemned priests for celebrating Mass in street clothes during the Feast of Fools and loading the altar with cured ham, cuts of beef, and bottles of wine. Jean Charlier de Gerson, the late-medieval theologian and rector of the University of Paris, sharply criticized the Feast of Fools ("things are impudently and execrably done that should be done only in taverns and brothels, or among Saracens and Jews").[28] But others realized their place. According to a defense issued by the Paris School of Theology in 1444, they functioned for the populace as venting barrels did for new wine. "All of us men are barrels poorly put together, which would burst from the wine of wisdom, if this wine remains in a state of constant fermentation of piousness and fear of God. We must give it air in order not to let it spoil."[29]

Letting off steam (or carbonic acid, as the case may be) prevents an explosion. A book on the Feast of Fools concurs. "To see in these scenes and games nothing but systematic criticism of the levels of power, wealth, and rule is to see too much from the outset. The spoof usually remained amusing—obliging, even—and any bitterness hid itself behind the guise of the happy fool. . . . Its displays [were] devised, planned, and performed in order to please, and were almost always without anything genuinely scathing."[30]

To consider moments of European carnival over the past five hundred years is to be reminded of the sheer variety of the season. Carnival may be spontaneous or scripted, harmless or explosive, disruptively seditious or decorously festive. It may stay within limits or violate them, and its transgressions may be authorized or genuine. It may let off steam in a burst of discontent or fizzle in the same tired routine. It may be used by the powerless to challenge authority or by the authorities to distract or divide the many. It may offer an occasion to deny or affirm one's roots. The particularities of history resist a universal description of carnival. Of special relevance are questions affecting life outside of carnival: how the church and state exercise authority, whether masks are seen only as a means of disguise or have uses not meant to conceal, and—of special relevance to the view that carnival liberates revelers from an attachment to the self—whether individuals believe that they can shape their own identities or are born into unchanging roles.

CHAPTER 19

The Mask of Sincerity

In the strange world of Venetian masking, where masks helped to preserve hierarchy by temporarily suspending it, the masking was by and large honest. Masks of course inspired acts of deception large and small. But their more common use was closer to dissembling than to feigning. Even for the Lauras of the city—the widow who sat alone in a café all afternoon—the mask was prudent and protective. It was "a veil of honest obscurity," as Torquato Accetto had put it in *On Honest Dissimulation,* rather than a cover for deceit.

Officials grumbled about the equalizing effects of the mask, but the threat they saw was not to identity itself. It was to proper public deference. They worried, probably for good reason, that the appearance of equality would undermine due subordination: of commoner to patrician, women to men, inexperience to wise seniority. Upon these unalterable conditions the solidity of the Republic depended. Masks might conceal identity, but they could not alter it.

This is how a population that embraced masks could abhor imposture. Grumbling about seeming equality was one thing. The outrage over those who assumed a false identity was something else altogether. To countenance masks while abominating imposture was no contradiction. Both grew from a culture that held one's essence as inalterable. Those who challenged that belief paid dearly.

In the early years of the eighteenth century, gamblers of the noble class across northern Italy began exchanging stories about a certain ostentatious stranger who was winning at cards with suspicious regularity. Judging by his dress—most especially the noble toga he wore—they presumed he was a patrician, some thought from Venice, others from Milan. The names he went by varied ever so slightly—Gerachi, Ghirardi, Rizzardi, Biccardi—and he occasionally added titles to them: *marchese, cavaliere, dottore, huomo d'honore.*[1]

Word spread that he was a master card shark. He was said to insinuate himself into noble circles with an easy manner and a quick wit. He won the players' confidence and cheated them of their money. He hid duplicate cards, doctored the deck with nicks and scratches, and paid hotel boys to produce tainted packs in the middle of games. Suspicions quickened when a former servant went public with what he knew. Letters detailing the gambler's trail of fraud appeared in Turin and Genoa. The servant, a man named Carlo Besia, also sent his accusations to a powerful Venetian committee, the Esecutori contro la Bestemmia, the Council against Blasphemy.

The letters stated Besia's case. Tomaso Gerachi was not a Venetian patrician but a commoner from Verona who disguised himself to seduce and defraud the nobility, Besia charged. In Milan he tried to pass himself off as a lawyer, distributing cards bearing the words *Dottore di Legge, Juris Consultus.* Elsewhere he called himself Don Tomaso, as if he were a priest. Besia called him an impostor, a man charming in success but violent when challenged. The council received other letters, among them complaints from the Venetian nobles Vetter Dolfin and Angelo Contarini, that Gerachi had cheated them. The evidence was enough to establish Gerachi's crime and launch a massive effort to track him down. He was guilty, the council wrote in its initial finding, "of counterfeiting his true essence to the shame of the sovereign law."

Today Besia's letters lie among other pieces of evidence in a bulging file of the Council against Blasphemy in Venice. Most of the files in the council's archive are thin and describe the same sequence of accusation, arrest, testimony, wholesale denial by the accused, and, more often than not, a guilty verdict. By contrast, the Gerachi file contains upward of five hundred manuscript pages of letters, pamphlets, notarized claims and rebuttals, and lengthy testimony from some twenty-three witnesses. Agents working for the Esecutori eventually tracked Gerachi down, and they duly crushed him with a penalty whose severity is still shocking. There is something disproportionate about what this fat file contains—about the zeal and determination to convict Gerachi, about the number of witnesses against him, about the sentence imposed, and not least about Gerachi's own unprecedented way of defending his innocence. Cheating alone doesn't justify the overkill. Gerachi's false titles and hollow trappings clearly touched a nerve.

Established in 1537 under the shadow of advances by the Turk against Venice's overseas empire, the Council against Blasphemy was charged with protecting Christianity against degrading words and actions.[2] Until then, the supreme authority in penal justice had been the Consiglio dei Dieci, the Council of Ten, established in the fourteenth century to guard against treason from within the noble ranks. As the powers of the Consiglio expanded and its domain widened, it spun off other bodies, including the Esecutori, to monitor the populace. The Esecutori's original jurisdiction was over all things that touched God, the Virgin, and "the celestial court." It was expected to "extirpate and eradicate blasphemers" in churches and other places of worship.

For the most part, the Esecutori prosecuted crimes committed only by nonnobles. By sending his accusations to this body instead of the Council of Ten, Besia underscored his point. Gerachi was no noble. Three men, nobles "of the highest conscience," served one-year terms on the Esecutori. According to its founding documents, it possessed "supreme authority to interrogate, attend, torture, sentence, and punish" the accused. It is a legitimate question to ask why a crime such as Gerachi's should fall under the category of blasphemy. One might also ask what exactly was criminal about "counterfeiting [one's] true essence," as the charge read. In Venice at the time, blasphemy was either "heretical," defined as actions or beliefs counter to the Church, or "ordinary," which described offenses against God. A tribunal of the Roman Inquisition in Venice heard cases of heretical blasphemy, while a secular body—either the Esecutori or the Council of Ten, depending on the status of the accused—heard cases of ordinary blasphemy. In accepting the case, the Esecutori determined that Gerachi's offense was against God rather than against the Church.

Gerachi was in his early twenties when gamblers began to suspect him. He was small and compact, and not especially a lady's man (although he did complain of suffering from the *male francese*). He was sophisticated, had a subtle intellect, and was unusually well read. One victim described him as "a Cicero with a deck of cards." He was also capable of ruthlessness. In a letter from Milan to a man who had not paid his debts, Gerachi wrote: "I tell you that I expect to be satisfied, or else I will do such things—things that cannot be written down—in such a manner, that the security of your family in Italy, I mean the security of your children, cannot be assured. Do not fail to reply to me immediately in Milan. I urge you not to give me any major occasion to demonstrate to you who Tomaso Gerachi truly is."

Who Tomaso Gerachi truly is. At this moment the council was urgently asking the same question. They received one answer in 1708 when copies of an anonymous pamphlet began appearing in the cafés and shops of San Marco. Its title, in bold letters, read, "THE INNOCENCE OF SIGNORE TOMASO GERACHI VINDICATED FROM THE IMPOSTURE OF CARLO BESIA." The pamphlet promised to tell the real story of the man. Until very recently, Gerachi had been a resident of Parma, where his family had immigrated after the Turkish conquest of Crete. At one time, the pamphlet continued in its third-person voice, Gerachi employed a servant named Carlo Besia, a coward who set out to destroy Gerachi's character in order to hide his own thefts. Besia had published slanderous letters in Turin and Genoa claiming that Gerachi was a swindler and impostor, that he had been banished from the Venetian domain on threat of arrest, and that his case was now being reviewed by the Council against Blasphemy.

This was calumny, the pamphlet said. Furthermore, Besia claimed that Gerachi was the illegitimate son of a washerwoman in Verona, born on the edge of a fountain in a squalid part of the city. This was not true: he was the scion of a great Venetian military line that had served for generations in Crete, the honored son of Captain Andrea Hiearchi and a Greek noblewoman named Giorgina Lugali, sister to the governor of the fortress at Lignano. His father died in 1692, the year of Tomaso's birth, and his mother raised him as a pious child in the bosom of the Church.

On the heels of this pamphlet came a second, certified by a notary public, which offered seven supporting items of fact about Gerachi's life, including a full account of why Besia nursed his vendetta. Gerachi had once caught Besia stealing his money, they fought, Gerachi bloodied Besia's nose, and he was on the verge of thrashing him with his cane when others intervened. The seventh item was the coup de grâce. It reported the text of a letter addressed to a priest in Milan written by Carlo Besia admitting that his accusations were false. In fear of the law and dread of divine justice, the sworn statement read, Besia disavowed his earlier letters and asked pardon of Gerachi.

It is unlikely that these two pamphlets were written by anyone other than Tomaso Gerachi. They are improbably vivid in the small matters and inadequate on the important ones. A tone of wounded vanity undercuts the third-person pretense. If the pamphlets were the work of Gerachi, he went to extreme lengths to clear his name, redeem his reputation, and avoid arrest. It would have been easier to stay quiet and keep away from Venice. Instead, Gerachi tried to justify his actions. The gamble proved fatal.

The first consequences came swiftly. Carlo Besia read the pamphlet and in December 1708 sent a longhand rebuttal to the council from Milan with more details. Besia wrote that he first met Gerachi in Turin, where, claiming to be of Venetian aristocracy and dressed as a patrician, he threw a lavish luncheon for local nobility. Besia was drawn to his energy and daring, and he accepted Gerachi's offer of employment. Gradually Besia learned his tricks and discovered his true origins as the son of a Greek prostitute in Verona. He began to fear for his safety and decided to leave his master. He had seen a copy of the notarized statement and categorically denied having renounced his letters.

Now others began to write to the council. A player from Milan reported Gerachi's fondness for gold medallions, which were no doubt stolen. Three players from Verona who believed they had been cheated described watching Gerachi replace the house cards with a pack from a leather pouch on his belt, which, on inspection, bore telltale marks. One said he knew for a fact that Gerachi's parents were not noble, adding that Gerachi degraded the very word *noble* by using it. His only legitimate titles were "thief, brigand, degenerate, and cheat." The Venetian noble Vettor Dolfin, also in response to the pamphlets, said that his trust had been "deceived by clothes and false appearances."

In early January 1710, Carlo Besia wrote to propose a dragnet. Gerachi would soon be in Venice for carnival, and Besia was willing to watch his former master's haunts. On the basis of mounting evidence, the Council of Ten alerted its agents. Besia wrote on the sixteenth to say that he had spotted Gerachi. Agents were advised. Three and a half weeks later, on the morning of February 12, Giorgio Aliprandi, captain of the Council of Ten's foot patrol, penned this triumphant (and meandering) report: "Pursuant to the course of the law, and after several days in the exercise of diligent service for the arrest of Tomaso Gerachi, finally yesterday at the twentieth hour it was my fortuity to receive him from my lieutenant, Captain di Gobbi, in the druggist's shop that faces the *calle del Ridotto* in San Moisè, wherefore, in which location, it transpired to him that he encountered the other, who, leaving the Ridotto with another masker, divided inside the said shop with this masker much money, that being the other with him, namely the said Gerachi, wearing a mask."

The Council against Blasphemy formulated its official charges against Gerachi after his arrest and began hearing testimony. Each new witness was eager to drive another nail into his coffin. Francesco Quinto testified to having met Gerachi in Venice, where he went by the title *gran cavaliere Milanese;* Giuseppe Melchior heard him call himself a *marchese;* Sebastian Antonii gambled with him as Marchese Tomaso Biccardi. On it went for twenty-three witnesses, who were questioned, in accordance with Venetian practice, without a representative present for the accused and before he could respond to the charges himself. The verdict seemed certain long before Gerachi presented his defense.

After considering the testimony, the council issued its indictment in five points: that Gerachi was a professional card shark; that he disguised his identity with false titles and noble clothes; that he associated with known criminals; that he was responsible for printing and distributing a pamphlet wrongly asserting his innocence; and that he had affronted the honor of Venetian nobles by cheating. The wording of the second count is noteworthy. Echoing virtually verbatim the earliest finding about his imposture, the council charged that Gerachi had "falsified his true essence, passing himself off wrongly as Marchese Rizzardi Milanese, Don Tomaso Gerardi, and Dottore."

In Italian, the indictment's key phrase reads, "il mentiva il vero suo essere." The accent falls only lightly on the false names and not at all on the clothes. The stronger emphasis is on Gerachi's "essence," as if the real crime were not against the city's statutes but against his own identity. That singular phrase appears on the cover of each thick register of testimony as well, noted in the hurried scrawl of the council's secretaries as a script for his interrogators. Ask them, the first question reads, "whether they have ever known Gerachi." Ask them, the second question reads, "if they know whether the accused referred to himself as the Marchese Ghiardi of Milan, thus falsifying his essence and his name."

Gerachi's defense comes in the form of a handwritten fifty-four-page document, which, like much else in this case, was exceptional in the council's proceedings. Where other statements begin with ornate flattery for the judges, Gerachi opens with a lament. He writes "from the dense shadows of a dark cell, in which I suffer." After questioning the motives of his accusers at some length, Gerachi moves to summarize the council's principal charge against him. It is, he writes, "that in availing myself of these various names I attempted to hide [*liquidandosi*] my crimes if not my own self as well." (One might as easily translate *liquidandosi* as "to destroy" or "to liquidate.")

He prepares his main point with a question. "What could be the crime in the change of a name that would bring the full force of Justice upon my head to paint me as a criminal and destroy me?" Merely altering a name could not justify this prosecution, he says. But here Gerachi takes an unexpected turn. He confesses to using false names, titles, and clothes, and, in the same breath, declares his unequivocal innocence. Yes, in Milan someone might have called him Don Tomaso, he writes, but that's a common title there. Yes, friends might have called him Dottore, but that's a minor matter. Yes, a few noblemen might have called him Marchese, but it was intended as a joke to deflate their own importance. Others addressed him by these titles, and he humbly accepted them. What was the harm in that?

With this light dismissal Gerachi comes to the heart of the matter, the question of whether he wore the noble toga. He writes:

> Clothes neither increase nor diminish the innocence and integrity of one's being. What good is dressing modestly if one is guilty? And what good are the most showy ornaments in covering the infamy of a criminal? Who isn't aware that in foreign cities one tries to dress with some distinction corresponding to the use of the city? I confess that in Milan, in Turin, and in other cities I dressed up a bit more than I usually do. But I can never be made guilty simply by my clothes.

Gerachi's answer to the council's charge changes its terms to hatch a paradox. He violated a law but is guilty of no crime. With this, Gerachi defies the principle on which the elaborate dress codes were built—that appearance mirrored social role—and rejects the related assumptions that yoked social role to individual essence. In so doing, Gerachi shifts the ground from attribute to intention—from the magistrates' criterion of innate essence (noble vs. commoner) to a standard of character (guilty vs. innocent). In the council's eyes, Gerachi's actions were wrong because he falsified his condition as a commoner. In his own view, Gerachi could not possibly distort his status, even if he did at times go by different names and dress in others' clothes. His identity was what he shaped it to be, not a fixed essence to be embraced, denied, or falsified.[3]

What brought him to this position? To have any success at all as an impostor you have to be believable, and to be believable, especially when you're lying, you must seem sincere. With a conviction refined by experience, Gerachi urged his judges not to ask whether he wore proscribed clothes or accepted false titles but instead to consider his character, which could never be made guilty by clothes. That might have been true in the abstract, but it was a thin reed on which to build a defense, especially since Gerachi gave no substantial reason to regard his character as pure. What he offered instead was a tone of sweet assurance that tried to convince with its ingenuousness.

Gerachi's fifty-four-page testament reveals the secret of all successful frauds, seducers, con men, and impostors: the mask of sincerity. Sincerity is not self-expression. It need not be consistent in its claims. It is as foreign to the principled earnestness of the nineteenth century as it is to our own time's demand for authenticity. In Lionel Trilling's classic definition, sincerity is "a congruence between avowal and actual feeling."[4] Gerachi was clearly lying about his identity to those he met—his avowals were at odds with his actual feeling—but the mask was apparently convincing. A little more than a century earlier, artists had pictured Sincerity with visible hearts and trampled masks (see figures 14, 16, and 17). In their terms, Gerachi's avowedly visible heart was a well-tended fiction. In claiming noble birth, he was a feigner through and through.

Challenges by impostors to hierarchies rooted in birth provide insight into the historical development of identity, since one effect of their tone was to assert a different kind of selfhood. Whether used to bear witness to the inmost conscience or to deceive shamelessly, the terms of sincerity assert the self as a legitimate authority against dominant beliefs, traditions, and institutions. Natalie Zemon Davis has written that boundaries of the thinkable self in early modern Europe were defined more by immediate circumstances than by any general consciousness of emergent individuality. (Davis had in mind the nineteenth-century Swiss historian Jacob Burkhardt, whose *History of the Renaissance in Italy* grandly announced the birth of the individual.) From within the constraining webs of religion, rank, gender, and community norms, Davis writes, "actors [made] use of what physical, social, and cultural resources they had in order to survive, to cope, or sometimes to change things."[5]

To survive, to cope, to change things. Also: to deceive. This is what Gerachi was attempting to do when he spoke with such seeming sincerity, first to his victims, then to readers of his pamphlets, and finally to his judges. He came to this particular tone as one of the few ways to achieve what in later centuries would be open to talent and unhindered by low birth—namely, social mobility, status, wealth, and power. In the nineteenth century, he might have been called a climber, a young man on the make, unprincipled perhaps but not a criminal. Depending on the company, he might have even been praised for his audaciously enterprising spirit. In Gerachi's testament, we see a new view of the self—as malleable, independent, and defined from within. The view would look increasingly familiar across Europe as the venturesome staked their claims against the privileged.[6]

Giacomo Casanova, who forged a series of identities consistent only in denying who he really was, comes to his readers wearing the same mask of sincerity. Ingenuous and immediate, Casanova seems to reveal everything, including his setbacks and humiliations, his illnesses and debilities, each time he was impotent, and the shame he felt when visiting prostitutes. Throughout the *Memoirs* Casanova repeats a single theme: that he was neither a seducer nor a deceiver. He writes: "I venture to say that I was often virtuous in the act of vice. Seduction was never characteristic of me; for I have never seduced except unconsciously, being seduced myself."

The fascination in Casanova's autobiography is how little this man's actions matched his declared intent. The denunciation that brought his arrest accused him of sorcery, irreligion, and dissipation. He quotes an enemy who has deemed him a counterfeiter and spy. His adventures provide instances of every charge. And yet he steadfastly asserts his innocence. Even as his stories change, Casanova insists that he was honorable and honest. Consider his defense of inventing the name Seingalt: "I assumed it because it is mine. . . . There is nothing more true than my name."[7] Casanova was a chameleon in a society whose colors were largely fixed. He was also more astute than Gerachi. In fabricating his serial selves, Casanova never claimed to be patrician, even if his tailored uniforms and ostentatious manner were nothing like the style of most commoners.

In the exquisitely imagined *Casanova in Bolzano* (1940), the Hungarian novelist Sándor Márai underlines the character's self-willed identity. "Venice is a city of miracles where everyone, even the street waif lurking among pigeon droppings by the campanile, can aspire to be an aristocrat," Márai's Casanova declares. "Mark my words, every Venetian is indeed an aristocrat, and you should address me with due reverence!" This Casanova follows "another law" that defies the petty norms of convention, a law "loathed by the guardians of morality but understood by the Almighty: the law of the truth to one's nature, one's fate, and one's desire."[8]

Gerachi and the historical Casanova both professed to act on the law of truth to one's nature. But Márai's Casanova was mistaken in one important respect. Every Venetian was not an aristocrat, and most commoners would have seen little use in aspiring to become one. The freedom to fashion an identity, an article of faith in contemporary discourse about the self, was unavailable to most Venetians of Gerachi and Casanova's century. It took privilege, wealth, and the gift of good birth to forge a future with relative autonomy, and even then the wellborn had responsibilities that limited their choices at every stage of life. To live solely by the law of one's nature was left to impostors, whom the state did all within its power to unmask and punish.

In Venice, rank was ingrained, and centuries of a virtually static hierarchy nourished the view that identity was immutable. The Venetian social structure was unique in all of Europe for its rigidity. Its patrician class was officially closed in 1297, with noble males constituting about 1 percent of the population. Patricians constituted a closed caste, which only the direst of crises could crack open. Ennoblement by marriage was strictly policed. Noble women who married nonnobles passed no nobility to their children. Nonnoble women who married patricians received noble status only after petitions were approved by members of the Senate and by ministers from the state offices of War, the Marine, and the Mainland. They had to be of legitimate birth, could never have practiced manual or mechanical labor, and were required to be free of any taint of "infamy." Any sons of such unions could sit in the Great Council and enjoy the privileges of nobility only upon further conditions: the woman's father or grandfather must not have dirtied his hands in the mechanical arts and her mother cannot have been "a servant, chambermaid, woman of the street, or of any other abject or vile condition." Intermarriages occurred, and through them came a measure of social mobility. But in most such cases, the ennobled women were born cittadine rather than commoner.[9] For the lowborn, the order was for all intents and purposes unchanging. One's social identity was fixed at birth.

Lacking conceivable mobility, most Venetians did not dwell on transforming their identities, even with a mask. A patrician's essence resided in the blood that flowed through his veins, in the political rights and functions he exercised daily, and in the family name preserved and protected by statutes that guarded noble descent. A commoner's "essence" was in the lack of such distinguishing qualities. In assuming noble clothes and titles, the commoner Gerachi went beyond wearing the clothes of another caste. In his accusers' eyes, he had attempted to alter a God-given quality. The charge of blasphemy begins to make sense.

In 1712, the Council against Blasphemy declared Tomaso Gerachi guilty as charged. It did not specify which offenses were decisive in its verdict. Perhaps we should take the crime of deception at face value and accept the unmasking. Gerachi was, after all, perfectly capable of taking others in. Polished, educated, able to cite the ancients and parrot the well-to-do, he executed his every encounter with consummate skill, mingling self-assurance and courtliness with indignation and sudden anger.

But it is fair to entertain another possibility. Might the nobles with whom he gambled have known all along that they were playing with a commoner? Aristocratic circles in Venice were small, elite families knew one another, and noble networks in other Italian cities could be easily consulted. Venetians were certainly practiced in scrutinizing the smallest details of a masker's appearance to discern his status. Gerachi's partners may well have subjected him to this same scrutiny, discovered his imposture, and played along for the sport of it. He had style, money, and an appetite for the game.

Rather than actually fooling his partners, the fiction would have licensed otherwise improbable games and provided players with plausible deniability in much the same way that masks at the Ridotto allowed patricians to rub shoulders knowingly with shopkeepers. As at the Ridotto, or when foreign dignitaries visited under false names, the ritual of disguise was perhaps sufficient. If this is what happened, then the discovery that Gerachi was a card shark was probably as decisive in instigating outrage as his noble clothes and sham titles. Cheating was a fundamental violation of the rules on which the temporary equality of gambling rested. More to the point, it was a brazen offense against aristocratic honor on the part of a commoner.

Whether Gerachi actually fooled his partners or was a participant in a more complicated ritual well known to Venetians, his punishment was tremendous: life in an unlit underground cell. In the notorious *pozzi*, the Venetian prisons where the water was often thigh-deep, this meant daily misery and eventual death. The severity of this sentence suggests that the case was about more than just a commoner dressing in a noble toga. That his prosecution came at a time when the noble order was under increasing strain surely worsened Gerachi's prospects. Perhaps the sentence was tinged with vindictiveness, a return in kind for his ignoble affront to the dignity of patricians. If council members at all registered Gerachi's attempts to shift the terms from appearances to intentions, they gave no explicit indication. But their insistence that the accused had falsified his essence was in itself a denial of the claims of character. That insistence was key to the political and social structure of eighteenth-century Venice. As representatives of a government built on unchanging identities, where social position mirrored essence, they had reason to worry when the self—with its pliancy, sincerity, and appeals to inner truth—became the touchstone.

CHAPTER 20

Carnival Contained

Carlo Goldoni's play *The Maidservants* is set in the waning days of carnival. Several domestics arrange to meet at an inn for dancing and a meal. Zanetta is the noblewoman Dorotea's servant, and she convinces Meneghina, a servant in another household, to join her and the others. Zanetta takes a dress from Dorotea's closet for Meneghina to wear as a costume. No sooner have the two masked maidservants entered the inn than they are greeted by the patrician Raimondo, who scorns his wife but dotes on his neighbor Dorotea. Recognizing her dress, he begins to sweet-talk and flatter Zanetta. It is the perfect opening for a carnival farce: the cocksure aristocrat is on the verge of embarrassing himself with a plebeian. But Goldoni plays it another way. Meneghina is terrified by Raimondo's advances. Scarcely able to speak, she rushes out of the tavern in a panic.[1]

Meneghina's response is consistent with Goldoni's other carnival plays, which include *The Party, One of the Last Nights of Carnival,* and *Hysterical Women.*[2] There is plenty of impertinence and manipulation, but the characters usually stick to their social roles, even when masked. As one of the world's leading Goldoni scholars, Franco Fido, puts it, characters "never lose their identity, just as they never lose their heads" during carnival. There are no moments of abandon or anarchic leveling, he writes. On the contrary, Goldoni retains the existing structures of rank and station in his carnival scenes. Carnival for Goldoni was not "an escape from social constraints" or "a permissive fulfillment of elemental impulses," Fido writes. Instead, its masks fostered "mingling and social integration" and brought "complicity or collusion based on the shared terms of servant and master."[3]

Goldoni affirms what his fellow Venetians reported: a carnival season full of high spirits and celebration but not fundamentally disruptive. In the eighteenth century, carnival was chaotic, crowded, exuberant, and ecstatic. But rarely were roles reversed or hierarchies inverted. Political defiance was seldom expressed. Religious sensibilities were largely respected. Pointed taunts and irreverent costumes were not numerous, and when they did appear they were challenged by other revelers. The identities of maskers were often known. With a handful of notable exceptions like the transvestites called gnaghe, carnival in Venice was conservative in both impulse and effect. In the eighteenth century, the carnival of Venice was not very carnivalesque.

One indication of the limits to social mockery during carnival resides in the long lists of costumes compiled during the season. They are notable for the absence of political and religious figures. The eighteenth-century *Codice Cicogna* lists some seventy different carnival costumes. Apart from two Jews (hardly a challenge to the powerful), there are no religious attributes—no false priests or bishops, no monks, saints, hermits, nuns, or popes.[4] Another daily chronicle of events in the city, the *Codice Gradenigo*, catalogues fifty-six carnival costumes its author had seen. Apart from a "Hebrew complaining about carnival," there are no religious designations. By far the bulk of eighteenth-century costumes consisted of tradespeople and fishermen, exotic foreigners, and commedia dell'arte figures. Giovanni Rossi, who filled 418 manuscript volumes with his recollections of the fallen Republic, noticed this, too. He wrote that the variety of costumes was limited only by the imagination, "provided one observes religious and political precautions."

Venetians were aware of their carnival's Janus face, its appearance of riot against a more sedate reality. Writing in the nineteenth century, Samuele Romanin described the paradox. "Saltimbancoes, Pulcinellas, marionettes, dancers everywhere—all of them as strange as the most twisted imagination might produce—comprised a single scene that appeared to parody the human intellect. . . . It was the time of madness, when all madness became forgivable; masks of every sort, of every style, so long as they weren't insulting to religion or the government. . . . And yet the truly admirable part of it was that in the midst of such throngs and disturbances, there wasn't an insult to a masker, not a theft, not an offense."[5] Romanin's glasses are indisputably rose-colored. During carnival there were insults, thefts, and offenses. But the general view is accurate if exaggerated, and it is far from Bakhtin's topsy-turvy utopia of human equality.

It isn't surprising that visitors mistook the tumult for subversion and the sheer force of numbers for social leveling. The memoirist Rossi took care to describe the several layers of the season, stressing by turns its seeming disorder, an underlying restraint, and its special kind of its freedom. "In no other place in the world did the people better keep within the bounds of order and tranquility in the midst of such uproar; in no other place did the mask give such liberty." Outside the carnival season, the mask fostered the same general qualities: respect among a mix of social orders, decency in public places, bounded liberty. This was the spirit in which the *Pallada Veneta* commended the "beautiful freedom" of carnival, whose revelers "know how to judge their pleasures honestly."[6]

Some discerned social segregation by costume. Antonio Lamberti, whose memoirs describe the final decades of the Republic, wrote that among plebeians one sees all manner of characters, including Sicilians, Turks, faux-gondoliers, thieves, and lawyers. But patricians and cittadini typically resisted such costumes. Rossi reports the same social segregation. Young nobles strutted along the *liston,* a fashionable area near the vast San Stefano church, like peacocks showing off their feathers, in the "most civilized mask," the tabàro and baùta. It wasn't exactly forbidden for commoners to walk there as well, Rossi writes, "but their education was such that commoners left the nobles their space in liberty."

Some also noticed separation by rank in Piazza San Marco. "Persons of status," Lamberti recalled, "did not circulate through the popular celebration." Instead, elites took one *brillante passagio* through the piazza—avoiding the throngs massed there if possible—and then retreated to their sumptuous dinners, the theater, or private balls. The *Gazzetta Urbana Veneta* reported that while nobles permitted themselves a mask and a certain liberty in speaking and responding during carnival, they avoided "uniting themselves with the plebeians in excessive transports of joy." Rossi put it more cruelly. Patricians absented themselves in the closing days of carnival "so they wouldn't have to mix with the dregs and the rabble." The English traveler William Bromley observed that wives and daughters were "seldom permitted to go in masquerade unless accompanied by their husbands and parents or other trusty person to watch over them," a judgment that sounds accurate given the degree of paternal supervision at other times of the year.[7]

Such reports speak powerfully against the notion that Venetians donned the mask, assumed alien identities, and acted out of station. There was at least one good reason for this. Even in carnival, masks did not always disguise. For six months of the year, Venetians were accustomed to going about their business in masks, whose function did not depend on concealment. The population of Venice was small in relation to other European cities, with about 137,000 residents in 1790 as compared to roughly 525,000 in Paris and close to one million in London.[8] The city's streets were narrow, its spaces were close, its neighborhoods a dense fabric of rich and poor, humble and elite. Venetians knew their neighbors by appearance if not by acquaintance. A single bridge spanned the Grand Canal. People squeezed by one another in the shop-lined Merceria; they took the air by the sea along the Riva degli Schiavoni or on the Fondamenta behind the towering church of SS. Giovanni e Paolo. It was an urban space that virtually obliged physical contact—a geography, as one scholar has written, that trained its inhabitants to display "a maximum of apparent attention and a minimum of real engagement." Neighbors knew who was noble and cittadino. They knew one another's occupations and trades. They recognized the character of a walk, the height and build of a body, the sound of a voice.

Part of the fun of carnival was therefore in guessing the identities of other maskers. If you couldn't place them or didn't know them, you could examine the small telltale signs that might reveal their status—things like the cut of the costume they wore or the quality of its cloth. So claimed the diarist Giovanni Rossi. "Not infrequently the clothes indicated the quality of the masker. In observing the clues to his condition, you examined the shoes, the stockings, and the gloves. No one observed as intently as then whether the woolen clothes of the masked and unmasked men were fine or coarse, brilliant or rough." The traveler Edward Wright noticed this in the theater, too. "Not a face is to be seen, but the chief Amusement is to find out, through the Disguise of the Masque, who such and such a one is, which those that are accustomed to the place can very readily do." A Venetian's account from the carnival of 1763 confirms Wright's intuition, identifying a group of about one hundred maskers as residents of the San Nicolò parish: "Nicoletti in various disguises, though known."[9]

To be sure, the devil's laughter rang during carnival. Some of it was promptly and effectively silenced by other maskers. At midcentury, two women exposed their "not small breasts" to the thick crowd in Piazza San Marco. According to an eyewitness, they were met with universal disapproval and took refuge in a café "to escape the jeers of a scandalized public." This was an example of the "civil police," a shared sense of what was and wasn't to be done, that one Venetian said was in force during the season. There was also the threat of arrest. In 1759, the carnival prank of two commoners ended with a night in jail. They had dressed themselves as government lawyers and gone through the piazza loudly criticizing the justice system and stopping in shops to levy fines for supposed infractions. They were accused of "impudence incompatible with the lower orders."[10]

There were cases in which revelers mocked their social betters, tweaking their pretensions and pointing up their officiousness. Nobles sometimes mocked the lowborn, too, as when well-to-do revelers dressed themselves in rags and went begging from café to café in the piazza. The agent who was watching them also records public outrage, especially over their rough way of demanding alms. He questioned whether begging was really something to joke about in a city with such visible poverty. Costumers who dressed as assassins received a similar rebuke in the pages of the *Gazzetta Urbana Veneta,* which called the costume odious and shameful.[11]

Such responses expose the sensitivities of those objecting, who believed that the behavior flouted decency, duty, or compassion. As for the revelers, the mischief found its target, which was of course the point. But exposed breasts or hilarity over the poor's struggles, however shocking or heartless, hardly threatened the status quo. Venetian maskers pressed beyond propriety during carnival, but they didn't press especially hard. There was little tolerance, and little apparent inclination, for genuine or sustained reversals.

Recalling carnivals late in the century, Giovanni Rossi said that however great the dissipation, some semblance of modesty always remained. "It did not displease the populace to unleash its hilarity, provided that religious and political subjects weren't touched." "Scandal was never carried in triumph." Antonio Lamberti commented on the piety of the Venetians at carnival's close. As midnight bells rang on Shrove Tuesday, revelers poured into parish churches, pulling off their masks to receive the ashes. No women were offended, and there were no thefts or injuries, which was proof, he wrote, of "the peoples' goodness and subordination to law."[12]

Are these reports to be believed? If so, what accounts for the overall sobriety during carnival they describe? The *Pallada Veneta* credited the paternal state structure. Elites carried a noble mien that had been refined over centuries, the newspaper explained. Part of that bearing was a perpetual cognizance of the example they set for their inferiors, which was present "even in the face of amusement." Clearly the author was not above flattery. The argument implied that commoners were like children who craved the approval of their parents. "The people take guidance from the example of the great. They do not give themselves to dissolution because they do not wish to lose the merit of imitating those who govern them. . . . This is why carnival proceeds with such calm. Certain to receive neither approval nor applause, no one has the courage to stir up a scandal in public."[13]

The social explanation for restraint during carnival is surely more complex. Common sense and the historical record contradict the description of a dutiful lower class looking above for its cues. Profligate and corrupt nobles are likewise not hard to find. But beneath the article's unctuous tone is an idea worth considering, one consistent with Goldoni's depictions of the season: that carnival revelers did not forget their social position when they put on masks. With little social mobility and a tradition that taught pious acceptance of one's God-given status, imagining oneself in another caste, even under the cover of a mask, could not have come naturally. The fate of the impostor Tomaso Gerachi demonstrates the power of a self-confirming worldview to enforce fixed roles, particularly when policed by the apparatus of the state. The city no doubt had other Gerachis and Casanovas, but most Venetians probably accepted the traditional view unreflectively.

Although acting out of station during carnival was not unthinkable for Venetians, its celebrations were not a testing ground for identities aspired to or under construction. This was not the case in eighteenth-century London, where commercial masked balls drew immense crowds from all ranks and the masquerade was a pervasive literary trope for the fluidity of position.[14] Benjamin Griffin's play *The Masquerade; or, An Evening's Intrigue* (1717) featured "a nobleman dressed like a cinderwench, a colonel of dragoons like a country rat-catcher, a lady of quality in Dutch trousers, and a woman of the town in a ruff and farthingale." In masquerade, as in much else, England was a bellwether for the continent. During the course of the nineteenth century, when the prospect of social mobility allowed an apothecary's son to imagine himself a stockbroker or a humble seamstress the bride of a businessman, carnival on the continent became a stage for auditioning one's "truer" self. The riotous Parisian masked balls of the 1820s and '30s were a measure of how disruptive this was to be.[15]

In Venice, the ruling elite openly discussed carnival as a means of strengthening the existing order. Pietro Franceschi, the government secretary who urged nobles in 1780 to mask themselves in theaters to avoid mixing too intimately with commoners, spoke forthrightly about using carnival to keep the lower orders happy. It was the only bright spot in an otherwise dismal accounting of the state of society.[16] Public festivities, Franceschi wrote, "have pleasantly diverted the thoughts of plebeians from more serious matters." Competitions between rival neighborhoods, moreover, have kept the populace "divided and balanced." Carnival events toughened participants for military service—here Franceschi mentioned the moresca and Labors of Hercules—but they also served a more immediate political objective. They distracted the populace from more serious subjects.[17]

The nobleman Giacomo Nani, who helped shape the debate over dwindling noble ranks, made a similar point without the Machiavellian undertone. Puppets, music, mountebanks, and masks were "useful means of keeping the populace happy and content." This view seemed only natural to the French traveler Maximilien Misson, who after viewing carnival observed that there was not much mystery in why the patriciate permitted this season of license. The monstrous Nero was also loved for the games he sponsored.[18] Far from calling carnival a threat, these officials welcomed it as a means of strengthening the established order.

From this, it is a short step to the safety-valve model that likens carnival to pressure cookers. An anonymous report from 1775 argued along these lines, although its terms were far less appetizing. Carnival and its pleasures are as essential to a healthy society as bowels are to the human body, the report observed. Close them off and waste will grow hard, clog the works, and damage the system. "Every civil society needs a sewer to drain its vices." Without carnival, "the Venetian people will have nowhere to meet and assemble, and when they cannot gamble, or mask, or dance. In a word, when they have nothing to do, only one great preoccupation will remain: to turn their eyes toward the government. And then . . ." The sentence trails off ominously. This was a train of thought, the author commented, that one shouldn't follow.[19]

Whether to dazzle, divide, distract, or purge, the carnival invoked in these accounts was not just domesticated. It was domesticating, an active means of keeping the established order intact. Judging by the responses of ordinary Venetians, at least one of these aims was met. Whatever else was in their minds during carnival, local maskers were not allowed to forget the might of the state. The centuries-old *giovedì grasso* tradition, which assembled the senators, judges, and heads of powerful councils to watch the festivities from their perch above, kept a potentially disruptive season firmly tied to the grandeur of the Republic.

There is little doubt that the state's intrusive presence touched the lives of citizens at other times of the year, as well. A visible reminder was the marble slots installed on public buildings in the 1670s, '80s, and '90s, which were meant to encourage anonymous reports of wrongdoing. (The only other places with such slots were Genoa and the Russia of Czar Paul I, who had been feted so lavishly in Venice with other "Counts of the North.") In the eighteenth century, internal surveillance in Venice was possibly more effective than ever before. With the apparatus for processing foreign intelligence in place long after overseas possessions had been lost, agents now focused on fellow Venetians. Conspiracy against the state was the ostensible threat. Few such plots were uncovered, but in the process of looking for them scores of so-called moral crimes were uncovered.

The perpetual threat of unnamed denunciation, made vivid by the slabs' grotesque face and gaping mouth, aroused the feeling that someone was always watching. Venetians reported on their neighbors for selling spoiled meat and bogus medicine, for mistreating animals, and for wearing fabrics or jewels forbidden by sumptuary laws. They reported on tramps and vagabonds, on charlatans and prostitutes, and on those whom they thought were atheists, adulterers, blasphemers, usurers, or sodomites.[20]

All credible charges were investigated, which helps to explain the legions of agents sent out by the State Inquisition and the large caseload heard by the Council against Blasphemy, whose jurisdiction in the eighteenth century had grown to include public indecency, sodomy, pornography, the rape of minors, and scandalous acts in sacred places. The more strident condemnations of Venetian justice as a despotism that denied basic rights to the accused—the future president John Adams's vision of "cruelty and assassination, which excite horror," for instance, or Lord Byron's "lazar-house of tyranny"—are misplaced. No Venetian was arrested without cause or condemned without due process, which included experienced defense attorneys and a rigorous review of accusations.[21]

Yet the reach of the law extended far into what later ages would call the private realm. The Council against Blasphemy's files are filled with transcripts of terrified citizens who had been snatched from the streets and were now insisting to magistrates that they hadn't eaten meat on Friday, hadn't cursed as their accusers claimed ("God's whore!" "Bloody Virgin Mary!"), hadn't deceived the girl and truly intended to marry her. In 1781, the council sentenced a man to three months in prison for living with a prostitute in the same dwelling as his child. In 1785, it sentenced a priest to three years in a dark cell for celebrating Mass while carrying condoms. The council was especially rigorous in prosecuting men who seduced women under the false promise of marriage. According to one study, it heard 125 such cases over the course of the eighteenth century and on most occasions ruled in favor of the plaintiff, which usually led to either exile for the man or matrimony. In the case of one Bartolo Fassetta, accused of having had sex with two women on the promise of marriage, the council ordered him to marry one and provide long-term financial support to the other.[22]

Vice and license were amply present in eighteenth-century Venice, which is what one would expect in a cosmopolitan port city with a flourishing tourist trade. But the prevailing spirit of the city, judging from the prosecution and sentencing of numerous would-be Casanovas, was far from the sexual decadence so often tied to the epoch. The debauches Casanova staged, which feed the image of a city lost to pleasure, do not typify the habits of the population.

The increased overall surveillance was one of the reasons why carnival in the eighteenth century was more contained than that of earlier centuries. The sudden appearance of state agents to arrest two commoners who dressed as lawyers to mock the profession suggests that surveillance was not suspended during carnival. But the restraint of Venetian carnival drew from another source as well. Ordinary Venetians called maskers to account for crossing a line of taste or offending decency. Presumably a tyrannized public, or one merely cowed before the glory of the state, would not enforce common standards on their neighbors so willingly. The "invisible restraint" a journalist noted during carnival went beyond the knowledge that masks didn't necessarily disguise one's identity. It expressed a general spirit of moderation among the population and the sense that carnival was not a transformative moment in which daily relations were remade.

The historian Peter Burke expresses skepticism over the supposed disorderliness of eighteenth-century carnival in Venice. He describes raucous celebrations of the Renaissance gradually yielding to restraint. For Burke, creeping commercialization drained the life and spontaneity from carnival. During the course of the seventeenth century, sacred pilgrimage gave way to tourism as a motive to travel, and Venice responded with what Burke calls "staged authenticity."

Professional merrymakers who stood to gain flooded into the city to sing, dance, act, tell fortunes, and sell cures. One modern estimate places the number of working Venetians at close to one in five who helped support the tourist industry in the mid-eighteenth century as hoteliers, innkeepers, café owners, and restaurateurs. At the threshold of the eighteenth century, a visitor calculated that some thirty thousand visitors came to the city for carnival. Peter Burke writes, "Venice was thus the pioneer in a process by which traditional festivals were replaced by permanent recreation of the modern sort."[23] The weight of foreigners deadened indigenous celebrations. Mistaking their own exuberance for that of their hosts, visitors pronounced carnival alive and well.

What then to make of the gnaghe, those men in dresses who preened and fought like cats in heat? Their inversions were overtly sexual, their language an irreverent assault on religion and morality, and their insults the crudest kind of leveling. Wasn't this an egregious example of carnival's reversals, with women mocked and love profaned? Gnaghe burst onto the scene in the last decade of the Republic and just as suddenly disappeared. In their defiance and outrage, they were an exception to eighteenth-century carnival. But their moment of fame, which offered everything scandal-seekers sought, is of genuine significance.

A series of laws dating back nearly four hundred years had punished the crime of sodomy with extraordinary brutality in Venice. In language that invoked Sodom and Gomorrah, legislation in the fifteenth century imposed the death penalty for those engaging in this "unspeakable and dreadful vice." The horrors one sodomite faced in 1552 were characteristic. Preceded by a herald broadcasting his sin, he was bound, tied by the legs to a horse's tail, and dragged through the streets to the Rialto, where his hands were cut off. He was then dragged to Piazza San Marco, where he was beheaded and burned.[24]

Lesser penalties included prison, the galleys, branding, whipping, and severing of the nose or ears. Over the next two hundred years, prosecution of sex between males continued, although the viciousness receded. Statutes defining the crime dropped the sin-drenched language; arrests for sodomy declined as those for blasphemy, illicit gambling, and petty theft rose; and corporal punishment for the convicted gave way to time in prison or as galley slaves. Explanations for this shift include a growing reluctance to explain catastrophe—the plague of 1630, for instance, which took forty-nine thousand lives, or the steady loss of overseas colonies—as divine retribution for unholy acts. At the same time, an economic crisis in the Ottoman Empire and the Thirty Years' War sent the Venetian economy into decline. Policing of "moral crimes" shifted to that of more immediate dangers such as theft and assault, which rose as conditions worsened.[25] None of this indicated a greater tolerance for sodomites, but the intolerance was growing less savage.

Profiles of 177 men arrested for sodomy in the seventeenth century reveal a range in status and occupation (27 nobles, 7 of middling rank, 47 from the lower classes, 49 clerics, 47 drifters). They also provide the types of offense, which included homosexual sodomy (13 percent), pederasty involving solicitation (6 percent), sodomy by force (43 percent), and sodomy with women (21 percent). The legal historian Gabriele Martini, who has studied these cases, finds evidence of significant numbers of "partners" among those in the first category, who engaged in consensual sex over a period of time. These included pairs "who emulated, at least in part, the prototypical heterosexual couple."[26]

This research points to an underground community of same-sex partners at a time when draconian punishments for sodomy were loosening. Is it possible that the men in dresses who danced and brawled in the late eighteenth century were not intending to mock their social or sexual opposites? Were the clothes of the gnaghe an honest disguise, a mask that told the truth according to their desires and in defiance of social norms? If so, their use of carnival's reputed liberty was ahead of its time in pointing to an age when greater numbers of revelers would use the mask to express more authentic selves.

In eighteenth-century Venice, such testing could be dangerous. The artist Grevembroch wrote that the shocking language and overfamiliar actions of gnaghe sometimes provoked violence. They were mocked, chased, and on occasion beaten. During festivities honoring a visiting German prince, the crowd turned on a single gnaga who was arguing from his boat on the Grand Canal with spectators near the Fondaco dei Turchi. Insults were exchanged, some threw stones and chunks of tile at the boat, and a Turk retrieved a gun and fired shots. The gnaga managed to escape. One detail from the account questions the notion that his cross-dressing was a carnival parody. The date was May 4, long after carnival had ended and a good three weeks before the renewed masking of Ascension.[27]

There was laughter in such moments, as there was in the ritualized violence that accompanied carnival in Venice. But its bloodlust showed few signs of the merry praise Bakhtin imagines. Its victims were identifiable, and the injury or humiliation they suffered was real, from the brutalized bulls and bludgeoned turkeys to Jews made to race naked down Rome's Corso or condemned in mock trials as surrogates for Judas. The laughter was not fondly inclusive. The abuse was not devoid of terrifying overtones.[28]

Venetian carnival in the eighteenth century fell short of the dissolute abandon foreigners described. It disappoints the modern view that sees in it a utopian moment of social leveling or mockery in inversion. Its supposed disguises were less sweeping and its confusions of class less wholesale than outsiders believed. Its festivity was real, but it was seldom uncontrolled. Its restraint grew from the combined effects of a state that policed the words and actions of its subjects and an overall reluctance on the part of citizens to defy the hierarchy or act out of station. Whether this reluctance stemmed from fear, approbation, or indifference is difficult to discern. Local maskers would have probably felt that same difficulty if asked to describe their restraint. Most, however, would have called their joy genuine as they watched their neighbors replay the script of Venetian domination on *giovedì grasso:* the butcher who felled the bull with a single stroke, the boy who plunged down the cable to deliver flowers to the doge, the nobles in robes who smashed wooden castles with their clubs, the shipyard workers who danced the moresca or performed the Labors of Hercules.

Venetian carnival was a spectacular instance of what the powerful states of Europe had learned to perfect using ceremony: the "sleight of hand" that disguised coercion and clothed obedience in glory.[29] But it was also the joyous production of a community in celebration of itself—segregated, divided perhaps, possibly distracted from the lofty concerns of governance and justice, but not strangers.

CHAPTER 21

Bitter Ash

When the nineteenth century dawned in Venice, the widow Laura's afternoon at the café Thistle seemed like ancient history. In a swift stroke, Napoleon had conquered the city with scarcely a shot. On May 12, 1797, under threat of imminent invasion and rumors of a planned bloodbath by Venetian revolutionaries, the Senate voted to dissolve the government. The Serenissima's millennium of proud independence was over. Before the next carnival, among the welter of decrees from the tumultuous first year of the new order, would come an edict banning masks in cafés, streets, and other public places. With this, the small piece of waxed carton, the inscrutable public face of Venice for more than a century, vanished as abruptly as the Republic itself.[1]

Napoleon's relentless drive through northern Italy had met little substantial resistance as city after city fell: Milan, Bergamo, Brescia, Mantua, Verona, Vicenza, Padua. When a skirmish in Venetian waters left a French commander dead, Napoleon seized the moment. An arrest warrant targeted the three State Inquisitors as the supreme authority. All other offices and magistrates were declared the "miserable instruments of [their] atrocities." He raged to stunned envoys that he would tolerate no "inquisitions." "Opinions must be free," he told them, "and I will liberate every man who has been detained for his opinions."[2]

Following the capitulation, the doge ceded authority to a sixty-member Municipality. Under the "protection" of more than three thousand foreign troops occupying the city, the body mimicked deeds from the

French Revolution's earliest days. Noble titles were abolished, a National Guard was established, and elaborately didactic civic festivals were staged. Among the first official acts was a patriotic luncheon that culminated with the planting of a Liberty Tree in Piazza San Marco, a ceremony repeated over the coming weeks and months in neighborhood squares throughout the city. Sometimes fasces were erected on either side of the trees. An explicit French borrowing from ancient Rome, the cluster of sticks symbolized strength through unity. Another official act commissioned six stonemasons to chisel all lions off the city's public facades as emblems of tyranny. When Venetians opposed to the new regime gathered in late July to protest, they were arrested. The Municipality then issued an edict formally outlawing opposition. It prohibited "incendiary" literature, forbade all acts of "insubordination," and criminalized the cry *Viva San Marco!* The penalty was death.[3]

Public discontent seethed. Crowds vandalized the shop of a printer who displayed images of a lion enchained by Liberty. The principal instigator of this act of protest, a twenty-four-year-old named Antonio Mangarini, was sentenced to death by firing squad. The presence of foreign troops led to brawls, which were sometimes fatal. For having caused the deaths of two Frenchmen, the authorities made an example of two Venetians, Giuseppe Marinato and Sebastiano Panadella. They were also executed by firing squad. When Nicolò Morosini, a military commander from an ancient noble family, published a letter harshly critical of the Municipality's direction, his property and possessions were seized, and he was banished for life. The case received considerable attention in the press, and the Municipality did its part to shape the story by publishing a decree that condemned Morosini's "nefarious talents against the fatherland" and declared him to be "a felon and an enemy." The decree was issued "in the name of the sovereignty of the people." It was clearly intended to silence other critics.[4]

Propaganda rewrote the past business of the Venetian judiciary from hearing criminal cases to terrorizing its population. Didactic engravings were commissioned that featured chilling scenes: a Christlike figure stands nobly to hear his death sentence, a manacled prisoner is dumped into a canal as a priest looks cooly on, wretches in fetid cells soak in seawater or swelter beneath the prison's lead roof. Pamphlets flooded public places describing the State Inquisitors as monsters and their deliberations as a chamber of horrors. One pamphlet, *The Mask Falls,* condemned "odious enemies of the fatherland" for their "pomposity, cruelty, ferocity, and inhumanity." Another, *Imposture Unmasked by Fact and by Truth*, called the malice of the aristocratic republic a sin against the sacred laws of nature.[5]

Over a period of six months, members of the Municipality replayed key moments from the French Revolution. It created a Committee of Public Safety, called for the nationalization of patrician wealth and property, and proposed a renewed Reign of Terror to intimidate conspirators and purify the population. The latter plan, which was not acted on, would begin with the mass arrest of former government officials and the execution of ex-aristocrats and cittadini.[6]

Taken together, the moves to demonize the ruling class and punish counterrevolutionaries made reforming the Venetian political system—and not the billeting of French troops, pillage of cultural patrimony (twenty paintings, five hundred manuscripts), or substantial transfers of arms and money to France—the main story. French and Venetian negotiators agreed not to make public these latter terms.[7] Napoleon possessed the ultimate secret, which staggered even his most ardent defenders. He held a tentative agreement, concluded before the Republic had fallen, to transfer a conquered Venice to Austria. In late January 1798, the French ceded the city to the Hapsburg throne, which nullified the ordinances of the Municipality, restored the rights of patricians, and, in the name of public tranquility and individual security, banned carnival and outlawed masks.[8]

Venice's past as a city of masks and its carnival tradition were easily recast to fit the narrative. Both were declared symptoms of the Republic's tyranny and marks of moral decline. Venice fell so suddenly because its extravagant pleasures, the mad orgies of a desperate people, had sapped the body politic of its vitality. Napoleon simply finished what the sickness had already begun. An official (i.e., Austrian-approved) newspaper account connected the dots, describing carnival as a poison that had infected its revelers and weakened their moral fiber. The language betrays morbid fascination.

> I still remember the immense, ever-swirling vortex of disguised, masked people in a thousand-thousand fashions and forms blocking every entry and obstructing every street with the clamor of bacchantes. Each access vomited forth this proud tumescent torrent into the vast magisterial piazza, the true marvel of the modern universe. I remember finally so many singers, players, and dancers all jumbled together, the endless charlatans, mountebanks, storytellers, and crooks that covered the piazza and the so-called Riva degli Schiavoni, and the inns crammed with foreigners and their banquets, feasts, and parties— in sum, an ordered disorder that delighted with the most surprising chaos of

sport and merriment that nevertheless harmed no one and made the carnival of Venice the first and most pleasing carnival of our mad hemisphere.

The writing is deft, discrediting the event without denying locals their remembered pleasures. A malign air of sexual disease hovers over the account. "To the consequent moral breakdown was added every physical corruption and misery, first convulsing and then destroying the delicious happiness now lost."[9] The city had tolerated its despots by chasing after mad pleasures, willingly distracted and oblivious to the decay.

Exceptions were eventually made to the decree banning masks, but only for the highly decent and closely monitored masquerade balls at the Fenice and San Benedetto theaters. Nearly twenty years after the decree, the press was defending it in vaguely patronizing terms. "It follows that after such an extended and dangerous illness—and even in its continuing convalescence—the patient cannot in full but only in part resume its habits."[10] The Ridotto, which had been closed for nearly seventy-five years, underwent substantial renovation to reopen in 1816 as a model of decorum. New lighting eliminated its dark recesses; marble columns shimmered in the new central hall; there was a restaurant for diners, a salon for conversation, and a large area for dancing. That year, it hosted seven balls in January and eight in February. High ticket prices insured that the participants were respectable. There were no reports of disorder.

Eventually the Austrians permitted popular carnival celebrations to resume, but they were policed to such a suffocating degree that the civic spirit known before the fall never returned. In its place was a weaker version, vapid, commercial, and staged primarily for wealthy tourists. Official accounts of carnival wear a forced smile for most of the nineteenth century, as bearded Austrians in top hats and greatcoats took the places of Venetians in mantles, masks, and tricorns. The descriptions conclude predictably. The population is happy, the festivities are at last decent, gratitude reigns.

Such is the history written by those who win wars.

Giandomenico Tiepolo offered an alternate eulogy for the mask that was not triumphant. His dark farewell to the Republic came in a collection of pen-and-wash drawings he called *Amusements for Children*. Despite the title, *Divertimenti per li regazzi* is neither simple nor innocent. The 104 images that make up the set depict a race of Pulcinellas living among ordinary Venetians. Their lives look much like those of other Venetians. They fall in love, marry, and raise children; they work as carpenters, tailors, barbers, and schoolteachers; they sing, drink, dance, and die.

Some deaths are not ordinary. Two are executed, one by hanging and the other by firing squad.[11]

Amusements for Children is the offspring of national collapse and personal withdrawal. It is also the unique product of a culture in which masking was widespread and not always festive. The masks of these Pulcinellas do not disguise or deceive. Their baggy blouses and trousers are not costumes. The strangeness of Venetian masking in the eighteenth century—its haunting blankness, its absurd coupling of hilarity with solemnity, its self-replicating uniformity—is captured in these drawings. In *Divertimenti per li regazzi,* Tiepolo extends the mask to all moments, public as well as private. Pulcinellas come into the world, go about their business, and are laid in the grave with their faces half covered.

Pulcinella was the one character of commedia dell'arte not to conform to a prescribed repertoire of roles. Some have supposed that Tiepolo chose the figure to stand as an Everyman in *Amusements*—"our *Doppelgänger,* our mirror or surrogate," as one art historian puts it.[12] In the collection, Pulcinellas are varied in the extreme. They populate all reaches of the social scale as masters and apprentices, schoolteachers and pupils, lords and tenant farmers, executioners and their victims. If Pulcinella is an Everyman, his pleasures and pursuits identify him as Venetian. Tiepolo's integration of this curious breed into the affairs of the city creates an uncanny sense of familiarity, as though commedia characters have finally managed to free themselves of the stage and are at last living as they wish. Like Goldoni, Tiepolo made these characters fully human, but in *Amusements for Children* he found a way to do so that was also faithful to the public face of this city of masks. In retaining their masks, Tiepolo sacrifices none of his subjects' dignity, individuality, or expression.

Tiepolo's Pulcinellas are likewise freed from commedia's degradations. They are passionate in love and high-spirited in play. They prepare meals with gusto and relish eating. They drink wine, doze, quarrel, and brawl. When they have to, they urinate or defecate by the roadside. They are not drunks, lechers, clowns, half-wits, or gluttons. They are not insolent, vulgar, or brazen, and there are no obvious displays of disobedience to authority. There is nothing demonic, or even particularly disruptive, about their masks or antics. A carnival scene, for instance, has two Pulcinellas on donkeys and a clutch of others dancing with banners and musical instruments. The mood is jubilant rather than raucous.

Their joy is full-throated and abundant. They link hands to dance with peasants in the country, clapping, prancing, playing pipes and tambourines. In a badminton match their glee is childlike; they carry the win-

FIGURE 31. Giandomenico Tiepolo, *At the Leopard's Cage (no. 38)*

ner on their shoulders in triumph. They marvel at the circus, and at the leopard's cage several speak at once, comparing observations (figure 31). The images draw a smile, but the humor is not easy to classify. There are few jokes at the Pulcinellas' expense, and they do not pull pranks on one another. Although distorted by hunchbacks and bulging bellies, the figures are not exactly caricatures. The exaggerations do not mock or deride. The public scenes lack Hogarth's scathing satire. Those with violence are far from the savagery of Goya. The elegance conveyed—in Pulcinella's wedding procession, for instance, or when Pulcinella escorts a masked woman—lacks Watteau's charm. A deliberate lumpiness in the images works against enchantment or sensuous delight. The line is tremulous, the shading splotchy.

Yet Tiepolo's mastery of bodily expression communicates human pathos, tenderness, and joy in situations that would otherwise be absurd. The effect both attracts and perplexes. A mother peers with wonder into the eyes of her baby-Pulcinella, masked and in swaddling clothes, who stares back intently at her (figure 32). Her Pulcinella-husband rests a protective arm across the chair and leans toward a visitor with pride and a little defiance. Only the dog is excluded from the group's interlocking gazes. Judging by his expression, he has already grasped what this means

FIGURE 32. *Pulcinella Swaddled in His Crib (no. 10)*

for him. (*Hangdog* in Italian is *cane bastonato,* "whipped pup.") Late in
the series, Pulcinellas work awkwardly to lower a dead companion into
the pavement (figure 33). The rump of one looms up; another twists his
torso and braces a foot to keep his balance. Three onlookers show more
fascination with the maneuver than sorrow. A young Pulcinella off to the
left—is he a son of the deceased?—has lost his hat in his grief.

An undertone of melancholy runs through *Amusements* and is present
even in the happy scenes. The overall mood is elegiac, a late-work sense
of leave-taking compounded by cultural loss. As one of the subtlest commentators on Tiepolo has written, the collection is "the disenchanted testimony of a dying society unaware of its own end."[13] Yet its moments of
anguish occur as if at a remove, lightened as they are by the masks and
attire. A Pulcinella has collapsed on a country road and others now gather
to comfort him. Pulcinella's sick lover vomits into a bedpan that he awkwardly holds for her. A dying Pulcinella, his hooked nose pointing toward heaven, receives the last rites. The Pulcinellas live with immediacy
and ardor, now dancing, now weeping, now flaring up in anger. Their delight is both ours and not ours. Their pain is real although felt from a
distance. The late Philipp P. Fehl, an artist and author who fled Vienna
as storm troopers swept the city for Jews, found both sweetness and ter-

FIGURE 33. *Burial of Pulcinella (no. 103)*

ror in these drawings. For him, they exhibit "the most significant use of poetry: the consolation it affords us by taking the measure of true things bravely, and with a wink."[14]

Tiepolo was seventy years old and living at the family's mainland villa when the Republic collapsed. His father, Giambattista, had died in 1770. For most of his professional career, Domenico had worked in the shadow of the elder Tiepolo, whose glorious rococo frescoes of saints and the holy family direct the eye upward: to pink-orange clouds, angels rocketing to heaven, martyrs clothed in blazing whites and silvers, and serenely imperious Madonnas. Domenico's works are mostly earthbound. His Mary and Joseph make their dusty way to Egypt. His saints endure agony. His *Stations of the Cross,* painted for the Oratory of the Crucifix in Venice's Campo San Polo when he was twenty-one years old, are emotionally raw. Christ stumbles through crowds of the beseeching and the indifferent. Lining the way are despots in their robes and turbans, brutish soldiers, affluent children, and Domenico's own plausible contemporaries, who look back at us helplessly from inside the frame. In Domenico's work, cruelty, ugliness, and banality defy—and at times sully—the pure. St. Stephen is martyred not by stones but by boulders dropped from

FIGURE 34. *Birth of Pulcinella (no. 1)*

above. A soldier braces a foot against Christ's leg to whip him. A bored dog stares off into the distance as Mary cradles her dead son.

In retirement, Domenico spent his days covering the interior walls of his villa with frescoes. Pulcinella is present in most of them, frolicking with a lover, strolling with country-folk, bunched in a tight group to watch acrobats leap and tumble. On the ceiling of a small interior room, a happy Pulcinella on a swing thrusts himself into the skies. *Amusements for Children* was drawn in this villa. Tiepolo likely began it sometime after the Republic's fall in 1797. It is not known when he finished the drawings or what his intentions for them were. In 1921, the set was shown publicly for the first time at an exhibit in Paris sponsored by Sotheby's. It was photographed and then auctioned off, print by print. Seventy-seven drawings survive in private and public collections; the other twenty-seven are unaccounted for. Although Tiepolo numbered the pages, the order defies any clear narration. The images are untitled. In the first drawing, Pulcinella is born in a stable from a turkey egg (figure 34).[15] A wedding follows, and a wedding feast. Then comes a courtship, and after that an infant. Is this the jumbled biography of an individual, or are we witnessing key moments from the lives of many Pulcinellas? The set's frontispiece

FIGURE 35. Frontispiece, *Divertimenti per li regazzi*

is mysterious. A marble monument set in a forlorn landscape bears the title, *Divertimenti per li regazzi* (figure 35). Before it stands a solitary Pulcinella clutching a doll that seems more alive than he. The monument could be a stage, or an altar, or a tomb. Is this an introduction to these lives or a desolate conclusion?

Read against the grim backdrop of events in Venice, the drawings reveal details rich in meaning. A third of the way into the set (no. 33), Pulcinella is taken into custody by officials wearing bicorn hats, headgear favored by the French as opposed to the tricorn, which Venetians preferred (figure 36). An unnumbered image (likely no. 34) shows Pulcinella in prison (figure 37). He holds a despairing hand to his head as a hooded woman speaks to him through the bars and a throng crosses the bridge before him. The busy action, which includes peddlers, women bending over a basket, a strapping lad with a pail on his head, and two idle or impatient Pulcinellas at the top of the bridge, distracts from what's happening in the far left. A local boy is trying to pickpocket a man in a bicorn.

No. 35 shows Pulcinella before a three-man tribunal (figure 38). A secretary reads an edict granting pardon as a jailer removes Pulcinella's shackles. One judge is fiercely resolute, a second registers disapproval,

FIGURE 36. *Pulcinella Arrested (no. 33)*

FIGURE 37. *Pulcinella in Prison (no. 34?)*

FIGURE 38. *Pulcinella before the Tribunal (no. 35)*

FIGURE 39. *Pulcinella's Farewell to Venice (no. 36)*

FIGURE 40. *At the Lion's Cage (no. 39)*

and a third shows sudden confusion or fear. The same hooded woman who appeared at prison and four Pulcinellas stand before the tribunal in bowed supplication, their cone hats deferentially removed. The next drawing (no. 36) suggests exile, as Pulcinella is embraced by a band of brethren on the quay before the prisons of the ducal palace (figure 39). Perhaps the four drawings are politically insignificant. This Pulcinella may be a thief or troublemaker. But no earlier crime is depicted. And what sort of regime arrests and imprisons a troublemaker only to pardon him grandly and send him into exile? One answer would be a regime intending to intimidate. The sequence evokes the fate of Nicolò Morosini, the former officer exiled for having criticized the Municipality.

No. 39 in the series, which immediately follows the visit to the leopard's cage, shows another group of Pulcinellas studying an animal, now in considerably different postures. Here an official in a bicorn and holding a pike points to a caged lion (figure 40). Its head is not visible, but its body looks scrawny and beaten down. A bird of prey waits above. The sentiments of six Pulcinellas are difficult to read. They are close-lipped, arguably distrustful or defiant, largely expressionless. A seventh turns out of the frame in what looks to be sudden grief. His posture is

FIGURE 41. *Pulcinellas Bring Down a Tree (no. 40)*

virtually identical to that of the boy who weeps as Pulcinella is lowered beneath the pavement in figure 33. The lion was famously the symbol of Venice. In the presence of occupiers, most locals would want to hide their thoughts or, if overcome with emotion, turn quickly away.

If the drawings beginning with no. 33 form a sequence, then the next two are defiant. In no. 40, a scene in the countryside, Pulcinellas bring down a tree as others lift their arms in triumph (figure 41). To the left stand two onlookers, one with a conquering foot on a bundle of sticks that resemble the iconic fasces of the French Revolution. An ax typically enwrapped in the cluster announced the terror of swift justice. Here a woodsman holds the ax. The symbols prompt a political reading: crowds cheer as Pulcinellas pull down a Liberty Tree and dismantle fasces.

The next image (no. 41) is a spirited scene in a tavern, where two Pulcinellas kick up their heels with drinks in their hands (figure 42). The same shirtless lad who crossed the bridge in front of the prison is here, still bearing a load on his head. On the back wall Tiepolo has drawn a robust lion of St. Mark's under two overlapping Vs. That piece of graffiti, then as now, sounds a cheer: *Evviva!* Together with the lion, it forms a rebus of the outlawed salute *Viva San Marco!* An earlier work by Tiepolo

FIGURE 42. *Tavern Scene (no. 41)*

gives evidence of the artist's changing intentions. It contains a substantially similar scene without the Pulcinella masks and clothes (figure 43). A single dancer hoists a glass in a tavern, with drinkers at a table to the left and a cellarer and casks on his right. A lion is pictured obscurely in the rear, near the steps. Moving the animal to the center and crowning it with double Vs turns the dance into a toast.

Domenico Tiepolo filled *Amusements for Children* with allusions to other artworks. One needn't identify them to sense incongruity: in the observing presence of turbaned foreigners, alone or in pairs; in the man and child who attend Pulcinella's burial in the pavement of Venice as if from another time; in a curious pair of miniatures before Pulcinella and his masked escort, as though Rembrandt's Blue Boy has come to life alongside one of Goya's *majas*. Near- or direct quotations add a cryptic layer to these drawings. The mother-and-son scene with Pulcinella in swaddling clothes resembles Giovanni Bellini's *Presentation at the Temple* (itself inspired by a painting of Andrea Mantegna). A wedding banquet of Pulcinellas restages Veronese's *Wedding at Cana*. A farmer-Pulcinella shovels earth in the exact pose of a worker digging a hole for a thief's cross in Jacopo Tintoretto's vast *Crucifixion*.[16]

FIGURE 43. *Tavern Scene*, 1791

FIGURE 44. *Execution by Firing Squad (no. 97)*

FIGURE 45. Jacques Callot, *The Firing Squad*

The two executions, both rich with allusion, come late in the series. The first is closely modeled on a scene from Jacques Callot's *Miseries of War* (1633). A blindfolded victim stands bound to a post with a heap of bodies off to one side as his executioners step into formation (figure 44). Tiepolo's modifications are worth noting. In the Callot print, the shot has just gone off (figure 45). We see a burst of smoke; a dog's tail stiffens in sudden interest. Tiepolo, by contrast, captures the instant before the shot. He replaces Callot's billowing plumes on the soldiers' hats with jagged feathers resembling a (Gallic?) rooster's tail. Tiepolo would have known about the execution of the Venetians Marinato and Panadella by a French firing squad in late December 1797, just two weeks before troops ceded authority to Austria.

In the second execution, a lifeless Pulcinella hangs from a noose (figure 46). A heavy mustache distinguishes the commanding officer, whose headgear has no rooster's tail. Near the foot of the gallows, amidst a mass of Pulcinellas, stands a boy who looks out of place in his glistening, square-shouldered doublet. His ears tilt outward. This boy is also present in Tiepolo's *Stations of the Cross,* seen from the back and gazing up as his mother speaks to Christ (figure 47). In Tiepolo's *Execution by Firing Squad,* a girl in the foreground hides her face and splays her fingers in horror. That same hand, with its thumb bent back and a wedge of shadow in the palm, rises above the heads of onlookers in his *Stations of the Cross* as Christ falls (figure 48).

The matches are not exact and are perhaps unintentional. But there are other echoes in the Pulcinella scenes from Tiepolo's depictions of

FIGURE 46. *Death by Hanging (no. 98)*

Christ that should be considered before discounting such similarities. The turbaned foreigners who appear on the road to Calvary are also witness to the two executions and other key moments in Pulcinella's life. The stance, hood, and turban of an observer outside the grate of Pulcinella's prison cell are virtually identical to Tiepolo's engraving of the seventh Station of the Cross, a reverse image of the painting (figure 49). The turbaned men are also present when Pulcinella is lifted high in triumph, taken into custody, whipped, and, after his death, viewed by mourners, a narrative (which necessarily omits and conflates) that retells the life and death of Christ from his entry into Jerusalem (figure 50). If Tiepolo meant *Amusements for Children* to carry intimations of divine sacrifice, this is how he would have accomplished it.

The frontispiece to *Amusements for Children* shares features with the engraved frontispiece to Tiepolo's *Stations of the Cross* done fifty years earlier. In the latter, a tomblike monument bearing the title is also set in a desolate landscape (figure 51).[17] Their attributes are of course different—in one, a toppled hat and discarded jacket, wine, and a plate of *gnocchi;* in the other, the cross, a rumpled cloak, the crown of thorns, and a

FIGURE 47. Station 8 from *Stations of the Cross*

FIGURE 48. Station 9 from *Stations of the Cross*

hammer—but both bear powerful witness to an absence. In one, it is the possessor of the jacket and hat. In the other, it is the man who wore the cloak and crown of thorns.[18] Both contain ladders, one made of planks and the other of rounded beams. The flat-planked ladder leans against the cross in Tiepolo's *Stations* to retrieve the body of Christ. The round-beamed ladder rests against the gallows in his *Death by Hanging* to cut Pulcinella down. It is also in the stable where, like Christ, Pulcinella was born (see figure 34, above).

In the late eighteenth century, a French traveler to Venice wrote that Pulcinellas proliferated in the city. He encountered them on the stage and in other entertainments, in paintings and literature, and especially among revelers during carnival. The procurator Marco Foscarini disapproved of these costumers' crude talk and weighed banning all Pulcinellas from Piazza San Marco. Pulcinella was also a favorite puppet in the city. In the 1770s, a government agent reported that children were imitating his vile language.[19]

In the urban dreamscape of *Amusements for Children*, Pulcinella also proliferates, but here he is far from the vulgar clowns these contemporaries

STAZIONE VII ·
CADE SOTTO LA CROCE LA SECONDA VOLTA .
Gesù ricade, e s'alza, e non si duole:
che nella Croce pur salvar ci vuole.

FIGURE 49. Station 7 from
Stations of the Cross

FIGURE 50. *Scourging of Pulcinella (no. 85)*

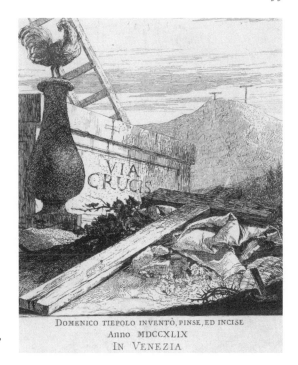

FIGURE 51. Frontispiece,
Stations of the Cross

knew. Tiepolo humanized Pulcinella by integrating him into civic life and
the attachments of family. This humanity brings a solemn, local cast to
Pulcinella's sufferings and especially to his death, whose intimations of
sacrifice lead us away from the irreverent flood of puppets and revelers.
The closer affinity lies with the "true Pulcinella" Diderot had reported
in Piazza San Marco, where a Venetian priest lifted a crucifix in the midst
of charlatans' stages.[20]

By conferring political and religious associations on a Venetian
Everyman, Tiepolo cast the fall of the Republic as tragedy. This was in
keeping with the ritual violence that marked the coming of spring every
year in and around Venice. Tiepolo probably knew that among those
ritually killed were effigies of Pulcinella. But there is one crucial difference that separates the recurring seasonal violence and the Republic's
immolation, which Tiepolo also understood. The demise of this carnival-
city carried no redemption. This death of carnival, Lent without end,
brought bitter ash.

The last image in *Amusements for Children* is horrific. Pulcinellas have
come to a tomb in what appears to be morning light as a skeleton bursts

FIGURE 52. *Pulcinella's Tomb (no. 104)*

hideously from the grave (figure 52). The decaying remains of another Pulcinella lie unburied. The living recoil in sudden fright, their arms raised in a tangle. The skeleton is in midair. His head turns back, but his toes have already begun to flatten against the ground. In a moment he will crash forward in a heap, his bones clattering across the rotting torso. There will be no resurrection.

After the Fall

Venice remains a city of masks. Masks greet visitors as they pour out of motorboats and buses. They line the vendors' racks just outside the train station and along the terraced steps of the Rialto Bridge. There are masks on sticks, masks with ribbons, masks glued to jewelry boxes. Tiny refrigerator-magnet masks are sold alongside the bottled water in small shops. Postcards show dreamy maskers in gondolas. Paintings at high-end galleries place them in moonscapes and snow scenes. Masks in Venice come in all forms: as bottle openers, brooches, pieces of porcelain, and objets d'art.

In a handful of workshops, carnival masks are still made by craftsmen. Their varieties are limitless, festooned with feathers, swathed in gauzy fabrics, bordered with a jester's fronds, topped with plaster hats or turbans. They may be a single color—white or dazzling gold—or elaborately painted with diamonds or arabesques. Some feature miniature scenes: St. Mark's by night, Pierrot serenading Colombine, a humanized sun embracing the moon. Some are inlaid with sequins, some fashioned from delicate filigree, and some cut as jagged leaves or crescents. There are double-faced masks of comedy and tragedy, Medusa masks with wreaths of snakes, masks with cherry lips pursed to kiss or spread wide in a joker's sly grin. There are unicorns, cats, birds, swans, and horses. Not many revelers are drawn to the eighteenth century's simple white *larva,* the waxed carton that permitted a city of unequals to go about their daily business with dignity and discretion. By comparison, this mask lacks character. It makes no statement.

Today's Venetian masks live up to everything we expect of them. Each is unique and there are so many to choose from! Modern masks come with a script. They evoke a self only loosely attached to its possessor. In ancient Rome, the mask was a *persona*, the outer shell actors wore to fix their characters. From *personāre*, "to sound through," the word originated in the belief that Greek theatrical masks amplified the voice. Today, personas—personalities, even—are a mask. The self, we tell ourselves, can be remade. Masks are an image of this freedom.

In the global imagination fed by travel ads and package tours, Venice generates a particular kind of fantasy. Whatever other attachments carnival suspends, it sanctions the urge to question one's identity. Modern revelers attribute that urge to the mask, forgetting or unaware that the article long predated such impulses. A twenty-first-century visitor to Venice describes her thoughts as she wandered masked through the city during carnival:

> A world of certainties is put on hold. I think this must have been always part of the charm of the Venetian Carnevale. Strange energies are released in a peculiar way. . . . [O]ne seems to meet forces within that nebulous entity that we like to think of as "the self," energies customarily involved in constructing what we call the "personality" but which now (briefly) do not have to manufacture a personality in the same way. . . . Once you have grown used to your "false" surface, you are less certain about the front you more ordinarily wear. The boundaries between subjective and objective are blurred or broken, for you become an object of your own gaze, and the mirror returns you a mask.[1]

Each age sees in the mask of Venice a reflection of its own face: its fears and convictions, its ideals and uncertainties, its passions and preoccupations. Our own vision is a product of the modern credo that stakes personal fulfillment on being true to one's inner nature. Its roots date to the early years of the twentieth century, when artists and intellectuals dreamed of liberating the self from society's unhealthy norms and expectations. This is from a book titled *Venice in the Eighteenth Century,* originally published in 1907. "To live carelessly, with no thought of the morrow, to be content with one's lot, to ward off the wicked onslaughts of melancholy, and to banish dull care as so much useless encumbrance, such was the aim of existence." The book's author, Philippe Monnier, describes Venetians as free to follow their desires without guilt or sin, whose pleasure-seeking inspired them to wear masks, and whose masks granted them what all humans truly want: genuine community. Here is Monnier's sketch of carnival, which he puts in the present tense.

There are no more lordlings now, nor beggars kissing their long sleeves; no more is heard of spy or nun, of *sbirro* or *zentildonna,* rope-walker or inquisitor, poor man or alien; there is but one rank, and one character, *Sior Maschera;* but one costume, and one free people, garmented, steeped, confounded in delight. A scrap of white satin on the face, a black silk hood upon the shoulders; and by virtue of this comic livery, the aristocratic city becomes a democracy; and the loose garb of Laughter levels all her sons.[2]

Monnier's Venice is of a piece with depictions from the belle époque, which were happy and carefree. Johann Strauss's 1883 opera *Eine Nacht in Venedig* is a frothy pastiche filled with waltzes and polkas. The visiting duke of Urbino is in love with the young wife of a doting and decrepit senator; she, however, fancies her aged husband's nephew. Inventing a tale to escape for the final night of carnival, she dresses a fisher-maiden in her own noble clothes, instructs the girl to amuse the duke, and slips off with her husband's nephew. Eros crackles just beneath the surface, and the couplings are most probably accomplished.

The opera premiered in Berlin in 1883 and played a week later in Vienna. For its Viennese audiences, the tolerant cosmopolitanism was a link to the Vienna of Joseph II and the Venice of Paisiello's *Il Re Teodoro.* The opera's open sensuality and willed superficiality keep the Republic's fall in an unimaginable future. Its placid setting not only leaps over more than a half century of Austrian occupation; it questions the reasons Napoleon gave for invading in the first place. The tone is cheerfully defiant of nineteenth-century mores. The duke's saccharine aria "Come into my gondola," which he sings to seduce the disguised fisher-maiden, is kitsch, to be sure, but it wears a knowing worldliness. *Eine Nacht in Venedig* offers a vision of carnival in which identities are inconstant and perhaps unimportant.[3]

Such depictions overturned an image of the mask that had held sway for most of the nineteenth century. The dominant narrative, put in place by Napoleon, cast Venice as a tyranny that harbored bloody crimes and housed a corrupt population.[4] John Ruskin assumed the tone of moralist in targeting the latter. Ruskin was disgusted by the indolence and irreverence he encountered. The idle and unemployed spend their days "basking in the sun like lizards," he writes. Their depraved children gamble and fight, "their throats hoarse with cursing." Such was the legacy of a civilization ruined by carnival. In *The Stones of Venice* (1851), Ruskin's contempt for the population is matched by a grim satisfaction in divine justice. "Mountebank and masquer laughed their laugh, and went their way; and a silence has followed them, not unforetold; for amidst them all, through century after century of gathering vanity and festering guilt, that white dome of St. Mark's had uttered in the dead ear of Venice, 'Know thou, that for all these things God will bring thee into judgment.' "[5]

Ruskin's mask of decadence was a variation on the view that linked the mask to despotism, a potent myth during the middle years of the nineteenth century. It appealed to crusading liberals who wished to show the backwardness of the Republic and to writers and artists who found in it rich material for villainy. The American James Fenimore Cooper combined both elements in his lurid novel *The Bravo* (1831). Here the mask is an instrument of tyranny and a shield from its atrocities. "Disguise was as often useful to the oligarchy of Venice," Cooper writes, "as it was necessary to elude its despotism." The book's nightmarish last scene takes place as revelers, numb with excess, watch a brutal spectacle. The Inquisitors have executed a poor fisherman for begging and framed a youth named Jacopo for his murder. Jacopo is to be beheaded during carnival. The doge knows of his innocence and has falsely promised him and his lover Gelsomina a last-minute stay.

Jacopo kneels at the block, a monk whispers prayers, and Gelsomina deliriously awaits a sign from the doge. The executioner brings down the ax, and Jacopo's head falls. "Take away this maniac!" says an officer, pointing to Gelsomina.

> The porticoes became brilliant with lamps, the gay laughed, the reckless trifled, the masker pursued his hidden purpose, the cantatrice and the grotesque acted their parts, and the million existed in that vacant enjoyment which distinguished the pleasures of the thoughtless and the idle. Each lived for himself, while the state of Venice held its vicious sway, corrupting alike the ruler and the ruled, by its mockery of those sacred principles which are alone founded in truth and natural justice.[6]

Cooper's image of the mask drew from a book published just after the fall, Pierre Daru's *History of the Venetian Republic* (1819). Daru was an *intendant* in Napoleon's War Ministry whose work narrates a tale of torture, stealth, flattery, and deceit. At the heart of the Venetian government, in Daru's description, was the three-member State Inquisition, which, like a malign spider at the center of its web, spread terror through "the capricious abuse of power . . . [and] the monstrous application of authority." The essential feature of its rule was the mask, an instrument of surveillance by the authorities and false comfort to their victims. It "seemed to authorize folly in the absence of liberty," Daru writes, adding that such appearances were deceptive. Despite the tide of foreign visitors and a semblance of festivity, Venice remained a silent city. "No green thing enlivened the view, no sound accompanied the movement." Menacing and mysterious, the mask cloaked all in the same sullen guise. It was a desperate response to tyranny, the last refuge of the oppressed.[7]

Lord Byron, who came to the city in 1816, consulted Daru's history in writing his two Venetian plays *Marino Faliero* (1820) and *The Two Foscari* (1821). In the latter, Doge Francesco Foscari is forced to preside over his son's condemnation for treachery before being stripped of his authority. Here the younger Foscari's wife denounces the system in terms that would influence a generation of Romantics:

> Your masked nobility, your sbirri, and
> Your spies, your galley and your other slaves,
> To whom your midnight carryings off and drownings,
> Your dungeons next the palace roofs, or under
> The water's level; your mysterious meetings,
> And unknown dooms, and sudden executions,
> Your "Bridge of Sighs," your strangling chamber, and
> Your torturing instruments, have made ye seem
> The beings of another and worse world![8]

Images of the Venetian mask from the end of the Republic to our own time reveal a sequence of singular visions, from tyranny to decadence to personal liberation. For Venetians before the fall, the daily reality of masking shared elements of these myths. Mountebanks laughed, maskers pursued hidden purposes, masked spies spied, and a kind of equality reigned. But no single myth from after the fall has captured the wide scope of what masking meant to Venetians in their last century and a half of independence. The myths' distortions and exaggerations, moreover, have served ideologies foreign to early modern Venice.

With a history stretching back to the thirteenth century, the Venetian mask was an improbable amalgam of ill-matched aims and associations. It was monstrous, raucous, obscene, and satanic. It was virtuous, face-saving, protective, and discreet. It meant solemnity, ceremony, and civility. It also licensed the raunchy and profane. It preserved identity and guarded hierarchy. It also eroded distinction and taught equality. It was the warrant of both privacy and openness in public places. It manufactured distance and inspired familiarity.

The Venetian mask's many faces were the product of separate strands that became enmeshed in the closing decades of the seventeenth century. Arlecchino's mask preserved his character across generations and taught audiences that the sins of the role need not be visited on the actor. His mask asserted identity while denying personality. Political dissenters and religious minorities refined dissembling to an honest response. Their mask defended rather than distorted truth. The virtuous prince's Reason of State distinguished between masks that falsified and those that merely omitted. His mask did not have to mean deceit. Women's veils and beggars' masks taught that covering the face could protect dignity without disguising the features. Their masks were conservative. Incognito notables and diplomats learned that going unacknowledged did not mean going unknown. Their masks signaled distinction. These associations shaped the practice of masking outside the carnival season, and, when carnival came, they tempered its license.

The same rigid social structure that prompted masks in Venice's theaters and cafés bounded the imagination of its residents. The worldview it sustained was especially resistant to the notions that make Venice and its masks so alluring today. Under such constraints, exceptional individuals fashioned masks of false names and fraudulent titles to push beyond the limits of their own status. Some succeeded, but for those who did not the punishment was harsh.

There was much about Venetian carnival that remains familiar. Happy maskers filled restaurants and theaters; they crowded into boats and sang out greetings from balconies; they romped, danced, and skipped through Piazza San Marco. Strangers spoke freely, inhibitions fell, and mockery was more often jolly than cruel. But there was also much that seems strange and even shocking. Animals were brutalized, parents put their children at mortal risk to take flowers to the doge, hunts continued after spectators were injured or killed, and throughout the city Venetians ate the flesh of bulls beheaded before the assembled citizenry. In the past, carnival led Venetians to celebrate what they held in common in spite of implacable divisions. Its violence was an essential part of that affirmation, as were the feats and dances that recalled a victory hundreds of years earlier. Venetian carnival emphasized a shared identity, rather than one questioned or contested.

Today, Venice's warren of streets leads carnival revelers on an inward journey. Its masks obscure former certainties in a widening circle of doubt, suspending civic and communal ties, denying recognition to others, and blurring the border between the real and the unreal. Modern masks feed the belief that identity is a performance and the self can be refashioned by its possessor. In this, they recall a moment more than two hundred years ago, as a gondola made its way from a convent on Murano to the teeming crowds near St. Mark's. Inside it was a reveler who spent his life fashioning his own identity. For Giacomo Casanova and a handful of extraordinary spirits like him, living in the perpetual present was the masker's prerogative. To us such freedom is within reach. For most of his contemporaries, masked and unmasked, it was inconceivable.

Notes

The following abbreviations are used in the notes:

A.M.A.E.   Archives du Ministère des Affaires Etrangères, Paris

A.S.V.   Archivio di Stato, Venice

B.C.P.   Biblioteca Civica, Padua

B.F.Q.S.   Biblioteca della Fondazione Querini Stampalia, Venice

B.M.C.   Biblioteca del Museo Civico Correr, Venice

B.N.M.   Biblioteca Nazionale Marciana, Venice

m.v.   *more Veneto,* or "Venetian style" in dates

PREFACE

1. Gasparo Gozzi, *L'Osservatore Veneto,* 3 vols. (Milan: Rizzoli, 1965), 1:175–76 (article dated April 29, 1761); Jean-Jacques Rousseau, *Émile, ou de l'éducation* (Paris: Garnier frères, 1964), 271; Oscar Wilde, "The Critic as Artist," from *Intentions,* in *The Complete Works of Oscar Wilde,* 4 vols. (Oxford: Oxford University Press, 2007), 4:185.

2. Stephen Greenblatt, *Renaissance Self-Fashioning: From More to Shakespeare* (Chicago: University of Chicago Press, 1980); Natalie Zemon Davis, *The Return of Martin Guerre* (Cambridge, MA: Harvard University Press, 1983), and *Fiction in the Archives: Pardon Tales and Their Tellers in Sixteenth-Century France* (Stanford, CA: Stanford University Press, 1987); Charles Taylor, *Sources of the Self: The Making of the Modern Identity* (Cambridge, MA: Harvard University Press, 1989).

CHAPTER 1. CASANOVA'S CARNIVAL

1. Giacomo Casanova, *History of My Life*, trans. Willard R. Trask, 12 vols. (New York: Harcourt, Brace & World, 1966–1971), 4:51.

2. Ibid., 5:184.

3. Ibid., 7:92.

4. Ibid., 4:80–84. Casanova's account of his affair with C. C. appears in 3:235–85.

5. "Mémoire pour servir d'instruction au Sr. abbé de Bernis, comte de Lyon, allant en qualité d'Ambassadeur de Roy auprès de la République de Venise," September 9, 1752, in *Corréspondance politique, Venise*, vol. 214, fol. 51, A.M.A.E.; Franco Venturi, *Settecento reformatore*, vol. 5, *L'Italia dei lumi*, pt. II, *La Repubblica di Venezia (1761–1797)* (Turin: Einaudi, 1990), 158.

6. On *casini* in the eighteenth century, see Giuseppe Tassini, *Feste, spettacoli, divertimenti e piaceri degli antichi Veneziani* (Venice: Filippi Editore, 1961), 135–38.

7. Giovanni Comisso, *Agenti segreti di Venezia, 1705–1797* (Milan: Longanesi & Co., 1941), 93.

8. Edward Wright, *Some Observations Made in Travelling through France, Italy, &c. in the Years 1720, 1721, and 1722*, 2 vols. (London: Tho. Ward and E. Wicksteed, 1730), 1:86.

9. Casanova, *History of My Life*, 4:103.

10. Ibid., 9:353.

11. Ibid., 11:58.

12. Ibid., 4:152.

13. Ibid., 4:83.

CHAPTER 2. NEW WORLD

1. Francesco Gemelli Careri, *Viaggi per Europa*, 2 vols. (Naples: Felice Mosca, 1722), 1:50.

2. Maximilien Misson, *Nouveau voyage d'Italie, avec un Mémoire contenant des avis utiles à ceux qui voudront faire le même voyage*, 3 vols. (The Hague: Chez Henry van Buldereu, 1698), 1:239.

3. Casimir Freschot, *Nouvelle relation de la ville & république de Venise* (Utrecht: Guillaume van Poolsum, 1709), 405; "Folega," in Giuseppe Boerio, *Dictionario del dialetto veneziano* (1856; reprint, Florence: Giunti, 1993), 278.

4. Quoted in Bruce Redford, *Venice and the Grand Tour* (New Haven, CT: Yale University Press, 1996), 57–58. John Eglin provides an excellent overview of British travelers to Venice in *Venice Transformed: The Myth of Venice in British Culture, 1660–1797* (New York: Palgrave, 2001).

5. Misson, *Nouveau voyage d'Italie*, 1:246.

6. Abbé Coyer, *Voyage d'Italie*, 2 vols. (Paris: La Veuve Duchesne, 1776), 2:79–80.

7. Stephania Bertelli, *Il carnevale di Venezia nel Settecento* (Rome: Jouvence Società Editoriale, 1992), 21.

8. Françoise Decroisette, *Venise au temps de Goldoni* (Paris: Hachette, 1999), 168.

9. Ibid., 170.

10. *Codice Cicogna*, n.d., 2991-II, 55, B.M.C.

11. "It is permitted to mask oneself not only in *bahute* or domino, but in every fashion, and in the clothes of particular characters. Nevertheless, I observed everyone wearing the same uniform." Joseph Jérome Le Français de Lalande, *Voyage en Italie*, 9 vols. (Paris: Chez la Veuve Desaint, 1786), 8:507.

12. *Codice Gradenigo*, February 16, 1756, 3:60, B.M.C.

13. Misson, *Nouveau voyage d'Italie*, 1:245.

14. Wright, *Some Observations Made in Travelling through France, Italy, &c.*, 1:86–87.

15. Comisso, *Agenti segreti di Venezia*, 173.

16. March 15, 1732, in Slava Klima, ed., *Joseph Spence: Letters from the Grand Tour* (Montreal: McGill–Queen's University Press, 1975), 95; *Codice Gradenigo*, February 17, 1759, 5:119, B.M.C.

17. Fabio Mutinelli, *Lessico Veneto* (Venice: Giambatista Andreola Editore, 1851; reprint, Arnaldo Forni Editore, 1985), 54.

18. Samuele Romanin, *Storia documentata di Venezia*, 10 vols. (Venice: P. Naratovich, 1861), 9:15–16.

19. *Pallada Veneta*, January 23–30, 1739 (m.v.). Until the late eighteenth century, Venetians dated the new year from March 1 rather than January 1; "m.v."— *more Veneto*, or "Venetian style"—designates this use. January 23–30, 1739 (m.v.) was recorded elsewhere as January 23–30, 1740.

20. Daniele Concina, *De' teatri moderni, contrari alla professione Cristiana* (Rome: Pasquino, 1755), 242.

21. *Gazzata Urbana Veneta*, January 26, 1788, no. 28, 1:61.

22. Wright, *Some Observations Made in Travelling through France, Italy, &c.*, 1:97.

23. Giacomo Nani, *Principi di una amministrazione ordinata e tranquilla* [1781?], 59, 118, B.C.P.

24. Nuove machiaveli
    le parla de politica
    al casin, al café
    sul leto e sul bidé,
    le fa novi sistemi,
    le xe legistrici,
    le giusta la republica
    le puza i senatori.

    Angelo Maria Barbaro, *Poesie Veneziane dell'abate A.M. B.*, quoted in Bianca Tamassia Mazzarotto, *Le feste veneziane* (Florence: Sansoni, 1961), 132.

25. *Inquisitori di Stato*, February 14, 1743 (m.v.), B. 914, A.S.V.

26. Comisso, *Agenti segreti di Venezia*, 123.

27. Ibid., 124–25.

28. Klima, *Joseph Spence*, 95.

29. *Inquisitori di Stato, Riferti dei Confidenti*, January 18, 1788 (m.v.), B. 611, A.S.V.; Comisso, *Agenti segreti di Venezia*, 276–78.

30. Comisso, *Agenti segreti di Venezia*, 279.

31. Ibid., 274.

32. Girolamo Lioni, *Inquisitori di Stato, Riferti dei Confidenti,* January 18, 1788 (m.v.), B. 611, A.S.V.

33. Comisso, *Agenti segreti di Venezia,* 276–77.

34. Angelo Tamiazzo, *Inquisitori di Stato, Riferti dei Confidenti,* February 6, 1782 (m.v.), B. 634, A.S.V.

35. Girolamo Lioni, *Inquisitori di Stato, Riferti dei Confidenti,* February 2, 1785 (m.v.), B. 611, A.S.V.

36. Chi vol goder un nobile sollazzo
vada in Piazza la sera a spassizzar.
Lè se vede el gran mondo messo a chiazzo,
el Lusso, e la lussuria tripudiar.
[. . .]
Chi vol veder un mondo allegro, e bello
vegna la sera in Piazza a spassizzar,
che i vederà su e zo, qua e là zirar
mille donne, che fa tirar l'osello.
Subito che le vien in sto bordello,
ghe scomenza la mona a sbocchizzar,
e, come el pesce alza la testa in mar,
cussì le fa vardando questo, e quello.

Giorgio Baffo, *Poesie di Giorgio Baffo, Patrizio Veneto* (Milan: Arnoldo Mondadori, 1991), 317.

37. Alexandre Toussaint Limojan de Saint-Didier, *La Ville et la république de Venise* (Paris: Chez Guillaume de Luyne, 1680), 368, 346.

38. Karl Ludwig, Freiherr von Pöllnitz, *The Memoirs of Charles-Lewis, Baron de Pollnitz,* trans. Stephen Whatley, 4 vols. (London: Daniel Brown, 1737–38), 1:411–14.

39. Joseph Addison, *Remarks on Italy* (1705), in *The Miscellaneous Works of Joseph Addison,* 2 vols. (London: G. Bell and Sons, 1914), 2:58.

40. Careri, *Viaggi per Europa,* 1:51.

41. Quoted in Redford, *Venice and the Grand Tour,* 56.

42. Ange Goudar, *L'Espion chinois, ou l'envoyé secret de la cour de Pekin, pour examiner l'état présent de l'Europe,* 6 vols. (Cologne: n.p., 1765), 2:169, 3:87.

CHAPTER 3. EVEN ODDS

1. Un logo dove ognuno pol zogar
el zechin, el filipo, el ducatelo,
no il se podeva per tal uso far
più nobile, magnifico e più belo.
Ne l'atrio gh'è la dea che invigilar
ch'à un volto in man e alegra invidia a entrar,
in maschera per altro, e questo e quelo.

Anon., "In lode del Nuovo Ridotto," quoted in Mazzarotto, *Le feste veneziane,* 132.

2. Lorenzo da Ponte, *Memoirs,* trans. Elisabeth Abbott (New York: New York Review of Books, 2000), 34.

3. Misson, *Nouveau voyage d'Italie*, 1:243.

4. Limojan de Saint-Didier, *La Ville et la république de Venise*, 371.

5. *I pettegolezzi delle donne* (1751), *Il vecchio bizarro* (1754). Carlo Goldoni, *Mémoires*, in *Tutte le opere*, 14 vols. (Milan: A. Mondadori, 1935–56), 1:293; Goldoni, "L'autore a chi legge," *Il vecchio bizzarro*, in *Tutte le opere*, 5:354.

6. Wright, *Some Observations Made in Travelling through France, Italy, &c.*, 1:87.

7. Comisso, *Agenti segreti di Venezia*, 120.

8. Da Ponte, *Memoirs*, 31.

9. *Consiglio dei Dieci, Comune*, August 27, 1703, R. 153, A.S.V.

10. Voltaire and Diderot, cited in Alexandre Stroev, *Les Aventuriers des lumières* (Paris: Presses Universitaires de France, 1997), 66–67, 196.

11. Pietro Garzoni, Βάσανος *cioè Paragone usato da Pietro Garzoni, Senatore sù la Repubblica di Venezia per fare prouva della sua qualità* [1725], 227, B.F.Q.S.

12. Giovanni Dolcetti, *Le Bische e il giuoco d'azzardo à Venezia 1172–1807* (Venice: Aldo Manuzio, 1903), 73. Garzoni relates that reversal of the ban on masks came after the appointment of new members to the Council of Ten (Garzoni, Βάσανος *cioè Paragone*, 227).

13. Andrea Degrandi, "Problemi di percezione e di rappresentazione del gioco d'azzardo," in Gherarado Ortalli, ed., *Gioco e giustizia nell'Italia di Comune* (Rome: Viella, 1993), 111.

14. Jonathan Walker, "Gambling and Venetian Noblemen, c. 1500–1700," *Past and Present* 162 (1999): 29, 56.

15. Comisso, *Agenti segreti di Venezia*, 48–49; *Inquisitori di Stato*, May 5, 1742, B. 560, A.S.V.

16. Cesare Biliotti, *Il Ridotto* (Venice: Pietro Naratovich, 1870), 15–19.

CHAPTER 4. BLOOD SPORT

1. Wright, *Some Observations Made in Travelling through France, Italy, &c.*, 1:88; Giorgio Busetto, "Le Opere del Bella," in Giandomenico Romanelli et al., *I Mestieri della moda a Venezia dal XIII al XVIII secolo* (Venice: Edizioni del Cavallino, 1988), 335–41.

2. *Codice Cicogna*, 1688, 3277–VIII, B.M.C.

3. Mazzarotto, *Le feste veneziane*, 1–4.

4. *Codice Cicogna*, 1708, 2991-II, 73, B.M.C.

5. *Relazione distinta in cui si dà piena contezza di quanto seguirà nel di 17 del corrente Febbrajo 1767* (Venice: Gio. Battista Occhi, 1767), n.p.

6. [Michele Battaglia,] *Cicalata sulle cacce di tori Veneziane* (Venice: G. B. Merlo, 1844), 30–31.

7. *Relazione distinta*, n.p.

8. Wright, *Some Observations Made in Travelling through France, Italy, &c.*, 1:90.

9. *Codice Cicogna*, 1688, 3277-VIII, B.M.C.

CHAPTER 5. FAT THURSDAY

1. Roberto Cessi, ed., *Seu Venetiarum (Chronicon Altinate et Chronicon Gradense)* (Rome: Tipografia del Senato, 1933), 26.

2. Giorgio Ravegnani, "Tra i due imperi. L'affermazione politica nel XII secolo," in Giorgio Cracco and Gherardo Ortalli, eds., *L'Età del comune*, vol. 2 of Vittore Branca et al., eds., *Storia di Venezia delle origini alla caduta della Serenissima*, 10 vols. (Rome: Istituto della Enciclopedia Italiana, 1991–98), 44–49; Bertelli, *Il carnevale di Venezia*, 13; Edward Muir, *Civic Ritual in Renaissance Venice* (Princeton, NJ: Princeton University Press, 1981), 160–64.

3. Marino Sanuto, *Diarii di Marino Sanuto*, 58 vols. (Venice: Tipografia Marco Visentini, 1879–1902), 27:12.

4. Francesco Sansovino, *Venetia: Città nobilissima et singolare*, 2 vols. (Venice: Steffano Curti, 1663; Venice: Filippi Editore, 1968), 1:406.

5. Nicolo Doglioni, *Le cose notabili, et maravigliose della città di Venetia* (Venice: Battista Cestati, 1671), 45.

6. *Gazzetta Urbana Veneta*, February 21, 1789, 118.

7. Giovanni Rossi, *Leggi e Costumi Veneziani*, n.d., 416 vols., 7:139, B.N.M.

8. Giustina Renier Michiel, *Origine delle feste veneziane*, 2 vols. (Venice: Gaetano Longo, 1852), 1:129–30.

9. Bertelli, *Il carnevale di Venezia*, 15.

10. For accounts of the *giovedì grasso* ceremonies, see Limojan de Saint-Didier, *La Ville et la république de Venise*, 391; Cristoforo Ivanovich, *Minerva al tavolino: Lettere diverse di Proposta, e Risposta à varij Personaggi, sparse d'alcuni componimenti in Prosa, e in Verso, con Memorie teatrali di Venezia*, 2 vols. (Venice: Nicolò Pezzana, 1688), 1:379; Wright, *Some Observations Made in Travelling through France, Italy, &c.*, 1:88–90; and *Codice Gradenigo*, February 18, 1772, 35:97–102, B.M.C. On the distribution of meat, see Martin da Canal, *Les Estoires de Venise: Cronaca veneziana in lingua francese dalle origini al 1275* (Florence: Leo S. Olschki, 1972), 263; Rossi, *Leggi e Costumi Veneziani*, 7:151, 227–28, B.N.M.; and Pino Correnti, *Il Carnevale di Venezia* (Milan: Edizioni Ecotur, 1968), 47.

11. A contemporary's account places the capture of Ulrich on February 9 (Ravegnani, "Tra i due imperi," in Cracco and Ortalli, *L'Età del comune*, vol. 2 of Branca et al., *Storia di Venezia, 75*).

12. The first mention of carnival comes in a document by Doge Vitale Falier from 1094 (Pompeo G. Molmenti, *La Storia di Venezia nella vita privata*, 3 vols. [Trieste: Edizioni Lint, 1973], 1:203).

13. Antonio Lamberti, *Memorie degli ultimi cinquant'anni della Repubblica di Venezia*, n.d., 3 vols., It. VII, 9345–47, 1:137, B.N.M.

14. *Gazzetta Urbana Veneta*, February 6, 1788, 88.

15. *Gazzetta Urbana Veneta*, February 9, 1788, 94.

16. Rossi, *Leggi e Costumi Veneziani*, 7:244, 18:212, B.N.M.

CHAPTER 6. ANYTHING GOES?

1. Goudar, *L'Espion chinois*, 3:87.

2. Johann Wilhelm von Archenholz, *Tableau de l'Italie*, 2 vols. (Brussels: Chez Le Francq, 1788), 1:16.

3. "Dissertazione: Storica-serio-piacevole intorno la letizia in Venezia del Carnovale," *Codice Cicogna*, n.d., 2991-II, 49, B.M.C.

4. Feliciano Benvenuti, "La città dei 'piaseri,' " in Piero Del Negro and Paolo Preto, eds., *L'Ultima fase della Serenissima*, vol. 8 of Branca et al., *Storia di Venezia*, 744. See also Benvenuti, "Classi e società alla caduta della Repubblica Veneta," in Gino Benzoni, ed., *Le metamorfosi di Venezia: Da capitale di stato a città del mondo* (Florence: Leo S. Olschki, 2001), 1–23.

5. James Christen Steward, "Masks and Meaning in Tiepolo's Venice," in Steward, ed., *The Mask of Venice: Masking, Theater, and Identity in the Art of Tiepolo and His Time* (Berkeley: University of California Press, 1996), 19. In Edward Muir's classic work *Civic Ritual in Renaissance Venice*, Bakhtin is said to provide some of the best clues for understanding sixteenth-century carnival. Misrule reigned; its world was "topsy-turvy." "Most masqueraders identified themselves ritually or dramatically with their social opposites," Muir writes, "*popolani* dressed themselves as officials, nobles as peasants, men as women, harlots as men; likewise, destruction led to birth and sex to death; the old became young and the decrepit potent" (Muir, *Civic Ritual in Renaissance Venice*, 177–78). See also Muir, *Ritual in Early Modern Europe* (Cambridge: Cambridge University Press, 2005), 94–106.

6. Lina Padoan Urban, "Il Carnevale veneziano," in Girolamo Arnaldi and Manlio Pastore Stocchi, eds., *Storia della cultura veneta*, 6 vols. (Vicenza: Neri Pozza Editore, 1976–86), 5/1:633; Mazzarotto, *Le feste veneziane*, 123.

7. Danilo Reato, *Storia del Carnevale di Venezia* (Venice: Filippi Editore, 1991), 12. Terry Castle frames her influential study of masquerade in English culture and literature of the eighteenth century in these terms.

> The masked assemblies of the eighteenth century were in the deepest sense a kind of collective meditation on self and other, and an exploration of their mysterious dialectic. From basically simple violations of the sartorial code—the conventional symbolic connections between identity and the trappings of identity—masqueraders developed scenes of vertiginous existential recombination. New bodies were superimposed over old; anarchic, theatrical selves displaced supposedly essential ones; masks, or personae, obscured persons. . . . The result was a material devaluation of unitary notions of the self, as radical in its own way as the more abstract demystifications in the writings of Hume and the eighteenth-century ontologists. (Castle, *Masquerade and Civilization: The Carnivalesque in Eighteenth-Century Culture and Fiction* [Stanford, CA: Stanford University Press, 1986], 4).

See also Peter Stallybrass and Allon White, *The Politics and Poetics of Transgression* (Ithaca, NY: Cornell University Press, 1986).

8. Benvenuti, "La città dei 'piaseri,' " 8:744.

9. Frederick C. Lane, *Venice: A Maritime Republic* (Baltimore: Johns Hopkins University Press, 1973), 434.

CHAPTER 7. CITY OF MASKS

1. Coyer, *Voyage d'Italie*, 2:82.

2. Comisso, *Agenti segreti di Venezia*, 114–15; *Esecutori contro la Bestemmia*, 1782–83, B. 38, A.S.V.

3. Wright, *Some Observations Made in Travelling through France, Italy, &c.*, 1:98–99.

4. Pierre-François, comte de Montaigu, to François-Joachim-Bernard Potier, duc de Gesvres, December 7, 1743, in Jean-Jacques Rousseau, *Corréspondence complète de Jean-Jacques Rousseau*, ed. R. A. Leigh, 11 vols. (Geneva: Institut et Musée Voltaire, 1965), 1:216–17. See Madeleine Ellis, *Rousseau's Venetian Story: An Essay upon Art and Truth in "Les Confessions"* (Baltimore: Johns Hopkins University Press, 1966), 59–68.

5. Tony Tanner's misconception is fairly common: "six months of the year were carnival time by the eighteenth century." See, inter alia, Hetty Paërl: "By the eighteenth century, Venice had become the capital of carnival. Carnival lasted six months a year, beginning on the first Sunday of October and continuing uninterrupted except by the week between Christmas and the New Year"; Frederick C. Lane: "The carnivals in which men and women went masked and indulged the liberties of make-believe created a spirit which lasted the year around"; and Lina Padoan Urban: "In the Serenissima, carnival embraced a vast period of time, beginning in the first days of October (with interruptions for Advent and Christmas) and continuing from St. Stephen's day until Shrove Tuesday." Denis Diderot typified many foreign contemporaries' view in reporting the same six-month carnival—"when even the monks go about in masks"—in a letter to Sophie Volland. Tony Tanner, *Venice Desired* (Cambridge, MA: Harvard University Press, 1992), 5; Hetty Paërl, *Pulcinella: La misteriosa maschera della cultura europea* (Rome: Apeiron Editori, 2002), 70; Lane, *Venice*, 434; Lina Padoan Urban, *Il carnevale veneziano nelle maschere incise da Francesco Bertelli* (Milan: Edizioni Il Polifilo, 1986); Denis Diderot, September 5, 1762, in *Oeuvres complètes*, ed. J. Assézat, 20 vols. (Paris: Garnier Frères, 1876), 19:123.

A rare exception is found in the work of Eleanor Selfridge-Field, who notes erroneous contemporaneous views about carnival's duration in the seventeenth and eighteenth centuries but attributes the greater influence in today's misconceptions to nostalgic accounts by Venetians writing just after the fall of the Republic. "It is through the lens of such nostalgia that [Giovanni] Rossi [1776–1852] might have seen the equation of carnival with the whole span of winter productions to be appropriate" (Eleanor Selfridge-Field, *Song and Season: Science, Culture, and Theatrical Time in Early Modern Venice* [Stanford, CA: Stanford University Press, 2007], 107–8, 291).

6. Eleanor Selfridge-Field, *A New Chronology of Venetian Opera and Related Genres, 1660–1760* (Stanford, CA: Stanford University Press, 2007), appendix 2, 649–56.

7. Pöllnitz, *Memoirs*, 1:411.

8. John Moore, *A View of Society and Manners in Italy: With Anecdotes Relating to Some Eminent Characters*, 2 vols. (Paris: J. Smith, 1803), 1:199.

9. Rossi, *Leggi e Costumi Veneziani*, 7:235, B.N.M.

10. François Marie Arouet Voltaire, *La Princesse de Babylone* (Paris: Émile-Paul Frères, 1920), 110; Misson, *Nouveau voyage d'Italie*, 1:239.

11. *Inquisitori alle Arti*, 1795, quoted in Bertelli, *Il carnevale di Venezia*, 75; Selfridge-Field, *Song and Season*, 98, 109–11; Pietro Antonio Pacifico, *Cronica sacra e profana, o sia, Un compendio di tutte le cose più illustri ed antiche della città di Venezia*, 2 vols. (Venice: Francesco Pitteri, 1751), 2:349. For a meticulous reconstruction of the Venetian theatrical calendar, see Selfridge-Field, *Song and Season*.

12. Lalande, *Voyage en Italie*, 8:507; Giambattista Albrizzi, *Forestiero illuminato intorno le cose più rare, e curiose antiche, e moderne, della città di Venezia* (Venice: n.p., 1772), 411–23; Lina Padoan Urban, "Il Carnevale veneziano," in Arnaldi and Stocchi, *Storia della cultura veneta*, 5/1:633.

13. Garzoni, *Βάσανος cioè Paragone*, 222, B.F.Q.S; *Codice Gradenigo*, February 7, 1756, and February 3, 1756, B.M.C.

14. Da Ponte, *Memoirs*, 19–20.

15. *Gazzetta Veneta*, January 31, 1761.

16. *Inquisitori di Stato*, April 18, 1741, B. 560, A.S.V.; Emanuele Kanceff, ed., *Voyageurs Étrangères à / Foreign Travellers in / Viaggiatori stranieri a Venezia*, 2 vols. (Geneva: Slatkine, 1981), 2:136–37; *Codice Gradenigo*, November 20, 1751, 2:3, B.M.C.; Rossi, *Leggi e Costumi Veneziani*, 7:236, B.N.M.

17. *Inquisitori di Stato*, 1761, B. 595, A.S.V.; *Esecutori contro la Bestemmia*, 1709–12, B. 6, A.S.V.; Jérôme Richard, *Description historique et critique de l'Italie, ou Nouveaux mémoires sur l'état actuel de son gouvernement, des sciences, des arts, du commerce, de la population*, 6 vols. (Paris: Chez Delalain, 1770), 2:464.

18. Comisso, *Agenti segreti di Venezia*, 52–53; *Inquisitori di Stato, Riferti dei Confidenti*, February 24, 1765, B. 613, A.S.V.

19. *Inquisitori di Stato*, November 20, 1696, B. 615, A.S.V.

CHAPTER 8. INFERNAL ASSOCIATIONS

1. Lane, *Venice*, 68–73.

2. Molmenti, *La Storia di Venezia*, 1:203; Maria Teresa Muraro, "Venezia," in *Enciclopedia dello spettacolo*, 13 vols. (Rome: Le Maschere, 1954–62), 9:1532.

3. On turbans and women's veiling in eleventh- and twelfth-century Byzantine society, see Leila Ahmed, *Women and Gender in Islam: Historical Roots of a Modern Debate* (New Haven, CT: Yale University Press, 1992), 27–30; Fadwa El Guindi, *Veil: Modesty, Privacy, and Resistance* (Oxford: Berg, 1999), 12–22; and Timothy Dawson, "Propriety, Practicality, and Pleasure: The Parameters of Women's Dress in Byzantium," in Lynda Garland, ed., *Byzantine Women: Varieties of Experience, 800–1200* (London: Ashgate, 2006), 41–64.

4. Franco Mancini et al., *I Teatri del Veneto*, 4 vols. (Venice: Corbo e Fiori, 1995), 1:6–91. For the beginnings of "commedia all'improvviso," as it was originally known, see Roberto Tessari, "Il mercato delle Maschere," in Roberto Alonge and Guido Davico Bonino, eds., *Storia del teatro moderno e contemporaneo*, 4 vols. (Turin: Einaudi, 2000), 1:119–35.

5. Nel lezzo del bestiale incendio
urlano streghe, masche buonerobe;
e in ruote di ventri
con essi i fratocci s'accoppiano.
Paolo Buzzi, "La fantasia di Magdeburgo," in *Versi liberi*
(Milan: Fratelli Treves, 1913), 158.

Masca and *Maschera* in Salvatore Battaglia et al., *Grande dizionario della lingua italiana,* 21 vols. (Turin: Unione Tipografico, 1961–2009); *Vocabolario della lingua italiana,* 4 vols. (Rome: Istituto della Enciclopedia Italiana, 1986–89).

6. Quoted in Raffaello Padovan and Andrea Penso, *La Repubblica delle maschere* (Venice: Corbo e Fiore Editori, 2000), 61.

7. *Larvæ* in Charles du Fresne, sieur du Cange, *Glossarium mediae et infimae latinitatis,* 10 vols. (Paris: Librairie des Sciences et des Arts, 1937–38), 5:32. See also *laruo, ~are,* in P. G. W. Glare, ed., *Oxford Latin Dictionary* (Oxford: Oxford University Press, 1982), 1003. See Satire 1.5.62–64 in Horace, *Satires, Epistles and Ars Poetica,* trans. H. Rushton Fairclough (Cambridge, MA: Harvard University Press, 1999), 69–70.

8. Dante Alighieri, *Purgatorio,* trans. Allen Mandelbaum (New York: Bantam Classic, 1983), 140–41.

9. *Larvarium,* in du Cange, *Glossarium,* 5:32.

10. The definitions of *larva* and *larvation* and the quotation from Phillips all come from William Murray et al., eds., *Oxford English Dictionary,* 22 vols. (Oxford: Clarendon Press, 1970), 6:79–80.

11. Ibid. See also Padovan and Penso, *La Repubblica delle maschere,* 62.

12. Karl Kerényi, *Dionysos: Archetypal Image of Indestructible Life,* trans. Ralph Mannheim (Princeton, NJ: Princeton University Press, 1976), illustrations 76A, 77, 78, 82, 83, 84, 85.

13. Eric Csapo and William J. Slater, *The Context of Ancient Drama* (Ann Arbor: University of Michigan Press, 1995), 103–21.

14. Henri Jeanmaire, *Dionysos: Histoire du culte de Bacchus* (Paris: Payot, 1951), 273–74, 332–51; Jan Kott, *The Eating of the Gods: An Interpretation of Greek Tragedy,* trans. Boleslaw Taborski and Edward J. Czerwinski (New York: Random House, 1970), 186–230; Heraclitus of Ephesus, quoted in Kerényi, *Dionysos,* 239–40.

15. Quoted in Jeanmaire, *Dionysos,* 54.

16. Richard Seaford, *Dionysos* (London: Routledge, 2006), 73–75.

17. Walter F. Otto, *Dionysus: Myth and Cult,* trans. Robert B. Palmer (Bloomington: Indiana University Press, 1965), 91. See also Françoise Frontisi-Ducroux and Jean-Pierre Vernant, "Divinités au masque dans la Grèce ancienne," in Odette Aslan and Denis Bablet, *Le Masque: Du rite au théâtre* (Paris: Éditions du Centre National de la Recherche Scientifique, 1985), 24–25; and A. David Napier, *Masks, Transformation, and Paradox* (Berkeley: University of California Press, 1986), 45–62.

18. Seaford, *Dionysus,* 126–27; Jeanmaire, *Dionysos,* 470–72.

19. Much has been written about the ancestral spirits African masks are thought to summon. According to John Emigh, masks are used in shamanistic

performances worldwide to help bring the "spirit helper" into the body of the performer. Emigh mentions such practices in Sri Lanka, Siberia, India, and New Guinea, and among North American Eskimos (Emigh, *Masked Performances: The Play of Self and Other in Ritual and Theatre* [Philadelphia: University of Pennsylvania Press, 1996], 14). In rites of passage among the Dogon peoples of western Africa, elders don masks to produce temporary union with the spirit world, leaping and dancing to the hypnotic pulse of drumming and the shriek of noisemakers. In this setting, masks "transform the officiants into gods, spirits, animal ancestors, and all types of terrifying and creative supernatural powers" (Roger Caillois, *Man, Play, and Games,* trans. Meyer Barash [New York: Free Press, 1961], 87–88). See also Germaine Dieterlen, "Masques: Sociétés traditionnelles d'Afrique occidentale," in Aslan and Bablet, *Le Masque,* 27–32. For masking in mourning worldwide, see Jennifer Heath, "What Is Subordinated, Dominates," in Heath, ed., *The Veil: Women Writers on Its History, Lore, and Politics* (Berkeley: University of California Press, 2008), 111.

20. Walter Map, *De Nugis Curialium: Courtiers' Trifles,* trans. M. R. James (Oxford: Clarendon Press, 1983), 27–31. The scholarship chronicling the name *Harlequin* and its relation to the commedia dell'arte character is considerable. For an excellent overview, see Delia Gambelli, *Arlecchino a Parigi: Dall'inferno alla corte del re sole* (Rome: Bulzoni Editore, 1993), 83–125. A classic work on the linguistic and literary history of the name is Otto Driesen, *Der Ursprung des Harlekin: Ein kulturgeschichtliches Problem* (Berlin: Alexander Duncker, 1904).

21. *The Ecclesiastical History of Orderic Vitalis,* trans. Marjorie Chibnall, 6 vols. (Oxford: Clarendon Press, 1969–80), 4:237–51.

22. *Croniques de Normandie* (1487) and *Exposition de la doctrine chrestienne,* quoted in Gambelli, *Arlecchino a Parigi,* 98–99. The historian Cesare Poppi describes a carnival scene on Shrovetide Sunday in the Italian Dolomites in 1981, where, in keeping with tradition, masked "Arlechign" figures suddenly appear with horse whips to wreak havoc among the tourists and villagers. "A thin but steady thread links together, across space and time, the masks, the living and the dead, witches and dream-like experiences, ritual violence, the illness induced by malevolent spirits and the cure provided by courageous young men" (Poppi, "The Other Within: Masks and Masquerades in Europe," in John Mack, ed., *Masks: The Art of Expression* [London: British Museum Press, 1994], 194).

23. Adam de La Halle, *Le Jeu de la feuillée, et Le Jeu de Robin et Marion* (Paris: E. de Boccard, 1964), 56–57; Gordon Douglas McGregor, *The Broken Pot Restored: "Le Jeu de la Feuillée" of Adam de la Halle* (Lexington: French Forum Publishers, 1991); Eugene Vance, "*Le Jeu de la feuillée* and the Poetics of Charivari," *Modern Language Notes* 100, no. 4 (1985): 815–28. Huon de Méry, *Le Tournoiement de l'antéchrist* (1235), and Jacquemars Giélée, *Renart le nouvel* (1292), are discussed in Gambelli, *Arlecchino a Parigi,* 110–11.

24. Vostre bele bouche besera mon cul
    Dame se vos fours est chaud
    En hellequin le quin nele en hel . . .
    Elles ont peux ou cu nos dames.

    Paul Helmer, ed., *Le Premier et le secont livre de fauvel* (Ottawa: Institute of Mediæval Music, 1997), 295–99.

25. See Dante Alighieri, *Inferno,* trans. Allen Mandelbaum (New York: Bantam Classic, 1982), 186–213.

26. "That Alichino is derived from the legendary character of fable and drama, and therefore from a stage figure, is a fact, which the homonym Hellequin affirms" (Riccardo Bacchelli, "Da Dite a Malebolge: La tragedia delle porte chiuse e la farsa dei ponti rotti," *Giornale storico della letteratura italiana* 131, no. 1 [1959]: 3). See also Albert S. Cook, ed., *The Earliest Lives of Dante* (New York: Haskell House, 1974), 17, 31; Thomas Caldecot Chubb, *Dante and His World* (Boston: Little, Brown, 1966), 549–50, 575–77; Robert M. Isherwood, *Farce and Fantasy: Popular Entertainment in Eighteenth-Century Paris* (New York: Oxford University Press, 1986), 22–23; Alfred Fierro, *Histoire et dictionnaire de Paris* (Paris: Robert Laffont, 1996), 394–95.

27. Puis faisoient une crierie
Onques telle ne fut oïe
Li uns montret con cul au vent
Li autre rompet un auvent
L'un cassoit fenestres et huis
[. . .]
Avec eux portoient deux bières
Ou il avoit gent trop avables
[. . .]
Je croi que c'estoit Hellequin
Et tuit li autre sa mesnie.

From Paulin Paris, *Les Manuscrits français de la Bibliothèque du Roi* (1836), quoted in Driesen, *Der Ursprung des Harlekin,* 106.

28. Ibid., 108.

29. "Songe doré de la pucelle" (1500?) and Gabriel Murier, *Recueil des Sentences notables, dicts et dictons communs, adages, proverbes et refrains* (1568), both quoted in Dreissen, *Der Ursprung des Harlekin,* 122, 124.

30. Gambelli, *Arlecchino a Parigi,* 195–200, 419–34; *Compositions de Rhétorique de M. Don Arlequin,* in Agne Beijer, ed., *Le Recueil Fossard* (Paris: Librairie Théâtrale, 1981), 45–62.

31. Siro Ferrone, *Attori, mercanti, corsari: La Commedia dell'Arte in Europa tra Cinque e Seicento* (Turin: Einaudi, 1993), 17.

CHAPTER 9. DEVIL'S DANCE

1. *Histoire plaisante de faicts et gestes de Harlequin, commedien italien* (1585), in Vito Pandolfi, *La Commedie dell'Arte: Storia e testo,* 6 vols. (Florence: Sansoni, 1959), 5:21–28.

2. *Reponse di gestes de arlequin au poete fils de Madame Cardine* (1585), in Gambelli, *Arlecchino a Parigi,* 401–5. See also 157–92. For a discussion of Gros Guillaume and French farce in this period, see Sara Beam, *Laughing Matters: Farce and the Making of Absolutism in France* (Ithaca, NY: Cornell University Press, 2007), 142–79.

3. Robert Henke, *Performance and Literature in the Commedia dell'Arte* (Cambridge: Cambridge University Press, 2002), 60, 50–53. Linda Carroll has chronicled the life and works of another important precursor to commedia del-

l'arte in Venice, Angelo Beolco, whose carnival plays were ribald and provocative (Carroll, *Angelo Beolco (Il Ruzante)* [Boston: Twaine, 1990]).

4. Luigi Riccoboni, *Histoire du théâtre italien* (Paris: A. Cailleau, 1731), 3–39; M. A. Katritzky, *The Art of Commedia: A Study in the Commedia dell'Arte, 1560–1620, with Special Reference to the Visual Records* (Amsterdam: Rodopi, 2006), 18, 34; Ferdinando Taviani, "Positions du masque dans la Commedia dell'Arte," in Aslan and Bablet, *Le Masque*, 126; Tomaso Garzoni, *La piazza universale di tutte le professione del mondo*, quoted in Ferruccio Marotti and Giovanni Romei, *La professione del teatro*, vol. 1, part 2, of *La commedia dell'arte e la società barocca*, ed. Ferdinando Taviani, 2 vols. (Rome: Bulzoni, 1969–1991), 20.

5. Katritzky, *The Art of Commedia*, 39; Kenneth McKee, "Foreword" to Flaminio Scala, *Scenarios of the "Commedia dell'Arte": Flaminio Scala's "Il Teatro delle favole rappresentative*," trans. Henry F. Salerno (New York: Limelight Editions, 1989), xiv.

6. Flavio Biondo, who lived in the mid-fifteenth century, reported that "under the trappings of religion, [*cerretani*] returned home very rich" (quoted in Roberto Tessari, *Commedia dell'Arte: La maschera e l'ombra* [Milan: Mursia, 1981], 37).

7. Roberto Tessari, "Il mercato delle Maschere," in Roberto Alonge and Guido Davico Bonino, eds., *Storia del teatro moderno e contemporaneo*, 4 vols. (Turin: Giulio Einaudi, 2000), 1:126.

8. Tomaso Coryat, *Coryat's Crudities*, 2 vols. (Glasgow: James MacLehose and Sons, 1905), 1:410–11; Atanasio Zannoni, *Generici brighelleschi, consistenti in sortite di scena, discorsi di bravura, motti dialoghi, alfabeti estratti da varj comici autori, particolarmente dal per uso della Commedia Italiana*, quoted in Carmelo Alberti, *La Scena Veneziana nell'età di Goldoni* (Rome: Bulzoni Editore, 1990), 105.

9. Quoted in Ferrone, *Attori, mercanti, corsari*, 18.

10. Henke, *Performance and Literature in the Commedia dell'Arte*, 9–10.

11. Allardyce Nicoll, *The World of Harlequin: A Critical Study of the Commedia dell'Arte* (Cambridge: Cambridge University Press, 1963), 24–39.

12. Anton Giulio Bragaglia, *Pulcinella* (Rome: Gherardo Casini, 1953), 97–118; Paërl, *Pulcinella*, 46.

13. Stage directions from *Flavio's Fortune, Isabella's Fortune*, and *The Three Loyal Friends*, in Scala, *Scenarios of the "Commedia dell'Arte*," 14, 24, 178; Marotti, *La professione del teatro*, xlvi.

14. Pietro Gambacorta, *Trattato fatto contro le comedie mercenarie oscene* (1652), and Giovan Domenico Ottonelli, *Della christiana moderatione del theatro* (1652), in Ferdinando Taviani, *La fascinazione del teatro*, vol. 1, part 1, of *La commedia dell'arte e la società barocca*, ed. Taviani, xci. For a more general account of the attitude of the Church and intellectuals toward commedia dell'arte, see Mario Apollonio, *Storia della Commedia dell'Arte* (Rome: Edizioni Augustea, 1930), 24ff.

15. Quoted in Tessari, *Commedia dell'Arte*, 22–23.

16. Cesare Franciotti, *Il giovane Christiano* (1661), and Francesco Maria del Monaco, *In actores et spectatores comoediarum nostri temporis paraenesis* (1621), in Taviani, *La fascinazione del teatro*, 168, 209.

17. Girolomo Fiorentini, *Comoedio-crisis sive theatri contra theatrum censura; cœlestium, terrestrium, e infernorum linguis, continatis ab orbe condito sæculis, firmata* (Lyon: Officina Anissoniara, 1675).

18. Nicolò Barbieri, *La Supplica discorso famigliare a quelli che trattano de' comici* (1634; reprint, Milan: Polifilo, 1971), 72.

19. Gambelli, *Arlecchino a Parigi*, 159; Siro Ferrone, *Arlecchino: Vita e avventure di Tristano Martinelli attore* (Rome: Laterza, 2006), 73–75.

20. Nicola Fano, *Le maschere italiane* (Bologna: Il Mulino, 2001), 14; Tessari, *Commedia dell'Arte*, 26–27; Paolo Toschi, *Le origini del teatro italiano* (Turin: Editore Boringhieri, 1955), 177–78, 215–16; Benedetto Croce, "Pulcinella e le relazioni della commedia dell'arte con la commedia popolare romana," in Croce, *Saggi sulla letteratura italiana del seicento* (Bari: Laterza & Figli, 1948), 187–240; C. G. Jung, "On the Psychology of the Trickster Figure," in Paul Radin, *The Trickster: A Study in American Indian Mythology* (New York: Schocken Books, 1956), 195–211; Tessari, *Commedia dell'Arte*, 106.

21. *The Jealous Old Man*, in Scala, *Scenarios of the "Commedia dell'Arte,"* 47–54.

22. Borromeo, *Memoriale di Monsignor Illustrissimo e Reverendissimo Cardinale*, and B. S., *Lettera inviata da Piacenza a Carlo Borromeo*, May 2, 1572, in Taviani, *La fascinazione del teatro*, 30, 21.

23. *The Faithless One*, in Scala, *Scenarios of the "Commedia dell'Arte,"* 197. I have slightly altered Henry Salerno's English translation, which reads: "Sir, you see these hands; notice that they are the very same hands." The original is: "Signor mio, vedete voi queste mie mani? fate conto che queste sieno come le sue istesse" (Flaminio Scala, *Il teatro delle favole rappresentative*, 2 vols. [Milan: Edizioni Il Polifilo, 1976], 2:277).

24. *The Disguised Servants* and *The Two Disguised Gypsies*, in Scala, *Scenarios of the "Commedia dell'Arte,"* 218–26, 235–41.

25. In his classic work on commedia, Mario Apollonio argues that the humor audiences found in a servant upbraiding his master formed the original core of commedia dell'arte. "The community, with its taste for laughter, tolerated this evident diminution in the prestige of authority. This retaliation, the revenge of the servant—which was not wholly underhanded or unconscious—gave substance to a caricature of the master while stopping short of wholesale satire: an amused audience is always a young audience, and these young masters tolerated mockery as long as its targets were old masters" (Apollonio, *Storia della Commedia dell'Arte*, 72).

26. *Capricci et nuove fantasie alla Venetiana di Pantalone de' Bisognosi* (1601), quoted in Henke, *Performance and Literature in the Commedia dell'Arte*, 150.

27. Barbieri, *La Supplica*, 35; October 4, 1786, from Goethe, *Italian Journey*, quoted in Margaret Doody, *Tropic of Venice* (Philadelphia: University of Pennsylvania Press, 2007), 75.

28. Taviani, "Positions du masque dans la Commedia dell'Arte," in Aslan and Bablet, *Le Masque*, 128; V. E. Meyerhold, "Two Puppet Theatres," in Edward Braun, ed., *Meyerhold on Theatre* (New York: Hill and Wang, 1969), 128–43.

29. Barbieri, *La Supplica*, 24–25. Anya Peterson Royce offers an insightful dis-

cussion of the role of masks in commedia dell'arte with emphasis on the distinction between actor and role in "The Venetian Commedia: Actors and Masques in the Development of the Commedia dell'Arte," *Theatre Survey* 27 (1986): 69–87.

30. Ferrone, *Attori, mercanti, corsari*, 244–47. Some have identified the portrait as Tristano Martinelli or, less often, Claudio Monteverdi (Ferrone, *Attori, mercanti, corsari*, 269). By comparing it with other images and descriptions of Andreini, Eduard A. Šafařík has established the subject's true identity (Šafařík, *Fetti* [Milan: Electra, 1990], 284–87).

31. September 9, 1614, quoted in Henke, *Performance and Literature in the Commedia dell'Arte*, 171.

CHAPTER 10. UNMASKING THE HEART

1. The ambition of the project is Borgesian. Here is a sampling from the 155 general categories that constitute its triple-column, six-page table of contents:

> Lords, Princes, and Tyrants; Governors; Religious people in general, and in particular Prelates, Ceremonialists, the Superstitious, Canons, Monks, Brothers, Cavaliers, and, finally, Preachers; Grammarians and Pedants; Doctors of Civil Law, Jurisconsults, Legists; Fashioners of Calendars; Surgeons; Makers of Prognostications, Charts, Lunaria, Almanacs; Academicians; Arithmeticians, Computists, Counters, Masters of the Abacus; Peckers and Grinders; Physicians; Noblemen, otherwise known as Gentlemen; Affixers of Seals, otherwise known as Bullists; Professors of Hidden Knowledge, Theologians, Cabalists, Sophists, Compositors of Books, Exorcists, Anatomists, Vates and Haruspices, Musicians, Grave-diggers, Translators and Linguists, Distillers, Goldsmiths, Shepherds and Cheese-makers, Mule-drivers, Bird-catchers, Practitioners of the Art of Memory, Courtesans, Heretics, Merchants, Duelists, Ruffians, Perfumers, Letter-carriers, Makers of Gloves, Lovers, Spies, Comedians and Tragedians, Drunks and Gluttons, Jesters and Riddlers, Cut-purses and Assassins, Loafers, Bandits, Buffoons, Soap-makers, Sock-sewers, Cobblers, Domesticators of Wild Animals, Barbers, Gondoliers, Gardeners, Collectors of Ancient Medallions, Poets, and Humanists. (Tomaso Garzoni, *La piazza universale di tutte le professione del mondo* [Venice: Gio. Battista Somasco, 1589], 34–39. The original 1585 title concluded with the words *e nobili et ignobili*, "both honorable and base." These were dropped in the 1587 edition.)

2. Ibid., 645–49.

3. *Discorso contra il Carnevale: Dove si tratta delle Maschere, et balli, et si dimostra, come per interesse di religione, e beneficio publico delle città e privato de cittadini, si dovrebbe in tutto estirpare dal commun uso de' Cristiani*, in Taviani, *La fascinazione del teatro*, 74–76.

4. *Descriptio et Explicatio pegmatum, Arcuum, et Spectaculorum . . . sub ingressum . . . Ernesti archiducis Austriae* (1594), quoted in Mario Andrea Rigoni, "Una finestra aperta sul cuore," *Lettere italiane* 26, no. 1 (1974), 437.

5. Cesare Ripa, *Iconologia, overo descrittione d'imagini delle virtù, vitii, affetti, passioni humane, corpi celesti, mondo e sue parti* (1611; reprint, New York: Garland, 1976), 485, 310, 53–54, 103.

6. Quoted in Leon Guilhamet, *The Sincere Ideal: Studies on Sincerity in*

Eighteenth-Century English Literature (Montreal: McGill–Queen's University Press, 1974), 15–16. John Martin singles out devotional works by Protestant reformers as essential in the construction of sincerity and the emergence of a new self-consciousness in "Inventing Sincerity, Refashioning Prudence: The Discovery of the Individual in Renaissance Europe," *American Historical Review* 102, no. 5 (1997): 1309–42.

7. Traiano Boccalini, *Ragguagli di Parnaso e Pietra del paragone politico,* 2 vols. (Bari: Giuseppe Laterza & Figli, 1910–12), 1:3.

8. Ibid., 1:260.

9. Ibid., 1:262.

CHAPTER 11. AGE OF DISSIMULATION

1. Boccalini, *Ragguagli di Parnaso,* 1:314–15, quoted in Rosario Villari, *Elogio della dissimulazione: La lotta politica nel Seicento* (Rome: Editori Laterza, 1987), 21. On the reception and diffusion of the term *ragion di Stato,* see Rosario Villari, "Introduzione" to Vallari, ed., *Scritti politici dell'età barocca* (Rome: Istituto Poligrafico e Zecca dello Stato, 1995), xiv–xv; and Maurizio Viroli, *From Politics to Reason of State: The Acquisition and Transformation of the Language of Politics 1250–1600* (Cambridge: Cambridge University Press, 1992), 266–80. See also Friedrich Meinecke, *Machiavellism: The Doctrine of Raison d'État and Its Place in Modern History,* trans. Douglas Scott (New Haven, CT: Yale University Press, 1957), 70–89. Jon R. Snyder discusses the themes of this chapter with skill and insight in *Dissimulation and the Culture of Secrecy in Early Modern Europe* (Berkeley: University of California Press, 2009).

2. Michel de Montaigne, "Of Giving the Lie" and "Of the Useful and the Honorable," in *The Complete Works: Essays, Travels Journals, Letters,* trans. Donald M. Frame (Stanford, CA: Stanford University Press, 1958), 505, 603.

3. Quoted in David Wootton, *Paolo Sarpi: Between Renaissance and Enlightenment* (Cambridge: Cambridge University Press, 1983), 119, 112; Perez Zagorin, *Ways of Lying: Dissimulation, Persecution, and Conformity in Early Modern Europe* (Cambridge, MA: Harvard University Press, 1990), 311; William J. Bouwsma, *Venice and the Defense of Republican Liberty: Renaissance Values in the Age of the Counter Reformation* (Berkeley: University of California Press, 1968), 512–55.

4. Wootton, *Paolo Sarpi,* 121.

5. Quoted in Bouwsma, *Venice and the Defense of Republic Liberty,* 554.

6. Zagorin, *Ways of Lying,* 254.

7. Poiché del sole ogni gradito raggio,
poiché vuol parte de la notte ancora
la servitù gentil, che sempre onora
il silenzio, la penna e 'l pensier saggio,
io, che la seguo (qual mi sia), non aggio
libera per le Muse e lieta un'ora
se non la scemi, o sonno, a la dimora
che toglie agli occhi stanchi il grave oltraggio.

Torquato Accetto, *Rime amorose,* ed. Salvatore Silvano Nigro (Turin: Giulio Einaudi, 1987), xi.

Salvatore Silvano Nigro provides a brief biographical account of Accetto in the introduction to this volume. See also Nigro, "Usi della pazienza," in Accetto, *Della dissimulazione onesta*, ed. Salvatore Silvano Nigro (Turin: Giulio Einaudi, 1997), xi–xxx; Nigro, *"Scriptor Necans,"* in Accetto, *De l'Honnête dissimulation*, trans. Mireille Blanc-Sanchez (Lagrasse: Éditions Verdier, 1990), 7–17; and Snyder, *Dissimulation and the Culture of Secrecy*, 68–105.

8. Battista Guarini, *Il segretario* (1594), quoted in Jean-Pierre Cavaillé, *Dis/simulations: Jules-César Vanini, François La Mothe Le Vayer, Gabriel Naudé, Louis Machon et Torquato Accetto* (Paris: Honoré Champion, 2002), 338; Gabriele Zinano, *Il segretario* (1626), quoted in Salvatore Silvano Nigro, "Le Livre masqué d'un secrétaire du XVIIe siècle," *Le Temps de la réflexion* 5 (1984): 185; Douglas Biow, "From Machiavelli to Torquato Accetto: The Secretarial Art of Dissimulation," in Giorgio Patrizi and Amedeo Quondam, eds., *Educare il corpo, educare la parola: Nella trattatistica del Rinascimento* (Rome: Bulzoni Editore, 1998), 219–38.

9. Acetto, *Della dissimulazione onesta*, 4, 12.

10. Ibid., 19–20.

11. Ibid., 19.

12. Jean de La Bruyère, "De la cour," in *Oeuvres complètes* (Paris: Éditions Gallimard, 1951), 235; Jean-Pierre Cavaillé takes up these points in *Dis/simulations*, 13.

13. Acetto, *Della dissimulazione onesta*, 6–7, 22.

14. Nigro, "Le Livre masqué d'un secrétaire," 192–93; *Oxford English Dictionary*, 8:593, 8:186, 8:520, 8:251, 8:341.

15. Acetto, *Della dissimulazione onesta*, 67.

16. Ibid., 59–60.

17. Ibid., 53, 54.

18. Villari, *Elogio della dissimulazione*, 13.

19. This reading draws on the observations of Salvatore Silvano Nigro in Accetto, *Della dissimulazione onesta*, 16 n. 4.

20. "One might nonetheless omit the memory of one's own wrong for a time, as I will discuss later; but the circuit of dissimulation stretches from the center of one's breast to the circumference of those surrounding us. This should mark the limit of our prudence, which, supported wholly by truth, proceeds in its own time and place, upholding and exhibiting its splendor" (Accetto, *Della dissimulazione onesta*, 17).

21. Villari, *Elogio della dissimulazione*, 25.

22. Accetto was not the only theorist of dissimulation in these decades. Others had contrasted it with simulation, but none embraced it as fully as he did. These include Isidore of Seville (*De differentiis verborum*, seventh century), Francesco da Buti (*Commento sopra la Divina Commedia di Dante Aligheri*, 1385–95), and Giovanni Botero (*Della ragion di Stato*, 1589) (Cavaillé, *Dis/simulations*, 11–24).

A significant treatment of the topic appears in Francis Bacon's essay "Of Simulation and Dissimulation," which was published in the 1625 edition of his *Essayes or Counsels, Civill and Morall*. Bacon's assessment of dissimulation is considerably more negative than Accetto's. It was "the weaker sort of politics," alienating friends and eroding one's credibility (Francis Bacon, "Of Simulation and Dissimulation," in *The Essayes or Counsels, Civill and Morall* [Cambridge, MA: Harvard University Press, 1985], 20–22). Accetto speaks of no such disadvantages.

An eccentric work from 1657 plagiarizes sections of Bacon's essay to cast dissimulation in a more favorable light. *A Dictionary of Falsehood,* appearing in the second volume of Pio Rossi's *Moral Symposium for the Ordering and Integration of Ethics, Economy, and Politics, Treating Reason of State and Essential Military Matters,* distinguishes simulation from dissimulation and insists that the latter is not deceit. Hypocrisy, by contrast, "is the foulest mask a villainous soul can wear" (Pio Rossi, *Dictionnaire du mensonge,* trans. Muriel Gallot [Nantes: Éditions Le Passeur-Cecofop, 1993], 54–56, 68). See also Snyder, *Dissimulation and the Culture of Secrecy,* 203 n. 128.

23. Niccolò Machiavelli, *The Prince,* trans. Harvey C. Mansfield Jr. (Chicago: University of Chicago Press, 1985), 70.

24. Meinecke, *Machiavellism,* 2–3, 29–30, 38–39; Maurizio Viroli, "The Revolution in the Concept of Politics," *Political Theory* 20, no. 3 (1992): 473–95; Snyder, *Dissimulation and the Culture of Secrecy,* 106–14.

25. *Epistola Wenceslai Meroschwa Bohemi ad Johannem Traut Norimbergensem de statu presentis belli et urbium imperialium* (1620), quoted in Villari, *Elogio della dissimulazione,* 20–21, 23.

26. Gianfranco Borrelli, *Ragion di Stato: L'arte italiana della prudenza politica. Catalogo della mostra* (Naples: Istituto Italiano per gli Studi Filosofici, 1994), 11–14.

27. Ludovico Settala, *Della ragion di stato,* in Benedetto Croce and Santino Caramella, *Politici e moralisti del seicento* (Bari: Guiseppe Laterza & Figli, 1930), 82, 72.

28. Those who wished to embrace the morally dubious aspects of his work typically masked their views under the cover of commentaries on Tacitus. See Giuseppe Toffanin, *Machiavelli e il "Tacitismo": La "Politica storica" al tempo della controriforma* (Naples: Guida Editori, 1972); Meinecke, *Machiavellism,* 117–26; and Jacob Soll, *Publishing the Prince: History, Reading, and the Birth of Political Criticism* (Ann Arbor: University of Michigan Press, 2005).

29. Carlo Ginzburg, *Il nicodemismo: Simulazione e dissimulazione religiosa nell'Europa del '500* (Turin: Giulio Einaudi, 1970), xiv; Albano Biondi, "La giustificazione della simulazione nel cinquecento," in Biondi, *Eresia e riforma nell'Italia del Cinquecento* (Florence: G. C. Sansoni Editore, 1974), 7–68; Giorgio Spini, *Ricerca dei libertini: La teoria dell'impostura delle religioni nel seicento italiano* (Rome: Editrice Universale, 1950). Jerome and Aquinas also used scripture to justify dissimulation in certain circumstances (Zagorin, *Ways of Lying,* 16–17, 30–31).

30. Quoted in John Jeffries Martin, *Myths of Renaissance Individualism* (New York: Palgrave, 2004), 33; Martin, *Venice's Hidden Enemies: Italian Heretics in a Renaissance City* (Berkeley: University of California Press, 1993), 125–46.

31. M. A. Overell, "The Exploitation of Francesco Spiera," *Sixteenth Century Journal* 26, no. 3 (1995): 619–37.

32. Jean Calvin, *Excuse de Jehan Calvin, à Messieurs les Nicodemites,* in *Three*

French Treatises (London: Athlone Press, 1970), 131–53; Overell, "The Exploitation of Francesco Spiera," 627–37.

33. Otto Brunfels, *Pandectarum veteris et novi Testamenti, libri XII,* quoted in Ginzburg, *Il nicodemismo, 78.*

34. Brunfels recounted the story of the leper Naaman, commander of the Syrian army, who, on instructions from the Hebrew prophet Elisha, dipped himself in the Jordan river, was healed, and declared his belief in the God of the Israelites. Naaman asked Elisha that he be permitted one thing: that if his master the king should command him to worship pagan gods, he might be pardoned for bowing. Brunfels takes the prophet's simple response as permission to practice religious simulation: "Go in peace " (II Kings 5:1–19).

35. Ginzburg, *Il nicodemiso,* 100, 102.

36. Ibid., 170–72, 160–61, 165–68; Martin, *Venice's Hidden Enemies,* 125–33, 145–46, 219–33; E. William Monter and John Tedeschi, "Toward a Statistical Profile of the Italian Inquisitions, Sixteenth to Eighteenth Century," in Gustav Henningsen and John Tedeschi, eds., *The Inquisition in Early Modern Europe: Studies in Sources and Methods* (Dekalb: Northern Illinois University Press, 1986), 130–57.

37. Anne-Marie Lecoq, "Une peinture 'incorrecte' de Lorenzo Lippi?' *Revue de l'Art* 130, no. 4 (2000): 10, 15.

38. Chiara d'Afflitto, *Lorenzo Lippi* (Florence: Edizioni Firenze, 2002), 244; Lecoq, "Une peinture 'incorrecte,' " 10.

39. Wendy Wassyng Roworth, *"Pictor Succensor": A Study of Salvator Rosa as Satirist, Cynic and Painter* (New York: Garland, 1978), 215. Roworth names Ariston of Chios, Diogenes Laertes, and Epictetus as possible subjects (253).

40. Filippo Baldinucci, *Dal Baroccio a Salvator Rosa* (Florence: G. C. Sansoni, 1914), 193.

41. Jonathan Scott, *Salvator Rosa: His Life and Times* (New Haven, CT: Yale University Press, 1995), 238.

42. Salvator Rosa, *Il teatro della politica sentenziosi afforismi della prudenza* (Bologna: Commissione per i testi di Lingua, 1991), 45, 15, 75.

43. In an article tracing the Greek origins of this phrase, Eckhard Leuschner credits Arnaldo Momigliano as the first to identify the source as Strobaeus, who claimed that the quotation came from Pythagoras (Leuschner, "The Pythagorean on Rosa's London Self-Portrait," *Journal of the Warburg and Courtauld Institutes* 57 [1994], 278–83).

44. For thoughtful commentary on these three paintings, see Cavaillé, *Dis/simulations,* 31–38.

CHAPTER 12. LEGISLATING MORALITY

1. *Consiglio dei Dieci, Comune,* August 13, 1608, R. 68, A.S.V.; *Parte presa nell'eccelso Consiglio di Dieci, 6 Aprile 1699: In materia d'assoluta prohibitione di maschere in tempo della Quadragesima* (Venice: Antonio Pirelli, 1699).

2. *Storia dell'anno 1736,* quoted in Bertelli, *Il carnevale di Venezia,* 41.

3. *Parte presa nell'eccelso Consiglio di Dieci, 16 Genaro 1718: In materia di maschere* (Venice: Pietro Pinelli, 1718); *Parte presa nell'eccelso Consiglio di Dieci,*

15 Genaro 1739: In materia di maschere (Venice: Z. Antonio Pinelli, 1739); *Parte presa nell'eccelso Consiglio di Dieci, 4 Genaro 1744: In materia di maschere* (Venice: Z. Antonio Pinelli, 1744). For earlier prohibitions, see *Codice Cicogna,* February 3, 1603, 2991-II, 53, B.M.C., and *Consiglio dei Dieci, Comune,* January 4, 1606, R. 56, A.S.V.

4. Comisso, *Agenti segreti di Venezia,* 37.

5. Urban, "Il Carnevale veneziano," in Arnaldi and Stocchi, *Storia della cultura veneta,* 5/1:634.

6. *Codice Cicogna,* n.d., 2991-II, 54, B.M.C.; *Compilazione delle Leggi,* December 31, 1628, B. 68, A.S.V.; *Maggior Consiglio, Ottobonus Primus, 1625–30,* December 31, 1628, A.S.V. See also *Parte presa nel Maggior Consiglio,* December 2, 1628, B.N.M. For the edicts prohibiting weapons, see *Proclama publicato per deliberatione delli Eccelentissimi Signori Capi dell'Eccelso Consiglio di Dieci, 15 Genaro 1658: In materia di maschere e baletti* (Venice: Pietro Pinelli, 1658); and *Proclama publicato per deliberatione delli Eccelentissimi Signori Capi dell'Eccelso Consiglio di Dieci, 23 Dicembre 1673: In materia di maschere e baletti* (Venice: Pietro Pinelli, 1673).

7. *Terminatione degl'illustrissimi Sig. Provveditori alla Sanità: In materia di meretrici,* December 20, 1628, B.N.M; *Provveditori alle Pompe,* September 23, 1598, and February 26, 1625, in *Leggi e memorie venete sulla prostituzione fino alla caduta della Republica* (Venice: Marco Visentini, 1870–72), 127.

8. *D'Ordine dell'Illustrisimi e Eccellentissimi Signori Esecutori contro la Bestemmia, 18 Dicembre 1651: In materia de meretrici, e di quelli che non rispettano le chiese, e lochi sacri* (Venice: Gio. Pietro Pinelli, 1651); *Provveditori alle Pompe,* January 12, 1681, B. 1, cap. III, fol. 65v, A.S.V.; *Provveditori alla Sanità,* December 2, 1582, in *Leggi e memorie venete sulla prostituzione,* 126.

9. *Compilazione delle Leggi, Parte presa nell'eccelso Consiglio di Dieci,* August 13, 1608, B. 68, fol. 106, A.S.V. A 1615 law from the same body explicitly forbade prostitutes from appearing masked in gondolas (*Leggi e memorie venete sulla prostituzione,* 137–38). See also Antonio Barzaghi, *Donne o cortigiane? La prostituzione a Venezia: Documenti di costume dal XVI al XVIII secolo* (Verona: Bertani Editore, 1980).

10. *Provveditori alle Pompe,* December 18, 1709, B. 2, cap. IV, fol. 160v, A.S.V. For later versions of this decree, see proclamations dated December 23, 1712; May 16, 1713; May 7, 1714; May 19, 1716; December 22, 1731; December 27, 1732; May 9, 1733; May 22, 1734; and May 18, 1736; B. 2, cap. V, A.S.V.

11. *Provveditori alle Pompe,* December 27, 1732, B. 2, cap. V, 44, A.S.V.

12. *Consiglio dei Dieci,* December 18, 1776, decree quoted in full in Comisso, *Agenti segreti di Venezia,* 423.

13. Carlo Zanidi, in *Inquisitori di Stato,* November 11, 1780, B. 914; Angelo Tamiazzo, in *Inquisitori di Stato,* May 30, 1777, and May 21, 1777, B. 633, A.S.V.

14. *Inquisitori di Stato,* February 8, 1776 (m.v.); Simon Bailo, in *Inquisitori di Stato,* May 24, 1777, and October 11, 1785, B. 914; Angelo Tamiazzo, in *Inquisitori di Stato,* May 24, May 30, and May 13, 1777, B. 633, A.S.V.

15. From the Council of Ten's decree, in Comisso, *Agenti segreti di Venezia,* 423.

16. Carlo Gozzi, *The Memoirs of Count Carlo Gozzi,* trans. John Addington

Symons, 2 vols. (New York: Scribner & Welford, 1890), 2:101. See also Gozzi, *Memorie inutili* (Turin: Unione Tipografico–Editrice Torinese, 1928).

17. *Inquisitori di Stato*, November 18, 1776, B. 538, A.S.V.; *Inquisitori di Stato*, "Misc.," n.d., B. 914, A.S.V.; Simon Bailo, in *Inquisitori di Stato*, October 11, 1785, B. 914, A.S.V.

18. Pietro Franceschi, *Memorie della Correzione 1780*, 120, 109, It. VII, 1810, B.N.M.

CHAPTER 13. SAVING FACE

1. Goudar, *L'Espion chinois*, 3:87. Carnival was "like a vice," Davanzo Poli writes, and "would have gone on continuously had particular laws not imposed restrictions on its duration" (Doretta Davanzo Poli, *Abiti antichi e moderni dei Veneziani* [Venice: Neri Pozzi, 2001], 106).

2. G. Grevembroch, *Gli abiti de Veneziani di quasi ogni età con diligenza raccolti e dipinti nel secolo XVIII*, 4 vols., 2:50, 3:80, B.M.C.

3. Cesare Vecellio, *Costumes anciens et modernes*, 2 vols. (Paris: Firmin Didot, 1859), 1:145.

4. Ibid., 1:101–2; Grevembroch, *Gli abiti de Veneziani*, 1:143, B.M.C.; Misson, *Nouveau voyage d'Italie*, 1:231.

5. See Jean-Jacques Boissard, *Habitus variarum Orbis Gentium* ([Cologne: Kaspar Rutz], 1581).

6. Jennifer Heath, "Introduction," to Heath, *The Veil*, 9. This collection of essays provides excellent historical and contemporary commentary on the complex meaning of women's veils. One author describes her own difficult choices regarding the head covering, which has variously been called oppressive, liberating, protective, and assertive. "As a Muslim, as a woman, as a feminist, I find it increasingly difficult to wear the hijab, which I have found so gratifying in my personal life, in the face of this political Islam that is gaining in popularity and is more and more being seen by non-Muslims as the 'true' face of Islam. I donned the hijab to reject the exploitation of women for their sexuality; I wonder if someday I will take it off again in order to reject the suppression of women for their sexuality" (Pamela K. Taylor, "I Just Want to Be Me," in Heath, *The Veil*, 125).

7. "Cendà o Cendal," in Boerio, *Dizionario del dialetto veneziano*, 158; "Zendà, Zendàl, Zendado," in Achille Vitali, *La moda a Venezia attraverso i secoli: Lessico Ragionato* (Venice: Filippi Editore, 1992), 428–32.

8. Vitali, *La moda a Venezia*, 263–67, 430; Davanzo Poli, *Abiti antichi e moderni dei Veneziani*, 96.

9. Grevembroch, *Gli abiti de Veneziani*, 3:90, B.M.C.

10. Gaetano Cozzi, *La società veneta e il suo diritto: Saggi su questioni matrimoniali, giustizia penale, politica del diritto, sopravvivenza del diritto veneto nell'Ottocento* (Venice: Marsilio, 2000), 144.

11. Lady Mary Wortley, writing from Adrianople in 1717 as she traveled with her husband to a diplomatic posting in Constantinople, admired the "perpetual masquerade" of women's veils there for giving them "entire liberty of following their inclinations without danger of discovery." "Upon the whole, I look upon the Turkish women as the only free people in the empire." The compari-

son is imperfect, but the observation is relevant to Venice. (Mary Wortley, *The Selected Letters of Lady Mary Wortley*, ed. Robert Halsband [London: Penguin, 1986], 97.)

12. Carlo Goldoni, *Il festino (dramma per musica)* (1757) and *Le donne di buon umore* (1758), in *Tutte le opere*, 11:589, 6:1025. In the play *Il festino* (1754), the Contessa di Belpoggio asserts that "according to city customs, masks permit honest wives to enter respectable cafés without the slightest impropriety" (5:479). See also Gastone Geron, *Carlo Goldoni cronista mondano: Costume e moda nel settecento a Venezia* (Venice: Filippi Editore, n.d.), 28.

13. Ellen Rosand, *Opera in Seventeenth-Century Venice: The Creation of a Genre* (Berkeley: University of California Press, 1991), 2, 77–81; Nicola Mangini, *I teatri di Venezia* (Milan: Mursia Editore, 1974), 9–21. For the chronology of provisional and permanent theaters in Venice, I have used dates given in Mancini et al., *I teatri del Veneto*, vols. 1–2. For additional discussion of the spread of theaters in Venice, see Remo Giazotto, "La Guerra dei palchi," *Nuova rivista musicale italiana* 2 (July–August 1967): 245–86; 3 (September–October 1967): 465–508; 5 (September–October 1969): 906–33; 6 (November–December 1971): 1034–52; and Ivanovich, *Minerva al tavolino*, 1:389–401. For a detailed survey of theaters and repertoires in the eighteenth century, see Taddeo Weil, *I teatri musicali veneziani del settecento* (Venice: Fratelli Visentini, 1897).

14. Antonio Persio, *Trattato dei portamenti della Signoria di Venezia verso la Santa chiesa* (pre-1593), quoted in Mancini et al., *I teatri del Veneto*, 1:95.

15. Ludovico Zorzi, *I teatri pubblici di Venezia (Secoli XVII–XVIII)* (Venice: Biennale di Venezia, 1971), 12; Limojan de Saint-Didier, *La Ville et la république de Venise*, 381–82; Maddalena Agnelli, "Il pubblico veneziano di Carlo Goldoni," *Problemi di critica Goldoniana* 2 (1995), 182–230; Siro Ferrone, *Carlo Goldoni: Vita, opere, critica, messinscena* (Florence: Sansoni Editore, 1990), 9–13.

16. Philip Skippon, *An Account of a Journey Made thro the Low-Countries, Germany, Italy, and France* (1682), quoted in Beth L. Glixon and Jonathan E. Glixon, *Inventing the Business of Opera: The Impressario and His World in Seventeenth-Century Venice* (Oxford: Oxford University Press, 2006), 314; Limojan de Saint-Didier, *La Ville et la république de Venise*, 379–80; *Pallada Veneta*, October 1687, in Eleanor Selfridge-Field, *Pallada Veneta: Writings on Music in Venetian Society, 1650–1750* (Venice: Fondazione Levi, 1985), 194.

17. Freschot, *Nouvelle relation de la ville et république de Venise*, 402–3.

18. *La putta onorata* (1748), in Goldoni, *Tutte le opere*, 2:498–506.

19. Zaccaria Seriman, *Viaggi di Enrico Wanton alle terre incognite australi, ed al paese delle scimie, ne' quali si spiegano il carattere, li costumi, le scienze e la polizia di quegli strarodinari abitaniti* (1749), quoted in Martha Feldman, *Opera and Sovereignty: Transforming Myths in Eighteenth-Century Italy* (Chicago: University of Chicago Press, 2007), 178.

20. For a detailed discussion of the seating in Venetian opera houses, see Glixon and Glixon, *Inventing the Business of Opera*, 17–19, 295–304. On the origins of private boxes in Venice, see Edward J. Johnson, "The Short, Lascivious Lives of Two Venetian Theaters, 1580–85," *Renaissance Quarterly* 55, no. 3 (2002): 936–68.

21. Ivanovich, *Minerva al tavolino*, 1:387–88.

22. Luigi Riccoboni, *An Historical and Critical Account of the Theatres in Europe* (London: R. Dodsley, 1741), 56–57.

23. Quoted in Monica Miato, *L'Accademia degli Incogniti di Giovan Francesco Loredon, Venezia (1630–1661)* (Florence: Leo S. Olschki, 1998), 67.

24. Ivanovich, *Minerva al tavolino*, 1:386. For a vivid contemporary description of Venetian academies in the seventeenth and eighteenth centuries, see Freschot, *Nouvelle relation de la ville et république de Venise*, 395–96; Edward Muir, *The Culture Wars of the Late Renaissance: Skeptics, Libertines, and Opera* (Cambridge, MA: Harvard University Press, 2007); and Peter Burke, *Venice and Amsterdam: A Study of Seventeenth-Century Elites* (Cambridge, MA: Polity Press, 1994), 80–81.

25. A. Lupis, *Vita di Giovan Francesco Loredano*, quoted in Miato, *L'Accademia degli Incogniti*, 68.

26. Ibid., 61; Muir, *The Culture Wars of the Late Renaissance*, 72; G. Brusoni quoted in Miato, *L'Accademia degli Incogniti*, 60.

27. Ivanovich, *Minerva al tavolino*, 1:377.

28. See chapter 3.

29. Comisso, *Agenti segreti di Venezia*, 59–60; Wright, *Some Observations Made in Travelling through France, Italy, &c.*, 1:87.

30. Comisso, *Agenti segreti di Venezia*, 49–50.

31. Dolcetti, *Le Bische e il giuoco d'azzardo*, 141–42.

32. *Inquisitori di Stato*, February 4, 1743, B. 914; May 5, 1742, B. 560; January 9, 1764, B. 613; January 16, 1743, B. 560; November 5, 1767, B. 614, A.S.V.

33. Pietro Garzoni, Βάσανος *cioè Paragone*, 228, B.F.Q.S.

34. Limojan de Saint-Didier, *La Ville et la république de Venise*, 372; Amelot de la Houssaye, *Histoire du gouvernement de Venise*, quoted in Freschot, *Nouvelle relation de la ville et république de Venise*, 419.

35. *Inquisitori di Stato*, March 15, 1746, B. 595; May 11, 1739, B. 560; October 6, 1764, B. 613, A.S.V.

36. Undated report filed by Felice Favretti [1761?], *Inquisitori di Stato*, B. 595, A.S.V.; Nani, *Principi di una amministrazione ordinata*, fol. 59v, B.C.P.; *Inquisitori di Stato*, February 16, 1777 (m.v.), B. 633, A.S.V.; Gozzi quoted in Bertelli, *Il carnevale di Venezia*, 55.

37. As James Van Horn Melton puts it, coffeehouses became "politicized spaces of public discussion." "As places where affairs of government were dissected and often judged, coffeehouses were antithetical to the absolutist assumption that politics were an arcane realm whose 'secrets' should be accessible to no one beyond sovereigns and their ministers" (James Van Horn Melton, *The Rise of the Public in Enlightenment Europe* [Cambridge: Cambridge University Press, 2001]), 243. For a treatment of the rise of public opinion in eighteenth-century Italy, see Sandro Landi, " 'Pubblico' e 'opinione pubblica': Osservazioni su due luoghi comuni del lessico politico italiano del Settecento," *Cromohs* 13 (2008): 1–11; Giuseppe Aliprandi lists occurrences of "public opinion" in eighteenth-century Venetian works in "Dalla 'opinione comune' alla 'pubblica opinione' nella seconda metà del Settecento," *Atti e memorie: Accademia Patavina di scienze, lettere ed arte* 77, no. 3 (1964–65): 483–503. See also Jürgen Habermas, *The Structural Transformation of the Public Sphere: An Inquiry into a Category of Bourgeois*

Society, trans. Thomas Burger (Cambridge, MA: MIT Press, 1989); Mona Ozouf, " 'Public Opinion' at the End of the Old Regime," *Journal of Modern History* 60 (1988): S1–S21; and Keith Michael Baker, "Defining the Public Sphere in Eighteenth-Century France: Variations on a Theme by Habermas," in Craig Calhoun, ed., *Habermas and the Public Sphere* (Cambridge, MA: MIT Press, 1992), 181–211.

38. Comisso, *Agenti segreti di Venezia*, 113–14.

39. *Pallada Veneta*, January 23–30, 1739 (m.v.).

40. Limojan de Saint-Didier, *La Ville et la république de Venise*, 435–36; *Pallada Veneta*, September 1687, in Selfridge-Field, *Pallada Veneta*, 189; *Mémoire de l'entrée et de l'audience publiques de M. Amelot* (1682), quoted in Armand Baschet, *Les Archives de Venise: Histoire de la Chancellerie secrète* (Paris: Henri Plon, 1870), 481–82.

41. Misson, *Nouveau voyage d'Italie*, 1:247.

42. *Provveditori alle Pompe*, September 24, 1677, in *Leggi e memorie venete sulla prostituzione*, 163; see also *Provveditori alle Pompe*, cap. I–II–III, 1488–1683, esp. cap. III (1673–1683), A.S.V.

43. Bertelli, *Il carnevale di Venezia*, 76; Davanzo Poli, *Abiti antichi e moderni dei Veneziani*, 98; Melton, *The Rise of the Public in Enlightenment Europe*, 240.

44. Freschot, *Nouvelle relation de la ville et république de Venise*, 404.

45. Gozzi, *L'Osservatore Veneto*, 1:175–76 (article dated April 29, 1761).

46. The conservative Edmund Burke comes close to Gozzi's substance and language in deploring the death of chivalry before the French revolutionaries' cold reason.

> All the pleasing illusions, which made power gentle and obedience liberal, which harmonized the different shades of life, and which, by a bland assimilation, incorporated into politics the sentiments which beautify and soften private society, are to be dissolved by this new conquering empire of light and reason. All the decent drapery of life is to be rudely torn off. All the superadded ideas, furnished from the wardrobe of a moral imagination, which the heart owns, and the understanding ratifies, as necessary to cover the defects of our naked, shivering nature, and to raise it to dignity in our own estimation, are to be exploded as a ridiculous, absurd, and antiquated fashion. (Edmund Burke, *Reflections on the Revolution in France* [New Haven, CT: Yale University Press, 2003], 66)

CHAPTER 14. VENETIAN INCOGNITO

1. This account of the Russians' visit is drawn from *Descrizione degli spettacoli e feste datesi in Venezia per occasione della venuta delle LL. AA. II. il Gran Duca e Gran Duchessa di Moscovia, sotto il nome di Conti del Nort nel mese di Gennajo 1782* (Venice: Vincenzio Formaleoni, 1782); *Les Fêtes Vénitiennes du mois de janvier 1782: Dediées à son Excellence Madame Morosina Corner Gradenigo* [n.p., n.d.]; *Inquisitori di Stato*, B. 922, A.S.V.; Lodovico Morelli, *Lettera scritta da un Patrizio Veneto ad un suo amico: Con cui si descrivono minutamente tutti li Grandiosi Spettacoli, co'quali si compiacque il Veneto Governo di trattenere li Signori Conti di Nord, dal giorno del loro arrivo, sino al giorno delle loro partenza dalla Dominante* [1781?]; and Giustiniana Wynne Rosenberg-Orsini, *Du Séjour des comtes du Nord à Venise en janvier 1782: Lettre de Mme*

La Comtesse Douairière des Ursins, et Rosenberg à Mr. Richard Wynne, son frère, à Londres ([Venice]: n.p., 1782).

2. *Inquisitori di Stato,* November 13, 1775, B. 922, A.S.V.; Urban, "Il Carnevale veneziano," in Arnaldi and Stocchi, *Storia della cultura veneta,* 5/1:642; Giovanni Battista Casti and Giovanni Paisielli, *Il Re Teodoro in Venezia* (Padua: Pietro Molinari, 1801).

3. John Julius Norwich, *A History of Venice* (New York: Alfred A. Knopf, 1982), 599; *Codice Cicogna,* 1708, 2991-II, 73, B.M.C.; Urban, "Il Carnevale veneziano," in Arnaldi and Stocchi, *Storia della cultura veneta,* 5/1:641.

4. "Instruzioni dell'Eccmo Senato di Venezia all'Ambr. Veneto Residente alla Corte Cesarea," in *Inquisitori di Stato,* B. 922, A.S.V. On the couple's European trip and its aims, see Roderick E. McGrew, *Paul I of Russia, 1754–1801* (Oxford: Clarendon Press, 1992), 105–42.

5. Rosenberg-Orsini, *Du Séjour des comtes du Nord,* 25–26; Luigi Ballarini, *I Conti del Nord a Venezia: Due lettere* (Venice: Marco Visentini, 1870), 19.

6. Ballarini, *I Conti del Nord a Venezia,* 15.

7. Morelli, *Lettera scritta da un Patrizio Veneto ad un suo amico,* 5.

8. Rosenberg-Orsini, *Du Séjour des comtes du Nord,* 71; Ballarini, *I Conti del Nord a Venezia,* 26.

9. Rosenberg-Orsini, *Du Séjour des comtes du Nord,* 15; "Venuta in Venezia dei Granduchi di Russia sotto il nome di Conti del Nord—1781," in *Inquisitori di Stato,* B. 922, A.S.V.

10. Rosenberg-Orsini, *Du Séjour des comtes du Nord,* 15, 35, 19–20. For a compelling account of Wynne's life, see Andrea di Robilant, *A Venetian Affair: A True Tale of Forbidden Love in the Eighteenth Century* (New York: Knopf, 2003).

11. "Instruzioni dell'Eccmo Senato di Venezia all'Ambr. Veneto Residente alla Corte Cesarea," in *Inquisitori di Stato,* B. 922, A.S.V.

12. "Risposta al'interpellazioni del Sigr. Ambr. Di Venezia," in *Inquisitori di Stato,* B. 922, A.S.V.

13. Rousseau to Anne-Françoise de La Chaise d'Aix, comtesse de Montaigu, November 23, 1743, in *Corréspondence complète de Jean-Jacques Rousseau,* 1:213; Rousseau, *Les Confessions,* in *Oeuvres complètes,* 3 vols. (Paris: Éditions Gallimard, 1959), 1:297–327.

14. Paolo Preto, "Le 'paure' della società veneziana," in Branca et al., *Storia di Venezia,* 6:215–38. See also Richard Mackenney, "'A Plot Discover'd?' Myth, Legend, and the 'Spanish' Conspiracy against Venice in 1618," in John Martin and Dennis Romano, eds., *Venice Reconsidered: The History and Civilization of an Italian City-State, 1297–1797* (Baltimore: Johns Hopkins University Press, 2000), 185–216.

15. Abbé de Pomponne, May 9, 1707, in *Mémoires et documents, Venise,* vol. 27, fol. 93, A.M.A.E.

16. *Mémoires et documents, Venise,* vol. 27, fols. 125–54, A.M.A.E.

17. Lalande, *Voyage en Italie,* 8:511.

18. *Mémoires et documents, Venise,* vol. 27, fols. 136–38, A.M.A.E.

19. *Mémoires et documents, Venise,* vol. 27, fols. 136, 138, 177, 70, 73–74, A.M.A.E.

20. Ibid., fols. 161–64.

21. Ibid., fols. 52–58.

22. *Codice Gradenigo*, 1736, "Commemoriali," 17:176, B.M.C.

23. *Corréspondance politique, Venise,* December 22, 1753, vol. 215, fols. 108–10, A.M.A.E.

24. Ibid., November 25, 1752, vol. 214, fols. 118–19.

25. Ibid., December 2, 1752, fols. 129–30.

26. *Ceremoniali*, February 3, 1684, B. 111, fol. 183; *Ceremoniali*, March 24, 1700, B. III, fol. 218; *Inquisitori di Stato*, n.d., B. 922, fols. 9–10, A.S.V.

27. Account from surveillance agent of the State Inquisitors, March 6, 1797, quoted in Daniele Ricciotti Bratti, *La Fine della Serenissima* (Milan: Alfieri & Lacroix, [1917?]), 115.

28. Letter from Cattaneo to the State Inquisitors, March 25, 1791, in *Inquisitori di Stato*, B. 922, A.S.V.

29. Charles de Secondat, Baron de Montesquieu, *Voyage de Gratz à La Haye*, in *Oeuvres complètes*, 2 vols. (Paris: Éditions Gallimard, 1949), 1:553–54.

CHAPTER 15. DEMOCRATIZING DRESS

1. Vitali, *La moda a Venezia*, 414–22; Doglioni, *Le cose notabili*, 15–18; Abraham-Nicolas Amelot de la Houssaye, *Histoire du gouvernement de Venise*, 2 vols. (Paris: Chez Frédéric Leonard, 1677), 1:244–381; Davanzo Poli, *Abiti antichi e moderni dei Veneziani*, 99–100.

2. Diane Owen Hughes, "Distinguishing Signs: Ear-Rings, Jews and Franciscan Rhetoric in the Italian Renaissance City," *Past and Present* 112 (1986): 17; Brian Pullan, *The Jews of Europe and the Inquisition of Venice, 1550–1670* (Oxford: Basil Blackwell, 1983), 54, 130.

3. Limojan de Saint-Didier, *La Ville et la république de Venise*, 317–18; Wright, *Some Observations Made in Travelling through France, Italy, &c.*, 1:91.

4. Gaetano Cozzi et al., *La Repubblica di Venezia nell'età moderna*, 2 vols. (Turin: Unione Tipografico–Editrice Torinese, 1992), 2:168–200.

5. Paraphrasing Gasparo Contarini, whose sixteenth-century *De Magistratibus et Republica Venetorum* is the classic articulation of Venetian uniqueness through its complex mechanisms of governing, J. G. A. Pocock comments: "Venetians are not inherently more virtuous than other men, but they possess institutions which make them so" (J. G. A. Pocock, *The Machiavellian Moment: Florentine Political Thought and the Atlantic Republican Tradition* [Princeton, NJ: Princeton University Press, 1975], 324). David Carrithers reviews the considerable literature on the mixed constitution of Venice and contemporary views of its authoritarian features in "Not So Virtuous Republic: Montesquieu, Venice, and the Theory of Aristocratic Republicanism," *Journal of the History of Ideas* 52, no. 2 (1991): 245–68. See also Myron Gilmore, "Myth and Reality in Venetian Political Theory," and William Bouwsma, "Venice and the Political Education of Europe," in J. R. Hale, ed., *Renaissance Venice* (London: Faber and Faber, 1973), 431–44, 445–66.

6. Vettor Sandi, *Principi di Storia civile della Repubblica di Venezia*, 3 vols.

(Venice: Presso Sebastian Coletti, 1772),1:351; *Provveditori alle Pompe*, April 26, 1663, B. 1, cap. II, fol. 58v; September 16, 1676, B. 1, cap. III, fol. 46v, A.S.V.

7. Rosita Levi Pisetzky, *Storia del costume in Italia*, 4 vols. (Milan: Istituto Editoriale Italiano, 1967), 3:271, 425–67; 4:342–43. See also Giulio Bistort, *Il magistrato alle pompe nella Republica di Venezia* (Venice: Tipografia–Libreria Emiliana, 1912).

8. Sandi, *Principi di Storia civilie della Repubblica di Venezia*, 1:351; report to *Inquisitori di Stato*, quoted in Comisso, *Agenti segreti di Venezia*, 44; *Provveditori alle Pompe*, April 30, 1701, B. 2, cap. IV, fol. 109v; September 16, 1676, B. 1, cap. III, fol. 45, A.S.V.

9. *Gazzetta Urbana Veneta*, March 9, 1793, 153; Bistort, *Il magistrato alle pompe*, 147; Cesare Vecellio, *Degli habiti antichi et moderni di diverse parti del mondo* (Venice: Damian Zenaro, 1590), 106.

10. Bistort, *Il magistrato alle pompe*, 147; *Maggior Consiglio, Ballarinus pater*, March 11, 1668, A.S.V.

11. Vitali, *La moda a Venezia attraverso i secoli*, 395–98, 120–24; Giuseppe Morazzoni, *La moda a Venezia nel secolo XVIII* (Milan: Museo Teatrale alla Scala, 1931), 20–24; Comisso, *Agenti segreti di Venezia*, 413–14.

12. Bistort, *Il magistrato alle pompe*, 147–48.

13. Casanova, *History of My Life*, 2:59–60; Bistort, *Il magistrato alle pompe*, 161.

14. See Molmenti, *La Storia di Venezia nella vita privata*, 3:167. Doretta Davanzo Poli also notes the similarity between women's veils and the baùta (Davanzo Poli, *Abiti antichi e moderni dei Veneziani*, 96); Bautta in *Vocabolario universale italiano*, 7 vols. (Naples: Tramater, 1829–40), 1:603.

15. Bistort, *Il magistrato alle pompe*, 159.

16. *Provveditori alle Pompe*, May 5 and May 18, 1707, B. 2, cap. IV, fols. 147v–148, 151v, A.S.V.; Bistort, *Il magistrato alle pompe*, 142–43, 150–55.

17. *Provveditori alle Pompe*, May 2, 1709, B. 2, cap. IV, 155; February 25, 1710 (m.v.), B. 2, cap. V, 1v; May 19, 1716, B. 2, cap. V, 25v; May 5, 1744, B. 2, cap. V, 69, A.S.V.

18. Anonymous poem quoted in Bistort, *Il magistrato alle pompe*, 158.

19. The times given are "le ore 21," "alle ore 23," and "alle ore 21 e meza." In Venice, time was recorded by the hour beginning at sunset. The last hour before sunset was "ore 24." *Inquisitori di Stato*, August 11, 1747, B. 595, A.S.V.

20. Bistort, *Il magistrato alle pompe*, 160.

21. Pöllnitz, *Memoirs*, 1:399.

22. Lalande, *Voyage en Italie*, 8:507.

23. Volker Hunecke, "Il corpo aristocratico," in Branca et al., *Storia di Venezia*, 8:363; Piero Del Negro, "Introduzione," in Branca et al., *Storia di Venezia*, 8:6; Giacomo Marcello (1646) and Michele Foscarini (1684), quoted in James Cushman Davis, *The Decline of the Venetian Nobility as a Ruling Class* (Baltimore: Johns Hopkins University Press, 1962), 76.

24. Paolo Preto, "Le riforme," in Branca et al., *Storia di Venezia*, 8:90.

25. Del Negro, "Introduzione," 8:74, 69.

26. Giacomo Nani, *Saggio politico del corpo aristocratico della Repubblica*

di Venezia per l'anno 1756 (1749–56), quoted in Hunecke, "Il corpo aristocratico," 8:363; Piero Del Negro, "Proposte illuminate e conservazione nel dibattito sulla teoria e la prassi dello stato," in Arnaldi and Stocchi, *Storia della cultura veneta*, 5/2:138–40; Venturi, *Settecento riformatore*, 5/2:13–16; Hunecke, "Il corpo aristocratico," 8:372.

27. Remo Giazotto, "La Guerra dei palchi," *Nuova rivista musicale italiana* 3 (September–October 1967): 491.

28. Garzoni, Βάσανος *cioè Paragone*, 221, B.F.Q.S.

29. Francesco Masotti, quoted in Bertelli, *Il carnevale di Venezia*, 47.

30. Franceschi, *Memorie della Correzione 1780*, 115, 100, B.N.M.

31. Clemente Bondi, *Le conversazioni: Poemetto* (Venice, 1783) and Stefano Zucchino Stefani, *Lo specchio del disinganno per conoscere la deformità del moderno costume* (Venice, 1754), quoted in Luciano Guerci, *La discussione sulla donna nell'Italia del Settecento: Aspetti e problemi* (Turin: Tirrenia Stampatori, 1988), 79–80, 108, 109. See also Feldman, *Opera and Sovereignty*, 357.

32. Nani, *Principi di una amministrazione ordinata e tranquilla*, 48v, B.C.P.

33. *Gazzetta Urbana Veneta*, January 16, 1793, 36; January 26, 1793, 58.

CHAPTER 16. TAMING THE DEVIL

1. Goldoni, *Le donne gelose* (1752), in *Tutte le opere*, 4:404–13.

2. "L'umana vita è una continua guerra, / Ma la pace chi ama, / aperto vede / Che più granelli son ch'uomini in terra." Quoted in Gerard Luciani, "Carlo Gozzi (1720–1806): L'Homme et l'oeuvre" (thesis, Université de Dijon, 1974), 2:71. Gozzi, *Memoirs*, 2:93–97. For an informative and largely sympathetic account of Gozzi's life and works, see John Louis DiGaetani, *Carlo Gozzi: A Life in the 18th Century Venetian Theater, an Afterlife in Opera* (London: McFarland & Company, 2000).

3. From Antonio Muratori, *Della perfetta poesia italiana* (1706), and Esteban de Arteaga, *La rivoluzione del teatro musicale* (1783), quoted in Giuseppe Ortolani, *La riforma del teatro nel settecento e altri scritti* (Florence: Istituto per la Collaborazione Culturale, 1962), 4–5.

4. Quoted in Ted Emery, "Gozzi in Context," in Carlo Gozzi, *Five Tales for the Theatre*, ed. and trans. Albert Bermal and Ted Emery (Chicago: University of Chicago Press, 1989), 4.

5. Ortolani, *La riforma del teatro*, 28.

6. *L'erede fortunata* (1759), *La vedova scaltra* (1748), *L'uomo prudente* (1748), *La putta onorata* (1748).

7. Paolo Bosisio, *Carlo Gozzi e Goldoni: Una polemica letteraria con versi inediti e rari* (Florence: Leo S. Olschki, 1970), 60.

8. Gozzi, *Memoirs*, 2:110, 2:122–23; Emery, "Gozzi in Context," 5.

9. Ortolani, *La riforma del teatro*, 51; Ferrone, *Carlo Goldoni*, 110; Gozzi, *Memoirs*, 2:112.

10. Goldoni, *La bottega del caffè* (1750), in *Tutte le opere*, 3:60; Goldoni, "L'autore a chi legge," *La bottega del caffè*, in *Tutte le opere*, 3:5.

11. Arnaldo Momo, *La carriera della maschere nel teatro di Goldoni, Chiari*,

Gozzi (Venice: Marsilio Editori, 1992), 19; Carlo Goldoni, *Mémoires* (Paris: Mercure de France, 1988), 254.

12. Goldoni, *Mémoires,* 258.

13. Carlo Goldoni, *Il teatro comico (1750),* in *Carlo Goldoni teatro,* vol. 3, part 1, of Guido Davico Bonino, ed., *Il teatro italiano,* 5 vols. (Turin: Giulio Einaudi, 1975–1991), 101–69. Goldoni ultimately found the effect a little too bizarre. In the 1753 edition, he gave the actors playing Arlecchino, Pantalone, and Brighella their own names (see Goldoni, *Il teatro comico,* in *Tutte le opere,* 2:1041–1105).

14. Goldoni, *Il teatro comico,* in *Carlo Goldoni teatro,* 129–30; Goldoni, *Il teatro comico,* in *Tutte le opere,* 2:1066–67.

15. Goldoni, *Il teatro comico,* in *Carlo Goldoni teatro,* 130; Goldoni, *Il teatro comico,* in *Tutte le opere,* 2:1067.

16. See chapter 9.

17. Goldoni, *Il teatro comico,* in *Carlo Goldoni teatro,* 144; Goldoni, *Il teatro comico,* in *Tutte le opere,* 2:1080–81.

18. Goldoni, "L'autore a chi legge," *Il cavaliere e la dama* (1749), in *Tutte le opere,* 2:627.

19. Goldoni, *Il cavaliere e la dama, La bottega del caffè,* and *Le donne gelose,* in *Tutte le opere,* 2:672, 3:38, 4:394.

20. Goldoni, *Le baruffe chiozzotte* (1762), in *Tutte le opere,* 8:127–203.

21. Goldoni, "L'autore a chi legge," *Le baruffe chiozzotte,* in *Tutte le opere,* 8:130.

22. Gozzi, "Ragionamento ingenuo e storia sincera dell'origine delle mie dieci fiabe teatrali," in *Carlo Goldoni teatro,* vol. 3, part 3, of Bonino, *Il teatro italiano,* 1373.

23. See Franco Fido, *Guida a Goldoni: Teatro e società nel settecento* (Turin: Einaudi, 1977), 18ff; Goldoni, *I portentosi effetti della Madre Natura* (1752), *Torquato Tasso* (1755), and *Bertoldo, Bertoldino e Cacasenno* (1749), in *Tutte le opere,* 10:1211, 5:793, 10:539.

24. Goldoni, *La famiglia dell'antiquario* (1749), in *Tutte le opere,* 2:911. Pietro Spezzani discusses the evolving role of Pantalone in Goldoni's comedies in *Dalla Commedia dell'Arte a Goldoni* (Padua: Esedra Editrice, 1997); Joseph Spencer Kennard, *Goldoni and the Venice of His Time* (New York: Benjamin Blom, 1967), 312–15.

25. Comitato di Pubblica Istruzione, October 27, 1797, in *Raccolta di carte pubbliche, istruzioni, legislazioni, ecc. del nuovo Veneto governo democratico,* 12 vols. (Venice: Gatti, 1797), 11:182–83; Franca R. Barricelli, " 'Making a People What It Once Was': Regenerating Civic Identity in the Revolutionary Theatre of Venice," *Eighteenth-Century Life* 23, no. 3 (1999): 38–57; Guy Dumas, *La Fin de la République de Venise: Aspects et reflets littéraires* (Rennes: Imprimerie Bretonne, 1964), 353–87.

26. For a summary of Gozzi's plays in these and later seasons, see DiGaetani, *Carlo Gozzi,* 107–54.

27. Goldoni's repudiation coincided with setbacks to liberal reform more generally. In early 1762, the Great Council rejected proposals to reduce the Coun-

274 | Notes to Pages 165-172

cil of Ten's powers. Citing Montesquieu and Voltaire, supporters had advanced arguments in terms of judicial transparency and freedom of expression. Opponents prevailed with the claim that secrecy and a firm hand best protected liberty; to change the Republic, they argued, risked its destruction. In 1764, censorship in Venice was tightened.

28. Quoted in Emery, "Gozzi in Context," 7.

29. Quoted in ibid., 6.

30. Alberto Beniscelli, "Introduzione," to Carlo Gozzi, *Fiabe teatrali* (Milan: Garzanti Editori, 1994), xv.

CHAPTER 17. REDEEMED BY THE BLOOD

1. The following account is drawn from Ivanovich, *Minerva al tavolino,* 1:164–73. Ivanovich's description appears virtually verbatim and without attribution in Galeno Belloratto [Angelo Bottarello], *Breve descrizione di Venezia, e de piacevoli trattenimenti, che godea prima, che s'introducessero i teatri, e che tutta via gode, in tutte le quattro stagione dell'anno, ed in particolare in tempo di Carnovale* (Venice: Giovanni de' Paoli, 1715), 20–27. The book includes the lyrics to the songs sung in this masquerade (28–30). See also Selfridge-Field, *A New Chronology of Venetian Opera,* 627–28.

2. Neither Ivanovich nor Belloratto indicates what the monsters were, but an account of the masquerade in the April 1769 *Mercure galante* reports that the riders "combatirent aux testes." *Courir les testes,* according to the 1694 *Dictionnaire de l'Académie française,* is "a type of drill on horseback in three passes done at full speed: the first to knock a head made of carton from the top of a barrel; the second to throw a javelin to strike the head; the last to lift the head from the ground with the point of a sword" (*Mercure,* quoted in Selfridge-Field, *Pallade Veneta,* 344; *Dictionnaire de l'Académie française,* 2 vols. [Paris: J. B. Coignard, 1694], 2:556).

3. Corner's spectacle closely resembled "Saracen Jousts" common elsewhere in Italy. In late February 1634, for instance, horsemen trailing plumes and ribbons gathered in Rome's Piazza Navona to compete for prizes by attacking wooden targets that represented Saracens. Costumes cast them as barbarians, Scythians, and Egyptians. Martine Boiteux writes: "In this festival, social inequality is seen objectively; its statues are fixed. The aristocratic festival, 'given to the populace,' rests upon a double affirmation: the assertion of a certain equality before festivity and an explicit recognition of the aristocracy's cultural hegemony" (Boiteux, "Carnaval annexé: Essai de lecture d'une fête romaine," *Annales E. S. C.* 32 [1977]: 356–58, 371).

4. Marino Sanuto, *Diarii,* February 4, 1529, quoted in Alessandro Pontremoli and Patrizia La Rocca, *La Danza a Venezia nel Rinascimento* (Venice: Nero Pozzi Editore, 1993), 193.

5. Sanuto, *Diarii,* February 8, 1528, quoted in Pontremoli and La Rocca, *La Danza,* 192; Sanuto, *Diarii,* February 15, 1504, 5:850–51.

6. Edward Muir provides a comprehensive general account of ritual violence coinciding with carnival across Europe in *Ritual in Early Modern Europe,* 112–21. See also Natalie Zemon Davis, "The Rites of Violence," in *Society and*

Culture in Early Modern France (Stanford, CA: Stanford University Press, 1975), 152–87; Toschi, *Le origini del teatro italiano,* 130–39, 234, 237.

7. Martine Boiteux, "Chasse aux taureaux et jeux romains de la renaissance," in Philippe Ariès and Jean-Claude Margolin, eds., *Les Jeux à la Renaissance* (Paris: J. Vrin, 1982), 38.

8. Toschi, *Le origini del teatro italiano,* 107–8; A. Barolo, *Folklore Montferrino* (Turin: Fratelli Bocca, 1931), 77; Toschi, *Le origini del teatro italiano,* 258–59.

9. Richard Bernheimer, *Wild Men in the Middle Ages: A Study in Art, Sentiment, and Demonology* (New York: Octagon Books, 1970). Cesare Poppi links the wild men hunts to animal hunts during carnival in Spain, France, Italy, and Russia, with the bear a common target. " 'To hunt the Bear out' can thus be a metaphor for human intervention in the seasonal transition, and 'to put the Bear to death' a redemptive sacrificial gesture. Before the masked figure of the Bear—and its dramatic equivalents—is finally harnessed and ritually put to death, it might be allowed to roam wild in villages, causing havoc, stealing and molesting women, as with the *Tschäggata* of Lötschental in Switzerland or the *Salvanel* in the Val di Fiemme" (Poppi, "The Other Within," in Mack, *Masks,* 211).

10. Sharp, quoted in Stephen D. Corrsin, "The Historiography of European Linked Sword Dancing," *Dance Research Journal* 25, no. 1 (1993): 5.

11. E. K. Chambers, *The Mediaeval Stage,* 2 vols. (Oxford: Oxford University Press, 1903), 1:190.

12. Toschi, *Le origini del teatro italiano,* 484–90.

13. Reato, *Storia del Carnevale,* 77–79; *Codice Cicogna,* 2991-II, 54, B.M.C.; January 26, 1760 (m.v.), *Codice Gradenigo,* 6:142, B.M.C.

14. Many have criticized aspects of Frazer's work for, among other things, disregarding specific contexts that gave meaning to myths, for attempting to convince more by accumulation than argument, for the naive positivism of equating magic and religion with superstition, and for achieving false coherence across time by omitting inconsistencies and contradiction among myths (Robert Ackerman, *J. G. Frazer: His Life and Work* [Cambridge: Cambridge University Press, 1987], 99).

15. James George Frazer, *The Golden Bough: A Study in Magic and Religion* (London: Macmillan Press, 1987), 315, 320.

16. Ibid., 325. Paolo Toschi's classic 1955 work on Italian theater, *Le origini del teatro italiano*—a book whose immense wealth remains in many ways unsurpassed—is strongly influenced by Frazer and by Wilhelm Mannhardt's *Wald- und Feldkulte* (1877) in its thesis linking both theater and carnival to spring fertility rites. "Let us repeat yet again that carnival is a propitiatory festival for the fertility of the earth and the abundance of crops," Toschi writes in a characteristic passage. "To produce new growth or a new plant, the seed must spend a period of time of greater or lesser length in the ground. From the darkness of the infernal realm, which contains the powers of regeneration with its subterranean deities and demons, the spirits of our forefathers, stirred by fitting rites, rise to earth to exercise their force on the fateful day of each New Year, an eternal return in this renewing cycle" (Toschi, *Le origini del teatro italiano,* 167).

17. Toschi, *Le origini del teatro italiano,* 351. From Prudentius (385–ca. 413),

Hymns, X, 1028–40: "The huge wound spouts a flood of hot blood ... which seethes in all directions. ... Through the countless channels provided by the perforations a stinking torrent falls. The priest enclosed in the pit gets the full force of it, exposing his befouled head to every drop; his robe and his whole body reek. Worse is to come! He tilts his head backwards, exposing his cheeks, his ears, his lips and nostrils, even his eyes. Without sparing his palate, he soaks his tongue in it, until his whole body is impregnated with this horrible, dark blood" (Robert Turcan, *Cults of the Roman Empire,* trans. Antonia Nevill [Cambridge, MA: Harvard University Press, 1996], 49–50).

18. Frazer, *The Golden Bough,* 583, 586. For Frazer's views on the scapegoat, see 494–583.

19. Julio Caro Baroja, *Le Carnaval,* trans. Sylvie Sesé-Léger (Paris: Gallimard, 1979), 20, 27, 359, 410–11. The French-trained anthropologist Arnold van Gennep countered Frazer's notion of an unbroken lineage in carnival practices by chronicling widely varying customs in towns and villages across France. Van Gennep suggested that any parallels among carnival practices were to be explained by "psychic and social constants" among humans (Arnold van Gennep, *Manuel de folklore français contemporain,* 4 vols. [Paris: Éditions Picard, 1937–58], 1:833–1088, 982).

20. Saturnalia (December 17–21) roughly coincided with the Feast of Fools (December 26–28) and came close to the official start of carnival in many locations; during Rome's *Kalendae Januariae* (January 1), a date corresponding to the Feast of the Ass, men dressed as women, women as men, and humans as animals; and the Roman Lupercalia (February 15–17), when young men raced through the streets joyously thwacking the bellies of young women with goatskin straps for fertility, coincided with the prime of carnival. Baroja, *Le Carnaval,* 150–54. For additional observations on the correspondence of Roman and Christian holidays, see Yves-Marie Bercé, *Fête et révolte: Des mentalités populaires du XVIᵉ au XVIIIᵉ siècle* (Paris: Hachette, 1976), 24–25. Recent work on Saturnalia casts doubt on Frazer's description of unbridled public license. Scholars now believe that its public festivities were mostly limited to ritual invocations of the god inside his temple in the Forum, that the so-called freedom of servants and slaves occurred largely within households, and that stories of wanton drunkenness, crime, and sex originated with early Christian writers intent on showing the depravity of pagans (Giorgio Brugnoli, "Il carnevale e i Saturnalia," *La ricerca folkloristica* 10 [1984]: 49–54).

21. "Until its abolition in the 1960s, the role of scapegoat was sustained in several towns in southern Spain by *La Mahoma,* a gigantic head of the Prophet that was exploded at the end of a mock battle between Christians and Moors" (Poppi, "The Other Within," in Mack, *Masks,* 210).

22. Boiteux, "Carnaval annexé," 365, 360–61; Alessandro Fontana, "La Scena," in Ruggiero Romano et al., eds., *Storia d'Italia,* 6 vols. (Turin: Giulio Einaudi, 1972–76), 1:852; Toschi, *Le origini del teatro italiano,* 335–56.

23. See, for instance, Timothy Gorringe, *God's Just Vengeance: Crime, Violence and the Rhetoric of Salvation* (Cambridge: Cambridge University Press, 1996), 11, 37, 45.

24. Walter Burkert, *Homo Necans: The Anthropology of Ancient Greek Sac-*

rificial Ritual and Myth, trans. Peter Bing (Berkeley: University of California Press, 1983), 22, 45. René Girard likewise links ritual violence to the sacred, but his guiding thesis—that such rites existed as an outlet to limit violence in communities without dependable judicial systems—does not fully account for the pervasive acts of ritual violence in settings where institutions minimized violence among groups and individuals (Girard, *Violence and the Sacred,* trans. Patrick Gregory [Baltimore: Johns Hopkins University Press, 1972], esp. 14–19, 124–25). Edward Muir's *Mad Blood Stirring* narrates the horrific course of carnival violence tied to factional strife. Muir offers this interpretation of its social meaning drawn principally from the logic of vendetta: mutilating the bodies of one's victims deprived them of masculinity and honor by equating them with criminals, was a "magical" means of tormenting them in the next world, and enacted a symbolic dismemberment of the body politic. Linking carnival violence against animals to vendetta, Muir writes that the "butchery of animals" was "the model for the killing of men" (Muir, *Mad Blood Stirring: Vendetta and Factions in Friuli during the Renaissance* [Baltimore: Johns Hopkins University Press, 1993], 198–200, xxix).

25. See chapter 4.

26. In describing the common response to carnival scapegoating in rural France and Switzerland, Yves-Marie Bercé uses similar terms. "All such episodes of frenzied joy, of the explosion of an aggressiveness without hatred or rancor, are instances of release. The community selects a fictive enemy whose effigy serves as an outlet for contained violence expressed in the full fury of youth. A game to satisfy fantasies and instincts, a psychodrama *avant la lettre,* the ceremony is also an exorcism. The figure, collectively humiliated, derided, and destroyed, is a vehicle who carries away the sorrow and indignity of the community. People feel stronger and more united after the sacrifice. The killing of a sacrificial victim plays its role as cleanser and liberator" (Bercé, *Fête et révolte,* 52).

27. Diderot, September 5, 1762, in *Oeuvres complètes,* 19:124.

CHAPTER 18. CARNIVAL TALES

1. Frazer, *The Golden Bough,* 322.

2. For bibliographies and historiographical reviews of the voluminous literature on European carnival, see, inter alia, Pier Giovanni d'Ayala and Martine Boiteux, eds., *Carnavals et mascarades* (Paris: Bordas, 1988), 187–88; Daniel Fabre, *Carnaval ou la fête à l'envers* (Paris: Gallimard, 1992), 152; Denis-Constant Martin, "Politics Behind the Mask: Studying Contemporary Carnivals in Political Perspective. Theoretical and Methodological Suggestions," *Questions de Recherche / Research in Question,* no. 2 (November 2001): 2–34; Muir, *Ritual in Early Modern Europe,* 121–24; Cesare Poppi, "Coutume, ethnicité et tradition: Formes de perpétuation dans le Carnaval Ladin du Val di Fassa (Dolomites, Italie du Nord)," in *Le Carnaval, la fête et la communication: Actes des premières rencontres internationales, Nice, 8 au 10 mars 1984* (Nice: Éditions Serre, 1985): 65–72; and Stallybrass and White, *The Politics and Poetics of Transgression,* 6–26.

3. Czeslaw Milosz, *The Captive Mind,* trans. Jane Zielonko (New York: Vintage Books, 1981), xii.

4. Katerina Clark and Michael Holquist, *Mikhail Bakhtin* (Cambridge, MA: Harvard University Press, 1984), 253–74, 321–25; Holquist, "Prologue" to Mikhail Bakhtin, *Rabelais and His World*, trans. Hélène Iswolsky (Bloomington: Indiana University Press, 1984), xix–xx.

5. Bakhtin, *Rabelais and His World*, 12, 410–12, 211, 165, 195, 205.

6. François Rabelais, *The Complete Works of François Rabelais*, trans. Donald M. Frame (Berkeley: University of California Press, 1991), 142, 152–58, 187.

7. Bakhtin, *Rabelais and His World*, 5, 10.

8. Ibid., 39.

9. Ibid., 19.

10. Rabelais, *The Complete Works*, 331–45; Bakhtin, *Rabelais and His World*, 224.

11. Bakhtin, *Rabelais and His World*, 7, 255. The Italian anthropologist Pietro Clemente likens the truth status of such declarations to "what one might say of an artwork or novel" rather than a work of historical scholarship (Clemente, "Idee del carnevale," in Clemente et al., *Il linguaggio, il corpo, la festa: Per un ripensamento della tematica di Michail Bachtin* [Milan: Franco Angeli Editore, 1983], 16).

12. Bakhtin, *Rabelais and His World*, 218.

13. Ibid., 245, 251.

14. Ibid., 265, 34. Caryl Emerson describes Bakhtin's attitude toward history harshly. She writes that his weaknesses include "facile analogies, indiscriminately 'open' documentation, overgeneralization, [and] a dismissal of history" (Emerson, *The First Hundred Years of Mikhail Bakhtin* [Princeton, NJ: Princeton University Press, 1997], 162.

15. Clark and Holquist, *Mikhail Bakhtin*, 312. Samuel Kinser offers considerable nuance in distinguishing text and context in Bakhtin's *Rabelais and His World* (Kinser, *Rabelais's Carnival: Text, Context, Metatext* [Berkeley: University of California Press, 1990], esp. 7–60 and 248–69).

16. Guido Ruggiero, *Binding Passions: Tales of Magic, Marriage, and Power at the End of the Renaissance* (Oxford: Oxford University Press, 1993), 3–23.

17. Ibid., 3, 12.

18. *Sant'Ufficio*, March 1 and 5, 1571, B. 30, A.S.V.

19. Umberto Eco, "The Frames of Comic Freedom," in Thomas A. Sebeok, ed., *Carnival!* (Berlin: Mouton Publishers, 1984), 3, 6–7. See also Feldman, *Opera and Sovereignty*, 157–58, 181.

20. *Le Modérateur*, February 17, 1790; *Révolutions de Paris*, February 18–25, 1792, 371; see also James H. Johnson, "Versailles, Meet Les Halles: Masks, Carnival, and the French Revolution," *Representations* 73 (2001): 93, 95–96.

21. Davis, *Society and Culture in Early Modern France*, 147.

22. Emmanuel Le Roy Ladurie, *Carnival in Romans*, trans. Mary Feeney (New York: George Braziller, 1979), 28, 68–69, 99, 190, 202, 239–40, 266–67.

23. Edward Muir describes a similarly explosive carnival in Friuli, when in 1511 social factions, fed by foreign invasion, economic crisis, and a cycle of vendetta, clashed on *giovedì grasso*. Rampaging carnival revelers, dressed in the clothes and insignia of their aristocratic opponents, burned castles and killed at

least fifty nobles, dismembering their bodies and throwing the remains into wells and latrines (Muir, *Mad Blood Stirring*, esp. 111–200).

24. Le Roy Ladurie, *Carnival in Romans*, 192.

25. Victor Turner, *The Ritual Process: Structure and Anti-Structure* (Ithaca, NY: Cornell University Press, 1969), 176. See also Muir, *Civic Ritual in Renaissance Venice*, 158. For a lucid discussion of leading views of religious and secular rituals and their social function, see Muir, *Ritual in Early Modern Europe*, esp. 1–6.

26. Roger Chartier and Domique Julia, "Le Monde à l'envers," *L'Arc*, no. 65 (1976): 43–53. See also Giuseppe Cocchiara, *Il mondo alla rovescia* (Turin: Editore Boringhieri, 1981).

27. Jacques Heers, *Fêtes des fous et carnavals* (Paris: Fayard, 1983), 108, 176–77, 136–39; Ingvild Salid Gilhus, "Carnival in Religion: The Feast of Fools in France," *Numen* 37, no. 1 (1990): 27, 24.

28. Heers, *Fêtes des fous et carnavals*, 181–82; Gilhus, "Carnival in Religion," 24.

29. Quoted in Bakhtin, *Rabelais and His World*, 75.

30. Heers, *Fêtes des fous et carnavals*, 244.

CHAPTER 19. THE MASK OF SINCERITY

1. All references to the Gerachi case are drawn from the records of the Esecutori contro la Bestemmia, B. 5, A.S.V.

2. A definitive essay on the Esecutori contro la Bestemmia is Renzo Derosas, "Moralità e giustizia a Venezia nell '500–'600: Gli Esecutori contro la Bestemmia," in Gaetano Cozzi, ed., *Stato, società e giustizia nella repubblica Veneta (sec. XV–XVIII)* (Rome: Jouvence, 1980), 431–528.

3. This point bears a certain resemblance to what Stephen Greenblatt has identified in poems, plays, and religious tracts from the sixteenth century. In his classic book *Renaissance Self-Fashioning*, Greenblatt describes an emergent view of identity as "a manipulable, artful process." Self-fashioning, he argues, was rooted in the conviction that the self might be shaped contrary to expected social or political roles (Greenblatt, *Renaissance Self-Fashioning*, 1).

4. Lionel Trilling, *Sincerity and Authenticity* (Cambridge, MA: Harvard University Press, 1972), 2; see also James H. Johnson, "Deceit and Sincerity in Early Modern Venice," *Eighteenth-Century Studies* 38, no. 3 (2005): 399–415.

5. Davis, *Society and Culture in Early Modern France*, xvii. According to Davis, elements of what we might recognize as modern individuality appear as reactions to specific expectations. Arnaud du Tilh, the false Martin Guerre, sought "to forge a new identity and a new life for himself" by mastering the intimate details of the real Martin's daily life against a backdrop of rigidly maintained and closely monitored boundaries of behavior. In *Fiction in the Archives*, Davis looks to judicial customs and conventions as boundaries within which the accused fashioned narratives of identity. " 'Imposture' stands not as an isolated form of behavior, not as a disconnected 'monstrosity' or disjoint 'prodigy,' but as an extreme and disturbing case on a sixteenth-century spectrum of personal change

for purposes of play, of advantage, or of 'attracting the benevolence of others' "
(Davis, *The Return of Martin Guerre*, 41; Davis, "On the Lame," *American Historical Review* 93, no. 3 [1988]: 590; Davis, *Fiction in the Archives*).

6. For a riveting account of an aristocratic impostor under Louis XIV who attempted to hide his nobility, see Jeffrey S. Ravel, *The Would-Be Commoner: A Tale of Deception, Murder, and Justice in Seventeenth-Century France* (Boston: Houghton Mifflin, 2008).

7. Casanova, *History of My Life*, 11:111, 8:35.

8. Sándor Márai, *Casanova in Bolzano*, trans. George Szirtes (New York: Alfred A. Knopf, 2004), 74, 103.

9. Volker Hunecke, *Il patriziato veneziano alla fine della Repubblica: 1646–1797, Demografia, famiglia, ménage*, trans. Benedetta Heinemann Campana (Rome: Jouvence, 1997), 43–46, 165–72. For an excellent discussion of the purchase of patrician status and the resistance new nobles encountered from old families, see Roberto Sabbadini, *L'acquisto della tradizione: Tradizione aristocratica e nuova nobiltà a Venezia (sec. XVII–XVIII)* (Udine: Istituto Editoriale Veneto Friulano, 1995). See also Stanley Chojnacki, *Women and Men in Renaissance Venice* (Baltimore: Johns Hopkins University Press, 2000), 224–33; and Dennis Romano, *Patricians and Popolani: The Social Foundations of the Renaissance Venetian State* (Baltimore: Johns Hopkins University Press, 1987), 50–51, 145.

CHAPTER 20. CARNIVAL CONTAINED

1. Goldoni, *Le massere* (1755), in *Tutte le opere*, 5:1002–4.

2. *Il festino* (1754), *Una delle ultime sere di carnovale* (1762), *Le morbinose* (1758).

3. Franco Fido, "Nobili, popolane, borghesi in maschera: (Ancora) sul carnevale in goldoniano," in *Le inquietudine di Goldoni* (Geneva: Costa & Nolan, 1995), 102–3.

4. *Codice Cicogna*, n.d., 2991-II, 55, B.M.C.

5. Molmenti, *La Storia di Venezia nella vita privata*, 3:253; Rossi, *Leggi e Costumi Veneziani*, 12:31; Romanin, *Storia documentata di Venezia*, 9:49.

6. Rossi, *Leggi e Costumi Veneziani*, 12:31; *Pallada Veneta*, January 23–30, 1716 (m.v.).

7. Lamberti, *Memorie*, 1:207, 1:138, B.N.M.; Rossi, *Leggi e Costumi Veneziani*, 3:60, B.N.M. A similar segregation prevailed in Rome during carnival. The privileged rode horses or traveled in coaches and were accompanied by attendants bearing baskets of perfumed eggs or confetti, which they threw at maskers like themselves. Most commoners went on foot and threw fruit or ordinary eggs at one another. Jews and the aged largely kept to their kind, as did the blind, hunchbacked, and lame. Roman carnival offered equality of access, one historian has concluded, but attachments governed how one participated. "Each had his place in the kingdom of carnival, as well as in the city" (Boiteux, "Carnival annexé," 371–72). *Gazzetta Urbana Veneta*, February 6, 1788, 88; Rossi, *Leggi e Costumi Veneziani*, 7:148, B.N.M.; William Bromley, *Remarks in the Grand Tour of France and Italy* (1692), quoted in Peter Burke, "Le Carnaval de Venise: Esquisse pour une histoire de longue durée," in Ariès and Margolin, *Les jeux à la Renaissance*, 58–59.

8. Daniele Beltrami, *Storia della popolazione di Venezia dalla fine del secolo XVI alla caduta della repubblica* (Padua: Cedam, 1954), 71.

9. Zorzi, *I teatri pubblici di Venezia*, 16; Rossi, *Leggi e Costumi Veneziani*, 12:34–35, B.N.M.; Wright, *Some Observations Made in Travelling through France, Italy, &c.*, 1:84; *Codice Gradenigo*, February 8, 1763, 11:35, B.M.C.

10. *Codice Gradenigo*, February 9, 1756, 3:133, B.M.C.; *Codice Gradenigo*, February 17, 1759, 5:119, B.M.C. See chapter 2.

11. Comisso, *Agenti segreti di Venezia*, 173–74; *Gazzetta Urbana Veneta*, January 26, 1788, 61–62.

12. Rossi, *Leggi e Costumi Veneziani*, 12:25, 7:244–45, B.N.M.; Lamberti, *Memorie*, 1:209, B.N.M.

13. *Pallada Veneta*, January 10–17, 1710 (m.v.).

14. "Unlike in certain parts of Europe," writes the historian Roy Porter, "no iron curtain of law or blood permanently divided bondman and freeman, trade and land, commoner and noble. Mobility was considerable, eroding traditional ideas of deference. . . . England was a society in which the fences dividing social ranks were, in theory and in practice, jumpable" (Porter, *English Society in the Eighteenth Century* [London: Penguin Books, 1990], 49–50). Dror Wahrman's terrifically rich *The Making of the Modern Self: Identity and Culture in Eighteenth-Century England* describes an "*ancien régime* of identity" in which personality, he contends, was malleable and the self was "relational" rather than fixed. His chapter on masquerade in the eighteenth century underscores how different the English experience of masking was from the Venetian. "The masquerade was not really about gender, any more than it was about any other category of identity," Wahrman writes. "Rather, it was a scene of bacchanalian experimentation with the protean mutability of identity on a more basic level and in all its possible manifestations" (Wahrman, *The Making of the Modern Self: Identity and Culture in Eighteenth-Century England* [New Haven, CT: Yale University Press, 2004], 160).

15. Griffen, quoted in Castle, *Masquerade and Civilization*, 29–30; see also 110–29. A letter published in the newspaper from one Julie Schott, who was smitten by a young masker at the Opéra-Comique ball, conveys the dream that masked balls inspired. "If he really is a former notary from one of our towns in the Midi, and if his family is rich and well-regarded, and if everything else he told me is true, then may he return to the ball this Sunday. I'll be there in the same costume, standing in the same place." A journalist at another masked ball overheard a young woman say this to a man who claimed to be a broker: "For us, a masked ball is our stock exchange" (*Vert-vert*, February 4, 1837; *Les Coulisses*, February 10, 1842).

16. A half century before Karl Marx, Franceschi quoted Carlo Contarini in a speech before the Great Council that described religion as "the opiate of the people." Franceschi lamented that it, too, was losing its hold over the populace, along with decency, modesty, and respect for hierarchy.

17. Franceschi, *Memorie della Correzione 1780*, 95, 126, B.N.M.

18. Nani, *Principi di una amministrazione ordinata e tranquilla*, 54v, B.C.P.; Misson, *Nouveau voyage d'Italie*, 1:235–36.

19. *Plan de réforme, proposé aux cinq correcteurs de Venise* (Amsterdam: n.p., 1775), xiv, xxviii. Robert C. Davis's work on the "War of the Fists" describing

pitched battles between rival neighborhoods in Venice cites the same line of reasoning among Venetian authorities: if the bloody brawls kept plebeians distracted from the affairs of the state, so much the better (Davis, *The War of the Fists: Popular Culture and Public Violence in Late Renaissance Venice* [Oxford: Oxford University Press, 1994], 158–59).

20. See Paolo Preto, *Persona per hora secreta* (Milan: Il Saggiatore, 2003), 57, 76. See also Preto, "Le 'paure' della società veneziana," in Branca et al., *Storia di Venezia,* 6:233–35.

21. Cozzi, *La società veneta e il suo diritto,* 66, 80, 126; Derosas, "Moralità e giustizia a Venezia nell '500–'600," in Cozzi, *Stato, società e giustizia,* 446–48; George Gordon, Baron Byron, *Marino Faliero,* in *The Complete Poetical Works,* 7 vols. (Oxford: Oxford University Press, 1986), 4:361; John Adams, *A Defense of the Constitution of Government of the United States of America* (1787), quoted in Preto, *Persona per hora secreta,* 176; see also 192.

22. See, for instance, *Esecutori contro la Bestemmia,* B. 4 (1700–1708), A.S.V.; Cozzi, *La società veneta e il suo diritto,* 224–27; Elizabeth Sepper, " 'Her Only Treasure Lost': Rape and Reputation in Eighteenth-Century Venice" (undergraduate honors thesis, Boston University, 2002), 3, 60.

23. Beltrami, *Storia della popolazione di Venezia,* 210; Misson, *Nouveau voyage d'Italie,* 1:236; Burke, "Le Carnaval de Venise," in Ariès and Margolin, *Les jeux à la Renaissance,* 61.

24. Patricia Labalme, "Sodomy and Venetian Justice in the Renaissance," *Review of Legal History* 52 (1984): 226, 241; Guido Ruggiero, *The Boundaries of Eros: Sex Crime and Sexuality in Renaissance Venice* (Oxford: Oxford University Press, 1985), 109, 140; Giovanni Scarabello, "Devianza sessuale ed interventi di giustizia a Venezia nella prima metà del XVI secolo," in *Tiziano e Venezia: Convengo internationale di studi, Venezia, 1976* (Vicenza: Neri Pozza Editore, 1980): 75–84. For an analysis of punishment as both purification and the display of state power, see Guido Ruggiero, *Violence in Early Renaissance Venice* (New Brunswick, NJ: Rutgers University Press, 1980), esp. 1–53.

25. Gabriele Martini, *Il "Vitio Nefando" nella Venezia del seicento* (Rome: Jouvence, 1988), 42–43, 73, 90; Labalme, "Sodomy and Venetian Justice," 251–52; Lane, *Venice,* 400–402.

26. Martini, *Il "Vitio Nefando" nella Venezia del seicento,* 132–35, 114.

27. Grevembroch, *Gli abiti de Veneziani,* 3:89, B.M.C.

28. "In Rabelais' novel the image of death is devoid of all tragic or terrifying overtones. Death is the necessary link in the process of the people's growth and renewal. It is the 'other side' of birth" (Bakhtin, *Rabelais and His World,* 407). For a reading of the violence of Venetian carnival that is consistent with Bakhtin's view, see Muir, *Civic Ritual in Renaissance Venice,* 177–79.

29. Muir, *Ritual in Early Modern Europe,* 254.

CHAPTER 21. BITTER ASH

1. Piero del Negro argues that in voting to end the aristocratic republic and install a democratic regime, the Great Council acted from neither panic nor a prudent regard for the preservation of the city but rather to protect their own

wealth and property on the mainland (Del Negro, "Il patriziato veneziano e la fine della Serenissima," in Cesare Mozzarelli and Gianni Venturi, eds., *Europa delle corti alla fine dell'antico regime* [Rome: Bulzoni Editore, 1991], 437). For a detailed account of the chaotic events of May 12, see the anonymous diary attributed to Piero Donà in Annibale Alberti and Roberto Cessi, eds., *Verbali delle sedute della Municipalità provvisoria di Venezia, 1797*, 3 vols. (Bologna: Nicola Zanichelli, 1928), 1/1:xxiii–xxvi; Giovanni Distefano and Giannantonio Paladini, *Storia di Venezia, 1797–1997*, 3 vols. (Venice: Supernova, 1996), 1:77–95.

2. *An Accurate Account of the Fall of the Republic of Venice*, trans. John Hinckley (London: J. Hatchard, 1804), 210, 184.

3. Alberti and Cessi, *Verbali delle sedute della Municipalità*, 1/1:23 (May 22, 1797), 50 (May 27), 61 (May 29), 247 (July 13), 490 (August 15); Distefano and Paladini, *Storia di Venezia*, 1:151–52, 159, 176; *Raccolta di carte pubbliche*, 1:53–61, 63; *Monitore universale*, July 26, 1797, 253; October 14, 1797, 507.

4. Alberti and Cessi, *Verbali delle sedute della Municipalità*, 1/1:xxv; *Raccolta di carte pubbliche*, 3:114; *Monitore universale*, June 28, 1797, 158; *Raccolta di carte pubbliche*, 8:189; Distefano and Paladini, *Storia di Venezia*, 2:17. See also Nicolò Morosini, *Lettera apologetica* [Venice: n.p., 1797].

5. Paolo Mariuz, "Francesco Gallimberti: Dai 'Fasti Veneziani' alle 'Carceri Sotterracquee,'" in Mozzarelli and Venturi, *Europa delle corti alla fine dell'antico regime*, 229. Pamphlets denounced the State Inquisitors as, among other things, "barbaric," "abominable," "a bloody tribunal," "perfect despots," "bestial," "infernal," "satraps," and "Neronic" (Paolo Preto, *I servizi segreti di Venezia. Spionaggio e controspionaggio: Cifrari, intercettazioni, delazioni, tra mito e realtà* [Milan: Il Saggiatore, 1994], 589); *La caduta della maschera* and *L'impostura smascherata dal fatto, e dalla verità, ragionamento libero*, in *Raccolta di carte pubbliche*, 2:64–67, 8:304–10.

6. Distefano and Paladini, *Storia di Venezia*, 1:189.

7. Ibid., 1:100.

8. For details on the treaties of Leoben and Campo Formio (signed on April 17 and October 18, 1797), the first promising and the second formally delivering Venice to the Hapsburg monarchy, see ibid., 1:204–31. For the February 17, 1798, law prohibiting masks, see ibid., 2:34–35, and Bertelli, *Il carnevale di Venezia*, 56. By an edict of January 18, 1801, Napoleon announced that "decent" masks would be permitted during carnival throughout the Cisalpine Republic (i.e., those areas in Italy still in French possession), but the edict "absolutely prohibited those masks of the so-called Italian theater, namely Brighella, Arlecchino, Pantalone, and others, as well as any masks representing religious subjects or institutions tolerated within the Republic, or those that might offend public morals." The edict was extended to Venice when France retook the city after Napoleon's victory at Austerlitz in 1805 (Emanuele Peraldi, "Storia del diritto d'autore nei teatri di Vercelli e Novara" [thesis in law, University of Pavia, 2002], 101).

9. *Gazzetta Privilegiata di Venezia*, February 21, 1816, 4.

10. Ibid.

11. For these pages I have drawn extensively from the excellent scholarship

on Tiepolo's *Divertimenti,* which includes Philipp P. Fehl, "Farewell to Jokes: The Last *Capricci* of Giovanni Domenico Tiepolo and the Tradition of Irony in Venetian Painting," *Critical Inquiry* 5, no. 4 (1979): 761–91; Adelheid M. Gealt and George Knox, eds., *Domenico Tiepolo: Master Draftsman* (Bloomington: Indiana University Press, 1996); Adelheid M. Gealt and Marcia E. Vetrocq, *Domenico Tiepolo's Punchinello Drawings* (Bloomington: Indiana University Art Museum, 1979); Adriano Mariuz, *Giandomenico Tiepolo* (Venice: Alfieri, 1971); Adriano Mariuz and Giuseppe Pavanello, *Tiepolo: Ironia e comico* (Venice: Marsilio, 2004); and James Byam Shaw, *The Drawings of Domenico Tiepolo* (Boston: Boston Book & Art Shop, 1962).

12. Adelheid M. Gealt, quoted in Adriano Mariuz, "I disegni di Pulcinella di Giandomenico Tiepolo," in Mariuz and Pavanello, *Tiepolo,* 58.

13. Adriano Mariuz, quoted in Giuseppe Pavanello, "'Tutta la vita, dal principio alla fine, è una comica assurdità,' ovvero 'Il segreto di Pulcinella,'" in Mariuz and Pavanello, *Tiepolo,* 32.

14. Fehl, "Farewell to Jokes," 782.

15. The scene points to the avian etymology of his name: *pulcino,* "chick," "nestling." In its gentler sound and associations, "Pulcinella" is closer in spirit to the character Tiepolo depicts than the pugilistic "Punchinello" or "Punch," names commonly used for the figure in English.

16. Mariuz and Pavanello, *Tiepolo,* 59.

17. James Byam Shaw was the first to observe this connection. See Adelheid M. Gealt and George Knox, eds., *Domenico Tiepolo: Master Draftsman* (Bloomington: Indiana University Press, 1996), 37.

18. For an extended religious reading of the frontispiece that views the plate of *gnocchi* as the host and the abandoned hat as a sign that Pulcinella's spirit now mingles with the *gnocchi,* see Paërl, *Pulcinella,* 69–70.

19. Marcia E. Vetrocq, "Domenico Tiepolo and the Figure of Punchinello," in Gealt and Vetrocq, *Domenico Tiepolo's Punchinello Drawings,* 24–25.

20. See chapter 17.

EPILOGUE

1. Doody, *Tropic of Venice,* 290–91.

2. Philippe Monnier, *Venice in the Eighteenth Century* (London: Chattus and Windus, 1910), 42, 32, 21.

3. Johann Strauss, *Eine Nacht in Venedig,* Serie I, Werkgruppe 2, Bd. 10 of *Neue Strauss Gesamtausgabe* (Vienna: Strauss Edition, 1999–2009); see James H. Johnson, "The Myth of Venice in Nineteenth-Century Opera," *Journal of Interdisciplinary History* 36, no. 3 (2006): 533–54; Anna Giubertoni, "Venezia nella letteratura austriaca moderna," in *Venezia Vienna: Il mito della cultura veneziana nell'Europa asburgica,* edited by Giandomenico Romanelli (Milan: Electra Editrice, 1983), 105–26.

4. For two excellent treatments of Venice in the nineteenth century, see John Pemble, *Venice Rediscovered* (Oxford: Oxford University Press, 1995); and Margaret Plant, *Venice: Fragile City, 1797–1997* (New Haven, CT: Yale University Press, 2002).

5. John Ruskin, *The Stones of Venice,* 3 vols. (New York: John Wiley & Sons, 1878), 2:76, 129.

6. James Fenimore Cooper, *The Bravo* (New Haven, CT: College & University Press, 1963), 340, 382.

7. Pierre Daru, *Histoire de la République de Venise,* 8 vols. (Paris: Firmin Didot, 1821), 6:173, 181–82.

8. George Gordon, Baron Byron, *The Two Foscari, an Historical Tragedy,* in *Five Romantic Plays, 1768–1821* (Oxford: Oxford University Press, 2000), 267–68. See L. Cattan, "La Venise de Byron et la Venise des romantiques français," *Revue de littérature comparée* 5, no. 1 (1925): 89–102.

Bibliography

ARCHIVES

Archives du Ministère des Affaires Etrangères, Paris (A.M.A.E.)
  Corréspondance politique, Venise
  Mémoires et documents, Venise
Archivio di Stato, Venice (A.S.V.)
  Ceremoniali
  Compilazione delle Leggi
  Consiglio dei Dieci
  Esecutori contro la Bestemmia
  Inquisitori di Stato
  Maggior Consiglio
  Provveditori alle Pompe
  Sant'Ufficio
Biblioteca del Museo Civico Correr, Venice (B.M.C.)
  Codice Cicogna
  Codice Gradenigo

UNPUBLISHED MANUSCRIPTS

Biblioteca Civica, Padua (B.C.P.)
  Nani, Giacomo. *Principi di una amministrazione ordinata e tranquilla* [1781?].
  MS C.M. 125.
Biblioteca del Museo Civico Correr, Venice (B.M.C.)
  Grevembroch, G. *Gli abiti de Veneziani di quasi ogni età con diligenza raccolti
  e dipinti nel secolo XVIII.* 4 vols.
Biblioteca della Fondazione Querini Stampalia, Venice (B.F.Q.S.)

Garzoni, Pietro. Βάσανος cioè Paragone usato da Pietro Garzoni, Senatore sù la Repubblica di Venezia per fare prouva della sua qualità [1725]. MS cl. IV 316.
Biblioteca Nazionale Marciana, Venice (B.N.M.)
[Conti, abbé.] Lettres de M. l'abbé Conti, noble vénitien, à Madame de Caylus. MSS Franc., 58 (12102).
Franceschi, Pietro. Memorie della Correzione 1780. It. VII, 1810.
Lamberti, Antonio. Memoire degli ultimi cinquant'anni della Repubblica di Venezia. 3 vols. It. VII, 9345–47.
Rossi, Giovanni. Leggi e Costumi Veneziani. 416 volumes. n.d.

NEWSPAPERS

Gazzetta Privilegiata di Venezia
Gazzetta Urbana Veneta
Gazzetta Veneta
Le Modérateur
Les Coulisses
L'Osservatore Veneto
Monitore universale
Pallada Veneta
Révolutions de Paris
Vert-vert

PUBLISHED SOURCES

Accetto, Torquato. Della dissimulazione onesta. Ed. Salvatore Silvano Nigro. Turin: Giulio Einaudi, 1997.
———. De l'Honnête dissimulation. Trans. Mireille Blanc-Sanchez. Lagrasse: Éditions Verdier, 1990.
———. Rime amorose. Ed. Salvatore Silvano Nigro. Turin: Giulio Einaudi, 1987.
An Accurate Account of the Fall of the Republic of Venice. Trans. John Hinckley. London: J. Hatchard, 1804.
Ackerman, Robert. J. G. Frazer: His Life and Work. Cambridge: Cambridge University Press, 1987.
Addison, Joseph. The Miscellaneous Works of Joseph Addison. 2 vols. London: G. Bell and Sons, 1914.
Agnelli, Maddalena. "Il pubblico veneziano di Carlo Goldoni." Problemi di critica Goldoniana 2 (1995): 182–230.
Ahmed, Leila. Women and Gender in Islam: Historical Roots of a Modern Debate. New Haven, CT: Yale University Press, 1992.
Alberti, Annibale, and Roberto Cessi, eds. Verbali delle sedute della Municipalità provvisoria di Venezia, 1797. 3 vols. Bologna: Nicola Zanichelli, 1928.
Alberti, Carmelo. La Scena Veneziana nell'età di Goldoni. Rome: Bulzoni Editore, 1990.
Albrizzi, Giambattista. Forestiero illuminato intorno le cose più rare, e curiose antiche, e moderne, della città di Venezia. Venice: n.p., 1772.

Aliprandi, Giuseppe. "Dalla 'opinione comune' alla 'pubblica opinione' nella seconda metà del Settecento." *Atti e memorie: Accademia Patavina di scienze, lettere ed arte* 77, no. 3 (1964–65): 483–503.

Alonge, Roberto, and Guido Davico Bonino, eds. *Storia del teatro moderno e contemporaneo.* 4 vols. Turin: Giulio Einaudi, 2000.

Amelot de la Houssaye, Abraham-Nicolas. *Histoire du gouvernement de Venise.* 2 vols. Paris: Chez Frédéric Leonard, 1677.

Apollonio, Mario. *Storia della Commedia dell'Arte.* Rome: Edizioni Augustea, 1930.

Archenholz, Johann Wilhelm von. *Tableau de l'Italie.* 2 vols. Brussels: Chez Le Francq, 1788.

Ariès, Philippe, and Jean-Claude Margolin, eds. *Les jeux à la Renaissance.* Paris: J. Vrin, 1982.

Arnaldi, Girolamo, and Manlio Pastore Stocchi, eds. *Storia della cultura veneta.* 6 vols. Vicenza: Neri Pozza Editore, 1976–86.

Aslan, Odette, and Denis Bablet. *Le Masque: Du rite au théâtre.* Paris: Éditions du Centre National de la Recherche Scientifique, 1985.

Bacchelli, Riccardo. "Da Dite a Malebolge: La tragedia delle porte chiuse e la farsa dei ponti rotti." *Giornale storico della letteratura italiana* 131, no. 1 (1959): 1–32.

Bacon, Francis. *The Essayes or Counsels, Civill and Morall.* Cambridge, MA: Harvard University Press, 1985.

Baffo, Giorgio. *Poesie di Giorgio Baffo, Patrizio Veneto.* Milan: Arnoldo Mondadori, 1991.

Bakhtin, Mikhail. *Rabelais and His World.* Trans. Hélène Iswolksy. Bloomington: Indiana University Press, 1984.

Baldinucci, Filippo. *Dal Baroccio a Salvator Rosa.* Florence: G. C. Sansoni, 1914.

Ballarini, Luigi. *I Conti del Nord a Venezia: Due lettere.* Venice: Marco Visentini, 1870.

Barbieri, Nicolò. *La Supplica discorso famigliare a quelli che trattano de' comici.* 1634; reprint, Milan: Polifilo, 1971.

Baroja, Julio Caro. *Le Carnaval.* Trans. Sylvie Sesé-Léger. Paris: Gallimard, 1979.

Barolo, A. *Folklore Montferrino.* Turin: Fratelli Bocca, 1931.

Barricelli, Franca R. " 'Making a People What It Once Was': Regenerating Civic Identity in the Revolutionary Theatre of Venice." *Eighteenth-Century Life* 23, no. 3 (1999): 38–57.

Barzaghi, Antonio. *Donne o cortigiane? La prostituzione a Venezia: Documenti di costume dal XVI al XVIII secolo.* Verona: Bertani Editore, 1980.

Baschet, Armand. *Les Archives de Venise: Histoire de la Chancellerie secrète.* Paris: Henri Plon, 1870.

[Battaglia, Michele.] *Cicalata sulle cacce di tori Veneziane.* Venice: G. B. Merlo, 1844.

Battaglia, Salvatore, et al. *Grande dizionario della lingua italiana.* 21 vols. Turin: Unione Tipografico, 1961–2009.

Beam, Sara. *Laughing Matters: Farce and the Making of Absolutism in France.* Ithaca, NY: Cornell University Press, 2007.

Beijer, Agne, ed. *Le Recueil Fossard.* Paris: Librairie Théâtrale, 1981.

Belloratto, Galeno [Angelo Bottarello]. *Breve descrizione di Venezia, e de piacevoli trattenimenti, che godea prima, che s'introducessero i Teatri, e che tutto via gode, in tutte le quattro stagione dell'Anno, ed in particolare in tempo di Carnovale.* Venice: Giovanni de' Paoli, 1715.

Beltrami, Daniele. *Storia della popolazione di Venezia dalla fine del secolo XVI alla caduta della repubblica.* Padua: Cedam, 1954.

Benzoni, Gino, ed. *Le metamorfosi di Venezia: Da capitale di stato a città del mondo.* Florence: Leo S. Olschki, 2001.

Bercé, Yves-Marie. *Fête et révolte: Des mentalités populaires du XVIe au XVI-IIe siècle.* Paris: Hachette, 1976.

Berengo, Marino. *La società Veneta alla fine del Settecento.* Florence: G. C. Sansoni, 1956.

Bernheimer, Richard. *Wild Men in the Middle Ages: A Study in Art, Sentiment, and Demonology.* New York: Octagon Books, 1970.

Bertelli, Stephania. *Il carnevale di Venezia nel Settecento.* Rome: Jouvence Società Editoriale, 1992.

Biliotti, Cesare. *Il Ridotto.* Venice: Pietro Naratovich, 1870.

Biondi, Albano. *Eresia e riforma nell'Italia del Cinquecento.* Florence: G. C. Sansoni Editore, 1974.

Bistort, Giulio. *Il magistrato alle pompe nella Repubblica di Venezia.* Venice: Tipografia–Libreria Emiliana, 1912.

Boccalini, Traiano. *Ragguagli di Parnaso e Pietra del paragone politico.* 2 vols. Bari: Giuseppe Laterza & Figli, 1910–12.

Boccardi, Virgilio. *L'Ambiente teatrale della Venezia musicale del '700.* Venice: Filippi Editore, 1998.

Boerio, Giuseppe. *Dizionario del dialetto veneziano.* Venice: Giovanni Cecchini, 1856; reprint, Florence: Giunti, 1993.

Boissard, Jean-Jacques. *Habitus variarum Orbis Gentium.* [Cologne: Kaspar Rutz], 1581.

Boiteux, Martine. "Carnaval annexé: Essai de lecture d'une fête romaine." *Annales E. S. C.* 32 (1977): 356–80.

Bonino, Guido Davico, ed. *Il teatro italiano.* 5 vols. Turin: Giulio Einaudi, 1975–1991.

Borrelli, Gianfranco. *Ragion di Stato: L'arte italiana della prudenza politica. Catalogo della mostra.* Naples: Istituto Italiano per gli Studi Filosofici, 1994.

Bosisio, Paolo. *Carlo Gozzi e Goldoni: Una polemica letteraria con versi inediti e rari.* Florence: Leo S. Olschki, 1970.

Bouwsma, William J. *Venice and the Defense of Republican Liberty: Renaissance Values in the Age of the Counter Reformation.* Berkeley: University of California Press, 1968.

Bragaglia, Anton Giulio. *Pulcinella.* Rome: Gherardo Casini, 1953.

Branca, Vittore, et al., eds. *Storia di Venezia dalle origini alla caduta della Serenissima.* 10 vols. Rome: Istituto della Enciclopedia Italiana, 1991–98.

Bratti, Daniele Ricciotti. *La Fine della Serenissima.* Milan: Alfieri & Lacroix, [1917?].

Braun, Edward, ed. *Meyerhold on Theatre.* New York: Hill and Wang, 1969.

Bromley, William. *Remarks in the Grand Tour of France and Italy.* London: n.p., 1692.

Brugnoli, Giorgio. "Il carnevale e i Saturnalia." *La ricerca folkloristica* 10 (1984): 49–54.

Burke, Edmund. *Reflections on the Revolution in France.* New Haven, CT: Yale University Press, 2003.

Burke, Peter. *Popular Culture in Early Modern Europe.* New York: New York University Press, 1978.

———. *Venice and Amsterdam: A Study of Seventeenth-Century Elites.* Cambridge, MA: Polity Press, 1994.

Burkert, Walter. *Homo Necans: The Anthropology of Ancient Greek Sacrificial Ritual and Myth.* Trans. Peter Bing. Berkeley: University of California Press, 1983.

Buzzi, Paolo. *Versi liberi.* Milan: Fratelli Treves, 1913.

Byam Shaw, James. *The Drawings of Domenico Tiepolo.* Boston: Boston Book & Art Shop, 1962.

Byron, George Gordon, Baron. *The Complete Poetical Works.* 7 vols. Oxford: Oxford University Press, 1986.

———. *Five Romantic Plays, 1768–1821.* Oxford: Oxford University Press, 2000.

Caillois, Roger. *Man, Play, and Games.* Trans. Meyer Barash. New York: Free Press, 1961.

Calhoun, Craig, ed. *Habermas and the Public Sphere.* Cambridge, MA: MIT Press, 1992.

Calvin, Jean. *Three French Treatises.* London: Athlone Press, 1970.

Caminer, Gioseffa Cornoldi. *La Donna galante ed erudita: Giornale dedicato al bel sesso.* Venezia: Marsilio Editori, 1983.

Canal, Martin da. *Les Estoires de Venise: Cronaca veneziana in lingua francese dalle origini al 1275.* Florence: Leo S. Olschki, 1972.

Careri, Francesco Gemelli. *Viaggi per Europa.* 2 vols. Naples: Felice Mosca, 1722.

Le Carnaval, la fête et la communication: Actes des premières rencontres internationales, Nice, 8 au 10 mars 1984. Nice: Éditions Serre, 1985.

Carrithers, David. "Not So Virtuous Republic: Montesquieu, Venice, and the Theory of Aristocratic Republicanism." *Journal of the History of Ideas* 52, no. 2 (1991): 245–68.

Carroll, Linda. *Angelo Beolco (Il Ruzante).* Boston: Twaine, 1990.

Casanova, Giacomo. *History of My Life.* Trans. Willard R. Trask. 12 vols. New York: Harcourt, Brace & World, 1966–1971.

Casti, Giovanni Battista, and Giovanni Paisielli. *Il Re Teodoro in Venezia.* Padua: Pietro Molinari, 1801.

Castle, Terry. *Masquerade and Civilization: The Carnivalesque in Eighteenth-Century Culture and Fiction.* Stanford, CA: Stanford University Press, 1986.

Cattan, L. "La Venise de Byron et la Venise des romantiques français." *Revue de littérature comparée* 5, no. 1 (1925): 89–102.

Cavaillé, Jean-Pierre. *Dis/simulations: Jules-César Vanini, François La Mothe Le Vayer, Gabriel Naudé, Louis Machon et Torquato Accetto.* Paris: Honoré Champion, 2002.

Cessi, Roberto, ed. *Seu Venetiarum (Chronicon Altinate et Chronicon Gradense).* Rome: Tipografia del Senato, 1933.

Chambers, E. K. *The Mediaeval Stage.* 2 vols. Oxford: Oxford University Press, 1903.

Chartier, Roger, and Domique Julia. "Le Monde à l'envers." *L'Arc*, no. 65 (1976): 43–53.

Chojnacki, Stanley. *Women and Men in Renaissance Venice*. Baltimore: Johns Hopkins University Press, 2000.

Chubb, Thomas Caldecot. *Dante and His World*. Boston: Little, Brown, 1966.

Clark, Katerina, and Michael Holquist. *Mikhail Bakhtin*. Cambridge, MA: Harvard University Press, 1984.

Clemente, Pietro, et al. *Il linguaggio, il corpo, la festa: Per un ripensamento della tematica di Michail Bachtin*. Milan: Franco Angeli Editore, 1983.

Cocchiara, Giuseppe. *Il mondo alla rovescia*. Turin: Editore Boringhieri, 1981.

Comisso, Giovanni. *Agenti segreti di Venezia, 1705–1797*. Milan: Longanesi & Co., 1941.

Concina, Daniele. *De' teatri moderni, contrari alla professione Cristiana*. Rome: Pasquino, 1755.

Cook, Albert S., ed. *The Earliest Lives of Dante*. New York: Haskell House, 1974.

Cooper, James Fenimore. *The Bravo*. New Haven, CT: College & University Press, 1963.

Correnti, Pino. *Il Carnevale di Venezia*. Milan: Edizioni Ecotur, 1968.

Corrsin, Stephen D. "The Historiography of European Linked Sword Dancing." *Dance Research Journal* 25, no. 1 (1993): 1–12.

Coryat, Thomas. *Coryat's Crudities*. 2 vols. Glasgow: James MacLehose and Sons, 1905.

Coyer, abbé. *Voyage d'Italie*. 2 vols. Paris: La Veuve Duchesne, 1776.

Cozzi, Gaetano. *La società veneta e il suo diritto: Saggi su questioni matrimoniali, giustizia penale, politica del diritto, sopravvivenza del diritto veneto nell'Ottocento*. Venice: Marsilio, 2000.

———, ed. *Stato, società e giustizia nella repubblica Veneta (sec. XV–XVIII)*. Rome: Jouvence, 1980.

Cozzi, Gaetano, et al. *La Repubblica di Venezia nell'età moderna*. 2 vols. Turin: Unione Tipografico–Editrice Torinese, 1992.

Croce, Benedetto. *Saggi sulla letteratura italiana del seicento*. Bari: Laterza & Figli, 1948.

Croce, Benedetto, and Santino Caramella. *Politici e moralisti del seicento*. Bari: Giuseppe Laterza & Figli, 1930.

Csapo, Eric, and William J. Slater. *The Context of Ancient Drama*. Ann Arbor: University of Michigan Press, 1995.

d'Afflitto, Chiara. *Lorenzo Lippi*. Florence: Edizioni Firenze, 2002.

Da Ponte, Lorenzo. *Memoirs*. Trans. Elisabeth Abbott. New York: New York Review of Books, 2000.

Dante Alighieri. *Inferno*. Trans. Allen Mandelbaum. New York: Bantam Classic, 2004.

———. *Purgatorio*. Trans. Allen Mandelbaum. New York: Bantam Classic, 1983.

Daru, Pierre. *Histoire de la République de Venise*. 8 vols. Paris: Firmin Didot, 1821.

Davanzo Poli, Doretta. *Abiti antichi e moderni dei Veneziani*. Venice: Neri Pozzi, 2001.

Davis, James Cushman. *The Decline of the Venetian Nobility as a Ruling Class*. Baltimore: Johns Hopkins University Press, 1962.

Davis, Natalie Zemon. *Fiction in the Archives: Pardon Tales and Their Tellers in Sixteenth-Century France.* Stanford, CA: Stanford University Press, 1987.

———. "On the Lame." *American Historical Review* 93, no. 3 (1988): 572–603.

———. *The Return of Martin Guerre.* Cambridge, MA: Harvard University Press, 1983.

———. *Society and Culture in Early Modern France.* Stanford, CA: Stanford University Press, 1975.

Davis, Robert C. *The War of the Fists: Popular Culture and Public Violence in Late Renaissance Venice.* Oxford: Oxford University Press, 1994.

d'Ayala, Pier Giovanni, and Martine Boiteux, eds. *Carnavals et mascarades.* Paris: Bordas, 1988.

Decroisette, Françoise. *Venise au temps de Goldoni.* Paris: Hachette, 1999.

Descrizione degli spettacoli e feste datesi in Venezia per occasione della venuta delle LL. AA. II. il Gran Duca e Gran Duchessa di Moscovia, sotto il nome di Conti del Nort, nel mese di gennajo 1782. Venice: Vincenzio Formaleoni, 1782.

Diderot, Denis. *Oeuvres complètes.* Ed. J. Assézat. 20 vols. Paris: Garnier Frères, 1876.

DiGaetani, John Louis. *Carlo Gozzi: A Life in the 18th Century Venetian Theater, an Afterlife in Opera.* London: McFarland & Company, 2000.

Di Robilant, Andrea. *A Venetian Affair: A True Tale of Forbidden Love in the Eighteenth Century.* New York: Knopf, 2003.

Distefano, Giovanni, and Giannantonio Paladini. *Storia di Venezia, 1797–1997.* 3 vols. Venice: Supernova, 1996.

Doglioni, Nicolo. *Le cose notabili, et maravigliose della città di Venetia.* Venice: Battista Cestati, 1671.

Dolcetti, Giovanni. *Le Bische e il giuoco d'azzardo à Venezia, 1172–1807.* Venice: Aldo Manuzio, 1903.

Doody, Margaret. *Tropic of Venice.* Philadelphia: University of Pennsylvania Press, 2007.

D'Ordine dell'Illustrisimi e Eccellentissimi Signori Esecutori contro la Bestemmia, 18 Dicembre 1651: In materia de meretrici, e di quelli che non rispettano le chiese, e lochi sacri. Venice: Gio. Pietro Pinelli, 1651.

Driesen, Otto. *Der Ursprung des Harlekin: Ein kulturgeschichtliches Problem.* Berlin: Alexander Duncker, 1904.

du Boccage, Mme. *Lettres sur l'Angleterre, la Hollande et l'Italie.* 3 vols. Lyon: Chez les Frères Perisse, 1762.

Du Cange, Charles du Fresne, sieur. *Glossarium mediae et infimae latinitatis.* 10 vols. Paris: Librairie des Sciences et des Arts, 1937–38.

Dumas, Guy. *La Fin de la République de Venise: Aspects et reflets littéraires.* Rennes: Imprimerie Bretonne, 1964.

The Ecclesiastical History of Orderic Vitalis. Trans. Marjorie Chibnall. 6 vols. Oxford: Clarendon Press, 1969–80.

Eglin, John. *Venice Transformed: The Myth of Venice in British Culture, 1660–1797.* New York: Palgrave, 2001.

El Guindi, Fadwa. *Veil: Modesty, Privacy, and Resistance.* Oxford: Berg, 1999.

Ellis, Madeleine. *Rousseau's Venetian Story: An Essay upon Art and Truth in "Les Confessions."* Baltimore: Johns Hopkins University Press, 1966.

Emerson, Caryl. *The First Hundred Years of Mikhail Bakhtin*. Princeton, NJ: Princeton University Press, 1997.

Emigh, John. *Masked Performances: The Play of Self and Other in Ritual and Theatre*. Philadelphia: University of Pennsylvania Press, 1996.

Enciclopedia dello spettacolo. 13 vols. Rome: Le Maschere, 1954–62.

Fabre, Daniel. *Carnaval ou la fête à l'envers*. Paris: Gallimard, 1992.

Fano, Nicola. *Le maschere italiane*. Bologna: Il Mulino, 2001.

Fehl, Philipp P. "Farewell to Jokes: The Last *Capricci* of Giovanni Domenico Tiepolo and the Tradition of Irony in Venetian Painting." *Critical Inquiry* 5, no. 4 (1979): 761–91.

Feldman, Martha. *Opera and Sovereignty: Transforming Myths in Eighteenth-Century Italy*. Chicago: University of Chicago Press, 2007.

Ferrone, Siro. *Arlecchino: Vita e avventure di Tristano Martinelli attore*. Rome: Laterza, 2006.

———. *Attori, mercanti, corsari: La Commedia dell'Arte in Europa tra Cinque e Seicento*. Turin: Einaudi, 1993.

———. *Carlo Goldoni: Vita, opere, critica, messinscena*. Florence: Sansoni Editore, 1990.

Les Fêtes Vénitiennes du mois de janvier 1782: Dediées à son Excellence Madame Morosina Corner Gradenigo. N.p., n.d.

Fido, Franco. *Guida a Goldoni: Teatro e società nel settecento*. Turin: Einaudi, 1977.

———. *Le inquietudine di Goldoni*. Geneva: Costa & Nolan, 1995.

Fierro, Alfred. *Histoire et dictionnaire de Paris*. Paris: Robert Laffont, 1996.

Fiorentini, Girolomo. *Comoedio-crisis sive theatri contra theatrum censura; cœlestium, terrestrium, e infernorum linguis, continatis ab orbe condito sæculis, firmata*. Lyon: Officina Anissoniara, 1675.

Frazer, James George. *The Golden Bough: A Study in Magic and Religion*. London: Macmillan Press, 1987.

Freschot, Casimir. *Nouvelle relation de la ville et république de Venise*. Utrecht: Guillaume van Poolsum, 1709.

Gambelli, Delia. *Arlecchino a Parigi: Dall'inferno alla corte del re sole*. Rome: Bulzoni Editore, 1993.

Garland, Lynda, ed. *Byzantine Women: Varieties of Experience, 800–1200*. London: Ashgate, 2006.

Garzoni, Tomaso. *La piazza universale di tutte le professione del mondo*. Venice: Gio. Battista Somasco, 1589.

Gealt, Adelheid M., and George Knox, eds. *Domenico Tiepolo: Master Draftsman*. Bloomington: Indiana University Press, 1996.

Gealt, Adelheid M., and Marcia E. Vetrocq. *Domenico Tiepolo's Punchinello Drawings*. Bloomington: Indiana University Art Museum, 1979.

Gennep, Arnold van. *Manuel de folklore français contemporain*. 4 vols. Paris: Éditions Picard, 1937–58.

Geron, Gastone. *Carlo Goldoni cronista mondano: Costume e moda nel settecento a Venezia*. Venice: Filippi Editore, n.d.

Giazotto, Remo. "La Guerra dei palchi." *Nuova rivista musicale italiana* 2 (July–August 1967): 245–86; 3 (September–October 1967): 465–508; 5 (September–October 1969): 906–33; 6 (November–December 1971): 1034–52.

Gilhus, Ingvild Salid. "Carnival in Religion: The Feast of Fools in France." *Numen* 37, no. 1 (1990): 24–52.

Ginzburg, Carlo. *Il nicodemismo: Simulazione e dissimulazione religiosa nell'Europa del '500*. Turin: Giulio Einaudi, 1970.

Girard, René. *Violence and the Sacred*. Trans. Patrick Gregory. Baltimore: Johns Hopkins University Press, 1972.

Giubertoni, Anna. "Venezia nella litteratura austriaca moderna." In *Venezia Vienna: Il mito della cultura veneziana nell'Europa asburgica,* edited by Giandomenico Romanelli, 105–26. Milan: Electra Editrice, 1983.

Glare, P. G. W., ed. *Oxford Latin Dictionary.* Oxford: Oxford University Press, 1982.

Glixson, Beth L., and Jonathan E. Glixon, *Inventing the Business of Opera: The Impressario and His World in Seventeenth-Century Venice.* Oxford: Oxford University Press, 2006.

Goethe, Johann Wolfgang von. *Italian Journey.* London: Penguin Classics, 1970.

Goldoni, Carlo. *Mémoires.* Paris: Mercure de France, 1988.

———. *Tutte le opere.* 14 vols. Milan: A. Mondadori, 1935–56.

Gorringe, Timothy. *God's Just Vengeance: Crime, Violence and the Rhetoric of Salvation.* Cambridge: Cambridge University Press, 1996.

Goudar, Ange. *L'Espion chinois, ou l'envoyé secret de la cour de Pekin, pour examiner l'état présent de l'Europe.* 6 vols. Cologne: n.p., 1765.

Gozzi, Carlo. *Fiabe teatrali.* Milan: Garzanti Editori, 1994.

———. *Five Tales for the Theatre.* Ed. and trans. Albert Bermal and Ted Emery. Chicago: University of Chicago Press, 1989.

———. *The Memoirs of Count Carlo Gozzi.* Trans. John Addington Symons. 2 vols. New York: Scribner & Welford, 1890.

———. *Memorie inutili.* Turin: Unione Tipografico–Editrice Torinese, 1928.

Gozzi, Gasparo. *L'Osservatore Veneto.* 3 vols. Milan: Rizzoli, 1965.

Greenblatt, Stephen. *Renaissance Self-Fashioning: From More to Shakespeare.* Chicago: University of Chicago Press, 1980.

Guerci, Luciano. *La discussione sulla donna nell'Italia del Settecento: Aspetti e problemi.* Turin: Tirrenia Stampatori, 1988.

Guilhamet, Leon. *The Sincere Ideal: Studies on Sincerity in Eighteenth-Century English Literature.* Montreal: McGill–Queen's University Press, 1974.

Habermas, Jürgen. *The Structural Transformation of the Public Sphere: An Inquiry into a Category of Bourgeois Society.* Trans. Thomas Burger. Cambridge, MA: MIT Press, 1989.

Hale, J. R., ed. *Renaissance Venice.* London: Faber and Faber, 1973.

Heath, Jennifer, ed. *The Veil: Women Writers on Its History, Lore, and Politics.* Berkeley: University of California Press, 2008.

Heers, Jacques. *Fêtes des fous et carnavals.* Paris: Fayard, 1983.

Helmer, Paul, ed. *Le Premier et le secont livre de fauvel.* Ottawa: Institute of Mediæval Music, 1997.

Henke, Robert. *Performance and Literature in the Commedia dell'Arte.* Cambridge: Cambridge University Press, 2002.

Henningsen, Gustav, and John Tedeschi, eds. *The Inquisition in Early Modern Europe: Studies in Sources and Methods.* Dekalb: Northern Illinois University Press, 1986.

Horace. *Satires, Epistles and Ars Poetica*. Trans. H. Rushton Fairclough. Cambridge, MA: Harvard University Press, 1999.

Hughes, Diane Owens. "Distinguishing Signs: Ear-Rings, Jews and Franciscan Rhetoric in the Italian Renaissance City." *Past and Present* 112 (1986): 3–59.

Hunecke, Volker. *Il patriziato veneziano alla fine della Repubblica: 1646–1797, Demografia, famiglia, ménage*. Trans. Benedetta Heinemann Campana. Rome: Jouvence, 1997.

Isherwood, Robert M. *Farce and Fantasy: Popular Entertainment in Eighteenth-Century Paris*. New York: Oxford University Press, 1986.

Ivanovich, Cristoforo. *Minerva al tavolino: Lettere diverse di Proposta, e Risposta à varij Personaggi, sparse d'alcuni componimenti in Prosa, e in Verso, con Memorie teatrali di Venezia*. 2 vols. Venice: Nicolò Pezzana, 1688.

Jeanmaire, Henri. *Dionysos: Histoire du culte de Bacchus*. Paris: Payot, 1951.

Johnson, Edward J. "The Short, Lascivious Lives of Two Venetian Theaters, 1580–85." *Renaissance Quarterly* 55, no. 3 (2002): 936–68.

Johnson, James H. "Deceit and Sincerity in Early Modern Venice." *Eighteenth-Century Studies* 38, no. 3 (2005): 399–415.

———. "The Myth of Venice in Nineteenth-Century Opera." *Journal of Interdisciplinary History* 36, no. 3 (2006): 533–54.

———. "Versailles, Meet Les Halles: Masks, Carnival, and the French Revolution." *Representations* 73 (2001): 89–116.

Kanceff, Emanuele, ed. *Voyageurs Étrangères à / Foreign Travellers in / Viaggiatori stranieri a Venezia*. 2 vols. Geneva: Slatkine, 1981.

Katritzky, M. A. *The Art of Commedia: A Study in the Commedia dell'Arte, 1560–1620, with Special Reference to the Visual Records*. Amsterdam: Rodopi, 2006.

Kennard, Joseph Spencer. *Goldoni and the Venice of His Time*. New York: Benjamin Blom, 1967.

Kerényi, Karl. *Dionysos: Archetypal Image of Indestructible Life*. Trans. Ralph Mannheim. Princeton, NJ: Princeton University Press, 1976.

Kinser, Samuel. *Rabelais's Carnival: Text, Context, Metatext*. Berkeley: University of California Press, 1990.

Klima, Slava, ed. *Joseph Spence: Letters from the Grand Tour*. Montreal: McGill–Queen's University Press, 1975.

Kott, Jan. *The Eating of the Gods: An Interpretation of Greek Tragedy*. Trans. Boleslaw Taborski and Edward J. Czerwinski. New York: Random House, 1970.

Labalme, Patricia. "Sodomy and Venetian Justice in the Renaissance." *Review of Legal History* 52 (1984): 217–54.

La Bruyère, Jean de. *Oeuvres complètes*. Paris: Éditions Gallimard, 1951.

La Halle, Adam de. *Le Jeu de la feuillée, et Le Jeu de Robin et Marion*. Paris: E. de Boccard, 1964.

Lalande, Joseph Jérome Le Français de. *Voyage en Italie*. 9 vols. Paris: Chez le Veuve Desaint, 1786.

Landi, Sandro. " 'Pubblico' e 'opinione pubblica': Osservazioni su due luoghi comuni del lessico politico italiano del Settecento." *Cromohs* 13 (2008): 1–11.

Lane, Frederic C. *Venice: A Maritime Republic*. Baltimore: Johns Hopkins University Press, 1973.

Lecoq, Anne-Marie. "Une peinture 'incorrecte' de Lorenzo Lippi?' *Revue de l'Art* 130, no. 4 (2000): 9–16.

Leggi e memorie venete sulla prostituzione fino alla caduta della Republica. Venice: Marco Visentini, 1870–72.

Le Roy Ladurie, Emmanuel. *Carnival in Romans.* Trans. Mary Feeney. New York: George Braziller, 1979.

Leuschner, Eckhard. "The Pythagorean on Rosa's London Self-Portrait." *Journal of the Warburg and Courtauld Institutes* 57 (1994): 278–83.

Levi Pisetzky, Rosita. *Storia del costume in Italia.* 4 vols. Milan: Istituto Editoriale Italiano, 1967.

Limojan de Saint-Didier, Alexandre Toussaint. *La Ville et la république de Venise.* Paris: Chez Guillaume de Luyne, 1680.

Luciani, Gerard. "Carlo Gozzi (1720–1806): L'Homme et l'oeuvre." Thesis, Université de Dijon, 1974. 2 vols.

Machiavelli, Niccolò. *The Prince.* Trans. Harvey C. Mansfield, Jr. Chicago: University of Chicago Press, 1985.

Mack, John, ed. *Masks: The Art of Expression.* London: British Museum Press, 1994.

Mancini, Franco, et al. *I teatri del Veneto.* 4 vols. Venice: Corbo e Fiori, 1995.

Mangini, Nicola. *I teatri di Venezia.* Milan: Mursia Editore, 1974.

Map, Walter. *De Nugis Curialium: Courtiers' Trifles.* Trans. M. R. James. Oxford: Clarendon Press, 1983.

Márai, Sándor. *Casanova in Bolzano.* Trans. George Szirtes. New York: Alfred A. Knopf, 2004.

Mariuz, Adriano. *Giandomenico Tiepolo.* Venice: Alfieri, 1971.

Mariuz, Adriano, and Giuseppe Pavanello. *Tiepolo: Ironia e comico.* Venice: Marsilio, 2004.

Marotti, Ferrucio, and Giovanni Romei. *La professione del teatro.* Vol. 1, part 2 of *La commedia dell'arte e la società barocca,* ed. Ferdinando Taviani, 2 vols. Rome: Bulzoni, 1969–91.

Martin, Denis-Constant. "Politics Behind the Mask: Studying Contemporary Carnivals in Political Perspective. Theoretical and Methodological Suggestions." *Questions de Recherche / Research in Question,* no. 2 (2001): 2–34.

Martin, John Jeffries. "Inventing Sincerity, Refashioning Prudence: The Discovery of the Individual in Renaissance Europe." *American Historical Review* 102, no. 5 (1997): 1309–42.

———. *Myths of Renaissance Individualism.* New York: Palgrave, 2004.

———. *Venice's Hidden Enemies: Italian Heretics in a Renaissance City.* Berkeley: University of California Press, 1993.

Martin, John Jeffries, and Dennis Romano, eds. *Venice Reconsidered: The History and Civilization of an Italian City-State, 1297–1797.* Baltimore: Johns Hopkins University Press, 2000.

Martini, Gabriele. *Il "Vitio Nefando" nella Venezia del seicento.* Rome: Jouvence, 1988.

Mazzarotto, Bianca Tamassia. *Le feste veneziane.* Florence: Sansoni, 1961.

McGregor, Gordon Douglas. *The Broken Pot Restored: "Le Jeu de la Feuillée" of Adam de la Halle.* Lexington: French Forum Publishers, 1991.

McGrew, Roderick E. *Paul I of Russia, 1754–1801*. Oxford: Clarendon Press, 1992.

Meinecke, Friedrich. *Machiavellism: The Doctrine of Raison d'État and Its Place in Modern History.* Trans. Douglas Scott. New Haven, CT: Yale University Press, 1957.

Melton, James Van Horn. *The Rise of the Public in Enlightenment Europe.* Cambridge: Cambridge University Press, 2001.

Miato, Monica. *L'Accademia degli Incogniti di Giovan Francesco Loredan, Venezia (1630–1661).* Florence: Leo S. Olschki, 1998.

Michiel, Giustina Renier. *Origine delle feste veneziane.* 2 vols. Venice: Gaetano Longo, 1852.

Milosz, Czeslaw. *The Captive Mind.* Trans. Jane Zielonko. New York: Vintage Books, 1981.

Misson, Maximilien. *Nouveau voyage d'Italie, avec un Mémoire contenant des avis utiles à ceux qui vourdront faire le même voyage.* 3 vols. The Hague: Chez Henry van Buldereu, 1698.

Molmenti, Pompeo G. *La Storia di Venezia nella vita privata.* 3 vols. Trieste: Edizioni Lint, 1973.

Momo, Arnaldo. *La carriera della maschere nel teatro di Goldoni, Chiari, Gozzi.* Venice: Marsilio Editori, 1992.

Monnier, Philippe. *Venice in the Eighteenth Century.* London: Chattus and Windus, 1910.

Montaigne, Michel de. *The Complete Works: Essays, Travel Journals, Letters.* Trans. Donald M. Frame. Stanford, CA: Stanford University Press, 1958.

Moore, John. *A View of Society and Manners in Italy: With Anecdotes Relating to Some Eminent Characters.* 2 vols. Paris: J. Smith, 1803.

Morazzoni, Giuseppe. *La moda a Venezia nel secolo XVIII.* Milan: Museo Teatrale alla Scala, 1931.

Morelli, Lodovico. *Lettera scritta da un Patrizio Veneto ad un suo amico: Con cui si descrivono minutamente tutti li Grandiosi Spettacoli, co'quali si compiacque il Veneto Governo di trattenere li Signori Conti di Nord, dal giorno del loro arrivo, sino al giorno delle loro partenza dalla Dominante* [1781?].

Morosini, Nicolò. *Lettera apologetica.* [Venice: n.p., 1797].

Mozzarelli, Cesare, and Gianni Venturi, eds. *Europa delle corti alla fine dell'antico regime.* Rome: Bulzoni Editore, 1991.

Muir, Edward. *Civic Ritual in Renaissance Venice.* Princeton, NJ: Princeton University Press, 1981.

———. *The Culture Wars of the Late Renaissance: Skeptics, Libertines, and Opera.* Cambridge, MA: Harvard University Press, 2007.

———. *Mad Blood Stirring: Vendetta and Factions in Friuli during the Renaissance.* Baltimore: Johns Hopkins University Press, 1993.

———. *Ritual in Early Modern Europe.* Cambridge: Cambridge University Press, 2005.

Mutinelli, Fabio. *Lessico Veneto.* Venice: Giambatista Andreola Editore, 1851; reprint, Venice: Arnaldo Forni Editore, 1985.

Napier, A. David. *Masks, Transformation, and Paradox.* Berkeley: University of California Press, 1986.

Nicoll, Allardyce. *The World of Harlequin: A Critical Study of the Commedia dell'Arte.* Cambridge: Cambridge University Press, 1963.

Nigro, Salvatore Silvano. "Le Livre masqué d'un secrétaire du XVIIᵉ siècle." *Le Temps de la réflexion* 5 (1984): 183–211.

Norwich, John Julius. *A History of Venice.* New York: Alfred A. Knopf, 1982.

Ortalli, Gherardo, ed. *Gioco e giustizia nell'Italia di Comune.* Rome: Viella, 1993.

Ortolani, Giuseppe. *La riforma del teatro nel settecento e altri scritti.* Florence: Istituto per la Collaborazione Culturale, 1962.

Otto, Walter F. *Dionysus: Myth and Cult.* Trans. Robert B. Palmer. Bloomington: Indiana University Press, 1965.

Overell, M. A. "The Exploitation of Francesco Spiera." *Sixteenth Century Journal* 26, no. 3 (1995): 619–37.

Ozouf, Mona. " 'Public Opinion' at the End of the Old Regime." *Journal of Modern History* 60 (1988): S1–S21.

Pacifico, Pietro Antonio. *Cronica sacra e profana, o sia, Un compendio di tutte le cose più illustri ed antiche della città di Venezia.* 2 vols. Venice: Francesco Pitteri, 1751.

Padovan, Raffaello, and Andrea Penso. *La Repubblica delle maschere.* Venice: Corbo e Fiore Editori, 2000.

Paërl, Hetty. *Pulcinella: La misteriosa maschera della cultura europea.* Rome: Apeiron Editori, 2002.

Pandolfi, Vito. *La Commedie dell'Arte: Storia e testo.* 6 vols. Florence: Sansoni, 1959.

Parte presa nell'eccelso Consiglio di Dieci, 6 Aprile 1699: In materia d'assoluta prohibitione di maschere in tempo della Quadragesima. Venice: Antonio Pirelli, 1699.

Parte presa nell'eccelso Consiglio di Dieci, 16 Genaro 1718: In materia di maschere. Venice: Pietro Pinelli, 1718.

Parte presa nell'eccelso Consiglio di Dieci, 15 Genaro 1739: In materia di maschere. Venice: Z. Antonio Pinelli, 1739.

Parte presa nell'eccelso Consiglio di Dieci, 4 Genaro 1744: In materia di maschere. Venice: Z. Antonio Pinelli, 1744.

Patrizi, Giorgio, and Amedeo Quondam, eds. *Educare il corpo, educare la parola: Nella trattatistica del Rinascimento.* Rome: Bulzoni Editore, 1998.

Pemble, John. *Venice Rediscovered.* Oxford: Oxford University Press, 1995.

Peraldi, Emanuele. "Storia del diritto d'autore nei teatri di Vercelli e Novara." Thesis in law, University of Padua, 2002.

Plan de réforme, proposé aux cinq correcteurs de Venise. Amsterdam: n.p., 1775.

Plant, Margaret. *Venice: Fragile City, 1797–1997.* New Haven, CT: Yale University Press, 2002.

Pocock, J. G. A. *The Machiavellian Moment: Florentine Political Thought and the Atlantic Republican Tradition.* Princeton, NJ: Princeton University Press, 1975.

Pöllnitz, Karl Ludwig, Freiherr von. *The Memoirs of Charles-Lewis, Baron de Pollnitz.* Trans. Stephen Whatley. 4 vols. London: Daniel Brown, 1737–38.

Pontremoli, Alessandro, and Patrizia La Rocca. *La Danza a Venezia nel Rinascimento.* Venice: Nero Pozzi Editore, 1993.

Porter, Roy. *English Society in the Eighteenth Century.* London: Penguin Books, 1990.

Preto, Paolo. *I servizi segreti di Venezia. Spionaggio e controspionaggio: Cifrari, intercettazioni, delazioni, tra mito e realtà.* Milan: Il Saggiatore, 1994.

———. *Persona per hora secreta.* Milan: Il Saggiatore, 2003.

Proclama publicato per deliberatione delli Eccelentissimi Signori Capi dell'Eccelso Consiglio di Dieci, 15 Genaro 1658: In materia di maschere e baletti. Venice: Pietro Pinelli, 1658.

Proclama publicato per deliberatione delli Eccelentissimi Signori Capi dell'Eccelso Consiglio di Dieci, 23 Dicembre 1673: In materia di maschere e baletti. Venice: Pietro Pinelli, 1673.

Pullan, Brian. *The Jews of Europe and the Inquisition of Venice, 1550–1670.* Oxford: Basil Blackwell, 1983.

Rabelais, François. *The Complete Works of François Rabelais.* Trans. Donald M. Frame. Berkeley: University of California Press, 1991.

Raccolta di carte pubbliche, istruzioni, legislazioni, ecc. del nuovo Veneto governo democratico. 12 vols. Venice: Gatti, 1797.

Radin, Paul. *The Trickster: A Study in American Indian Mythology.* New York: Schocken Books, 1956.

Ravel, Jeffrey S. *The Would-Be Commoner: A Tale of Deception, Murder, and Justice in Seventeenth-Century France.* Boston: Houghton Mifflin, 2008.

Reato, Danilo. *Storia del Carnevale di Venezia.* Venice: Filippi Editore, 1991.

Redford, Bruce. *Venice and the Grand Tour.* New Haven, CT: Yale University Press, 1996.

Relazione distinta in cui si dà piena contezza di quanto seguirà nel di 17 del corrente Febbrajo 1767. Venice: Gio. Battista Occhi, 1767.

Riccoboni, Luigi. *Histoire du théâtre italien.* Paris: A. Cailleau, 1731.

———. *An Historical and Critical Account of the Theatres in Europe.* London: R. Dodsley, 1741.

Richard, Jérôme. *Description historique et critique de l'Italie, ou Nouveaux mémoires sur l'état actuel de son gouvernement, des sciences, des arts, du commerce, de la population.* 6 vols. Paris: Chez Delalain, 1770.

Rigoni, Mario Andrea. "Una finestra aperta sul cuore." *Lettere italiane* 26, no. 1 (1974): 434–58.

Ripa, Cesare. *Iconologia, overo descrittione d'imagini delle virtù, vitii, affetti, passioni humane, corpi celesti, mondo e sue parti.* Padua: Pietro Paolo Tozzi, 1611; reprint, New York: Garland, 1976.

Romanelli, Giandomenico, et al. *I Mestieri della moda a Venezia dal XIII al XVIII secolo.* Venice: Edizioni del Cavallino, 1988.

Romanin, Samuele. *Storia documentata di Venezia.* 10 vols. Venice: P. Naratovich, 1861.

Romano, Dennis. *Patricians and Popolani: The Social Foundations of the Renaissance Venetian State.* Baltimore: Johns Hopkins University Press, 1987.

Romano, Ruggiero, et al., eds. *Storia d'Italia.* 6 vols. Turin: Giulio Einaudi, 1972–76.

Rosa, Salvator. *Il teatro della politica sentenziosi afforismi della prudenza.* Bologna: Commissione per i testi di Lingua, 1991.

Rosand, Ellen. *Opera in Seventeenth-Century Venice: The Creation of a Genre.* Berkeley: University of California Press, 1991.

Rosenberg-Orsini, Giustiniana Wynne. *Du Séjour des comtes du Nord à Venise en janvier 1782: Lettre de Mme La Comtesse Douairière des Ursins, et Rosenberg à Mr. Richard Wynne, son frère, à Londres.* [Venice]: n.p., 1782.

Rossi, Pio. *Dictionnaire du mensonge.* Trans. Muriel Gallot. Nantes: Éditions Le Passeur-Cecofop, 1993.

Rousseau, Jean-Jacques. *Corréspondance complète de Jean-Jacques Rousseau.* Ed. R. A. Leigh. 11 vols. Geneva: Institut et Musée Voltaire, 1965.

———. *Émile, ou de l'éducation.* Paris: Garnier frères, 1964.

———. *Oeuvres complètes.* 3 vols. Paris: Éditions Gallimard, 1959.

Roworth, Wendy Wassyng. *"Pictor Succensor": A Study of Salvator Rosa as Satirist, Cynic and Painter.* New York: Garland, 1978.

Royce, Anya Peterson. "The Venetian Commedia: Actors and Masques in the Development of the Commedia dell'Arte." *Theatre Survey* 27 (1986): 69–87.

Ruggiero, Guido. *Binding Passions: Tales of Magic, Marriage, and Power at the End of the Renaissance.* Oxford: Oxford University Press, 1993.

———. *The Boundaries of Eros: Sex Crime and Sexuality in Renaissance Venice.* Oxford: Oxford University Press, 1985.

———. *Violence in Early Renaissance Venice.* New Brunswick, NJ: Rutgers University Press, 1980.

Ruskin, John. *The Stones of Venice.* 3 vols. New York: John Wiley & Sons, 1878.

Sabbadini, Roberto. *L'acquisto della tradizione: Tradizione aristocratica e nuova nobiltà a Venezia (sec. XVII–XVIII).* Udine: Istituto Editoriale Veneto Friulano, 1995.

Šafařík, Eduard A. *Fetti.* Milan: Electra, 1990.

Sandi, Vettor. *Principi di Storia civilie della Repubblica di Venezia.* 3 vols. Venice: Presso Sebastian Coletti, 1772.

Sansovino, Francesco. *Venetia: Città nobilissima et singolare.* 2 vols. Venice: Steffano Curti, 1663; reprint, Venice: Filippi Editore, 1968.

Sanuto, Marino. *Diarii di Marino Sanuto.* 58 vols. Venice: Tipografia Marco Visentini, 1879–1902.

Scala, Flaminio. *Il teatro delle favole rappresentative.* 2 vols. Milan: Edizioni Il Polifilo, 1976.

———. *Scenarios of the "Commedia dell'Arte": Flaminio Scala's "Il Teatro delle favole rappresentative."* Trans. Henry F. Salerno. New York: Limelight Editions, 1989.

Scott, Jonathan. *Salvator Rosa: His Life and Times.* New Haven, CT: Yale University Press, 1995.

Seaford, Richard. *Dionysos.* London: Routledge, 2006.

Sebeok, Thomas A., ed. *Carnival!* Berlin: Mouton Publishers, 1984.

Secondat, Charles de, Baron de Montesquieu. *Oeuvres complètes,* 2 vols. Paris: Éditions Gallimard, 1949.

Selfridge-Field, Eleanor. *A New Chronology of Venetian Opera and Related Genres, 1660–1760.* Stanford, CA: Stanford University Press, 2007.

———. *Pallada Veneta: Writings on Music in Venetian Society, 1650–1750.* Venice: Fondazione Levi, 1985.

————. *Song and Season: Science, Culture, and Theatrical Time in Early Modern Venice.* Stanford, CA: Stanford University Press, 2007.

Sepper, Elizabeth. " 'Her Only Treasure Lost': Rape and Reputation in Eighteenth-Century Venice." Undergraduate honors thesis, Boston University, 2002.

Snyder, Jon R. *Dissimulation and the Culture of Secrecy in Early Modern Europe.* Berkeley: University of California Press, 2009.

Soll, Jacob. *Publishing the Prince: History, Reading, and the Birth of Political Criticism.* Ann Arbor: University of Michigan Press, 2005.

Spezzani, Pietro. *Dalla Commedia dell'Arte a Goldoni.* Padua: Esedra Editrice, 1997.

Spini, Giorgio. *Ricerca dei libertini: La teoria dell'impostura delle religioni nel seicento italiano.* Rome: Editrice Universale, 1950.

Stallybrass, Peter, and Allon White. *The Politics and Poetics of Transgression.* Ithaca, NY: Cornell University Press, 1986.

Steward, James Christen, ed. *The Mask of Venice: Masking, Theater, and Identity in the Art of Tiepolo and His Time.* Berkeley: University of California Press, 1996.

Strauss, Johann. *Eine Nacht in Venedig.* Serie I, Werkgruppe 2, Bd. 10 of *Neue Strauss Gesamtausgabe.* Vienna: Strauss Edition, 1999–2009.

Stroev, Alexandre. *Les Aventuriers des lumières.* Paris: Presses Universitaires de France, 1997.

Tanner, Tony. *Venice Desired.* Cambridge, MA: Harvard University Press, 1992.

Tassini, Giuseppe. *Feste, spettacoli, divertimenti e piaceri degli antichi Veneziani.* Venice: Filippi Editore, 1961.

Taviani, Ferdinando. *La fascinazione del teatro.* Vol. 1, part 1, of *La commedia dell'arte e la società barocca,* edited by Ferdinando Taviani, 2 vols. Rome: Bulzoni, 1969–91.

————, ed. *La commedia dell'arte e la società barocca.* 2 vols. Rome: Bulzoni, 1969–91.

Taylor, Charles. *Sources of the Self: The Making of the Modern Identity.* Cambridge, MA: Harvard University Press, 1989.

Tessari, Roberto. *Commedia dell'Arte: La maschera e l'ombra.* Milan: Mursia, 1981.

Tiziano e Venezia: Convengo internationale di studi, Venezia, 1976. Vicenza: Neri Pozza Editore, 1980.

Toffanin, Giuseppe. *Machiavelli e il "Tacitismo": La "Politica storica" al tempo della controriforma.* Naples: Guida Editori, 1972.

Toschi, Paolo. *Le origini del teatro italiano.* Turin: Editore Boringhieri, 1955.

Trilling, Lionel. *Sincerity and Authenticity.* Cambridge, MA: Harvard University Press, 1972.

Turcan, Robert. *The Cults of the Roman Empire.* Trans. Antonia Nevill. Cambridge, MA: Harvard University Press, 1996.

Turner, Victor. *The Ritual Process: Structure and Anti-Structure.* Ithaca, NY: Cornell University Press, 1969.

Urban, Lina Padoan. *Il carnevale veneziano nelle maschere incise da Francesco Bertelli.* Milan: Edizioni Il Polifilo, 1986.

Vance, Eugene. "*Le Jeu de la feuillée* and the Poetics of Charivari." *Modern Language Notes* 100, no. 4 (1985): 815–28.

Vecellio, Cesare. *Costumes anciens et modernes.* 2 vols. Paris: Firmin Didot, 1859.

———. *Degli habiti antichi et moderni di diverse parti del mondo.* Venice: Damian Zenaro, 1590.

Venturi, Franco. *Settecento riformatore.* 5 vols. Turin: Einaudi, 1969–90.

Villari, Rosario. *Elogio della dissimulazione: La lotta politica nel Seicento.* Rome: Editori Laterza, 1987.

———, ed. *Scritti politici dell'età barocca.* Rome: Istituto Poligrafico e Zecca dello Stato, 1995.

Viroli, Maurizio. *From Politics to Reason of State: The Acquisition and Transformation of the Language of Politics, 1250–1600.* Cambridge: Cambridge University Press, 1992.

———. "The Revolution in the Concept of Politics." *Political Theory* 20, no. 3 (1992): 473–95.

Vitali, Achille. *La moda a Venezia attraverso i secoli: Lessico Ragionato.* Venice: Filippi Editore, 1992.

Vocabolario della lingua italiana. 4 vols. Rome: Istituto della Enciclopedia Italiana, 1986–89.

Vocabolario universale italiano. 7 vols. Naples: Tramater, 1829–40.

Voltaire, François Marie Arouet. *La Princesse de Babylone.* Paris: Émile-Paul Frères, 1920.

Wahrman, Dror. *The Making of the Modern Self: Identity and Culture in Eighteenth-Century England.* New Haven, CT: Yale University Press, 2004.

Walker, Jonathan. "Gambling and Venetian Noblemen, c. 1500–1700." *Past and Present* 162 (1999): 28–69.

Weil, Taddeo. *I teatri musicali veneziani del settecento.* Venice: Fratelli Visentini, 1897.

Wilde, Oscar. *The Complete Works of Oscar Wilde.* 4 vols. Oxford: Oxford University Press, 2007.

Wootton, David. *Paolo Sarpi: Between Renaissance and Enlightenment.* Cambridge: Cambridge University Press, 1983.

Wortley, Mary. *The Selected Letters of Lady Mary Wortley.* Ed. Robert Halsband. London: Penguin, 1986.

Wright, Edward. *Some Observations Made in Travelling through France, Italy, &c. in the Years 1720, 1721, and 1722.* 2 vols. London: Tho. Ward and E. Wicksteed, 1730.

Zagorin, Perez. *Ways of Lying: Dissimulation, Persecution, and Conformity in Early Modern Europe.* Cambridge, MA: Harvard University Press, 1990.

Zorzi, Ludovico. *I teatri pubblici di Venezia (Secoli XVII–XVIII).* Venice: Biennale di Venezia, 1971.

Acknowledgments

This book would not have been possible without the generous help of many others. May these acknowledgments serve as a token of my gratitude. The research for the book was done with the financial assistance of the American Council of Learned Societies, the Bogliasco Foundation, the Boston University Humanities Foundation, the Fulbright Foundation, and the Gladys Krieble Delmas Foundation. In Venice, I benefited from the expert advice of personnel in the Archivio di Stato, the Biblioteca del Museo Civico Correr, the Biblioteca della Casa di Carlo Goldoni, the Biblioteca della Fondazione Querini Stampalia, and the Biblioteca Nazionale Marciana. Michela del Borgo of the Archivio di Stato was eager with her suggestions and advice, which were immensely valuable. Gianluigi Passuello of the Centro Studi di Storia del Tessuto e del Costume in the Palazzo Mocenigo was kind and resourceful. Dennis Cecchin and Francesco Turio Böhm spent time over several visits helping me find relevant illustrations. I am particularly grateful to the staff of the Archives du Ministère des Affaires Etrangères in Paris for squeezing me into a crowded reading room against all protocol. Susan Halpert of Harvard University's Houghton Library helped smooth the way for securing photographs from that extraordinary collection.

Adelheid Gealt's guidance was essential in locating drawings from Tiepolo's *Divertimenti per li regazzi* to use in this book; her abundant help was invaluable. Sophie Botstock was similarly generous in sharing her expertise on the Pulcinella drawings. I am especially grateful to Francis

Ford for granting me permission to reproduce *The Birth of Pulcinella* from the private collection of his father, the late Sir Brinsley Ford, and to Joan K. Davidson for permitting *Pulcinella's Tomb* to be photographed for this book.

I wish to express my appreciation to Boston University for the leaves and sabbaticals that made my work abroad possible. In particular, I thank Charles Dellheim, chair of the History Department, and Dean Jeffrey Henderson. The Boston University Humanities Foundation provided valuable support for the production of this book.

I am grateful to my copyeditor, Madeleine B. Adams, whose many small suggestions have improved my prose in a big way. I have appreciated the strong support of Niels Hooper, my editor at the University of California Press, as well as the warm encouragement of Sheila Levine.

Conversations and correspondence with friends and colleagues have aided me at every stage. Among them, I wish to acknowledge Franca R. Barricelli, Arianne Chernock, Stephen Esposito, Aaron Garrett, Frederick Ilchman, Suzanne Lye, John Jeffries Martin, Sarah Maza, Robert Nye, Michael Prince, Blythe Alice Raviola, Bruce Redford, Christopher Ricks, Jean Paul Riquelme, Dennis Romano, Guido Ruggiero, Stephen Scully, Eleanor Selfridge-Field, Roger Shattuck, Parker Shipton, Francesca Trivellato, Zsuzsanna Várhelyi, James Q. Whitman, and Larry Wolff. Steve and Nancy Ortega introduced us to Venice in the early years, and Ugo Trivellato and Mariolina Toniolo helped open doors more recently. I gained much from conversations with Piero Del Negro and Paolo Preto as the book neared completion. I am especially grateful for the unfailing kindness and encouragement of Roberto Poli, who helped me through numerous conundrums translating from Italian and Venetian dialect.

I profited from the opportunity to present parts of this book in Patrice Higonnet's Early Modern Europe seminar at Harvard's Center for European Studies; in the Cultural and Intellectual History seminar organized by Peter Gordon and Judith Surkis also at the CES; in a conference at Princeton on Opera and Society organized by Theodore K. Rabb; among musicologists and historians of music at the University of Oslo; and on panels of the American Historical Association in Boston and New York City. Portions of part 4 appeared in *Eighteenth-Century Studies* and the *Journal of Interdisciplinary History,* and I am grateful for permission to use them here.

I want to acknowledge a particular debt to those who have read earlier versions of this book. Edward Muir has been generous with his support from the start; his encouragement helped to ease my reservations about entering a new field. Theodore K. Rabb has been of tremendous help in matters of both detail and structure; his professionalism is an inspiration. In our many conversations over the years, Jeffrey Ravel has taught me a great deal about masking and imposture, lies and truth-telling, early modern fraud, and much else. Suggestions from all three have made this a better book.

I owe more than I can ever say to my wife, Lydia Moland, whose immeasurable love sustains me in everything I do. We discovered Venice together in the months after we were married as I started the research for this book, and we have returned regularly over the past thirteen years. Her presence animates these pages. Venice is unimaginable without her.

Photo Credits

Figures 1, 2, 23, 24: G. Grevembroch, *Gli abiti de Veneziani di quasi ogni età con diligenza raccolti e dipinti nel secolo XVIII.* Images courtesy of Museo Civico Correr, Venice.

Figure 3: Frontispiece to Giacomo Casanova, *Icosameron* (1788). Image courtesy of Museo Civico Correr, Venice.

Figure 4: Musée du Louvre, Paris. Photo credit: Réunion des Musées Nationaux / Art Resource, NY.

Figure 5: National Gallery, London. © National Gallery, London / Art Resource, NY.

Figures 6, 10: Image courtesy of Museo Civico Correr, Venice.

Figure 7: G. Grevembroch, *Gli abiti de Veneziani.* Image courtesy of Archivio Osvaldo Böhm, Venice.

Figure 8: Ca'Rezzonico, Venice. Photo credit: Erich Lessing / Art Resource, NY.

Figure 9: *Il gran teatro di Venezia, ovvero, Raccolta delle principali vedute e pitture che in essa si contengono,* Venice, 1720; Typ 725.20.435 P. Image courtesy of Houghton Library, Harvard University.

Figures 11, 12: Luigi Riccoboni, *Histoire du théâtre italien,* Paris, 1731; Ital 6247.1.3*. Images courtesy of Houghton Library, Harvard University.

Figure 13: Hermitage, St. Petersburg. Photo credit: Scala / Art Resource, NY.

Figure 14: *Descriptio et explicatio pegmatum: arcuum et spectaculorum quae Bruxellae,* Brussels, 1594; * 57–697. Image courtesy of Houghton Library, Harvard University.

Figures 15, 16, 18, 19: Cesare Ripa, *Iconologia di Cesare Ripa,* Siena, 1613; *IC6 R4802 593ie. Images courtesy of Houghton Library, Harvard University.

Figure 17: Pierio Valeriano, *Hieroglyphica sive de Sacris Aegyptiorum Literis Commentarii,* Basil, 1556; Typ 565.56.865F. Image courtesy of Houghton Library, Harvard University.

Figure 20: Musée d'Angers, Angers. Photo credit: Réunion des Musées Nationaux / Art Resource, NY.

Figure 21: Galleria Palatina, Palazzo Pitti, Florence. Photo credit: Finsiel / Alinari / Art Resource, NY.

Figure 22: National Gallery, London. © National Gallery, London / Art Resource, NY.

Figure 25: Carlo Goldoni, *Commedie,* Venice, 1788–95, vol. 21; Typ 725.88.432. Image courtesy of Houghton Library, Harvard University.

Figures 26, 27: Giacomo Balduino, *Imagini degl'abiti con cui va vestita la nobilità della Serenissima Republica di Venezia,* Venice, 1702; Typ 725 03.262F. Images courtesy of Houghton Library, Harvard University.

Figure 28: Brustolon, "Solenne Serenissimi Principis convivium, quo cum electis Proceribus, exterorum Principum Legatos excipit." Image courtesy of Archivio Osvaldo Böhm, Venice.

Figure 29: Carlo Goldoni, *Delle commedie di Carlo Goldoni,* Venice, 1761, vol. 1; Typ 725.61.432. Image courtesy of Houghton Library, Harvard University.

Figure 30: Carlo Gozzi, *Opere del Co: Carlo Gozzi,* Venice, 1772–74, vol. 1; *IC7 G7497 C7720. Image courtesy of Houghton Library, Harvard University.

Figure 31: National Gallery of Canada, Ottawa. Photo © National Gallery Canada. Gift of Mrs. Samuel Bronfman, O.B.E., Westmount, Quebec, 1973, in honor of her late husband, Mr. Samuel Bronfman, C.C., LL.D.

Figure 32: Copyright 2010, Indiana University Art Museum: Evan F. Lilly Memorial, gift of Thomas T. Solley, 75.52.2.

Figures 33, 41, 50: The Metropolitan Museum of Art, New York. Images copyright © The Metropolitan Museum of Art / Art Resource, NY.

Figure 34: The Brinsley Ford Collection, London. Image courtesy of Photographic Survey, The Courtauld Institute of Art, London.

Figure 35: The Nelson-Atkins Museum of Art, Kansas City, Missouri. Purchase: William Rockhill Nelson Trust, 32–193/9. Photograph by Mel McLean.

Figure 36: The Cleveland Museum of Art. Purchase from the J. H. Wade Fund 1937.570.

Figures 37, 39: Gift of Robert H. and Clarice Smith. Images courtesy of the Board of Trustees, National Gallery of Art, Washington DC.

Figure 38: The Cleveland Museum of Art. Purchase from the J. H. Wade Fund 1937.569.

Figures 40, 42, 45: Public domain.

Figure 43: Image courtesy of École nationale supérieure des beaux-arts, Paris.

Figure 44: Private collection. Image courtesy of Hazlitt, Gooden & Fox.

Figure 46: Iris & B. Gerald Cantor Center for Visual Arts at Stanford University; gift of Mortimer C. Leventritt.

Figures 47, 48: San Polo, Venice. Photo credit: Cameraphoto Arte, Venice / Art Resource, NY.

Figures 49, 51: Copyright 2010, Indiana University Art Museum: Collection of Deither Thimme, 98.299.8, 98.299.16.

Figure 52: Private collection. Image courtesy of Joan K. Davidson. Photo credit: Eileen Travell.

Index

TEXT
10/13 Sabon

DISPLAY
Sabon

COMPOSITOR
Integrated Composition Systems

PRINTER AND BINDER
Thomson-Shore